# TEACHING READING AND
# THE LANGUAGE ARTS

# Teaching
# READING and
# the LANGUAGE ARTS

JAMES A. FITZGERALD

PROFESSOR OF ELEMENTARY EDUCATION
UNIVERSITY OF SCRANTON

PATRICIA G. FITZGERALD

FORMER TEACHER
ELEMENTARY EDUCATION

THE BRUCE PUBLISHING COMPANY
MILWAUKEE

*Library of Congress Catalog Card Number: 65–24243*
© 1965 THE BRUCE PUBLISHING COMPANY

MADE IN THE UNITED STATES OF AMERICA

# Preface

INSTRUCTING children to communicate pleasantly and effectively is a continuing challenging problem and a serious weighty responsibility because language training and reading instruction affect immeasurably the activities, progress, and outcomes of children's lives. Courteous language and thoughtful reading practiced by children under guidance in home and school are invaluable attainments for learners and rewarding accomplishments for parents and teachers.

The purpose of this book is to expedite learning and facilitate teaching of reading and the other language arts. Experiences with children and discussions with teachers have impressed the authors with the basic truth that the learning and development of the communication skills are best approached and cultivated through integrating procedures. Reading, speaking, listening, and writing are used outside the school in relation to each other in work projects and in leisure activities. The individual listens and talks about his problems. He reads and writes to plan his projects. He uses each communication skill, not in isolation, but in connection with others. Consequently, the authors propose that the receptive and expressive communication arts be learned insofar as possible in integration, for the improvement of each skill promotes facility in acquiring and cultivating the others. Listening and speaking complement each other; reading and writing are reciprocal. Good speaking stimulates effective listening and vice versa. Writing is enhanced through well-directed reading, challenging listening, and fruitful speaking experiences. Similarly reading is stimulated by oral discussion and purposeful studious writing. The function of instruction is, consequently, to teach children to speak, listen, read, write, and spell so that they will be able to communicate effectively in life situations.

The substance of this book is indicated in the table of contents. Emphasis is given to children's needs and potentialities for language and reading in Chapter I. Oral language instruction is discussed in Chapter II, and listening procedures are treated in Chapter III. Reading materials and methods are considered sequentially in five chapters: in

v

IV, objectives and preparatory technics are set forth; in V, beginning reading, phonics, structural analysis, and other word attack activities are described; in VI, a developmental reading program — including class, group, and individualized procedures — is outlined; in VII, the development of thoughtful processes is clarified; in VIII, suggestions for recreational and work-type reading are made. Written language is presented as follows: guiding social and creative writing in Chapter IX; teaching and learning spelling in X; handwriting instruction in XI; developing good usage in XII; building vocabulary and language power in XIII. The cultivation and use of integration, enrichment, and mass media are suggested in Chapter XIV, and procedures for evaluation and testing are examined in Chapter XV.

The authors wish to express their appreciation to thousands of individuals who contributed in one way or another to this book: to children eager for learning and to pupils anxious for knowledge, with whom the authors have been privileged to work; to students who stimulated the thinking of the authors by their class discussions and research reports; to dedicated public and parochial school teachers, supervisors, principals, curriculum workers, and superintendents who cooperated with the authors in planning instruction and guiding the activities of children; to co-workers, whose activities and writings contributed to background; to investigators of reading and the other language arts, whose researches were analyzed and read; to publishers and editors of periodicals and textbooks for materials and permissions to use quotations.

# Acknowledgments

The authors acknowledge their gratitude to learned societies, especially the National Society for the Study of Education, the Department of Elementary School Principals, the American Educational Research Association, the National Conference on Research in English, the National Council of Teachers of English, the International Reading Association, the Association for Supervision and Curriculum Development, the American Association of School Administrators, the National Education Association, and Phi Delta Kappa, whose yearbooks, monographs, and periodicals were sources of knowledge and inspiration. Acknowledgment is made to the editors of and contributors to the three editions of the *Encyclopedia of Educational Research* for authentic reports of research. The authors also are indebted to the New York State Education Department, the Pennsylvania State Education Department, the United States Department of Health, Education, and Welfare, and UNESCO, whose publications proved valuable and stimulating.

A special debt of gratitude is owed to the officials of the University of Scranton especially for two summer sabbatical leaves used to facilitate the completion of the book. Acknowledgment is made to the librarian and staff of the university library for help given. Finally, thanks are expressed to Dr. Richard F. McNichols, Superintendent of the Scranton Public Schools; to Mr. Eugene M. Langan, Curriculum Coordinator; and to Mr. Anthony Musso, Director of Audio-Visual Aids, for photographs used for illustration.

THE AUTHORS

# Contents

# TEACHING READING AND
# THE LANGUAGE ARTS

# Chapter I

# Communication: Learners, Needs, Principles

## LANGUAGE USEFUL THROUGH THE AGES

LANGUAGE is a most important instrument for living happily and effectively. From ancient times to the present day, it has been the principal means of communication. It has been the vital process by which peoples of the world expressed and recorded the beginnings and advances of social science, literature, and other disciplines. From the rise of civilization throughout the centuries, communication has been developed as a two-way process in which signals made by the sender were understood by the viewer, sounds voiced by the speaker were interpreted by the listener, and symbols formed by the writer were read and studied by recipients. For thousands of years, messages have been sent by one individual to another, who upon receipt of the communication replied in whatever medium he could best employ. So conversation and discussion developed, and written correspondence was invented and utilized.

As centuries went by language was enriched. As needs for communication grew in the many areas — business, government, and social life — technics to satisfy those needs were designed and perfected. Instruments were invented to enhance communication. History was written, and the achievements of civilizations were recorded for the following generations to read and use. Problems were defined, and solutions to some of them may be found in the written treatises of philosophers and scientists. When problems defied solution because of lack of facts or deficiency of method, reports were recorded for those who undertook later to carry on new investigations. Without the use of communication, the rate of advance in many fields would have been pointedly reduced.

At present, language is a medium for understanding among individuals and among peoples of all cultures and inheritances. Considerate

1

language builds goodwill in the home, in the school, on the playground, and on the street. Effective oral language assists a teacher in instructing children in the school, while interesting printed language motivates pupils to read, to study, and to evaluate projects of people in this and in other lands. Language is, therefore, a most essential vehicle for learning, study, and research.

## LANGUAGE AN INTEGRATING FACTOR

### Language in Living

Language is an integral part of living for it functions almost every moment of the day. The child learns to talk as he lives. For example, he is taught to act in a polite manner at the breakfast and dinner tables. He learns to speak in a considerate way — to say "please" when he wants something and "thank you" when he receives it. Mothers of families use language in the home, when shopping, and in social relations in the community. Fathers of families, in addition to using language at home, employ it in every life situation in which they engage.

Business people use language as they converse, discuss, work on problems, find evidence, draw conclusions, read reports, and handle correspondence necessary in their respective lines of endeavor. Professional men — lawyers, scientists, teachers, physicians, newspaper editors, and bankers — use language almost continually. Invariably, success in a business or in professional ventures is predicated to a large degree upon the efficiency with which communication is carried on. Governments also function principally through various processes of language and communication in the many affairs of state and in the interrelationships of nations.

### The Expressive and Receptive Language Arts

Teachers no doubt recognize the important relationships that exist among the various aspects of language. Chart I indicates the two general reciprocal communication activities: expression and reception. It is obvious that speaking and writing are expressive and that listening and silent reading are receptive. To make reception effective, expression must be accurate and clear.

There are many related and reciprocal activities in the home. Boys and girls learn many things by listening to their parents. They react by following suggestions, obeying instructions, answering questions, and repeating language which they hear. They communicate with their

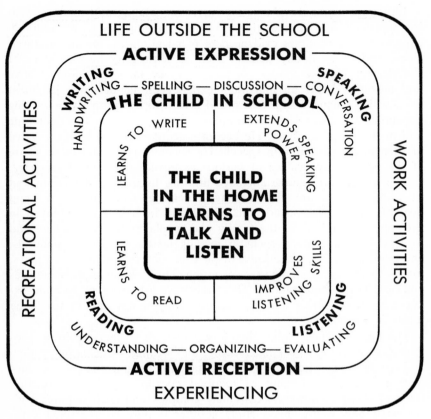

CHART I

Communication, Reading, and Language Arts

brothers, sisters, and others, and so develop skills of language. Observation and viewing are important also. The child in a rural area is exposed to the world of vibrant life and growth. His reactions may be expressed in joyous exclamations of wonder and surprise. A child in a city views many astonishing activities — people hurrying down the street, riding on buses or trains, and working in stores and shops. He sees massive buildings. He is fascinated with machines that are used in construction — the engines, the derricks, the steam shovels. He looks and listens, and sometimes reads. He is impressed and these intensive experiences are likely to remain with him a long time — perhaps for life.

Important *expressional* language arts are: talking, oral reading, writing, spelling, and handwriting (including manuscript). In addition, expression is sometimes evidenced in facial grimaces, manual gestures, signs, and other bodily actions such as shrugging the shoulders or shuddering. These activities combine to make the expression effective and meaningful. As an individual experiences, he develops judgment as to which language skill to use and how to use it properly in varying situations. He recognizes the importance of speaking at the right time and in the proper manner. He becomes acquainted also with the value of silence and of timing in speech. He becomes more and more aware of the comparative values of various expressional facets of language.

The principal *receptive* language arts are listening and reading, but in addition there are also viewing, observing, and sensing. A great deal of time in life outside the school and in school is employed in listening to members of the family and to playmates, to teachers and to schoolmates. Time is spent in reading textbooks, library materials, and periodicals. The child looks at pictures, observes games, sees plays, listens to the radio, and views television. He looks at motion pictures and observes demonstrations. These receptive arts combine to build experiences from which the child learns many things and to which he reacts in various ways.

The basic language skills, therefore, which all teachers desire to promote, are listening, speaking, reading, and writing — including spelling and handwriting. These are fundamental in communication as an integrating whole, functioning as required coordinately or reciprocally. Each of these is, however, extremely complex and each requires concentrated and well-planned study so that it may be perfected sufficiently to perform its proper function in the integrating gestalt of communication. Some of these skills are used more frequently than others. Mackintosh indicated the average person "probably 'listens' a book in a day, speaks a book in a week, reads a book in a month, and writes a book in a lifetime."[1]

Unsatisfactory results in reading and language have disturbed not only school personnel but people in general, and scholars have emphasized the importance of linguistics in instruction. Linguistics treats of the structure of language, and the translation of speech into written communication. The use of words and their positions in sentences are important in teaching reading and writing. The understanding and appro-

---

[1] Helen K. Mackintosh, "The Elementary School in the City — a Conference Report," *School Life,* 45:16, July, 1963.

priate use of oral language have favorable effects upon the learning of both reading and writing.[2] The integrative approach in learning is strongly emphasized because of the interrelationships of the communication arts.

## CHILDREN: THE LEARNERS

The likenesses and differences of children must be understood in order to teach them the many concepts and processes of communication.

### The Likenesses of Children

Important among the similarities of children is their marvelous potentiality to think, to communicate, to express their thoughts, to make themselves understood, and to interpret the expressions of others. Even in the early years of life, normal children learn to communicate their thoughts. As they grow in years and experience, their expressional abilities and skills develop. They come to be more or less cognizant of their environment, of the stimuli around them, and of the people in their homes, schools, and communities. They become interested in other children, in music and singing, in looking at pictures, and in engaging in conversations. Generally they develop a sense of satisfaction in participating in situations in which they are recognized as members of a group or in which they acquire worthwhile knowledge. Although differing in their responses they do react to the environment in which they live. Normal boys and girls are highly sensitive to and favorably impressed with learning situations carefully chosen and developed. They respond readily to pleasant and fruitful experiences and look forward to opportunities for using outcomes of their thinking and activity.[3] Situations which are boring or distasteful frustrate positive language learning and promote negative communication tendencies. Pupils learn, and their learnings will be richly developmental if teachers understand their needs and provide interesting and useful instruction. Learners will react unfavorably if materials are uninviting or if the methods are distasteful and unrewarding. Children are human, in a class far above animals, and alike in the qualities of humankind. Those who associate with boys and girls recognize them in a "class by themselves" capable of thought, emotion, expression, and communication.

---

[2] *Ibid.*, pp. 16–18.
[3] See David P. Ausubel, "Emotional Development," *Encyclopedia of Educational Research,* third edition (New York: The Macmillan Company, 1960), pp. 448–454.

Normal children are alike in many qualities. They show similarities as they progress from level to level. McCarthy traced their growth in language, sentence, and vocabulary from first words spoken in infancy up into school levels. The behavioral aspect of language is shown to be important for them. They tend to talk about objects or experiences in an emotional tone. They seem in general to develop a tendency toward completeness of sentence as they increase sentence length.[4] Carroll, after summarizing pertinent research, implied that the normal child comes to school with a rather extensive variety of concepts reflected by a large vocabulary, but in need of experiences and instructional procedures to improve meaningful language. In the early stages of school, children require instruction and practice in listening, understanding, and talking in order that reading and writing may be begun successfully.[5]

## Differences Among Children

Individual backgrounds and potentialities of children vary amazingly. Mental, achievement, environmental, and emotional differences complicate the instructional problems in a class. In order to promote efficient learning, it is necessary that these be recognized and appraised.

*Mental ability.* The middle 96 percent of children of first grade "have mental ages between four and eight years," according to Tyler, and variability increases in the grades above the first. The spread in the sixth grade runs almost double that in the first.[6]

*Achievement.* The achievement differences in various school levels are astounding also. Several years of spread have been recorded in subject areas in a classroom in the middle grades. Generally greater variations are found in the higher than in the lower grades.[7] These should be carefully recognized so that instruction may be carried on at proper levels for individuals. A most effective way of recording and using these variations is by means of a cumulative record kept in a folder for each individual. Learning is in its final analysis individual, and each

---

[4] Dorothea McCarthy, "Child Development — VIII. Language," *Encyclopedia of Educational Research,* revised edition (New York: The Macmillan Company, 1950), pp. 165–172.

[5] John B. Carroll, "Language Development," *Encyclopedia of Educational Research,* third edition (New York: The Macmillan Company, 1960), pp. 744–752.

[6] Fred Tyler, "Individual and Sex Differences," *Encyclopedia of Educational Research,* third edition (New York: The Macmillan Company, 1960), pp. 680–681.

[7] *Ibid.,* p. 680.

child should actively use the abilities he possesses to improve competency in the various language arts.

*Environment.* The impact of environment is important in the appraisal of children's language. Homes differ greatly in culture. In some homes, youngsters receive loving consideration from parents and older brothers and sisters with the result that they enter school with good habits of talking and listening. They are accustomed to meaningful conversation and acceptable television and radio programs. They develop habits of thinking and talking which are a basis for growth. Other children, not so fortunate, grow up in homes deprived of many facilities and opportunities conducive to language training. In some situations, children are forced to shift for themselves while both parents work. When parents return home, they are tired and often do not have the time or energy to communicate appropriately with their children. Another factor in the environment is the type of community, which varies greatly from slum to suburb, each with its problems considered now to be among the most difficult in American education.[8]

*Emotions.* Emotion is evidenced, generally, by a type of response more or less overt which reflects an inner feeling toward someone or something. It is an aspect of living, important in child education. Love, fear, and anger develop in children. Properly cultivated and controlled, emotions are an asset; uncontrolled, they can lead to trouble. Great social movements in history have derived strength from the persistent cultivation of emotional drives. People have been swayed by songs and speeches and have responded to stimulating, exciting, or disturbing stimuli. The great "Give Me Liberty or Give Me Death" address of Patrick Henry is an example.

Feelings of young children are sometimes expressed in uncontrolled anger, in demonstrative affection, or in unrestrained fear. The desirable and the undesirable manifestations in each child should be recognized. Emotional expression is not to be suppressed or eliminated in the child; it is rather to be cultivated and guided. Some undesirable traits are expressed by aggressive behavior, while others, sometimes more serious, are evidenced in withdrawal tendencies. Some children fortunately manifest a high feeling tone; they "feel good" about almost everything and see the bright side of their problems. Others unfortunately have a low emotional tone; they worry and fret and are sad and depressed. Some youngsters express their feelings by temper tantrums or by fighting.

---

[8] See James Bryant Conant, *Slums and Suburbs* (New York: McGraw-Hill Book Company, Inc., 1961), p. 147.

Others withdraw "within themselves" and build undesirable habits and attitudes of regression or seclusion and become isolated from their fellows. The elimination of some undesirable emotional reactions may be brought about by freeing the child from unnecessary tension, by consistent reasonable discipline, by social facilitation, or even by application of a sense of humor.[9]

Language is expressive of a child's emotional tendencies. In an individual's development of communication, he must learn to control his expression. The crude utterance of feelings is not to be encouraged, but a considerate indication of them can be favorable to educational growth. The proper control and use of emotions aid individuals to achieve acceptable social relationships.

## CHILDREN'S NEEDS FOR LANGUAGE

If children are to live wholesomely in these times of rapid change, evolving concepts, and amazing inventions, it is important that they develop ability and skill in understanding, thinking, communication, interpersonal relationships, language control, and reading.[10]

### Language and Understanding

The child needs guidance to understand his world as it grows for him from year to year. He learns to recognize and use such concepts in the home as *eat, come, go, stop, chair, sit,* and *run.* These are developed early in the child's life. As he learns to eat, he associates the word *eat* with the act of eating. He learns the meanings of the words *chair* and *sit* by association and use. He connects the word *sit* with the act of sitting on a *chair* at the table. Frequently the words *stop* and *go* are made meaningful to the child first in the home by members of the family who tell him to "go to the table" or to "stop running." He begins to speak the words he hears. By imitation, instruction, and practice he gradually improves and extends his language. On the way to school he learns to stop when the red traffic sign or the word STOP confronts him, and to go when the green light or the word GO flashes as a signal to advance. In like manner, some children learn to react properly to the WALK and DON'T WALK signs.

[9] See Florence L. Goodenough, "Child Development — XIV. Emotions," *Encyclopedia of Educational Research,* revised edition (New York: The Macmillan Company, 1950), pp. 187–190.

[10] Commission on English Curriculum of the National Council of the Teachers of English, *Language Arts for Today's Children* (New York: Appleton-Century-Crofts, Inc., 1954), pp. 3–17.

In school, the child extends his understanding, not only to new concepts, but he enriches familiar ones. For example, he learns to sit at his desk or to sit on a chair at a table to discuss a project with others. So the concept *sit* is expanded. Later in school, the child learns to read the words which he has used at home or at play, such as *sit, eat, come, go, stop,* and *run.* Still later, he spells and writes them. Accordingly, the individual hears, speaks, reads, and writes words that represent common ideas or acts. His understanding grows as he experiences, and his language develops facility with useful concepts.

## Language and Thinking

Language activities are useful in developing thought. For example, a pupil reads to obtain information for thinking, and writes to record notes he needs for a report. He talks and listens in thinking about a problem or a project. Language aids thinking, and, conversely, thinking guides language. What a child says in a real situation or what he writes is flavored by the content and the method of his thinking. As he develops thinking power, he learns to decide what types of language skills — listening, observing, reading, talking, writing, or spelling — are necessary for the communication of his thoughts. He will learn to think positively if he is guided to recognize his problems and to search for appropriate procedures for solving them.[11]

## Developing Facility in Communication

Communication involves listening, talking, reading, writing, "sending," and "receiving." The process connotes the transfer of meaning from the mind of the speaker or writer to the mind of the listener or reader. The pupil must learn that communication between individual and individual is modified to a greater or lesser degree by tone, gesture, feeling, facial expression, rhythm, and other visual and auditory symbols and processes. He should learn that written communication is modified also by the choice of words, formation of sentences, considerateness of expression, style of writing, spelling, and handwriting, and use of pictures, diagrams, or charts.

In oral communication words are used to convey thought. The speaker must know exactly what he wants to say, and select the correct combination of words, phrases, and sentences to give the precise meaning. The listener hears these words, phrases, and sentences. If he

[11] Joseph Mersand, "English Meets the Challenge," *Elementary English,* 37:69–80, February, 1960.

listens carefully to language which is familiar, he should be able to interpret fairly well what the speaker says. If the speaker is careless in word selection, in pronunciation, enunciation, or in sentence structure, the idea will not be clearly expressed, and the hearer is likely to be confused. Furthermore, if the listener is careless or distracted, or if he cannot comprehend a specific word or a particular sentence, the message will not be received correctly. The speaker's need for some understanding of the listener, his background, and his education is obvious. Clear thinking and the precise use of both speaking and listening skills are mandatory if oral communication is to be successful.

Written communication, in like manner, requires clear purpose, careful selection of words, exact sentence structure, correct spelling, proper punctuation, and legibility on the part of the writer. The reader of the communication must be able to interpret the written words and sentences in order to reconstruct the thought that the writer had in mind. He should not only "know the meanings" of the words but he must recognize the meanings in the sense that the writer intended. It is necessary that he be alert in his reading to understand the concepts which prompted the message. To miss a word in reading, to read a sentence incorrectly, or to ignore a punctuation mark may cause a faulty reception of the message intended. Accordingly, written communication between individual and individual depends to a great degree upon clarity of thinking, understanding of concepts, knowledge of words, and ability to use and interpret sentences by writer and reader.

In achieving the goals of acceptable writing and reading, and of effective talking and listening, the structure and the mechanics of language must be studied. Important also are the attitudes of participants toward communication and toward each other.[12]

## Language in Personal Relations

Delicacy and taste in social and personal relations require proficiency in language. Courtesy to others is evidenced often by tone of voice, by the words enunciated, and by the sentences used. Letters are interpreted by the meanings of the sentences in them and also by the meanings sensed "between the lines."

Personal relationships require the use of thoughtful language. Thinking is evidenced by words and sentences, spoken or written. Comprehensible expression reflects clarity of thought, but inadequate wording

[12] See Margaret J. Early, "Communication Arts," *Encyclopedia of Educational Research,* third edition (New York: The Macmillan Company, 1960), pp. 306–312.

often connotes confused thinking. Success in many types of interpersonal activity depends upon appropriate language to communicate thought exactly and considerately. Social situations require propriety in written correspondence and sensitivity in conversation. Consideration of the correspondent or discussant and care and courtesy in the use of language bring joy and good feeling; the lack of considerateness often invites tension and ill feeling. The child has the right to expect the type of instruction that will help him to realize the highest objectives possible to him in language learning.[13]

## Language Discipline and Control

Language control should be an objective of every person. Without control, an individual is handicapped in dealing with others. With it, his success in communication improves. Purpose, instruction, and practice are essential in achieving language control.

In any real speaking situation, whether it is in conversation, formal speaking, or telephoning, the speaker must use understandable patterns of speech to best achieve his purposes. A learner must be taught to plan his objectives for speaking. He should learn the importance of acceptable language, a pleasant voice, and agreeable manner. He should know when to talk, how to begin, how to express what he has to say, and how to conclude. He must appreciate the value of hearing correctly what other people say. Benefits are rich to the accurate listener as well as to the effective talker. Successful experience should not be negated in improving oral language. Drill upon the pronunciation of troublesome words contributes to control of speech.

Correct written language will be achieved not so much by memorizing the rules of grammar and drill upon the mechanics as by purposeful writing. When the individual begins school he has spoken millions of words and generally has written none. He must write. He cannot learn to write without practice in writing. The objectives must be clarified so that he will espouse them vigorously. Writing must become correct, first in simple situations, and later in complex projects. Worthwhile experience is gained by writing in real or lifelike situations. Rich experience should be supported by practice in recording and communicating thought. Proofreading and correction of errors should lead to improvement. Dictation is a useful procedure. Control of language will be

---

[13] Dora Smith, "Growth in Language Power as Related to Child Development," *Teaching Language in the Elementary School*, Forty-Third Yearbook of the National Society for the Study of Education, Part II, 1944, pp. 52–97.

effected by study, active challenging practice, and use of dictionary and stylebooks.[14]

## Symbols and Reading

Reading requires understanding of symbols as well as experience in order to function properly as a medium of communication, for without symbols — words, letters, punctuation, numerals, and other characters — reading as we know it would not exist. Before the appearance of the alphabet — the first form of which was invented about 1500 B.C. — pictures, signs, and hieroglyphics were made to stand for things and sounds. This ancient type of communication was cumbersome and difficult. The invention of the alphabet was a big step forward in reading because letters and their combinations which represent sounds *by common agreement* are meaningful to writers and readers. But it should be understood that the connection between a letter or combination of letters and a sound or an idea is arbitrary. The English language is particularly rich because the science of word usage is constantly growing. The alphabet, its mastery and its use, is basic for communication. In addition, signs and symbols such as the cross, the flag, $, &, +, ×, ÷, and % are employed; their meanings are clear to adults and become understandable to children through instruction.

By means of the alphabet and other symbols, the world's history and literature have been perpetuated for the education of ever present youth. Through reading, young learners assimilate the knowledge and experiences of ancient and modern men and with these as a basis build a future which reaches outward and upward to new thoughts and the attainment of goals not dreamed of in the past. Reading functions as a vital medium for reflection and understanding in every field of endeavor — literature, science, mathematics, art, and philosophy. Employed properly, reading and study guide students to investigate questions, solve problems, communicate results, and record accomplishments to be read by those who live today and by those who will live in the future. Through study of past accomplishments and present endeavors in any field new ideas are formulated, new theories are validated, old principles are clarified, and improved methods of work are originated, refined, and employed.

It is the duty of the school to motivate and guide reading in such a way that learners will experience the exciting world of past and present,

---

[14] See **Ruth C. Strickland,** "Improving Language Arts in the Elementary School," *The National Elementary Principal,* 39:37–43, April, 1960.

develop stimulating interests in recreational and work-type materials, and build up effective skills and habits of reading.[15]

Mastery of the communication arts is necessary to successful living. No halfway measures of learning these arts should be tolerated. The child has the right to expect to attain proficiency in listening, speaking, reading, writing, and the related language arts.

## SOME SUGGESTIONS FOR TEACHING AND LEARNING

Communication is facilitated by skill in each of the language arts and predicated upon the interaction of an individual with his environment and with the personalities with whom he associates. Language arts are an integration of listening, speaking, reading, writing, handwriting, and spelling. Although each of these is related more or less directly to the others, an individual must study each not only in integration, but also specifically, purposefully, and intensively to become efficient in the totality of communication.

The following suggestions should be of value to a teacher in formulating principles for instruction and learning.

1. Children must be understood and recognized as intelligent human beings capable of extraordinary development.

2. An individual should be taught a communication skill when he becomes ready or when he is guided to readiness for it by instruction.

3. Language potentialities from year to year should be recognized so that guidance may be afforded as the pupil becomes ready and able to master the various communication skills.

4. Integrating procedures are highly effective in teaching the closely related language skills.

5. Differences among children should be determined and instruction provided to fit individual needs and capabilities.

6. An objective is necessary in every plan of instruction in language teaching.

7. Interest is a vital factor in the successful instruction of youth.

8. Life situations should be utilized in the teaching of reading and the communication arts.

9. The materials selected should be adequately evaluated by standards of validity, usefulness, need, and interest.*

---

[15] *Report of the National Committee on Reading,* Twenty-Fourth Yearbook of the National Society for the Study of Education, Part I, 1925, 335 pp.

* For example, the ten words *a, and, I, in, is, it, the, to, we, you* comprise almost 25 percent of usage in the six communication areas.

10. Each boy and girl should be given dynamic and challenging instruction at successive maturation levels.

11. As the individual's capabilities expand and sharpen he should be presented with materials that meet his increasing needs and challenge his developing powers.

12. Fundamental concepts and processes must be learned before more complex ones can be taught.

13. Learners will profit most when they see the needs, understand the values, enjoy the procedures, and assess the outcomes of study.

14. Methods and activities should be varied to engender interest and to meet changing situations and problems.

15. Developmental instruction should be planned and carried out for each child.

16. Testing should be carried out before, during, and after instruction and study in order to prevent waste in effort and to motivate dynamic learning.

17. An individual should learn to test himself while studying in order to identify his difficulties and needs.

18. A skill once mastered should be maintained at an effective essential standard for use.

19. Diagnosis should determine the difficulties and their causes in order that essential remediation may be applied effectively.

20. The outcomes of learning and instruction in language arts should become evident in individuals who speak and write enthusiastically and competently and listen and read inquiringly, thoughtfully, and joyously.

## SUMMARY

The following factors were considered in this presentation: the values of language in the past and present; interrelations of the communication skills; likenesses and differences of learners; children's needs for language; and considerations for formulating some principles in teaching the communication arts.

### ACTIVITIES, PROBLEMS, QUESTIONS

1. Explain why language has been so important in civilization.
2. Why is language said to be an integrating factor in living?
3. Make lists of the expressive and receptive communication activities. Draw lines indicating reciprocal connections between them.
4. Compare and contrast the likenesses and differences of children.
5. In what grade levels of the elementary school are the differences among children most pronounced? Give reasons for these variations.

6. Discuss the nature of individual differences of children.
7. State several needs for language and their comparative importance.
8. Explain the importance of language in: understanding, thinking, facility in communication, personal relationships, discipline, reading.
9. Set up a comprehensive statement of principles for teaching communication.

## SELECTED REFERENCES

Baldwin, Alfred L. *Behavior and Development in Childhood.* New York: Dryden, 1955. 619 pp.

Barnett, Lincoln. *The Treasure of Our Tongue.* New York: Alfred A. Knopf, 1964. 304 pp.

Dunn, Lloyd M., ed. *Exceptional Children in the Schools.* New York: Holt, Rinehart & Winston, 1963. 580 pp.

*Early Childhood Education.* Forty-Sixth Yearbook of the National Society for the Study of Education, Part II. Chicago: University of Chicago Press, 1947. 390 pp.

*Education for the Gifted.* Fifty-Seventh Yearbook of the National Society for the Study of Education, Part II. Chicago: University of Chicago Press, 1958. 420 pp.

*Education of Exceptional Children, The.* Forty-Ninth Yearbook of the National Society for the Study of Education, Part II. Chicago: University of Chicago Press, 1950. 350 pp.

*Encyclopedia of Educational Research.* 3rd ed. New York: Macmillan, 1960. 1564 pp.

——— Rev. ed. New York: Macmillan, 1950. 1520 pp.

Fuller, Elizabeth Mechem. *About the Kindergarten.* What Research Says to the Teacher. No. 22. Washington, D. C.: DCT and AERA of the NEA, 1961. 32 pp. (In this and other references of this type: DCT = Department of Classroom Teachers; AERA = American Educational Research Association; NEA = National Education Association.)

Gallagher, James J. *The Gifted Child in the Elementary School.* What Research Says to the Teacher. No. 17. Washington, D. C.: DCT and AERA of the NEA, 1959. 32 pp.

Johnson, Orville G. *Education for the Slow Learners.* Englewood Cliffs, N. J.: Prentice-Hall, 1963. 330 pp.

Landreth, Catherine. *The Psychology of Early Childhood.* New York: Knopf, 1958. 412 pp.

Mussen, Paul Henry, John Janeway Conger, and Jerome Kagan. *Child Development and Personality.* 2nd ed. New York: Harper and Row, 1963. 625 pp.

Ojemann, Ralph. *Personality Adjustment of Individual Children.* What Research Says to the Teacher. No. 5. Washington, D. C.: DCT and AERA of the NEA, 1954. 32 pp.

Strang, Ruth. *Guided Study and Homework.* What Research Says to the Teacher. No. 8. Washington, D. C.: DCT and AERA of the NEA, 1955. 33 pp.

*Theories of Learning and Instruction.* Sixty-Third Yearbook of the National Society for the Study of Education, Part I. Chicago: University of Chicago Press, 1964. 430 pp.

Torrance, E. Paul, ed. *Talent and Education.* Minneapolis: University of Minnesota Press, 1960. 210 pp.

# Chapter II

# Developing Oral Language

## THE CHILD AND COMMUNICATION

THE normal child vocalizes shortly after birth. He uses about seven sounds in the first two months of life, and by the time he is two and one half years old, he employs twenty-seven different sounds.[1] At first, the child uses vowels at an approximate proportion of 2:1 over consonants, but at the end of year one, more consonants are used than vowels, and at the end of two and a half years of life the ratio is 3:2 in favor of consonants. The first "meaningful" word is spoken when the normal child is perhaps eleven or twelve months old. Gifted children probably use the first word a little earlier, and slow starters much later.[2]

Madorah Smith's often-quoted study of the vocabularies of 273 children, ranging from less than a year to six years, indicated that four-year-old children employ 1540 words, five-year-old children use 2072, and six-year-old children utilize 2562 words.[3]

When the child comes to school, he has an amazing amount of practice in the use of vocabulary. At the age of four he is probably speaking at the rate of from ten to twelve thousand words a day. At the age of six he has progressed further in vocabulary usage. Some authorities indicate that he may utter words at a rate as high as thirty thousand a day.[4] An important point to be kept in mind is

---

[1] Dorothea McCarthy, "Child Development — VIII. Language," *Encyclopedia of Educational Research,* revised edition (New York: The Macmillan Company, 1950), p. 165.

[2] *Ibid.,* p. 166.

[3] *Ibid.,* p. 167.

[4] John E. Anderson, "Principles of Growth and Maturity in Language," *Elementary English Review,* 18:250, November, 1941.

that when he comes to school, he is not just beginning to talk, but has talked millions of words in varying situations — some productive of, and others not conducive to good language. In general, the child has learned language in situations without the aid of formal grammar. Generally, he has talked about subjects and topics of his own choosing. He has in a sense learned to talk by talking. He has used simple, compound, and complex sentences, and statements, questions, and requests. The length of the sentence used by children grows gradually from one word at a year and a half to about seven words when they enter school. Children use complete sentences quite generally at the ages from three to four, but they do not discontinue the incomplete sentences entirely. The development of sentence structure continues in upper elementary school and into higher levels of education.

Children who come to school vary in many ways — in intelligence, experience, background, and readiness for learning; some are strong and healthy, others not so well — perhaps malnourished and often easily fatigued because of lack of sleep and proper care. The normal child can be properly guided in the regular classroom, but the deviants, particularly the slow learners, require special treatment. The girls seem to have a small but real advantage over the boys in most phases of language, and the boys more often than girls show evidence of language difficulty. However, the sex differences are not pronounced and some recent research has shown that there are a number of differences which favor boys.[5]

In planning language development, it is important to consider two problems: (1) how to develop new abilities, habits, and skills of expression; and (2) how to guide each child to change from ineffective or defective language habits to effective and acceptable ways of communicating with others. In considering these problems in the early grades, it should be recognized that although language is an integrating unitary process, the development of speaking and listening skills and habits should rightly precede to some extent reading and writing procedures.[6]

## Importance of Oral Language

Oral language is the center — the heart of the communication arts. Speech is unquestionably one of the most useful of the language arts.

---

[5] John B. Carroll, "Language Development," *Encyclopedia of Educational Research,* third edition (New York: The Macmillan Company, 1960), p. 749.
[6] *Ibid.,* p. 750.

Rankin reported that talking ranked next to listening in the amount of time that is given to it in living communication. Talking, which was used so frequently in preschool periods, is curtailed considerably in school.[7] Because children are not permitted to talk so much as they did before they began school, the adjustment for many of them requires considerate guidance.

Oral language is important in every walk of life — to the citizen, the businessman, the farmer, the lawyer, the statesman, the minister, the teacher, and the salesman. Oral communication is necessary to the average person in his vocation, in his home life, and in recreation. Everyone should be able to carry on a conversation, use the telephone, give directions, explain processes, use anecdotes, recount experiences pleasantly, make reports succinctly, and buy groceries for example, as it becomes necessary for him to do so.

A child should learn to meet people with poise, understand the importance of talking at the right time and of not talking when an occasion calls for silence. Every pupil must educate himself to speak clearly in all situations that call for such talking, learn an acceptable vocabulary and use it in good taste, understand the principles of good colloquial speech, and develop competence in listening and speaking.

## Need for Instruction in Oral Language

Every child has many needs for instruction in oral language. Before he comes to school, he learns to vocalize. He begins to comprehend the way of life in his society, and the etiquette of communicating with others. He tries to understand the way of behaving in getting along with his parents, with other children, and with the neighbors. He recognizes the necessity for expressing himself by actions, words, and behavior, and knows the needs for listening to others and of giving thought to their expressions.

Some children enter school with high aims and purposes because they want to learn to read and write and spell, while others do not recognize the importance of speaking correctly. Since they will converse almost constantly in life outside the school, even more than they will read, write, spell, and use handwriting, they must be guided to learn to talk well and to overcome wrong habits developed in their preschool life.

---

[7] Paul T. Rankin, "Listening Ability," *Chicago Schools Journal,* 12:177–179, June, 1930.

## Objectives of Oral Language

The objectives of oral language should be presented so potently that children will strongly desire to achieve them. It should be clear that learning to talk is not just a matter of saying anything and everything that comes to mind. A child should be stimulated to express himself properly in social situations in and out of school, and appropriately on all other occasions which call for oral communication.

Among the aims which a child should be guided to achieve are:

1. To talk appropriately and naturally with others — parents, neighbors, children, teachers
2. To speak courteously at all times in giving directions, making introductions, and presenting announcements and explanations
3. To engage in conversation with poise and courtesy, and to enter into the "give and take" of discussion intelligently and pleasantly
4. To listen attentively and speak correctly and in good taste on the telephone
5. To tell stories interestingly and to participate acceptably in plays and choral speaking
6. To prepare reports and other contributions for meetings by reading, thinking, studying, and organizing what is to be presented
7. To develop proper voice control, correct pronunciation, good enunciation, and distinct and pleasant speech
8. To evaluate critically one's speech and manner of talking, to diagnose deficiencies, and to take proper measures for correction of shortcomings.

It is obvious that to achieve these objectives in oral language, the aims of listening and those of the other language arts must be kept in mind. One cannot engage in conversation properly without listening attentively to what the others in the group say. One cannot talk appropriately in any social situation unless he comprehends the thoughts of others. One cannot be effective in discussion without evaluating the statements made by the others. Furthermore, a child can learn to speak effectively in public or in class only by careful study and preparation. In striving to achieve the aims suggested, it will be well to consider such problems as the use of words, phrasing, sentence structure, and organization. The correct pronunciation of a particularly difficult word, for example, may require careful study and exacting practice in saying the word in order that it be used properly.

Objectives of speaking should be acquired in social situations, but they may require specific preparatory practice and dynamic drill in order that competence be achieved. While teachers should be considerate of pupils' striving for naturalness, they should not be blind to carelessness and slovenliness in speech. However, it should be recognized that conversation on the street may well be easier in manner and more colloquial than that used when speaking to an audience, making a report in a class discussion, or answering questions in an oral quiz. The individual should become sensitive to the requirements and needs in every situation, and recognize the importance of understanding, poise, and correct expression in each.

## SITUATIONS FAVORABLE TO TALKING AND ITS DEVELOPMENT

The situations which call for talking naturally in and out of school should be utilized in developing the skills and abilities for speaking informally yet appropriately. Among them are the following:

1. Sharing experiences
2. Conversation
3. Informal discussion
4. Making explanations
5. Giving directions
6. Making announcements
7. Using the telephone
8. Audience talking — making reports and talks
9. Storytelling
10. Dramatic play
11. Choral speaking
12. Parliamentary procedure.

### Sharing Experiences

Experiences are enriching to children whether they are real or vicarious. Those who have experienced a thrilling ride, an exciting game, or an enjoyable summer vacation usually desire to tell about it to another child, to a group on the playground, or to the whole class, perhaps in the English period. Such experiences should be made use of in oral language. One boy who had spent his summer traveling in the Rocky Mountains with his father had many things to tell his classmates about the Yellowstone Park, the Old Faithful Geyser, bears, and other animals. A girl who returned from Europe had fascinating stories of experiences to relate to her classmates about London, Paris, Rome, and Lisbon. This child who had the pleasure of riding on the liner *United States,* described the ship and answered questions about it. A child who has had rich experiences will be richer for talking about them, and the youngsters who listen will learn vicariously.

No child in a second-grade class could think of anything which he deemed worthwhile, but questioning by the teacher brought out the telling of several interesting experiences. One child spent a half day at a zoo; another saw a circus; a third visited a mink ranch; a fourth viewed an exhibit of athletic goods; a fifth watched builders construct a bridge across a river; a sixth described work he saw in a factory; a seventh visited a farm.

## Conversation

Conversation is a give-and-take communication activity in which two or more people converse — talk with and listen to each other. It is an oral exchange of ideas, opinions, sentiments, and observations. While it is thought of principally as talking and listening, it frequently employs gesturing, facial grimaces, observing, and reacting to the expressions of others. Conversations are more frequently used than other types of oral communication. Youngsters talk to themselves or to imaginary beings. They engage in parallel conversations in the presence of others. Often they talk with their parents about many topics — asking innumerable questions and listening to answers. As these children become acclimated to school and as they grow up, they continue to talk in and out of school in almost every situation which permits vocal expression. As they mature, there is evident need for improving abilities, skills, and habits in conversation.

Conversation requires thinking and ability to listen and respond appropriately to what others say, and the aptitude to understand other personalities. A conversation is often incidental, and the talk may change almost instantly from one topic to another. The topics seem to be selected on the initiative of one or another of the participants. Sometimes the topic is brought about by a question which one asks another. Often an event or an activity becomes the topic of conversation. Occasionally, a conversation may be concentrated about only one topic, but frequently it is concerned with several different things.

*Requisites of conversation.* Conversation requires on the part of a conversationalist: (1) consideration of the other members of the group; (2) clear thinking and effective expression; (3) tact in selecting a topic and in conversing about it; (4) understanding of desirable topics to be discussed; (5) sensitivity and skill in avoidance of undesirable topics; (6) ability to change the conversation topic; (7) ability to talk clearly about topics of interest; and (8) aptitude in utilizing knowledge about a topic gained from experience or reading. A good conversationalist is aided by a sense of humor, geniality, broadmindedness, originality, and sincerity.[8] He is sensitive, pleasant, and considerate.

*Instruction in conversation technics.* Although a conversation is generally not a preplanned activity, a teacher may arrange for pupil conversations about interesting topics. Desirable qualities of such conversations are:

1. Beginning a conversation in a socially acceptable manner at the proper time
2. Terminating a conversation graciously
3. Knowing when and where not to initiate a conversation
4. Speaking appropriately in a conversation
5. Maintaining an agreeable attitude in conversation
6. Listening attentively and understandingly and responding considerately to another's statement
7. Using acceptable language and vocabulary
8. Knowing how to indicate in an agreeable fashion that there might be two sides to a proposition
9. Following an introduction with appropriate and interesting talk
10. Changing a topic of conversation when it seems advisable because of the feelings, thinking, or attitudes of other members of a group.[9]

*Planning topics for instruction in conversation.* Children in the kindergarten have interests in topics often different from those of a primary grade group, and children of a second-grade class frequently indicate choices differing from those of pupils in intermediate grade

---

[8] Harry A. Greene and Walter T. Petty, *Developing Language in the Elementary School* (Boston: Allyn and Bacon, Inc., 1959), p. 83.

[9] See Maude McBroom and others, *The Course of Study in Oral Composition,* unpublished report, University Elementary School, State University of Iowa, Iowa City, Iowa. Referred to by Paul McKee, *Language in the Elementary School* (Boston: Houghton Mifflin Company, 1939), pp. 97–98.

groups. Some suggestions follow for selection of topics to be used in instruction in conversation. Youngsters will offer excellent topics and their topics should frequently precede those suggested here. Sometimes a teacher may need to make suggestions from which children will choose one in which the whole group is interested.

Among the topics often selected are: pets, toys, games, dolls, animals in the circus or on the farm, trips, gardens, picnics, plays, sports, airplanes, parties, books, TV programs, music, singing, cars, clothes, the weather, excursions, projects, problems, news items, poems, stories, and many topics from various units and activities.

*Using sources.* As the child develops, he will recognize the importance of using valid sources of information in making conversation. An intermediate grade pupil may state, "I read about a sailor who said he saw a sea serpent." Another may bring in a report from *Compton's Encyclopedia, Britannica Junior,* or the *World Book Encyclopedia* about atomic energy or wild life. Stories and anecdotes from periodicals may add greatly to a conversation. Materials found in good books of literature, history, or science may be used effectively in conversation as well as in discussion. They not only add interest to talking but make the activity worthwhile as a learning procedure.

*Developing correct attitudes.* Some children have little knowledge of acceptable conversation skills, particularly those concerning right attitude and social grace. A teacher by her own example has an opportunity to assist an egocentric pupil in achieving an altruistic and considerate attitude in conversing with others. Children imitate a dynamic, refined, and considerate teacher. Often they go so far as to imitate a teacher's mannerisms, which may not be desirable. But it is desirable to develop courtesy, sincerity, and good manners. A teacher will influence a child to want to learn to talk correctly and courteously by her own attitude toward a topic or problem. She may talk with a child individually after a conversation is concluded concerning mistakes he made in voicing his opinion too loudly, in speaking too critically, or in disagreeing objectionably.

Perhaps there is no one group of factors which causes people to be disliked or liked more than the types of attitudes evidenced in a conversation. The attitudes toward people and the method of approach to problems become evident to members of a group. A sense of humor, a wide interest, a receptivity toward the sayings of others, and sympathy for the difficulties of companions are desirable in a conversationalist. The recognition for the need of trying to understand a problem and to find a solution to it receives favorable consideration from one's associates and classmates. Instruction which develops these characteristics should be planned and carried out.

*Teaching the child to avoid undesirable practices.*    The learner must differentiate between good and bad practices in conversation. By example, through instruction, and in individual interviews, a teacher has a responsibility to help each child to avoid such practices as the following: playing with chains, rings, ornaments, pencils, buttons, beads, and fingers; fingering clothing, hair, neck, face; gesturing excessively; making peculiar grimaces; using affected accent or pronunciation; talking too loud or too low; employing slang; using incorrect language; assuming a slovenly posture; behaving in an undesirable manner; showing discourtesy in word or act.

Other bad practices which should be avoided in conversation are: arguing; being blunt in denying another's statement; developing peculiar mannerisms; monopolizing a conversation or attempting to do so; interrupting another who is speaking, or interrupting a conversation unnecessarily; saying unpleasant or unkind things about individuals either present or absent; using ridicule or sarcasm; acting bored; not listening; speaking about a topic embarrassing to others; and talking persistently about experiences or topics of interest only to two or three of the group.

*Evaluating conversations.*    Instruction in developing conversation should include appraisal of the topic, procedures in talking, and outcomes. Purposing, planning, and carrying out a program of conversation should be scrutinized and improved when possible. The teacher and the pupils may generally discuss the strong points and the unfavorable points. Children will know whether a conversation was interesting, and they should be guided to appreciate the reasons for appeal and pleasure in some conversations and the dullness and lack of interest in others.

Questions concerning the desirability of the topic, the effectiveness of participants, the contributions of members of the group, and the attitudes of each can be discussed. Children will be interested in knowing the reasons for favorable or unfavorable appraisal. By means of evaluative procedures, they should recognize whether the purpose — obtaining information, enjoyment, helping a person feel at home, or assisting a speaker to pass the time until the beginning of a program — has been achieved. Children will sometimes question whether the expressions were clear, whether the thinking was adequate or in-

An informal discussion

adequate, whether enunciations were correct or faulty, whether listening and attention were appropriate, whether the attitudes gave evidence of sincerity or insincerity, of good humor or lack of humor, of considerateness or inconsiderateness, and whether the conversation began purposively, moved forward smoothly, and achieved desirable goals.

## *Discussions*

The informal discussion is generally a purposeful oral consideration of a topic or topics by a group. It is one of the most used of technics in the elementary school. It resembles a conversation, but it is generally a planned project in which definite problems are considered by a group in a more or less systematic manner, usually with a teacher or pupil as leader. The discussion is purposive because it is planned and executed with goals in mind, while the conversation may be quite incidental. The informal discussion usually develops about a question or topic and moves forward to a goal or conclusion while the conversation may shift from one topic to another. Although argument is not a necessary ingredient of an informal discussion, it would seem that a discussion should consider varying views of a question and ought to permit the presentation of facts to support the different positions taken.

The suggestions made about listening, speaking, articulation, pronunciation, and attitudes concerning conversation apply to discussion.

*Situations and needs for discussion.* Many school situations promote a discussion on problems such as the following:

1. How to induce better behavior in the lunchroom
2. How to keep the classroom neat and clean
3. How to keep a notebook in language
4. How to write a friendly letter
5. How to find materials for discussion
6. How to make a graph.

These are examples of practical problems for study; there are many other types of problems which arise from reading, such as the following:

1. What nursery rhymes are most enjoyable?
2. What stories give us the most pleasure in our first grade?
3. What poems do we like best in our second grade?
4. Why do we like a poem and what causes us to want to listen to it?
5. Why did the Pilgrims come to our country?
6. Describe the colonists in New York, Massachusetts, Pennsylvania, Virginia. How were they different?
7. Why did our forefathers want to be free from England?
8. How did the colonists treat the Indians?

As important as these selected from work in reading, literature, and history are many others in science, for example, which may be used from the lower to the upper elementary school levels:

1. When do flowers grow? What makes them grow?
2. How can we of the third grade plant a garden?
3. How can we of the fifth grade make a self-sustaining aquarium?
4. What causes day and night?
5. What is the cause of the seasons?
6. How do animals live in the winter?
7. Why can birds fly? Why can men fly?
8. What causes rain?
9. What causes lightning?
10. What does $E = MC^2$ mean?
11. How does sound travel?
12. Why is a rose red?
13. How are tides caused?
14. How can atoms be split?
15. How can we preserve wild life?
16. How can we conserve our natural resources?[10]

---

[10] Glenn O. Blough, Julius Schwartz, and Albert J. Huggett, *Elementary School Science and How to Teach It,* revised edition (New York: Henry Holt and Company, Inc., 1958), 608 pp.

Such questions and problems as the above promote discussion. Many types may be carried out quite naturally and profitably in work on projects and activities. The following projects have been used successfully: (*a*) the planning of an assembly; (*b*) the planting of a tree on Arbor Day; (*c*) the writing of a class history; (*d*) the collection of news for an issue of the school paper. These are examples of activities which promote oral communication: (*a*) operating a school store; (*b*) managing a library; (*c*) maintaining a lost and found station; (*d*) keeping a bulletin board; (*e*) running a bank.

*Planning and carrying out a discussion.* The leader should have a plan in mind for a discussion or he may enlist the aid of a committee to formulate agenda. Among the main points are the following:

1. The purpose should be made clear by presenting a mimeographed agenda or by writing a series of questions on the chalkboard.

2. The chairman should suggest a plan of working. Points may be stated in order that all members of the group will have an opportunity to study them.

3. The members should consider the points or issues, one after another; facts and information may be supplied, opinions given, and judgments made.

4. A summary of the discussion may be prepared by a recorder or secretary appointed to report the findings.

If there seems to be need for further study, committees may be appointed to consider respective problems. A time should be set for a second meeting at which they will be discussed in the light of new evidence. Minutes of the meeting may be recorded.

*Sources of information.* The library should be visited and sources consulted. Letters may be written to agencies, boards, commissions, and governmental bodies for suggestions, materials, and facts. Pupils should exhaust the resources of the library before requesting information from commercial firms.

*Committee work.* A class may be divided into several committees to consider phases of a project. Committees generally function under a chairman and follow an orderly procedure.

A committee may request permission of the principal to make an excursion. A committee may be asked to study the possibility of staging an operetta. A committee may visit a bank to obtain information about initiating a school bank.

A report by two or three members should be reviewed by the committee before presentation to the class. The report should be made clearly and completely, and this can be done by one pupil, or by three or four in a type of panel discussion. The report may be written out and read, or an outline may be mimeographed, copies distributed to the class, and explanations made. Questions should be asked and answered.

*Using the results of committee work.*    Outcomes, findings, and results of committee work should be made available to the class. If the report is deficient, it should be amended; if it is valid, the materials should be accepted by the whole group as a part of their stock of knowledge. The results of a properly recorded project should be useful to a class during a year, and to other groups the following year.

*Asking and answering questions.*    Perhaps there is nothing better in education than a well-thought-out question. Pupils should learn to formulate intelligent questions and to present them in an effective manner. The ability to answer questions is a valuable technic. To comprehend a question, to recognize its importance, to remember its parts, to utilize information from many sources in answering it, are desirable skills.

*Evaluation.*    Children will enjoy orderly, informal, interesting discussions. Among the values of such work are the following: listening is enhanced; oral English is improved; leadership is developed; thinking is fostered; getting along with others is practiced. Discussion that is worthwhile guides class action and pupil behavior. Each pupil's participation should be evaluated by the teacher and by the learner himself. Sharing in a discussion and in the outcome of study preparatory to it will stimulate motives for improving communication.

## Making Explanations

Making preparation for explanations and presenting them with clarity are valuable activities. The following points should be made clear to pupils to make acceptable explanations:

1. Know the purpose for the explanation.
2. Learn about the process, product, or topic that is to be explained.
3. Prepare an organized plan for presenting the explanation, step by step.
4. Emphasize the main points properly; omit the extraneous materials and unnecessary details.

5. Plan the explanation so that the listeners will recognize and appreciate its value.

6. Choose words and form sentences carefully in order to convey precise meanings.

7. Use pictures, drawings, graphs, and audio-visual aids, if necessary to make the subject clear.

8. Summarize the process or topic succinctly to help the listeners obtain the whole picture of it and to appreciate its significance.

9. Answer questions on the subject or product patiently and clearly.

Pupils who have studied or experienced processes such as "running a school store," sketching a map, caring for a car, or making a doll have a basis for presenting explanations. Constructive criticism by the teacher and the group and self-criticism by the pupil should help in developing skill in this important activity.

### Giving Directions

Directions given by the average person — child or adult — are frequently perplexing to one who needs them. Confusion is caused generally by lack of facility in the language and by failure to anchor directions to a point known by the one who is in need of them.

The pupil may be guided to give directions acceptably by planning exercises for directing someone to a church, library, courthouse, or bank. The following suggestions to the learner should be helpful in giving directions:

1. Base directions upon the knowledge of the inquirer.

2. Speak courteously; use language the listener or listeners can comprehend.

3. Give the necessary information clearly; state steps in direct sequence.

4. Emphasize prominent principal points or landmarks in the directions.

5. If necessary make a sketch or drawing.

6. Summarize the important points to follow in carrying out the directions.

7. Answer questions pleasantly and explicitly.

### Making Announcements

Among the occasions in which it is necessary to make an announcement are: notice of extra practice; the postponement of a rehearsal; the availability of materials for a project; the statement of plans for an activity. The following points should be extremely helpful:

1. Know the purpose of the announcement.
2. Plan the announcement before beginning to speak.
3. The opening sentence should arouse interest.
4. All essential facts should be presented clearly.
5. The announcement should be complete but as brief as possible.
6. The speaker should be enthusiastic and pleasant.

## Telephoning

In our modern society nearly everyone uses a telephone. A few lessons in the early grades will pay high dividends later. Courtesy should be fostered and proper etiquette developed. As science changes, a learner should be curious about the new telephone technics and study their advantages.

*Preparing to call.* A teacher should have several copies of telephone books to pass around. Pupils should be taught how to find numbers by looking up names alphabetically in the directory, and how to make local, emergency, and long-distance calls. They should become acquainted with the technics of phoning, the method of calling the fire and police departments, and the use of direct dialing. The importance of releasing the phone in case of an emergency call for a doctor, police officer, or fire station should be taught. Recognition of the "beep" signal indicating that a recording is being made of the conversation, recognizing the busy signal, acquaintance with the person-to-person technic, and knowledge of collect calls are interesting to pupils in the middle grades and become increasingly useful to them.

*Dialing long distance.* A pupil may become adept at dialing a local call, but many adults are hesitant and confused in using the improved methods for dialing numbers in distant cities. The introductory pages of a telephone book present valuable information about problems that a telephone user faces.

*Initiating a call and answering the phone.* One who calls another on the phone should give his name when someone answers, and ask for the person with whom he wishes to speak. There are varied suggestions for answering the phone. The pupil should learn that in ordinary business situations it is proper to indicate the firm, the department, the extension, and the name of the one answering. Answering a phone call at a residence may be similarly executed, but sometimes people answer simply by saying "hello."

*Talking on the phone.* The child should be taught to talk clearly in a moderate voice, courteously, and at normal speed. If, as sometimes happens, one cannot understand another, it is helpful to inform the operator and a new connection will generally remedy the difficulty. One should learn to keep the lips at a distance of about one inch from the transmitter when speaking, and the receiver in contact with the ear when listening. In taking a call for another, transmit the message either verbally or in writing to the person for whom it is intended. It is advisable to telephone at opportune times — not at mealtime or midnight unless a request has been made for a call at such a time. Telephone conversations should be comparatively brief and to the point. The telephone should not be used for extended visiting.

## Speaking and Reporting

There is need for the teaching of speaking and reporting in the elementary school, principally because there are many situations in which children talk and report about interesting experiences and work activities.[11] Lundin emphasized the importance of speaking in the elementary school. "The ability to give a short talk before one's group with reasonable effectiveness is one of the most important objectives of oral language instruction in the elementary school."[12] Some teachers negate the importance of making talks or speeches in the elementary school. If, however, we are to teach excellence in our schools, it would be wrong to ignore the opportunities for such speaking and to avoid giving instruction from which children can benefit. In the instruction on speaking, real situations should be utilized. Short talks should be made more or less informally particularly in the lower elementary grades and practice of such speaking should be promoted. To be satisfied with mediocrity from those who can produce excellency is to neglect opportunities for developing oral language.

*Real situations favorable to speaking.* A real need and a desire to express are motives for guiding children to make short informal talks. The child who has an experience to relate, a story to tell, or a report

[11] Harry A. Greene and William S. Gray, "The Measurement of Understanding in the Language Arts," *The Measurement of Understanding,* Forty-Fifth Yearbook of the National Society for the Study of Education, Part I, 1946, p. 179.

[12] Ethel H. Lundin, "Learning to Make Short Talks," *Language Arts in the Elementary School,* Twentieth Yearbook of the National Elementary Principal, July, 1941, p. 296. By permission.

to give will have a motive for speaking effectively. If the occasion is real, the child will receive pleasure in preparing — outlining, planning, and practicing — his talk, and the talk will be an intensive and satisfying experience. The following are a few real situations used by elementary school children in the early and middle grades:

1. The introduction of a police official who has been invited to talk to the class
2. Presenting a bouquet to a child who is in the hospital
3. A farewell talk presenting a gift to a classmate who is leaving for another city
4. A plea for keeping the school grounds clean
5. An appeal for a donation to charity
6. A report of a trip to a city
7. A description of a polar bear viewed in the zoo
8. A presentation of an experiment showing that air has weight
9. An introduction of a topic to a group for discussion
10. A talk about a trip to the Rocky Mountains
11. A description of a bridge
12. A funny story remembered from reading a periodical
13. Relating an anecdote.

*The purpose of talks.*   Children who spoke in the situations listed above had the purposes: (1) to inform, (2) to explain, (3) to convince, (4) to move listeners to act, and (5) to entertain.

Seven-year-old John related an experience on a fishing trip to Brant Lake with his father. He held the attention of the class by describing breathlessly how his fish pole "bent nearly double" when he hooked his fish. He told of catching a large lake trout, so strong that it nearly "tipped the boat over." After a long struggle and with some assistance from his father which he did not emphasize, the twelve-inch fish was landed securely in the boat. Questions from the group brought out the reluctant admission that he had considerable help in the episode, and that the near capsizing of the boat was caused by his excitement and not by the size of the fish. The purpose of this talk was to inform.

Mary had reported on the "First Winter of the Pilgrims in America," and was asked by the third-grade teacher to explain her method of preparing the report. She told enthusiastically that she selected the topic because of her interest in history and because she thought her classmates would like the story. She read what she could find in *Compton's Pictured Encyclopedia* and in books the librarian helped her locate. She said she talked to a scholarly neighbor. She told how she made some notes about her topic from the three sources. Following that, she made a little outline with (1) an introduction, (2) a main body, and (3) a conclusion. Finally, she explained, "I said my report over and over several times last night and once again this morning."

In a talk about keeping the school lawn free of debris, a fifth-grade speaker asked pupils to use waste receptacles and not to throw refuse on the school grounds. Reasons were given to convince his schoolmates of the importance of neatness in and around their school building. In his talk, he tried to cause them to throw wastepaper, candy wrappings, fruit peelings, and apple cores into trash cans. This talk sought to convince and move listeners to act.

A speaker who relates a funny story does so generally to entertain, and practice in storytelling is encouraged in many elementary classrooms.

*Preparation for speaking.* In general, every speaker faces the problems of: knowing what to say; saying it effectively; and of stopping when he has given his message. A child in preparing to speak should know his purpose and what he has to offer to the audience. He should try to plan for the particular group to whom he will talk; he should strive for clarity of thinking and speaking.

The child who wishes to make a report orally must know where to find the materials — books, periodicals, encyclopedias, and other sources — that will help him talk intelligently. His introduction should be brief but should gain attention. His purpose should be made clear to his audience. The discussion should contain a specific number of main points — two or three — perhaps. Practice in stating them will be worthwhile. The end of the speech may well be a conclusion or a summary, given in such a way that the main points will be clear. It is not difficult for a child to remember an introduction and the main points of discussion if they are his own. His summary will be simple if he practices planning, thinking, and saying the talk over to himself. Practice in thinking through the talk is an aid to facility in expression.

*Characteristics to be developed by a speaker.* Learners should understand the importance of trying to develop the following qualities:

1. Good posture — naturalness in standing or sitting
2. Poise — mental, physical, and emotional control
3. Honesty — telling the truth
4. Sincerity — being in earnest about one's message
5. An enthusiastic approach to delivering the message
6. A sense of humor

7. A pleasant voice and facial expression, variety in tone and speed of delivery
8. Good language, correct English, clarity in speaking
9. Correct pronunciation, distinct enunciation and articulation
10. Adaptability — alertness to sense the need for change and the ability to meet unforeseen eventualities
11. Originality — the power to state thoughts effectively in one's own way.

A teacher must appraise a child's strong and weak points. Deficiencies must be made matters for remediation, and the strong points should be used as means of motivation.

*Important factors in teaching oral expression.* The following factors should be stressed in oral language, particularly in a prepared report or talk: purpose, interest, essential principles of speaking, use of life situations, value of pacing and success, importance of integration and correlation.

1. *Purpose guides the speaker.* Purpose is denoted by answers to the questions: Why is the talk to be made? What is to be accomplished? Answers must be clear to the speaker if the talk is to succeed.

2. *Interest is the secret.* If the speaker is enthusiastic about his subject, studies it with a desire to learn much about it, and becomes imbued with a driving desire to tell others about it, to explain it, to describe it, to convince others of its importance, or move them to act in a specific way, he has achieved important factors which will generally guide him to success in oral language.

3. *Essential principles of speaking must be followed.* The child should learn three important principles of speaking to an audience: (*a*) Know what to say. (*b*) Say it. (*c*) Stop when through. Knowing what to say comes about by thinking, study, experiencing, reading, appraisal, organization. Expression can be improved by both practice and by experience. The study of ways of speaking is important. Knowing when to stop speaking should not be difficult for one who knows both his message and his audience.

4. *When possible, life situations should be used for speaking.* Speaking in real situations cannot be duplicated by any other kind of talking. Practice is valuable, and preparation by thinking, reading, pronunciation of words, phrasing, and expressing sentences is very important, but real speaking on natural occasions and in life situations should be utilized at every opportunity.

5. *Pacing and success.* An understanding teacher will lead an individual gradually from the simple to the complex and from the easy

type of speaking opportunities to more difficult situations. When success has been attained by the pupil in familiar or easy kinds of speaking, he will be more likely to succeed in a difficult speaking engagement. The value of pacing should be understood by teacher and pupil in developing success in speaking.

6. *Integration and correlation.* Perspective must be developed; balance should be achieved. Adequate knowledge of the subject, use of properly selected words, correct diction, variation in delivery, and courtesy in talking and listening should be integrated in speaking. The knowledge gained in social studies, science, reading, and experience should be employed in speaking, and the many procedures used in written language may be made bases for performing acceptably in oral language.

## Storytelling

A good story is a joyous experience both for the listener and for the teller. An accomplished storyteller is an artist. Few people tell stories exceedingly well, and no teacher should place the goals for children too high, but elementary school teachers should formulate aims for storytelling which can be achieved. A first-grade teacher can help a child to tell a story about his ride with his father. A second-grade child will probably tell a story about his dog chasing a squirrel or a rabbit.

An acceptable story may be true or it may be imagined. Whether true or imaginary, it should be interestingly related. Children are good listeners to fascinating tales told by anyone — parent, neighbor, teacher, or other pupils.

*Value of storytelling.* The pupil learns by practice and through reading the importance of a story well told — its interest and its utility. An intermediate pupil may have read exciting stories — the *Adventures of Kit Carson* or the *Battle of Lexington*. He will have listened to other stories and enjoyed them. He should know that a story is important in making a talk, and he may have heard someone who began a speech with a story. Perhaps the fireman who addressed the class told the story of a terrible oil fire. Perhaps a pioneer told the story of a prairie fire. Experiences such as these will convince him of people's interest in a well-related tale and the use of stories in various activities.

*Sources for obtaining stories.* Among the sources for obtaining stories are: experience, books, listening to others, newspapers, magazines, and imagination. Fables, folktales, fairy stories, Indian stories, tales of ancient times, and stories of pioneers may be gleaned from many sources. Reading and storytelling may be correlated in such a way that the child will read avidly to search for stories, and will tell enthusiastically the most attractive ones. Among the library books which are interesting to children are: *Aesop's Fables, Grimm's Fairy Tales, Children's True Book Series, Chandler's Cowboy Series,* and the *Filmore Folk Tales.* Reading to discover stories and anecdotes for the purpose of relating them is a fruitful activity, and the telling can be rewarding and very motivating for further reading. A book club, a story club, or an anecdote club may be an avenue for story enrichment.[13]

*Some tentative principles for guiding storytelling in the classroom.* Each teacher will develop tentative principles for guiding storytelling. The following may be helpful in setting up worthwhile practices:

1. The child should select stories to tell that are interesting to him.

2. He should select stories to tell that he thinks will be enjoyed by his listeners.

3. An informal procedure should be developed in storytelling.

4. The types of stories told may vary from the funny anecdote to the sublime event in order that experiences and interests may be widened.

5. A free reading program should motivate storytelling, and the storytelling urge should motivate wider reading.

6. Each child should prepare carefully for the telling of his story, using the dictionary, reading and rereading, and thinking about the sequence of the story.

7. The child should be permitted to tell his story in his own way, but suggestions for improvement are helpful.

8. An informal discussion may be valuable after the story is told so that questions of listeners may be answered.

9. Dramatization of stories may be encouraged.

10. Encouragement may be enhanced by praise, by thoughtful teacher criticism, by applause, and by suggestions of classmates.

11. Each child should consciously strive to improve his voice, fluency, expression, pronunciation, and technics of storytelling.

12. The teacher should tell a story occasionally in order that children may enjoy her ability and learn through imitation.

---

[13] See lists of supplementary books, magazines, and periodicals in Albert J. Harris, *Effective Teaching of Reading* (New York: McKay Company, 1962), pp. 352–356.

Play production

13. A child may be called upon by the class to retell a story which was very well received.

14. The shy child may tell his story to the teacher, to another child, or to a small group before attempting to talk to the whole class.

15. In order to give more experience and practice, a gifted class can be divided into several groups of from three to ten children according to their interests, and the storytelling may be carried on in each group. Such a plan gives each child more opportunities to tell stories.

16. A storytelling contest may be interesting and valuable as a motivation exercise in some situations.

17. On special occasions, representatives from groups may tell selected stories to the whole class.

### Dramatic Play and Dramatization

Dramatic play and dramatics are important because they provide a high type of motivation for expression as well as the joy of enthusiastic activity. They provide a means of combining expression with

exciting incidents of living and of imagination. Pupils from kindergarten to high school become characters in scenes they play and in
dramas they imagine. They live the parts they play of parents, teachers,
explorers, pioneers, soldiers, and statesmen. They also play the parts
of animals and fairies. Such play animates expression and stimulates
originality.

*Some suggestions for dramatic play.*    Dramatic play and play acting
have a real part in developing poise and confidence. Our literature is
rich in folk tales, fables, and Mother Goose rhymes that are useful
for dramatics in the elementary school. Among the Mother Goose
rhymes that may be dramatized in the primary grades are the following:

> "Baa, Baa, Black Sheep"
> "Hey, Diddle, Diddle"
> "Come, Butter, Come"
> "Pussy-cat, Pussy-cat, Where Have You Been?"
> "Jack Be Nimble"
> "Little Jack Horner"
> "Little Miss Muffet"
> "Peter, Peter, Pumpkin-Eater"
> "Old King Cole"
> "Where Are You Going, My Pretty Maid?"

While the above and many others may be acted out after they have
been told and enjoyed in the first grade, others may be used in second
grade and grades above. Among them are:

> "Yankee Doodle Went to Town"
> "I Had a Little Pony"
> "This Is the House That Jack Built"
> "Old Mother Hubbard"
> "The 500 Hats of Bartholomew Cubbins"

Fables also may be made the basis of dramatic play. After children understand the trend of a story they can plan a presentation
based upon it. A discussion about the presentation and the appraisal
of it are valuable for the purpose of improving language. "The
Wolf in Sheep's Clothing" may be used as a basis for acting. When
the shepherd decided to kill one of the sheep and killed the wolf
instead the youngsters feel that the bad wolf was trapped in his
own mischief. "The Lion and the Mouse" has great possibilities for
playacting, and although some authorities think that a moral should
not be thrust at the child, the thoughtful child may see that friends
are important in life.

Fables such as the following may be used as bases for dramatic
play:

"The Shepherd's Boy and the Wolf"
"The Dog and His Shadow"
"The Fox and the Crow"
"The Hare and the Tortoise"
"The Grasshopper and the Ants"
"The Fox and the Grapes"

Folktales, fairy tales, myths, legends, biblical stories, nature stories, fiction, true stories of heroism and of perseverance of people may be used for plays. Children can create dramatic sketches from real incidents in the lives of people. Poetry is filled with intriguing episodes which may be dramatized.

*Children's dramatics develop thinking and originality.* Children play house, store, and school. They imitate their parents, the storekeeper, the inventor, the scientist, the doctor, and the teacher with discerning insight and in some detail. In varying ways children depict life in natural situations. They portray the Americans at Concord and Lexington, at Valley Forge, at Bull Run, at Saint-Mihiel, at Pearl Harbor, and in Korea. In their portrayals, they learn that war is not all glory, but that it is filled with heartaches and sorrow and sacrifice. They learn that the life of the settler was not glamorous, but rather permeated with work, and challenged with struggle against many forces — wind, dust, storm, insects, grasshoppers, locusts, wild beasts, starvation, and disease. They learn not only to express, but they learn about the way our forefathers and our fathers worked and lived.

Dramatics promote thinking about the way historic and literary characters felt and acted in varying situations. What might have been a dry recital of historical narrative becomes a vivid vicarious experience. Children become interested, try to think the thoughts and re-enact the behavior of people who were participants in historic events. They become creative in their attempts to play the roles of these people and eventually they design original plays and skits. They banish their fears of expression, and act out the landing of the Pilgrims, the Boston Tea Party, the First Constitutional Convention, the Lincoln-Douglas debates, the first telephonic conversation, and the discovery of oil in Pennsylvania. In differing episodes, they think thoughts original for them; they express these thoughts, often selecting words they never used before; they devise for themselves new ways of talking and new patterns of action. They lose their timidity and act the part of people in many vocations both of the past and present. Children in their role-playing develop voice control, self-confidence, poise, and self-assurance. They are guided to improve enunciation, pronunciation, vocabulary, and diction.

## Nonverbal Communication

Words are aided greatly by nonverbal means of communication. When one drives on a street, he is directed by red and green lights when to *stop* and *go*. Traffic signs of various shapes indicate the types of roads to expect ahead. Smoke signals have been used since ancient times to send news. Clouds portend the weather. Signals "one, if by land, and two, if by sea" were to indicate the plans of the British. Listening for sounds was an important means of receiving messages by peoples of all eras. We still note the class bells, school bells, church chimes, fire sirens, and the alarm clocks to warn and direct us in our modern life. Odors, aromas, perfumes, and smells make us aware of drugs, cooking, flowers, and types of animals. The senses of taste and touch are constantly utilized to give information about materials and objects. It is probable that the senses combine more than people surmise to communicate various types of information. The present-day individual surely should become sensitive to many nonverbal types of communication.[14]

## Pantomime Aids Expression

Pantomime, although not oral, sometimes takes the place of oral language in communication. Gestures, posture, and facial expression have a place in communicating ideas to a recipient. While words are the media for transmitting and receiving a message in oral and written language, they are frequently quite inadequate for conveying complete understanding. A slight hand movement as a word is spoken gives emphasis to a thought. The raising of an eyebrow often connotes a subtle meaning which a word or sentence alone could not convey. The significance of a phrase or clause may be made more meaningful by the tensing of the body or the drooping of the shoulders. Such expression is important in striving for originality and effectiveness of communication. The eyes, the face, the hands, the arms, the feet, the body can become important tools for thought conveyance, and for giving the right direction, the correct amount of emphasis, and delicacy of tone to an idea.

In order to develop the use of these instruments, pantomime is

---

[14] Darold R. Beckman, "The Fifth Language Arts: Non-Verbal Communication," *Elementary English*, 40:191–193, February, 1963.

helpful because it can be made to reinforce the intent of words and to stimulate creativity. Plays may be given in pantomime. Characters of a play may be portrayed by acting. A child may depict or demonstrate the steadfastness of General Israel Putnam at Bunker Hill, the valor of General Philip Sheridan at Cedar Creek, the hardihood of George Washington crossing the Delaware, the courage of Sam Houston at the Alamo, and the dogged bravery of the soldiers who raised the American flag at Iwo Jima. The landing of Columbus at San Salvador may be played in pantomime. These, and other great moments, acted out nonverbally, add to a child's expression media, and at the same time help him to appreciate many of the vital and fascinating moments in history.

Pantomime is a type of expression which develops skill for adding color and luster to communication. Graubard suggested its use in depicting current events, describing embarrassing occurrences, and narrating fairy tales, fables, Mother Goose rhymes, and proverbs. In such activities and situations, opportunity is presented for "acting out" a headline event such as Major John Cooper returning from his orbital flight. In such nonverbal exercises, the actor or actors present the event and the audience tries to recognize it.[15]

A fairy tale such as "The Three Bears" or "Mr. Vinegar" may be pantomimed and recognized. A poem such as "The Highwayman" or "Casey at the Bat" permits a variety of nonoral expressional activities. Songs such as *America the Beautiful* or hymns such as *Rock of Ages* provide bases for the development of originality in nonoral expression. The general procedure in such activities is to have a small group plan and present an act, event, theme, or skit. Another group is challenged to recognize the first group's act. The second group may then give its presentation to challenge the first group, and so on. The activities are pleasurable and challenging, but the values go far beyond fun and play.

The learner can, by practicing nonverbal types of expression, develop tools which will enhance his communication. Pantomiming helps learners to know the importance of nonverbal actions to support verbal expression, and the advantage of avoiding wordiness becomes clear.

## Choral Speaking

Choral speaking has many values. It brings pleasure to children.

---

[15] Paul S. Graubard, "Pantomime: Another Language," *Elementary English,* 37:302–306, May, 1960.

A choral speaking group

It helps them to appreciate the beauty and appeal of poetry. It causes the shy child to begin to cooperate with others and to lose his self-consciousness. The aggressive youngster is helped because he learns to realize the importance of controlled expression in cooperative group presentation. Choral speaking gives children an opportunity to become creative in planning, sharing, and perfecting a presentation. In short, as Hedde and Brigance indicated, the values to be achieved are self-confidence, greater bodily expression, rhythmic appreciation, and co-ordination of voice and body.[16] Choral speech assists youngsters to interpret poetry in such a way that a child aids the group and is aided by the group. Rasmussen pointed out that as folk poetry is a product of group cooperation, it is quite natural that the recitation of poetry by a group would be highly enjoyable to children.[17] A teacher can guide children to enjoy and appreciate certain types of poetry through the medium of choral speaking. Dawson, Zollinger, and Elwell

[16] Wilhelmina G. Hedde and William Norwood Brigance, *Speech* (Chicago: J. B. Lippincott Company, 1937), pp. 376–377.
[17] Carrie Rasmussen, *Speech Methods in the Elementary School* (New York: The Ronald Press Company, 1949), pp. 234–235.

indicated four dangers which should be avoided in choric speaking: poor planning, use of mediocre verse, a type of singsong effect, straining of voices.[18]

To make it most effective, choral speaking should be planned carefully and cooperatively by teacher and children. A poem should be well understood by and highly pleasurable to the group in order that the speaking may be enjoyable and educative. Choral speaking can be a truly aesthetic experience. Children often make suggestions about the choice of poems they wish to speak. They present excellent ideas for plans of speaking when they are really interested. Sometimes they may even make up simple melodies to which poems of their liking may be sung.[19] Among the selections which are often chosen for the early grades are "Hickory Dickory Dock," "Little Miss Muffet," "Ding Dong Bell," "Hot Cross Buns," "There Was a Man in Our Town," and "Polly Put the Kettle On." If the reading is to be successful as a real experience, the children must know and like the selection. Thought and feeling are nicely conveyed especially when the children are free to create new ways of presentation. Children, when they realize that they are gaining in power of expression, are exhilarated and generally ask to have more of such activities. Pupils in the intermediate grades enjoy choral reading. Poems such as "Some One" (de la Mare), "Up the Airy Mountain" (Allingham), "The Duel" (Field), "Wynken, Blynken, and Nod" (Field), and "This Is the House that Jack Built" may be read effectively. "The Lamb" (Blake), "Sweet and Low" (Tennyson), "Silver" (de la Mare), "The Pirate Don Durk of Dowdee" (Meigs), and "The Wind" (Stevenson) may be used with the upper elementary school pupils.[20]

In the beginning, activities in which the children engage joyously and wholeheartedly are to be selected. Pronovost emphasized the idea that the first experiences with choral speaking should be for fun. In the early grades a beginning with unison speaking is productive.[21] Sometimes when the teacher reads a poem, the children may join

[18] Mildred A. Dawson, Marian Zollinger, and Ardell Elwell, *Guiding Language Learning,* second edition (New York: Harcourt, Brace and World, Inc., 1963), pp. 112–113.

[19] Miriam Blanton Huber, *Story and Verse for Children,* revised edition (New York: Macmillan Company, 1955), p. 102.

[20] See May Hill Arbuthnot, *Children and Books* (Chicago: Scott, Foresman and Company, 1947), pp. 177–198.

[21] Wilbert Pronovost and Louise Kingman, *The Teaching of Speaking and Listening in the Elementary School* (New York: Longmans, Green and Company, 1959), p. 208.

with her in the expression of thought. She may read a poem with a refrain, and the children come in at that point. Second, part arrangement may be planned and executed. Later, antiphonal (one group answers another), cumulative (a successive addition of voices), and sequential (voices following in order) types of speaking may be introduced. The extent to which a teacher will proceed in choral speaking must depend upon her purposes and the types of voices of the class.

## Parliamentary Procedure

Order in committee work, in assemblies, and in meetings of any kind is always to be desired so that the program may be carried on efficiently. Parliamentary procedure suggests an orderly means for accomplishing business of a meeting. In the elementary school, it is not too early to have children plan to do their work in a systematic manner. As a talk, a story, or a discussion should have an ongoing plan, so should a meeting.

A chairman requires understanding of fundamental principles of parliamentary law, although the principles need not necessarily be labeled as such, in order to preside effectively at a meeting. Among the procedures which pupils should learn are: how to make a motion, how to second it, how to amend a motion, and how to vote on it. They should learn how to keep minutes and how to use them. They should learn that only an individual recognized by the chairman should be permitted to speak. They should learn how to be recognized by the chair. They should understand how nominations are made and seconded, and how elections are carried out.

The four essential elements of parliamentary procedure follow: (1) *Orderliness:* Business should be conducted systematically; one point should be taken up at a time. (2) *Majority rule:* The principle of majority rule should be developed. Pupils should learn that in a democratic society, the majority rules and that it is important to accept this rule graciously. (3) *Minority rights:* The rights of the minority should be respected. Pupils should be taught that even a small minority has rights which are inviolable, and these rights must be protected. (4) *Courtesy to all:* Courtesy should be practiced by all who participate in meetings. Very early, children should learn that nothing is ever gained by discourtesy, but many things are gained by courtesy.

The four principles and some of the more specific points of procedure may be introduced in an informal way. Children will catch the spirit by engaging in meetings in which there is order, courtesy, and proper consideration of prerogatives of both the majority and the minority. Our way of life is democratic. If we are to improve this way of living, the child must learn to function properly and behave correctly. Early training in participating in meetings as members and taking turns in conducting a meeting are conducive to language development in modern schools.

## SOME PROBLEMS IN TEACHING AND GUIDING ORAL LANGUAGE

The teacher of oral language in the elementary school has many problems. She must lead and guide rather than demand and exhort. She must make use of opportunities for pupil speaking and plan situations which will help children to grow into using acceptable and effective oral language. She needs to appraise voice, fluency, articulation, and other factors in each child's speech.[22]

### The School and Class Climate

Language learning in the kindergarten and in the early grades is largely informal. The teacher will meet each child and greet him cordially as he comes into school the first day and the days following. Each child should be encouraged to develop a sense of security and of belonging to the class. He must not feel coerced or frustrated. The classroom should offer pleasant and stimulating experiences. Communication should be natural and there should be no undue tension. Children should be happy and enthusiastic about their work and their study. Discipline should be educative. Appropriate climate is achieved by a well-trained teacher who is considerate of children's interests, potentialities, and differences.

### Helping Pupils Improve Oral Language

Although informality is to be desired, talking without thinking is not to be encouraged. Although a child may vocalize without thinking in his first attempts at talking, as he matures and proceeds through the grades he should be guided to prepare for purposeful oral communication. On the first day of one of the author's schooling, he read on the blackboard, or the teacher read, "Think before you

---

[22] Nancy E. Wood, "Identifying Speech Disorders in the Classroom," *School Life,* 45:6, March, 1963.

speak." Ideally, a child should learn not to speak unless he has something to say, but he should be able to talk when the situation requires it. As he develops he should be guided to use sources for location of materials, to study, to plan, and to organize. Among the sources for consultation in preparation for talking are selected books, dictionaries, encyclopedias, and bibliographies found in the room or school library. Pupils should have recourse to real experiences and make use of home and community activities and events.

A pleasant voice is an important asset to anyone. The elementary school can exert great influence in guiding a child to speak appropriately by providing opportunities in interesting situations. Because the child may imitate an adult's voice and mannerisms, the teacher must provide example, situations, and suggestions which will promote acceptable pitch, good quality, and proper tone.

The pitch of a child's voice may be too high because of tension developed in talking about a topic concerning which he knows only what he remembers from a textbook. Measures should be taken to ease the strain by promoting discussion about life experiences and events with which the child is well acquainted. The child's voice may be raspy or grating, thin or dull; vocalization may be too loud, too low, throaty, or nasal. The causes of difficulties should be determined and remediation provided.

A child may speak too rapidly. He may "clutter" his expression, or talk so excitedly that his communication is unintelligible.[23] Sometimes he may require the aid of a speech therapist, but often a teacher who promotes rapport by considerateness may guide him to speak more slowly and intelligibly. To say to a pupil, "John, you talked too fast," is probably quite ineffective in improving expression. It would be more acceptable to say, "That was a good thought, John, but we might understand it better, if you talked a little slower. What do you think?"

A pupil may insert sounds such as "Ah, ah, ah," or "anda, anda," in his expression. These are sometimes used to fill in the time while he searches for a necessary word or desired phrase. They may be eradicated by practice in making brief carefully prepared reports. If a pupil thinks the thoughts he wishes to communicate and prepares the two or three sentences he needs to express them, generally the "ah" and the "anda" will be gradually omitted, and fluency will be developed.

[23] *Ibid.*

A child who has articulation difficulties will require careful instruction and individual practice to improve his speech. Articulation disorders are comprised of omissions, distortions, and substitutions of sounds in words. These may be due to emotional disturbance, mental disorders, or environmental influences. Sometimes they will disappear with growth and development, but generally careful diagnosis and remediation are required to overcome them. Examples of omissions are saying *doin'* for *doing, singin'* for *singing. Muver* for *mother, free* for *three,* and *axt* for *ask* are examples of substitutions and distortions of sounds. Continued patient effort must be exercised for correction of such difficulties. Once a mistake is pointed out, the pupil should substitute the correct form for the incorrect one, and practice it at every opportunity. If practice is as perfect as possible, the distortion will be eliminated in a reasonable time by a normal pupil.

A teacher should make every effort to have pupils avoid loud talk, slang, or contentious bickering by a positive approach to the practice of correct and appropriate conversation, discussion, storytelling, and other forms of communication. Youngsters should be encouraged to discuss problems thoughtfully and to report findings interestingly. The shy child particularly should be encouraged to share experiences and to converse with others on topics of his interest.[24]

The teacher should diagnose each pupil's deficiences, help him to correct his mistakes, note his successes, and encourage him to improve. She should teach each pupil enthusiastically, considering him an important human being who has a strong desire to know and cultivate correct language. She should promote speech experiences, devise enrichment activities, and share a pupil's joy in overcoming mistakes and his satisfaction in success.[25]

## Practice and Drill on Enunciation and Pronunciation

Meaningful and progressive practice in oral language must be provided. The purpose of practice — to develop a skill or to overcome a difficulty — should be clear to the pupil. Among the many skills which require drill are: enunciation, phrasing, and selection of proper words to convey exact meaning. The dictionary should be used as soon as

[24] George C. Balz, "Promoting Oral Expression," *The Elementary Principal,* 42:41–43, April, 1963.
[25] See Catherine J. Carmody, "I Thought I Taught Speech," *The Role of Speech in the Elementary School* (Washington, D. C.: Department of Elementary School Principals, NEA, 1946–1947), pp. 30–32.

a pupil is able to profit from it. Among the many things which he should look up in the dictionary when necessary are pronunciation and accent. A pupil in the intermediate grades may need to determine the correct pronunciation of words such as *truth, then, this, those, thousand, teeth.* He may find that his difficulty is with the *th* sounds. Some individual practice or drill may help, but a constant alertness for the *th* sound in such words will be highly valuable. A further example is the word *whether* which pupils sometimes pronounce as *weather.* Again the dictionary will help. When a pupil has studied *whether* (hwĕᵺ′ ēr) and *weather* (wĕᵺ′ ēr) carefully, he will recognize the difference in pronunciation. Consequently he should appreciate the necessity for constant vigilance and specific practice on his own special needs.

## Developing Considerateness in Oral Language

One of the marks of a lady or a gentleman is considerateness of others in thought, word, and act. The young pupil in developing kindliness in thought and manner will be aided by good example of teachers and others, by positive instruction in the many types of speaking in which he engages, and by opportunities to practice courtesy in speech and good manners in everyday behavior. Everyone should learn to be considerate of another's point of view. Learning and practice of agreeableness with others should be constantly purposed. The appraisal of one's successes and failures in extending courtesies in oral language is important in attaining the highest degree of success in talking.

## Developing a Critical Attitude of Self

It is important for a child to develop a critical attitude about his own speech. It is quite probable that no one ever becomes an accomplished conversationalist, discussant, storyteller, or speaker unless he carefully appraises his own efforts and outcomes in speaking. Without voicing criticisms, a child may be able to learn a great deal from the talking, conversation, and storytelling of others. He should learn from his companions procedures to be desired and sometimes those to avoid. One who is able to think critically has opportunities to evaluate what another says and also the manner of presentation. If a pupil is anxious to improve his own expression he may be aided by both the successes and deficiencies of others. If he recognizes the mistakes in the language of others and learns to avoid them, he is profiting. If he is able to appreciate a really fine performance of another, he is experiencing a production of value — perhaps a model to be imitated — which should stimulate him to improve his own voice, diction, pronunciation, thinking, and presentation. A pupil learns in different ways in every situation that calls for language. Guidance is necessary to motivate a learner to develop a thoughtful critical attitude about performance in oral communication. An individual should not be satisfied with only a pleasant voice, an enthusiastic attitude, or with correct diction. Each should be guided to strive to become excellent in all qualities of an accomplished speaker. This should be the aim, but it cannot be achieved by all pupils. Some who fail to attain excellence will benefit by trying to attain it.

## Developing Originality

The learner should be guided to think and to talk freely and naturally. If the climate is favorable, he will develop a feeling of security in a group, and as the sense of security increases, expression will become more and more normal to him. Natural expression tends to be flavored by personality. A pupil can become creative to some extent in thinking and talking if he has opportunities to experience, read, study, and listen. Freedom to study his own problems, freedom to critically evaluate books and reports, and freedom to say with courtesy what he thinks about problems should be approved. However, attempts at creativity should not promote slovenly pronunciation, wrong sentence construction, or nonsensible expression. A learner who is guided to evaluate his expression of thought critically and to improve it assiduously is likely to develop orginality in speaking.

### SUMMARY

Oral communication is a two-way process in which speaking and listening are necessarily complementary. Speaking is the reciprocal of listening and should be thought of as a means of communicating ideas by word of mouth to listeners. An infant just after birth has need to communicate and, as he grows to childhood, learns to talk and listen. The objectives of talking must be clearly understood by teacher and learner in order that acceptable speech may be developed in the situations which require it.

Some skills and abilities in oral communication are developed by the time a child enters school. His early habits which have become firmly implanted, however, require careful appraisal, and some generally demand remediation. General types of activities favorable to the development of talking are sharing experiences, conversation, discussion, making explanations and announcements, giving directions, speaking, reporting, telephoning, storytelling, dramatic play, nonverbal communication, pantomime, choral speaking, and parliamentary procedure.

In teaching oral language, the climate of the classroom should be pleasant. The learner should recognize the importance of talking correctly and should understand the purpose of each activity promoted. In responding to instruction he should gradually develop competency in planning communications and in expressing them considerately and enthusiastically.

Acceptable oral language requires thoughtful preparation and alert response to situations which call for talking. A pleasant voice, appropriate pose, and acceptable articulation should be developed. Effective instruction should be supported by well-planned practice. Considerateness in speech, a thoughtful critical attitude, and a developing mellowing originality are to be desired in oral communication.

## ACTIVITIES, PROBLEMS, QUESTIONS

1. Why is oral language so important to an individual? to the race?
2. Trace the growth of communication in a normal child from infancy to six years of age.
3. State the objectives of oral language in order of their importance.
4. List at least ten types of situations in which children will find oral language valuable.
5. How can acceptable communication be developed to fulfill the needs in each type of situation?
6. Evaluate the suggested requisites of a conversation. Explain how skill in conversation can be developed.
7. Compare desirable and undesirable qualities of conversationalists.
8. Show the similarities and differences between conversation and discussion.
9. Explain how oral expression can be helpfully supplemented by nonverbal means such as gesture or posture.
10. There are at least five general purposes for making a talk. Describe briefly one situation in which each of these purposes might be achieved.
11. State in the order of importance the characteristics of an effective speaker. Support your choices with reasons.
12. What are the values of storytelling?
13. Formulate the problems which a teacher meets in appraising and improving the speech of pupils who need remediation.
14. How can pupils help themselves to better speech?

## SELECTED REFERENCES

Anderson, Virgil A. *Improving the Child's Speech.* New York: Oxford University Press, 1953. 333 pp.

Backus, Ollie L., and Jane Beasley. *Speech Therapy With Children.* Boston: Houghton Mifflin, 1951. 441 pp.

Clark, Margaret Mary, Chairman. *Adventuring with Books.* Chicago: National Council of Teachers of English, 1950. 115 pp.

Howard, V. *Puppet and Pantomime Plays.* New York: Sterling, 1962. 108 pp.

Huber, Miriam, ed. *Story and Verse for Children.* New York: Macmillan, 1940. 857 pp.

Johnson, Wendell, ed. *Speech Problems of Children.* New York: Grune and Stratton, 1950. 265 pp.

———— *Stuttering in Children and Adults.* Minneapolis: University of Minnesota Press, 1955. 472 pp.

Johnson, Wendell, *et al. Speech Handicapped School Children.* Rev. ed. New York: Harper, 1956. 575 pp.

*Language Arts for Today's Children.* Commission on the English Curriculum. New York: Appleton-Century-Crofts, 1954. 431 pp.

Larrick, Nancy. *A Teacher's Guide to Children's Books.* Columbus, Ohio: Merrill, 1960. 316 pp.

Ogilvie, Mardel. *Speech in the Elementary School.* New York: McGraw-Hill, 1954. 318 pp.

Powers, David. *Fundamentals of Speech.* New York: McGraw-Hill, 1951. 380 pp.

Rasmussen, Carrie. *Speech Methods in the Elementary School.* New York: Ronald, 1962. 340 pp.

Sawyer, Ruth. *The Way of the Storyteller.* New York: Viking, 1942. 318 pp.

Siks, Geraldine Brain. *Creative Dramatics: An Art for Children.* New York: Harper, 1958. 472 pp.

Stevenson, Robert Louis. *A Child's Garden of Verses.* New York: Duell, Sloan & Pearse, 1963. 98 pp.

Van Riper, Charles. *Voice and Articulation.* Englewood Cliffs, N. J.: Prentice-Hall, 1958. 566 pp.

See also references for Chapters III and XII.

# Chapter III

# Listening: Learning and Teaching

## ORIENTATION

LISTENING means to hear with comprehension, to give attention to a sound, to receive and understand an oral message, to discriminate among noises of various kinds. It means to pay attention to spoken words, sentences, and discourse; to attend to instructions or advice; to analyze the import of what is said by another; and to critically evaluate it. Listening is part of everyday living and includes a large part of our waking time. It is an important component of communication. Listening is responding through understanding to oral expression.

Listening can be differentiated from hearing. We may hear something and not listen to it except in an inattentive sort of way, or we may listen attentively. When we hear the sounds of words, the ear — which is composed of the outer, middle, and inner parts — picks them up and sends them through our complex and wonderful nerve system to the brain. Our minds translate these impulses in the light of our experiences into images, concepts, thoughts. Every word is distinguishable from every other word; *bill* is different, for example, from *bell*. The vowel sounds of the two words are different, and the image created by the impact of one word upon the mind is different from that of the other. Our experiences have guided us to recognize that difference. Our experiences help us also to differentiate various meanings of words when they are used in context. For example, think: a five dollar *bill;* the duck's *bill;* a grocery *bill;* a *bill* of fare; *bill* of sale. This word *bill* conveys many meanings to us. Careful analytical listening is necessary to recognize the various thoughts communicated when the word is used in different sentences. Listening really brings forth thinking, understanding, recognition, and evaluation. Listening is an active process, a useful process, and a most necessary one.

## The Importance of Listening

"Listening skill is of major importance today in personal, social, economic, and civic affairs."[1] In school and out of school, from morning until night, listening is important to every individual. At work, adults confer with others in connection with their duties, sometimes for information or direction. In like manner children confer with their teachers, with other children, with the school nurse, and with the librarian.

At home, the child listens to the cautions of his mother about crossing the street. On the playground or in the gym, he listens to the instructions of the physical education teacher about playing a game. In baseball, he listens attentively for instruction about the exact movements in batting, throwing the ball, sliding into a base; in basketball, he listens to coaching in order to dribble correctly, perfect team play, or assume the right stance and motion in making free throws. In like manner, children should listen intently as the teacher explains a process in science or arithmetic. But do they? Often they are not listening attentively. Sometimes a teacher can be deceived by passive and silent children who, as Logan stated, "can turn their ears 'off and on.'"[2]

Rankin, years ago, studied the comparative importance of listening and other language arts. His results showed that 42 percent of language time was spent in listening, 32 percent in talking (conversation time was split equally for tabulation between listening and speaking), 15 percent in reading, and 11 percent in writing.[3] Wilt's investigation of the listening performance of 530 elementary school children in representative Pennsylvania schools indicated that they "were supposed to listen" more than 50 percent of their school time, that their listening varied in purpose and quality, and that there was no evidence that they were motivated or instructed to improve their technics or habits of listening.[4]

Listening is becoming increasingly important because of mass media of communication which operate in our society. The child listens to

---

[1] Miriam E. Wilt, "Listening Skills Can Be Improved," *The Instructor*, 72:6, January, 1963.

[2] Lillian M. Logan, *Teaching the Young Child* (Boston: Houghton Mifflin Company, 1960), p. 173.

[3] Paul T. Rankin, "Listening Ability: Its Importance, Measurement, and Development," *Chicago Schools Journal*, 12:177–179, January, 1930, and 12:417–420, June, 1930.

[4] Miriam E. Wilt, "A Study of Teacher Awareness of Listening as a Factor in Elementary Education," *Journal of Educational Research*, 43:626–636, April, 1950.

the news reports on the radio. He goes to the movies. He views and listens to the television. He experiences — sees and listens to — plays, programs, and various other broadcasts. Smythe reported that the average TV viewing (seeing and listening) time was four hours per day, and the average radio time for families that had no television was a little less.[5]

## The Need for Discriminating Listening

Every kind of advertising is broadcast. Programs of every nature — political, social, scientific, and economic — are sent over the air. Stimulating and educational programs are interspersed with "soapbox" presentations. The worthwhile are presented indiscriminately with programs of potential harm, particularly to the inexperienced and immature child. Accordingly, the learner must differentiate the good from the worthless.

A child who listens to a radio or television haphazardly for hours is likely to become habituated to a type of partial listening which dulls his sensibilities for understanding and critical evaluation. A free television and free radio have great advantages but also present dangers and disadvantages. To cope with indiscriminate telecasting and broadcasting, it is necessary for an individual to be trained in selective and critical listening. A pupil must be educated to discern good from bad, value from trash, and the worthwhile from the unworthy. Enemies of freedom are broadcasting their message of hate and untruth to billions of people. Intelligent and well-educated people are not easily misled, but the uneducated and the immature are prey to such broadcasts. Indiscriminate and uncritical listening may lead the unwary into difficulty. Discriminating listening requires the ability to comprehend what is broadcast, and the discernment to evaluate the information given. A skilled listener develops the ability to remember and use the materials and information presented.

Purposeless listening is a waste of time generally. Purposes may include listening to learn, to enjoy, to evaluate, to review, to experience. As Lee and Lee suggested, "The critical purpose of listening is to comprehend, from the speaker's point of view, what he is saying."[6] Such a skill requires instruction and practice.

[5] Dallas W. Smythe, "Television," *Education and Mass Media of Communication,* Research Bulletin of the National Conference on Research in English (Chicago: National Council of Teachers of English, 1950), pp. 47–57.

[6] J. Murray Lee and Dorris May Lee, *The Child and His Curriculum* (New York: Appleton-Century-Crofts, Inc., 1950), p. 129.

## Why Listening Is Ineffective

Listening is ineffective in our schools at the present time principally because it has not been adequately taught. In the first place, children have not learned the values to be achieved by listening purposively because our schools have not given emphasis to the teaching and learning of listening. If it is stressed as it should be, school learning could be greatly improved. Listening is valuable as a receptive language art, and ordinary people use it more than reading. Accordingly, the conditions and preparation for learning to listen need to be emphasized.

Second, causes for poor listening are found often in the listener himself, who sometimes shows little interest and displays a poor attitude toward the topic being discussed. The materials presented may be too difficult for him. Frequently he cannot understand the vocabulary or the language. Sometimes he cannot hear the instructor or the speaker because of an auditory deficiency. The ineffective listener may think of listening as boring. Instead of purposing to learn, he may be critical of the teacher or the subject. He sometimes presents an outwardly attentive mien but his mind is far away. His attention is diverted by the slightest interruption. When once diverted he makes no effort to "tune in" quickly on the lesson. A poor listener generally becomes lost in details, often because he does not relate them to the main points of the talk.[7]

Third, another cause of ineffective listening is related to the talker. A speaker may be colorless, lack enthusiasm, or be poorly prepared. His message may be devoid of organization. A well-prepared dynamic instructor guides a class by stating his plan, carrying it out, helping the listeners to understand relationships of details to main points, and by guiding them from one clear point to the next. He carefully summarizes what he has done, asks for questions to clear up misunderstandings, invites comment, and listens patiently to opposing points of view. Dale stated, "A poor speaker covers ten points. A good speaker uncovers one."[8] A good speaker develops effective listeners, just as a poor speaker invites poor listening.

In the fourth place, inferior listening eventuates often because measures are not taken to improve conditions for communication. Listening is not good when the climate of the room is bad. A classroom

[7] Ralph G. Nichols, "What Can Be Done About Listening?" *The Supervisor's Notebook* (Chicago: Scott, Foresman and Company, Vol. 22, Spring, 1960), pp. 2–3.

[8] Edgar Dale, "Why Don't We Listen?" *The News Letter*, 28:1–3, March, 1963.

Spontaneous listening

may adjoin a noisy street, highway, or railroad track. What goes on outside may invite distraction. The seating may be such as to hinder rather than promote communication. The acoustics may be poor or the ventilation bad. Whatever the difficulties, the conditions for listening and speaking must be improved as much as possible.

## Types of Listening

There are many kinds of listening: compulsive, spontaneous, curious, imitative, passive, inattentive, exploratory, appreciative, concentrative, critical, and creative. These types overlap somewhat, but in the teaching of listening each may well be kept in mind — some to be emphasized and others to be avoided.

*Compulsive listening.* Compulsive listening is of two types: listening compelled by another person or agency, and that initiated or imposed by an individual himself. When a child is told by a parent or teacher to listen "or else," he is in a sense compelled to listen against his will. Such listening may not be productive of educational values. However, when a student forces himself to listen for any reason, he is compelling himself to achieve discipline or self-control and at the same time to take in knowledge of a process or information of importance. Compulsive listening is practiced by many pupils before they have become curious about a project or process. This type of listening can be useful, and usually leads to worthwhile and more pleasurable processes of spontaneous listening.

*Spontaneous listening.* Spontaneous listening requires no compulsion; it is engendered by the listener himself. It is generally born of interest in a subject, a topic, a unit, or a project. For example, an individual who wants to improve his game of tennis will listen eagerly to a tennis coach. A child who hears a musical sound will require no compulsion to listen but will pay attention spontaneously. In like manner, when a pupil recognizes the importance of correcting articulation errors, he will listen to criticism and to corrections from his teacher. It has been said that in learning and teaching, interest is the secret of success.

*Curious listening.* A child is curious about many things. He is interested in birds, dogs, horses, airplanes, trains, missiles, and inventions. He is generally interested in stories of adventure. Girls like to hear about dresses and styles that go with living in homes and communities. A little boy who lived across the street from the authors wondered about the green of the grass and the colors of the leaves. He asked why and how birds fly. He wanted to know why the Japanese beetle was so pretty. A hundred questions were asked, some of which were difficult to answer even for a teacher of science or of art. He would listen to any explanation given to him. He was curious and took pleasure in specific definite answers.

*Imitative listening.* A young girl may listen to her mother and imitate her tone of voice and accent. A boy may, through listening, reproduce what he thinks is his father's way of talking. Boys and girls have been known to imitate their teacher's speech. A little girl, by listening to a newcomer in the community, developed a lisp which she outgrew after a few months when the fascination of the newcomer had worn off. The ability to imitate or mimic another has been developed by entertainers. Many people have quite successfully reproduced sounds similar to those emitted by animals — cows, horses, dogs, cats, chickens, ducks, turkeys.

*Passive listening.* Some pupils are satisfied with passive listening —

the type which accepts the spoken word without analysis or evaluation. People have listened to agitators or troublemakers without appraisal of their statements. They have accepted the word of pitchmen, barkers, or solicitors to their disadvantage. Children should be trained not to accept everything they hear as absolute truth. If pupils do listen passively and accept statements without analysis, they are not truly educated to the important values of listening.[9]

*Inattentive listening.*   Inattention to instruction or discussion may be caused by a listener's inability to understand a speaker, or because the presentation is monotonous. It may occur, however, because of poor attitude or low interest on the part of the listener, or because the conditions are unfavorable for communication.

*Exploratory listening.*   Exploratory listening is closely allied with curious listening. In exploratory listening, the pupil may question others less and independently experiment or explore more. One who beats the snare drum at first loudly and then faintly is exploring the possibilities of the loudness of sound. One who uses a tuning fork in connection with tubes of varying lengths is exploring the causes of pitch variation. A young explorer goes into the woods or the forest to hear the sound of the leaves as he walks along, to hear the sound of the limbs of the trees swaying back and forth in the wind, or to hear the songs of birds. One who listens to time the sound of the thunderclap after the lightning flash is exploring and using listening as a part of his equipment for understanding.

*Appreciative listening.*   When one listens to the sound of music with rapt attention, he is usually appreciative, especially if the program is thought to be excellent. Children learn to enjoy an exciting story. They like to hear an attractive voice. They appreciate instruction that is well organized and meets their needs. Even in such a subject as spelling, they want to hear the correct spelling of a demon that they have misspelled frequently. Children generally know what is valuable and interesting. Appreciation is developed through listening and listening enhances learning.

*Concentrative listening.*   Concentrative listening is giving studious attention to a communication. For example, a teacher explains a correct technic for making a joint in woodworking and the boys concentrate upon "every word" in the presentation. Pupils listen with concentration to the directions for carrying out an experiment. They focus their

---

[9] Sheila Schwartz, "What Is Listening?" *Elementary English,* 38:221, April, 1961.

Concentrative listening

interest on directions for making a softball diamond. A primary group concentrates with intensity upon the reading of a story about boats. A fifth-grade class considers carefully the explanation of the process of dividing an integer by a fraction.

*Critical listening.* Critical listening requires careful differentiation of value and of worthlessness, of truth and of falsity. A teacher may assign to pupils of the intermediate grades a project requiring critical listening. They will listen to advertising on the radio or television to determine unreliable statements. They learn to be critical of an advertiser who states that he is selling the best car on the market or of the pitchman who says that he has a cleanser that makes an old pan look like a new one. Pupils should be given opportunities of discerning the truth or falsity of statements. They should learn to determine the deficiencies of talks and to note the lack of organization or the poorly worded statements in reports.

*Creative listening.* Listening to good literature is a basis for the writing of acceptable English. A pupil who listens to a well-delivered speech may be impelled to strive for the development of an effective style of speaking. Listening to exciting stories should encourage a learner to tell or write original stories. A child who experiences nature deeply in some form or another may become interested in writing a poem about his experience in a tornado. His beginning effort may fall far short of creativity, but he has begun to strive for originality and a way of his own for telling a story. Creative listening, although not purposed in all schools, is beginning to be considered, along with the other types discussed, as an important kind of listening to be developed in learners.[10]

These types of listening — compulsive, spontaneous, curious, imitative, passive, inattentive, exploratory, appreciative, concentrative, critical, and creative — do not include all the kinds of listening, but they do suggest some of the aspects certainly to be purposed and utilized and others obviously to be avoided or remedied. Oral communication requires two, at least two individuals — mentally active and alert — in order that a message may be transmitted and received with understanding.

## Neglect of the Teaching of Listening

Instruction in the areas of listening has not been properly carried on in the schools, and research in this field has also been neglected. During the time that three thousand respectable studies were published in the field of reading only approximately fifty worthwhile ones were carried out in the field of listening. Much can be done both in research and method to improve the listening of children.[11] Nichols indicated that because listening is one of our main avenues of information, it should be investigated.[12]

We still hear in some schools, the admonitions: "Pay attention," "Listen carefully," and "You are not listening to what I am saying." Packard pointed out that students do not listen properly, and that

---

[10] Carrie Rasmussen, *Speech Methods in the Elementary School* (New York: The Ronald Press Company, 1949), pp. 95–97.

[11] Harold A. Anderson, "Needed Research in Listening," *Areas of Research Interest in the Language Arts,* Research Bulletin of the National Conference on Research in English (Chicago: National Council of Teachers of English, 1952), pp. 27–36.

[12] Ralph G. Nichols, "Teaching of Listening," *Chicago Schools Journal,* 30:273–278, June, 1949.

improved habits of careful listening would result in improved oral language.[13] Improved listening would help in learning, but admonitions and statements commanding attention are hardly the way to obtain it. Wilt concluded, after a careful study of listening in the elementary schools, that most of the teachers who participated in her investigation were unaware of the listening needs of children, and consequently devoted little time to the development of listening skills.[14]

These reports and others seem to warrant the conclusion that listening is a highly important language art, but a most neglected one. Children no doubt have a potentiality for listening as they do for reading, but training is necessary to develop the power. It is a mistaken idea that one grows into listening through incidental learning. On the contrary, it may be truthfully said that people have built up a resistance to listening because of circumstances of their environment. Therefore they should be taught the purposes, values, and procedures of profitable listening.

## OBJECTIVES IN TEACHING LISTENING

The objectives in teaching listening should be considered with regard to the maturity, ability, and background of pupils. Many children cannot master all the attitudes, skills, competencies, and uses of listening in one semester, one year, or in two or three years. Accordingly, instruction in listening should be purposed from the first day of kindergarten and emphasized throughout the elementary school. Pupils should be guided to achieve the following objectives:

1. To listen courteously and attentively to others in conversation and discussion

2. To recognize the trend of a conversation and to comprehend its outcomes

3. To understand the ideas of a speaker, and to be able to recall the main points in sequence

4. To analyze the thoughts set forth in a discussion and to be able to report the main points and significant details

5. To obtain information desired from answers to questions addressed to teachers or speakers

---

[13] Frederick C. Packard, "Learning to Listen," *Harvard Educational Review,* 15:198, May, 1944.

[14] Miriam E. Wilt, "A Study of Teacher Awareness of Listening as a Factor in Elementary Education," *Journal of Educational Research,* 43:626–636, April, 1950.

6. To appraise objectively statements of speakers, teachers, pupils, and others for accuracy and pertinence

7. To differentiate the essential from the nonessential and the valid from the invalid

8. To interpret, critically evaluate, and use the essence of a report, interview, or instruction.

If a teacher endeavors systematically to instruct pupils in the objectives as they are needed in each stage of development in the elementary school, listening competency should be achieved.

## SOME FACTORS OF GOOD LISTENING

Important among the basic motivators for listening are: purpose, points of interest, health elements, mental and emotional factors, and background of the learners.

### Purposes of Listening

Worthwhile purposes of listening are exemplified by the following: to acquire culture, to learn a method, to satisfy a need, to report a message, and to enjoy an entertainment.

*To acquire culture.* The pupil may purpose to listen to recordings and instructions of many types to understand and appreciate our culture and heritage. Brotherhood, neighborliness, and love of country grow in the youngster who listens to the fascinating stories of heroism and sacrifice of the pioneers and of men and women in later times. The child thrills to music such as *The Star Spangled Banner* and Sousa's *Stars and Stripes Forever.*

A teacher may plan activities in which pupils will listen to the Declaration of Independence, Lincoln's second inaugural, and stories, anecdotes, episodes, poems, and plays. Accounts of such battles as Corregidor, Coral Sea, and the Bulge may be given. The stories of explorers, the winning of the West, the Gold Rush, the extension of the railroads, and space travel may be discussed. The accomplishments of Fulton, Edison, Einstein, Lawrence, and other inventors, scientists, and pioneers will be both informative and motivating to pupils who desire to strive for excellence. Children will enjoy hearing the poems of Longfellow, Whittier, Poe, Whitman, Rose Fyleman, Robert Louis Stevenson, Vachel Lindsay, and eventually Alfred Tennyson, Robert Browning, and Shakespeare. Listening to readings of many types aids greatly in the understanding and appreciation of our heritage. The concepts of honesty, integrity, fellowship, justice, charity, and patience are learned in many ways, not the least of which is listening about individuals who made them part of their lives.

*To learn a method.* Listening is used in integration with other language arts in learning methods and technics. For example, in learning to pronounce a word especially in the early grades, the child listens to the teacher say the word. He then pronounces it. If he makes a mistake, he listens to a second pronunciation and practices it. Careful listening will guide him to correctness. A boy may want to hold his breath as long as possible in order to compete in an underwater race. The coach tells him to take several short breaths before completely filling the lungs with air. The learner finds that by practice based partly on listening he can master a method for lengthening considerably the time of holding his breath.

*To satisfy a need.* A pupil may need to find a procedure for working an experiment. The teacher suggests that he go to the library for a specific source book. The pupil who has an impelling need will remember the title of the book and the procedure for obtaining it.

The learner will be helped in a real situation in which he needs directions. He may ask, "How may I go to the courthouse in this city?" He listens carefully while the one questioned gives him the directions: "Go south from here three blocks on Sheridan Street to Main. Turn left on Main Street; go east two blocks to Monroe. Turn right and go two blocks south to Maple. The courthouse is the first building in the third block on the right or west side of the street."

*To report an oral message.* When a pupil is requested to carry a message from a teacher to the principal, he must listen. He will listen carefully in order to transmit the message correctly. It may be necessary to ask a question or two about the message. He should understand it, concentrate on it, remember it, and deliver it correctly.

*Entertainment and enjoyment.* Listening is fun. A great deal of enjoyment can result from listening to orchestras, bands, tape recordings, television, and radio. Upper-grade children listen long stretches on the telephone — too long to suit other members of the family. People listen to their favorite records periodically. Pupils listen to a gifted storyteller, and use the television to see and listen to a play. In these activities, pupils learn to be considerate of others.

## Points of Interest

An individual will listen to what he wants to hear. He may be conditioned by concentrating on the attractiveness in sound, the importance of meaning, his mind set, or by his prejudices.

*The speaker.* The listener will be attracted to a speaker, or a pupil to a teacher, who captures his attention and engages his listening powers. The pleasant voice of a speaker, a well-trained voice of a singer, a friendly smile, a kindly face, and a well-thought-out message will engage an audience of one or of one hundred. A teacher who has something to say, who says it well, will gain the attention of the pupil. A teacher who understands the individual, his problems, his hopes, his aspirations, his difficulties and deficiencies, will appeal to him. A teacher who sees the pupil's side of things, who is considerate, and who holds forth good objectives and worthy standards, will inspire good listening. She will be heard, understood, and quoted. Her counsel will be sought, accepted, and generally acted upon.

*The group.* The group is important in listening. Elementary school groups vary greatly in size, in personnel, in mentality, and in culture. The pupils enter into many kinds of discussions which help them recognize the value of listening. They learn to pay attention to questions, listen to answers, understand inferences, and draw conclusions. Appropriate listening in a group discussion is noting the comments and reactions of members of the group, keeping them in mind, comprehending, analyzing, and evaluating the whole. A group discussion well planned and carried out has tremendous appeal for listening to learn and value for learning to listen.

*The topic.* Another center of attractiveness which will induce good listening is the topic of the conversation, discussion, instruction, lecture, or telecast. Impelling topics will induce intensive and extensive listening. A discussion of a picnic, the planning of an athletic contest, the winning of an important football game, the World's Series, or the Olympic Games will generally motivate appreciative and concentrative listening. The coach of a basketball or track team requires this type of listening and receives it from his athletes. The coach of a play, which is to be the crowning event of the year, has little difficulty in gaining attentive listening. The reading lesson, the spelling lesson, and the language lesson will motivate good listening if these lessons are well planned and dynamically carried out.

## Health and Physical Elements

Health and physical condition are important factors in any type of learning. Physical well-being, strength, nutrition, rest, exercise, relaxation, and hearing itself, are important factors in stimulating listening.

*Physical well-being.* The physical tone, condition, and growth of the child should be appraised. An unwell child cannot learn as effectively as he might if well. A normal child, healthy and vibrant, has the potentialities for listening. A fatigued child will not have the stamina to listen with concentration.

*Strength, nutrition, and rest.* Among the many causes for poor listening are weakness, malnutrition, and fatigue. The school physician's appraisal of the child is important. Whether a child gets sufficient rest or whether he does not, whether he is well nourished or poorly nourished are factors to be considered. Very young children need a short rest and a drink of milk in the middle of the morning in order that they may function alertly.

*Exercise and relaxation.* Young children in the kindergarten or first grade cannot give attention for a long period of time. Between periods of work, they should have periods of relaxation. Periods of intensive listening should be interspersed by relaxing types of activity — music, games, or manipulative exercises.

*Hearing.* Millions of American children have subnormal or partial hearing. By use of the audiometer, the pupil's hearing can and should be tested. Hearing deficiency should be determined and treated by a specialist. A hard-of-hearing child should be guided most considerately. He should be seated in a favorable place in the room — in a position where he can see those who talk — at a desk where listening is least likely to be difficult.

## Mental, Psychological, and Emotional Factors

Rapport, mental alertness, and emotional factors affect a pupil's active listening.

*Rapport.* Considerateness toward the child will beget good feeling toward the teacher. A pupil will listen to a friendly teacher more attentively and receptively than to one who is distant and aloof. A pupil who has pleasant relationships with classmates gains more in listening to them than he would if the relationships were unfavorable. One who is well accepted by his group will be listened to with more consideration than an isolate.

*Mental alertness.* The child who is interested in ideas and concepts, who asks questions, who is able to use facts for making inferences and for arriving at conclusions, will listen better than one who has not developed these abilities. Listening cannot be carried on effectively without thinking. Some authorities use the word *auding* to include all the abilities and skills which are connected with the complex of listening. Auding is the process of listening to, recognizing, understanding, and interpreting spoken language. To carry on the process of auding effectively, a mentally alert individual listens, thinks, comprehends, organizes, evaluates, and uses facts.

*Attitudes and emotions.* Emotion plays an important part in listening. If one is emotional about something, he may not be able to think about it in an objective manner. On the other hand, emotion to a certain extent may be useful in listening. If one has the attitude that he must learn because it is necessary for his improvement, or if he strongly desires to solve a problem, his feeling will spur him to listen more effectively than if he has a "don't care" attitude. Nevertheless, if a pupil is upset emotionally, it is probable that his attention will be diverted from the critical content of the instruction and he will miss important points. Accordingly, attitudes and emotions must be considered as well as rapport and the mental processes.

## Background of the Listener

It is obvious that a speaker and a listener with approximately the same background, education, and similar experiences will have little difficulty conversing with one another. On the other hand, two people of varying experiences and different backgrounds may have extreme difficulty in understanding each other. For example, an Englishman uses many terms relating to common things which are not necessarily familiar to an American. The former's use of *lift* for *elevator,* and *tram* for our own *streetcar,* and *apothecary* for *druggist* may not be readily understood by the latter. Colloquial expressions used in one part of the country may be quite unheard of in another part. Pronunciations and the articulation of sounds in one section differ to some extent from those of another part. Accordingly, a listener who differs in experience and background from a speaker often has difficulty in comprehending what is being said even though he hears every sound.

The child who has listened to his mother and perhaps to an older brother or sister may have difficulty at first in understanding the oral statements of his teacher. A child may hear words in school that are new to him. For him, listening is difficult and he must be helped. Life experiences and mass media assist pupils in becoming familiar with a broad workable vocabulary and in comprehending an extensive range of concepts.

## PLANNING LISTENING INSTRUCTION

An instructional program in listening should be planned just as carefully and carried out just as enthusiastically as programs in speaking and writing. Anderson suggested instruction in listening should be provided which is as systematic as that offered in teaching developmental reading.[15] Preparation is necessary for effective instruction if optimum results are to be achieved.

### Making Arrangements for Listening

Preparations and arrangements must consider the maturity of the children who are to be listeners. For example, a science instructor may purpose to show variations in pitch, and bring before the class several tubes filled with water to different heights. During the class, he may demonstrate the difference in the pitch of sounds when a tuning fork struck with a mallet is placed over the tubes — one at a time. He may also plan to show the variance in pitch by changing the water level in one of the tubes. These materials must be ready for use when the class is begun.

Another example of preparation concerns the use of audio-visual materials. If a sound film is to be shown, the teacher should run it before showing it to the class to check the working order of the machine and also to appraise the picture. The class should be prepared for listening and viewing. A prediscussion may be followed by the viewing, and the viewing by a postdiscussion in which children can ask questions and talk about the film.

### The Room and Atmosphere

A properly constructed classroom is important for listening. The walls should be soundproof in order that noise from the halls and other classrooms will not disturb listening and discussions. The atmosphere in the room should be one of work, study, and cooperation. Frequently the class may be divided into committees to consider different problems. Sometimes a group — even as large as half of the class — may have an oral language program in which several pupils report what they have discovered and prepared while others study individually or in committees. It is often necessary to rearrange the seating in a room to meet

---

[15] Harold A. Anderson, "Teaching the Art of Listening," *The School Review*, 57:66, February, 1947.

changing needs for listening and speaking. Circular or semicircular seating for some discussions will improve rapport greatly among listeners and speakers. Opportunity for discussion, time for reflection, and facilities for reading and study of a problem will expedite and improve communication — listening and speaking.

## The Length of the Listening Period

The length of the listening period or of a discussion in which listening plays an important part should be adjusted to the maturity and experience of the pupils and to the type of listening in which they are to engage. Periods of too great length are likely to tire young children. Periods of too little duration may not permit others to become oriented before the period is terminated. Changes in the length of listening periods may be made to suit the interests of a group studying different problems.

## Organizing Materials to Be Presented for Listening

Organization connotes order and proper sequence in listening and speaking. It promotes thinking and efficiency in learning. Listening may be promoted by a dynamic personality without organization, but a combination of a dynamic personality and good organization will enhance results. Organization will vary with types of materials and the maturity of the group, but the concept of effective organization should be purposed from the kindergarten through the elementary school.

*A plan.* A good talk or report requires three basic parts — the beginning, the main body, and the ending — the introduction, the discussion, and the conclusion or summary. The individual who would get the most from a presentation must be trained to listen for the three parts. For young children, although the whole report may consist of only three or four sentences, the organization must be clear. For pupils in the middle grades, the introduction may consist of one or two brief sentences followed by the discussion. The speaker should so plan that in the discussion he will present, for example, two points. His ending may be a summary in one sentence of what he has said. These the listeners must recognize and comprehend.

*Statements designed for listening.* In the early grades, children will listen to and understand simple statements. The simple sentence, the simple compound sentence, and a complex sentence too, may be introduced as the children are able to comprehend and retain thought so expressed. Inverted sentences are difficult for many young children and long sentences will not be easily retained by them. Colorful words and phrases are enjoyed and remembered by children.

*Listening enhanced by examples and stories.* The elementary school child likes a story that he can understand. Although some people feel that children do not have a sense of humor, pupils generally have a liking for amusing incidents. A story which illustrates a point of a talk is enjoyed and remembered.

*Transitions as signposts.* In an instruction or report, the pupil will be benefited by transitions from one part to the next and an introduction which indicates what the plan of the report is to be. In the body, he will be guided by the transition which indicates that the first main point of a process has been explained, and that the speaker is proceeding to the second point. Such transitions make it possible for the listener to fix in his mind the organization of the talk. In other words, in the introduction he learns what the discussion is about. If he hears that there are to be, for example, two points in the discussion, he awaits eagerly their presentation. After comprehending the first, he notes that the speaker is moving from the first to the second point. After comprehending this, he is gratified to note the transition from the final point to the summary. He feels secure when the speaker mentions the two points (or other number) in the summary. An alert pupil reviews the whole presentation, the beginning, the main part, and the summary.

*The Summary.* A good organizer and a teacher who understands the psychology of learning and teaching will summarize what he has done in presentation. Dr. Ernest Horn stated in one of his classes that there should be a summary in every lesson. Every unit should have a culminating exercise. Every project should begin somewhere, achieve something, and end with a design or product. An effective listener identifies, comprehends, and remembers well-organized presentations properly summarized.

## The Use of Machines and Instruments

Machines are always interesting and often useful in presenting materials for listening. The record player may be used to bring to the children some of the finest music. The tape recorder may be used to play back to the child his own voice for appraisal. By means of a recording he is able to note his mistakes in enunciation, articulation, and pronunciation. The TV, the radio, and the motion-picture projector are useful in language teaching. Through them, a pupil or a group may study expression by seeing, listening, and auding.

## SITUATIONS WHICH PROMOTE LISTENING

Situations which require and which motivate good listening, such as the following, should be utilized.

### Situations for Listening Outside the School

1. Talking and listening to a neighbor
2. Buying some groceries at the store
3. Conversations with parents and with other children
4. Listening to an explanation at a fair or exhibit
5. Listening to a church service
6. Listening to a lecture in the community club
7. Listening to a news report
8. Listening to the singing of the birds
9. Listening to the sound of waves, or to the sound of the wind and the rain in a storm
10. Listening to directions for finding a place
11. Listening to a concert or operetta
12. Listening carefully to a telephone message for a parent
13. Listening critically to a salesman expounding the wonders of a gadget
14. Listening to a report of a vacation trip of a friend.

### Listening Situations in School

A teacher will select worthwhile situations for promoting listening in school. Some of the following will be useful:

1. Conversations among members of a group
2. Informal discussions about plans for a picnic, assembly, or other project
3. Listening to a speaker at a school assembly
4. Listening to or participating in a culminating activity of a unit developed by the class
5. Listening to others in "audience reading"
6. Listening to stories, poems, or anecdotes
7. Listening to and carrying oral messages
8. Listening to safety instructions
9. Listening critically to a report to evaluate the validity of the facts and inferences contained in it

10. Interviewing a prominent actor to report the interview in the school paper

11. Listening carefully to an assignment

12. Listening attentively to the questions in a test

13. Listening to an explanation of a process in arithmetic, science, or other field of interest

14. Listening to a travelogue.

These partial lists of possible opportunities involve listening and skills of other language arts. It should be remembered that listening is used generally not in isolation but in integration with speaking, for example, and that the activities selected for improving listening should have value for enhancing speaking.

## METHODS OF TEACHING LISTENING

### Some Research Findings and Classroom Evidence

Research indicates that listening can and should be taught. Objectives, planning, system, organization, taking stock of sequence, and summarization from time to time in listening should be purposed by the elementary school pupil.

Hollow matched one hundred intermediate pupils of an experimental group with one hundred of a control group on the basis of listening ability, intelligence quotients, and chronological age. Her purpose was to determine whether a systematic program of teaching children to listen was beneficial.

For the experimental group, she planned lessons to develop basic listening abilities, to summarize, to grasp main ideas, to recall ideas accurately in sequence, and to make inferences in three types of composition — narrative, descriptive, and expository. All listening lessons were twenty minutes long and included preparatory, presentation, and postlistening periods. Provision was made for practice as well as for instruction. The control group continued the language arts program generally followed in the schools.

The results indicated that the children who were taught listening systematically for six weeks improved significantly more than those who received no systematic listening instruction. Pupils of low, medium, and high IQ's benefited quite comparably from the listening instruction. The main implication was that since listening is so important in life, and so undeveloped in elementary school youngsters, it should be carefully taught — not in isolation — but in integration with the whole program of elementary education.[16]

Canfield compared six weeks of listening improvement of three groups of fifth-grade pupils — two experimental and one control. It was the purpose of the investigation to determine whether direct listening instruction or indirect listening teaching was superior. The children in both experimental groups listened for and undertook to determine main ideas, attempted to distinguish between main ideas and details, tried to differentiate between relevant and irrelevant statements, listened for opinions, and searched for transitions. The control group received no specific instruction to improve listening. Canfield reported that there was no significant difference between gains of the pupils taught by direct or indirect methods. However, both experimental groups made gains significantly greater than the control group. The main implication of this study was that instruction in listening pays good dividends and that plans made to teach listening to elementary school pupils should be carefully carried out.[17]

Adams suggested four phases in using audio aids in teaching listening: (1) careful choice of selection; (2) preparation for the presentation — enhancing of interest and promoting the desire to learn; (3) an active reception — listening analytically for points to fit into an organization of understanding of the whole; and (4) evaluative exercises, consisting of testing, questions, and discussion.[18] Hadfield presented a procedure by which listeners could use effectively their background of experience while listening. He emphasized the value of stopping during a discussion or presentation to stimulate recall of important points, and advocated discussion immediately following an instruction to compare what is recalled with past learning.[19] Hook proposed that the alert listener actively select main ideas and determine the organization of the theme as it is developed. He warned of certain dangers such as hasty generalization and ignoring the important questions.[20]

[16] Sister Mary Kevin Hollow, "An Experimental Study of Listening Comprehension at the Intermediate-Grade Level," unpublished doctor's dissertation, Fordham University, New York, 1955, p. 264.

[17] G. Robert Canfield, "How Useful Are Lessons on Listening?" *The Elementary School Journal,* 62:147–151, December, 1961.

[18] Harlen M. Adams, "Teaching the Art of Listening," *The Nation's Schools,* 34:51–54, November, 1944.

[19] Wilbur W. Hadfield, "Parallels in Teaching Students to Listen and to Read," *English Journal,* 35:553–558, December, 1946.

[20] J. N. Hook, "Developing Good Listeners," *Journal of Education,* 132:110, April, 1949.

Berry showed that listening is improved by a pupil adjusting to his group and his work. She suggested the importance: of recognizing the relationships of listening to the other language arts, of conditions for listening, of the use of opportunities for listening, of developing goals for listening, and of employing improved equipment and instruments in listening programs.[21]

Neville presented a plan for teaching listening which he reported works at primary levels as well as higher levels. A teacher may tell children about a record, for instance, *Daniel Boone*. She may say, "While you listen to this record, I will make a test to see how well you can listen." She plays the record and while they listen makes up an objective test. A discussion of the recording follows. Next the teacher reads the test items and children react to them; results are then discussed with the children. A second playing guides them to recognize their mistakes and to make note of corrections.[22]

An analysis of the procedure suggests five steps:

1. Motivation — the remarks about the record and testing
2. Presentation — playing the record
3. Discussion of important points after playing the record
4. Testing by oral reading of the test and reacting to the items by the children
5. Checking the results to indicate deficiencies in listening, and making note of corrections.

Sister Mary Ethel emphasized auditory discrimination and purpose in a successful six-month program in training first-grade children to comprehend by listening. She used from ten to fifteen minutes of the language period for teaching eight basic skills. All the exercises used were set up in the form of games in which children listened carefully to a definite set of directions and a story, riddle, or poem. They reacted attentively in each situation to build one of eight listening skills: (1) to grasp a main idea in a paragraph; (2) to follow a sequence of ideas; (3) to understand instructions; (4) to recognize the central thought; (5) to recall details; (6) to get the main idea from context; (7) to recognize relationships; and (8) to predict outcomes or to draw con-

---

[21] Althea Berry, "Listening Activities in the Elementary School," *Elementary English Review,* 23:69, February, 1946.

[22] Mark A. Neville, "Listening Is an Art: Practice It," *Elementary English,* 26:226–233, April, 1959.

clusions.[23] These skills were presented in rotation. Her program resulted in significant improvement in development of listening power and a favorable effect upon reading development also.

The studies reviewed warrant the conclusion that primary grade children and other elementary school pupils enjoy listening, profit from listening instruction of many types, and make use of opportunities to listen. The results of instruction in listening pay high dividends in learning.

### Listening to Recordings

Listening is reciprocal to talking, but it is also an aid to reading and an approach to literature and culture. A listening center makes possible the appreciation of many types of literature. Through listening to records played on audio devices, individuals may enjoy a great variety of selections.

Many schools have such a center equipped with ten or a dozen sets of individual earphones so that pupils may listen privately without annoying others. Listening to a record may be the inroad to wide and intensive reading in a field or on a topic.

Hoffman described clearly the advantages of a listening center, the economy of setting one up in a school, the procedure for operating it, and its value for improving listening. Among the values listed were: purpose, discussion after listening, the promotion of critical thinking, self-selection, and the development of listening pleasure.[24]

The selection of the best recordings is a serious problem. Research has indicated children's choices in literature, particularly of poetry.[25] Teacher's experiences with and judgment of such materials should be used. Many sources are now available from which information about musical and other recorded materials may be obtained.[26] Although

---

[23] Sister Mary Ethel, "Listening for Comprehension," *The Catholic School Journal,* 62:21–24, May, 1962.

[24] Miriam Hoffman, "Our Listening Center Livens Language Arts," *Elementary School Journal,* 63:381–385, April, 1963.

[25] See Chapter VIII.

[26] Among the companies and concerns from which information and materials may be obtained are the following: National Council of Teachers of English, Chicago, Illinois; Columbia Records Education Department, New York, New York; Coronet Films, Chicago, Illinois; Educators Guide to Free Tapes, Scripts, Transcriptions, Randolph, Wisconsin; Encyclopaedia Britannica Films, Inc., Wilmette, Illinois; Enrichment Records — Landmark Books Dramatizations — New York, New York; McGraw-Hill Book Company, Text-Film Department, New York, New York; R C A Victor Division, Radio Corporation of America, Educational Services, Camden, New Jersey; Society for Visual Education, Inc., Chicago, Illinois.

catalog descriptions are generally quite indicative, it is advisable to listen to a recording before purchasing it in order to satisfy desirable standards of content, authenticity, voice, rhythm, and enunciation.

## Plan for Teaching Listening

A program for teaching listening may well involve the situation, purpose, plan, presentation, evaluation, and use.

*The selection of a situation.* A favorable situation for listening should be selected from history, literature, or any appropriate area. For example, a group may want to learn about sets or numeration bases other than ten. Another group may be interested in a science experience. Interest is important.

*Purposing.* The teacher and the pupils should be clear about the purpose of an activity. For example, the pupils should know whether to strive to remember the main points of a story, or whether the objective is to master the sequential details of a process.

*Planning.* The lesson should be planned so that the materials will be readily available for presentation. The sequence of principal activities should stand out. If the purpose is to retain details as well as to master main points, both should be logically organized.

*Presentation.* This step can be executed by speaking in a pleasant and enthusiastic manner. An audio-visual device is useful — a motion picture, a record player, or television. A small group may present a panel discussion. The presentation, no matter how developed, should be clearly and interestingly delivered.

*Evaluation.* Testing may be carried on during the lesson, after the presentation, or after a postdiscussion in which listeners are invited to ask questions and to make comments and criticisms. A delayed recall test may be made after a period of a week, two weeks, or a month, and the results compared with a test previously given. Evaluation should consider not only test results, but also the evidence on attitudes, attention, comprehension, and use. Have the listeners learned the materials? Have they enjoyed the experience? Have they become more interested in the activity or area? Such questions are important in determining the value of a listening activity.

*Use.* Many presentations worth hearing are worth remembering and using. If a story is remembered it may be retold. If a process is valuable, it can be used in an appropriate situation. If an experiment is properly heard and retained, it becomes part of the pupil's background of learning.

Note-taking is effective in retaining, analyzing, and using materials heard. A good listener hears the entire thought. He gets the "gestalt" of the lecture and makes a mental note of the main points. After the session, but while the presentation is still clear, he may write an organized brief to be used later for review or as a basis for further study.

## Some Illustrative Exercises for Listening

*Imitation of sounds.*    Have children imitate sounds that they know: (1) of animals — the pig, cat, dog, cow, and horse; (2) of birds — the bluejay, the robin, the crow, the whippoorwill, the duck, the goose, the turkey, the chicken; (3) of the wind, a waterfall, the ocean, the rustling of leaves when walking through them. Members of the group listen and keep account of the ones they selected correctly.

*Remembering a story.*    To children in the kindergarten or first grade, a teacher tells a simple story and asks a volunteer to repeat the story. A second child may add points omitted.

*Listening to and reporting a message.*    Have the children form a circle. Whisper a statement to the first child. Have him listen and whisper the statement to the second. The second will transmit the message in a whisper to the third child and so on until the message is delivered to the teacher by the last child. A distorted statement will generally result on the first attempt. Practice of this type will sharpen the interest and skill in listening carefully and in speaking clearly.

*A game: "Captain says."*    Organize a game similar to "Simon says," or as the soldiers played it, "McGready says." The leader gives a command prefaced with "Captain says." The captain says, "Stand up." Everyone stands. The following orders illustrate some commands which may be given:

> Captain says, "Walk."
> Captain says, "Jump."
> Run to the window.
> Captain says, "Raise your right hand."
> Raise both your hands above your head.
> Captain says, "Touch your forehead with your right hand."
> Stand on your right foot.

The commands preceded by "Captain says" are to be obeyed. Those which are not prefaced with "Captain says" are to be ignored. The one who excels in obeying when he should, and who ignores the commands not prefaced by "Captain says" wins the game and becomes the captain.

*Listening to remember the main idea of a paragraph.*    A teacher reads a paragraph, for example, about a boy who made a snowman. The story includes rolling snowballs, placing them, and decorating them. The child listens to the story and decides that the main thought is that the boy made a snowman.

*Listening for the main points in a talk.* The teacher reads a paragraph which presents two main points. She asks the pupils to write them.

Another paragraph may include three major points. Pupils can be asked either to state them or to write them.

A third paragraph may include two or three subpoints under each of two major points. The requirement at first might be to list the two major points. Instruction will be necessary to help some children differentiate between a main and a subpoint. Later the pupils will be able to note the first major point and the minor points which support it, and the second main point with the supplementary ones. When such listening has been developed and practiced, a pupil has improved his organization ability.

*Listening for details.* Read an explanation about "How to Write a Letter" or "How to Make a Talk." Have pupils try to remember the important facts.

*Listening for sequence.* A teacher reads a story to the pupils. After the story has been completed she may ask the children: (1) to determine which of three statements came first, which second, and which third in the story; and (2) which of three characters was mentioned first, which second, and which third.

*Summarizing.* Have pupils, who discussed the problem of orderly retention, summarize the discussion.

*Remembering words that rhyme.* A teacher may ask the children to listen for words that rhyme with the word *say,* for example, in the following group: *bay, cake, day, look, hay, run, sun, may, right, think.* The one who can repeat all rhyming words or more than any other in the group may be the leader and speak the next exercise of a similar nature.

*Listening for meaning.* Pupils may be asked to listen for synonyms of the word *fight* among these: *battle, peace, skirmish, work, strive, struggle, combat, sing, talk, figure, fun, friend, day.*

*Retention of exact context.* The teacher reads five words or more at random to a group. She may ask children to write or repeat the words in the order they heard them.

The teacher reads a sentence to test ability of pupils to repeat it verbatim. Examples follow:

1. The old man walked slowly up the steep hill.
2. The children ran pell-mell from the school door to the diamond and began to play baseball.
3. Tommy, a Great Dane, was the favorite pet of the Smith children who lived in the foothills of the Rocky Mountains not far from a beautiful park.

*Listening for beginning consonant sounds.*    Have pupils listen for beginning consonant sounds in words. Ask them to remember those that begin with the same sound as *big*. Pronounce the words: *be, bite, boy, cow, car, bill.*

*Listening for words with vowel sounds that are long.*    Direction to pupils: Listen and repeat words that have the sound of *e* as in *me: be, leap, meat, hot, bake, seat, feet, do, come.*

*Listening for and remembering words with vowel sounds that are short.* Direction: Listen and repeat words with the sound of *i* as in *if: sit, hit, hope, lift, bat, it, is, but, lot, fit.*

*Listening for words with final consonant sounds.*    Direction: Listen and repeat the words that end with the *t* sound as in *cat: hat, dot, cap, hop, fat, boat, rat.*

*Listening for words that mean more, better, or larger than.*    Have pupils listen to a number of pairs of words. Have them remember the words that mean *better, bigger,* or *more* than the other words: *big, bigger; large, larger; fine, finer; soft, softer; loud, louder; high, higher; tall, taller.*

*Listening for superlatives.*    Ask the pupils to remember the words that mean *most* or *least* of all among the following: *large, larger, largest; big, bigger, biggest; fast, faster, fastest; fierce, fiercer, fiercest; heavy, heavier, heaviest; low, lower, lowest; small, smaller, smallest;*

*Listening to a spelling test, and writing the words.*    The teacher pronounces carefully the words of a spelling lesson. Have the children write them. Have each child correct his own paper as the teacher reads the spellings.

*Listening to tape recordings.*    Use a tape recorder to record statements made by members of the class and have these statements played back. (1) Have each child listen for errors in articulation of sounds, such as those in voicing *th, ing,* in such words as *the, these, with, sing, inning, beginning.* (2) Have children listen to statements recorded for qualities of voice, pitch, loudness, and tone.

Such exercises will help pupils to develop listening skills. Similar activities may be planned when necessary to meet special needs of children.

## EVALUATION OF LISTENING AND ITS IMPROVEMENT

A learner's listening technics should be evaluated in many types of situations — in conversation, in discussion, in instruction, in obtaining directions, in understanding explanations, in reporting a message received on the telephone, and so on. The teacher, the pupil, and the teacher and the pupil together should plan evaluation as a necessary continuing phase of striving to improve listening.

### Teacher Evaluation

The teacher should appraise listening in the light of such questions as the following, always considering of course the pupil's ability to learn:

1. Does the learner show interest, courtesy, and good attitudes toward the speaker and the topic?

2. Can the learner summarize the essentials of the presentation given in a discussion, a panel, a conversation, or in a culminating activity of a unit?

3. Is a learner able to report correctly the main points of an instruction, an explanation, a broadcast, or a lecture?

4. Is a learner capable of delivering correctly a message which was received by him in direct communication or on the telephone?

5. Does a learner show ability in distinguishing between oral assertions of opinion and statements of fact?

6. Is a learner critical of faulty or questionable statements or assumptions made by a speaker?

7. Is a learner developing and improving listening?

### Pupil Appraisal

The pupil can evaluate his technics in listening by setting up questions such as the following and rating his performance by answering them:

1. Why should I listen?
2. Am I always ready to listen when listening is essential?
3. Do I start to listen at the beginning of an instruction?
4. Do I listen carefully to every part of the instruction?
5. Do I understand what is being said?
6. Do I recognize the main ideas and the important details?
7. Do I follow the speaker from one point to another?

8. Do I take stock as I listen from part to part of a talk?

9. When the talk is over, can I summarize it by stating the main and the subpoints?

10. After the period is over do I try to remember what the teacher or speaker said?

11. Do I make use of information I gained by listening?

## *The Teacher and the Pupil Discuss Listening*

One of the best procedures for improving and developing proficiency in listening is through cooperative evaluation made by pupils and teacher. It is suggested that pupils and teacher talk over the methods for listening effectively and also ways of speaking to engender good listening. The kinds of talking that are liked and disliked will become evident. Some pupils will state frankly that they do not like a high-pitched "squeaky" voice, and others that they cannot "stand" shouting. They will identify the "good" talkers in the class. Some favorable constructive comments as well as some critical ones will be made. The members of the group will indicate that they like to listen to someone who has something to say and who talks in a courteous and agreeable manner. Some will criticize speaking so low that the message is not clear. Under guidance, pupils set up standards for listening which will probably include such points as the following:

1. Listen courteously.
2. Listen attentively.
3. Try to understand what is said.
4. Do not interrupt the speaker.
5. Ask necessary questions when the speaker is finished.
6. Try to remember the main points of the discussion.
7. Try to see both sides of a question — yours and the other person's.
8. If it is necessary to disagree, do so considerately.

Since listening and speaking are reciprocal, it should be recognized that effective speaking will stimulate attentive listening, and considerate listening will stimulate acceptable oral presentation.

## SUMMARY

Listening is highly important in the daily lives of people, because there is need for it in all occasions of oral communication. Investigations have shown that listening of pupils of varying abilities in school is often quite ineffective, but that it can be improved by all — the gifted, the normal, and the slow learners — through instruction.

The objectives of listening must be presented enthusiastically. Factors to be considered in promoting good listening are purpose, points of interest, health, mental ability, attitude, and the background of the learner. Objectives in each instruction should be clear. Listening to a dynamic teacher on a vital topic is pleasurable to healthy alert pupils of adequate background.

Listening instruction should be planned. Children will listen if listening is worthwhile. Instruction should be made attractive in a pleasant atmosphere and in an environment properly controlled. Vital life situations and well-planned activities are useful in motivating dynamic learning exercises. Research has shown the value of listening instruction, and authorities have suggested effective methods and exercises for the teaching of listening.

The appraisal of listening learning by the pupils and the evaluation of listening instruction by the teacher should suggest cues for remediation practices and the development of skills and abilities which make listening effective.

### ACTIVITIES, PROBLEMS, QUESTIONS

1. Explain how listening and hearing differ.
2. State four causes for ineffective listening in schools.
3. Make a list of the types of listening you have engaged in during the past week. Describe each. Differentiate them.
4. List the important objectives in teaching listening, and explain how each can be achieved.
5. State five major factors which favor effective listening. Why is each important to elementary school pupils?
6. What arrangements should be made to assure good listening?
7. Devise plans for teaching effective listening. Consider situations, the use of content, procedures, and instruments.
8. Summarize findings of research in the field of listening, and make recommendations for teaching listening to elementary school pupils.
9. Search for games or other activities that will stimulate effective listening. Present a clear account of the three you think would be most useful.
10. How can listening be best evaluated? What procedures are useful in: (a) teacher appraisal; (b) pupil appraisal?
11. How can teacher-pupil discussions improve the quality of listening?
12. Compare listening and reading. How do they differ? Which do you find most useful in living? in school? Give reasons for your answers.

## SELECTED REFERENCES

Hirsh, Ira J. *The Measurement of Hearing.* New York: McGraw-Hill, 1952. 364 pp.

Johnson, Wendell. *Your Most Enchanted Listener.* New York: Harper, 1956. 215 pp.

Nichols, Ralph, and T. R. Lewis. *Listening and Speaking: A Guide to Effective Communication.* Dubuque, Iowa: Brown, 1954. 250 pp.

Nichols, Ralph, and Leonard Stevens. *Are You Listening?* New York: McGraw-Hill, 1957. 235 pp.

Pronovost, Wilbert, and Louis Kingman. *The Teaching of Speaking and Listening in the Elementary School.* New York: Longmans, Green, 1959. 338 pp.

Russell, David H., and Elizabeth F. Russell. *Listening Aids Through the Grades.* New York: Bureau of Publications, Teachers College, Columbia University, 1959. 112 pp.

Taylor, Stanford E. *Listening.* "What Research Says to the Teacher." No. 29. Washington, D. C.: DCT and AERA of the NEA, 1964. 33 pp.

Witty, Paul A., and Robert A. Sizemore. "Studies in Listening, I, II, III, and a Postscript," *Elementary English,* 35:538–552, December, 1958; 36:59–70, January, 1959; 36:130–140, February 1959; 36:297–301, May, 1959.

See also references for Chapters II and XII.

# Chapter IV

# Reading: Objectives, Preparatory Phase, Readiness

## GENERAL CONSIDERATIONS

READING is perhaps the most important approach to knowledge and understanding for individuals in school and after leaving school. In the United States, according to the American Book Publishing Council, more than a billion dollars were spent in 1959 on reading matter, approximately six hundred millions on textbooks and encyclopedias.[1] An individual must learn to read and read to learn in order to take his place properly in our democratic society. Without reading skills and abilities a person is illiterate, but a facility in reading opens up the whole history of the world and the great thoughts of men. "He who reads has many teachers." Reading is an avenue through which an individual may enjoy the most heroic exploits experienced by man and the wisest pronouncements of the sages of all races and eras. Through reading one may experience vicariously life of all peoples. Reading, properly selected, leads to truth.

Carlyle said a hundred years ago, "All that a university or a final highest school can do for us is still but what the first school began doing — teach us to read." Accordingly, it is necessary that the elementary school teach children the basic processes of reading. Some pupils need more time and more intensive instruction than others. Even the most accelerated who read far beyond their grade levels will profit from instruction in reading throughout elementary school and high school.

## The Nature of Reading

Reading is receiving thought through printed and written symbols. It is comprehending the expression by a writer of a book or article. It

[1] *New York Times,* July 31, 1960.

is the understanding of a message — printed or written — of the sender. It involves interpretation by means of the application of experience to the symbols formed by a writer.

Reading is thinking about meaning conveyed through symbols. It includes many activities: finding sources of knowledge, discovering facts and information, recognizing concepts, perceiving inferences, using effective procedures, determining valid generalizations, making critical analyses of materials, selecting essential data, organizing notes made from many sources, and determining relationships and interrelationships of research findings.[2]

Reading is not a narrow mechanical skill; it is cogitative, and frequently involves reflective and deep thinking. Reading is not just a tool or an instrument; it is a complex configuration of thought, feeling, and active organization. Reading comprises word recognition and sentence understanding; it utilizes discovery, comprehension, reflection, reasoning, appreciation, analysis, evaluation, synthesis, organization, and application. Reading affects personality, gives spiritual sustenance, arouses emotions, develops understanding, and promotes activity. Reading is a means to action and to wholesome living.[3]

## Need for Reading in Life

Life is enriched and facilitated through reading. Almost every vocation requires it. It is necessary, for example, in business and law, in medicine and science, in philosophy and education. A professional man who does not read adequately cannot very well advance in his profession or give required service. Among the materials that require reading and must be interpreted by one or more classes of people are: formulas, recipes, reports, articles, explanations, descriptions, research, analyses, signs, graphs, tables, and maps. Without effective reading, these are not properly understood. Reading is a highly valuable and entertaining art for recreation. Books, periodicals, and plays are important materials for recreational activity. History, science, mathematics, business, and transportation require studious, diligent reading. Reading is a guide to achievement and progress "on the job" and an avenue for enrichment and recreation "off the job."

---

[2] William S. Gray, "The Nature and Types of Reading," *The Teaching of Reading: A Second Report,* Thirty-Sixth Yearbook of the National Society for the Study of Education, Part I, 1937, pp. 26–28.

[3] Arthur I. Gates, "The Nature of the Reading Process," *Reading in the Elementary School,* Forty-Eighth Yearbook of the National Society for the Study of Education, Part II, 1949, pp. 3–4.

## Disability and Retardation in Reading

Learning to read is a complex process and a difficult one for many children. The inability to read effectively is one of the chief causes of failure at any level — from the first grade through college. Percival found, thirty-five years ago, that the first grade was the grade of greatest failure in school, and that 99 percent of the failures in this grade were caused by reading disabilities. He reported that 90 percent of those failing promotion in the second grade and 68 percent of those failing in the third grade were retarded because of reading disabilities. In the fourth grade, 56 percent were kept back, in the fifth grade 40 percent, and in the sixth grade 33 percent were retarded because of reading deficiencies. In the seventh and eighth grades, 25 percent of failures were caused by reading deficiencies.[4]

Despite the improvement in methods and the development of elaborate materials in the past three or four decades, there is at the present time a large incidence of retardation in reading in all elementary grades. Long reported word analysis and word recognition deficiencies in lower grades and silent and oral reading deficiences in upper grades. She stated that teachers overestimate retarded children's reading ability, are not aware of their reading difficulties, and fail to instruct them on reading levels at which they can profit.[5] Furthermore, it seems evident at the present time that pupils with high IQ's and those with low IQ's have some quite similar difficulties in learning to read.

## The Importance of Reading Instruction

Reading skills are necessary to the mastery of every level of school — elementary to graduate. Instruction in reading requires most careful consideration of individual learners because of the frequent tendency to failure in subject areas.[6] The increasing necessity for reading in school and in life outside the school has upgraded the importance of reading instruction. Because reading is required to locate information, to promote understanding, to stimulate thinking, to develop appreciations, to evaluate written statements, and to organize findings, it must be taught

---

[4] Walter P. Percival, "A Study of the Causes and Subjects of School Failures" (unpublished doctor's dissertation, Teachers College, Columbia University, New York, 1926).

[5] Donna Janet Long, "An Analysis of Reading Difficulties of Retarded Readers in Second, Fourth, and Sixth Grades," *Epsilon Bulletin, Phi Delta Kappa,* 35:33–34, 1960.

[6] Arthur I. Gates, *The Improvement of Reading,* third edition (New York: Macmillan Company, 1947), p. 1.

not only as a way of recognizing words and sentences but more importantly as a basis for comprehending concepts, events, and processes, and interpreting relationships both in schoolwork and in lifework.

## A Balanced Reading Program Necessary

The National Committee in its second report on reading in 1937, indicated the increased emphasis which had developed in the teaching of reading in the preceding decade. Among the developments were: (1) the increase of interest in problems of reading, (2) progress in reading readiness, (3) enrichment of reading activities, (4) provision of improved materials for unit study, (5) stronger emphasis upon obtaining meanings, (6) consideration of reading instruction in other subject areas, (7) drives for library facilities, (8) development of testing materials and procedures, (9) careful appraisal of reading difficulties, and (10) adequate programing of remedial activity.[7]

In the decade considered, several undesirable trends appeared. Some schools emphasized reading to the neglect of other types of experiencing. More serious, however, was the tendency to negate reading in stressing other types of instruction — oral and visual — particularly in the lower and middle grades. Oral reading in many quarters had been seriously neglected. A formalized type of silent reading without the interest factor had been frequently practiced. Unbalanced programs in some systems emphasized recreational reading to the neglect of study reading. Work-type programs in others were predominant without much regard for recreational reading. Considerable emphasis was placed upon diagnostic and remedial reading with the result that developmental teaching of reading was neglected.[8]

Those who plan a reading program should do so with a clear understanding of the needs for and importance of a well-balanced program. Young emphasized "four major factors in the process of learning to read in school for the educator to consider: the child who is to learn, the teacher who is to teach him, the material the child will be given, and the methods, skills, or techniques of teaching."[9]

Wardeberg suggested the coordination of reading and language in teaching children. She emphasized strongly the teaching of vocabu-

---

[7] William S. Gray, "A Decade of Progress," *The Teaching of Reading: A Second Report,* Thirty-Sixth Yearbook of the National Society for the Study of Education, Part I, 1937, pp. 5–9.

[8] *Ibid.,* pp. 9–10.

[9] *When Shall We Begin to Teach Reading?* (Albany: University of the State of New York, Bulletin No. 1367, 1949), p. 5. By permission.

lary, comprehension, study, and oral reading skills, and the value of developing in the pupil the habit of personal reading. She stressed the importance of having available carefully selected reading — current, classical, biography, poetry, plays, and information materials — to fit a wide variety of interests and abilities. She set forth suggestions for evaluating a reading program, diagnosing reading difficulties, appraising progress in reading, and remediation.[10]

A well-balanced developmental program should include the teaching of basic fundamental phases: preparation; beginning reading; acceptable skills, habits, and attitudes; wide reading; refinement. It should involve both oral and silent reading in recreational materials. It should present instruction in work-type reading and include procedures in various fields of study. It should also contain a plan for diagnosis and remedial instruction when such measures are necessary.

## READING AIMS AND OBJECTIVES

The teaching of the children of America to read is a vital national activity, and the motivation of our American youth to read over a period of this decade and the following decades is a cooperative activity in which millions of parents, teachers, educators, and citizens engage purposively. Because reading is so important to the life of the individual, to the lives of people in our society, and to the welfare of the nation, the objectives of reading instruction should be clearly understood and dynamically undertaken. Purpose is crucially important. Without it, the teacher cannot direct reading effectively.

### General Objectives

General essential objectives of reading instruction have been stated by the National Committee on Reading to achieve in learners:

    I. Rich and Varied Experiences Through Reading
    II. Strong Motives for and Permanent Interests in Reading
    III. Desirable Attitudes and Economical and Effective Habits and Skills.[11]

The first aim suggests the importance of experiencing through read-

---

[10] *The Teaching of Reading* (Albany, N. Y.: University of the State of New York, State Education Department, Bureau of Elementary Curriculum Development, 1963), p. 129.

[11] "Essential Objectives of Instruction in Reading," *Report of the National Committee on Reading,* Twenty-Fourth Yearbook of the National Society for the Study of Education, Part I, 1925, pp. 9–19. By permission of the National Society for the Study of Education.

ing. Reading should be, when directed properly, one of the most useful approaches to thinking clearly, to working effectively, and to problem-solving. Through reading, one may comprehend the best of culture that our heritage offers. Those who direct reading must purpose the uplift of the learner and guide him in his search for knowledge.

The second aim is one of interest and motivation. "Interest is the secret" is a principle of motivation. Some claim that *Johnny will read what he wants to read,* and it is true that children generally will read eagerly what they really enjoy. It is furthermore a fact that learners will read with compulsive attention materials that they find valuable in their activities. Interest alone is important, but interests in materials of high value are of supreme significance to the growing personality and the developing mind. It is the responsibility of the school and the duty of the supervisors and teachers to stimulate the young to read materials that will benefit them at each level of development. If children acquire a love for reading they will continue to read. A child must be guided to read materials of value and interest in school so that he will use reading enthusiastically and habitually after he has graduated and must rely upon his own initiative.

The third aim suggests the development of desirable attitudes toward reading. A child who dislikes the reading period, who fails to enjoy reading, and who does not find reading helpful in learning will not develop desirable attitudes toward it. Accordingly, the teacher and child should plan the program, select the materials, and utilize activities which foster good attitudes and build strong desires for reading of various kinds. All this can be accomplished only when the programs are organized to fit the varying needs and the wide-ranging interests of individuals in a class.

The third aim also includes the development of economical and effective habits and skills. Among the skills which the child should acquire are those involved in independent identification and recognition of words, phrases, and sentences. The learner should become aware that many words are used varyingly to convey thought from the writer to the reader. The child should learn to identify and recognize words by use of phonics, structural analysis, pictures, and context. He should learn to read meaning into the symbols on the page. He should become proficient in reading sentences and groups of sentences; he should learn how to comprehend ideas that are expressed and also those which are implied — that become evident "between the lines." He should learn to interpret figurative language.

The learner should develop the habit of reading with clearly defined purposes in the various situations which arise. He should develop the habit of reading for enjoyment as well as for understanding; he should build up the habit of reading for pleasure as well as the habit of reading to locate information. He should strive to improve his skills and to develop effective habits of knowing how to read flexibly, studiously, rapidly, and even skimmingly as judgment tells him the materials require. These skills and habits will be considered more completely in a later chapter. They are implied at this time because they are included in the purposes of reading, and purpose should guide the method of learning to read.[12]

Gray reviewed reports of reading requirements in children's community relationships, and primary programs of reading in selected countries of the world. He presented summaries of aims for reading instruction under the headings of (1) values and (2) attitudes and skills:

1. *Values* to be secured through reading. Every lesson should contribute to pupil development through emphasis on one or more of the following aims:

To extend the experiences of children concerning things within the range of their environment

To make their lives more meaningful through an understanding of the experiences of others

To extend their knowledge of things, events, and activities to other places, countries, people, times

To deepen interest in their expanding world

To develop improved attitudes, ideals, and behaviour patterns

To enable pupils to find the solution of personal and group problems appropriate to their age level

To enrich their cultural background

To provide pleasure and enjoyment through reading

To develop improved ways of thinking and expressing ideas

To help them become more familiar with the interests, activities, and problems of the community.

2. *Aims* concerned with the development of the reading *attitudes* and *skills* needed to attain the various values listed above:

To develop keen interest in learning to read

To stimulate the development of an inquiring attitude or a demand for meaning in reading

To develop accuracy in word recognition

To promote efficiency in solving simple personal or group problems as one reads

---

[12] *Ibid.*

To develop habits of effective oral reading

To increase the speed of silent reading

To cultivate interest in reading and the habit of regular reading for information and pleasure.[13]

## Crucial Factors and Activities of Reading Instruction

*Teacher purposes.* One of the most prevalent difficulties in the teaching of reading is the lack of understanding of objectives. In many of the otherwise fine books on reading, the statement of the aims and objectives is neither definite nor dynamic. Because reading is a complex sequence of acts, it is difficult to present all the objectives simply. McKee's statement should be emphasized particularly to the beginning teacher. He states that the process of reading consists of carrying out three important series of acts:

1. Identifying and recognizing printed words quickly and accurately
2. Arriving at an adequate understanding of the meaning intended by the writer
3. Making use of the meaning arrived at.[14]

Some children will learn to say words on a page without understanding, and others who may be even slower in the beginning may learn to understand quite readily after a slow start. It is claimed that the upper third of the class will succeed without difficulty in beginning reading, that the middle third will learn to read with some success because of definite instruction by the teacher, and the lower third will have considerable difficulty in learning to read at all. Although there is severe retardation at the present time, it is probably true that every child with normal intelligence can be taught to read by a well-trained and dedicated teacher. The teacher should consider carefully each of the following, which may be thought of as purposes in teaching reading:

1. Make use of the child's readiness to read and, when necessary, motivate activities to develop readiness for various types of reading.
2. Interest the child in reading, and develop permanent interests by use of appropriate materials and activities.

---

[13] William S. Gray, *The Teaching of Reading and Writing* (Chicago: UNESCO Scott, Foresman and Company, Educational Publishers, 1961), pp. 120–121. Published in 1956 by the United Nations Educational, Scientific and Cultural Organization and Scott, Foresman and Company.

[14] Paul McKee, *The Teaching of Reading* (Boston: Houghton Mifflin Company, 1948), p. 12. By permission.

3. Appraise and utilize a child's background and expand his experiences through reading.

4. Stress thinking and comprehension in reading — getting meaning through printed symbols.

5. Teach the child to identify and recognize the words and other symbols in and out of context.

6. Guide the child to use reading in discovery and problem-solving.

7. Stimulate the child to value and enjoy silent and oral reading.

8. Instruct the child how to become independent in finding information, in critically evaluating materials, in the selection of what he needs for his purposes, in organizing it, in remembering it, and in using it effectively.

*Teach when the child is ready.* Psychologists have shown the importance of readiness in learning, and teachers have demonstrated the crucial value of the "teachable moment." It is obvious that an unready child will not learn as eagerly as he would if he were ready. A child's readiness should be appraised, and he should be taught to read at the right time in favorable conditions. This means simply that the right opportunity should be grasped. When a child shows interest in learning a skill and shows evidence of ability to master that skill, he should be taught at that time. The precious opportunity should not be ignored.

"Reading to learn" is a concept which follows closely after the desire for "learning to read." When a child wants to use reading as a tool for learning, for problem-solving, or for enjoyment, he is in the right frame of mind for instruction. It should be understood that this involves a type of readiness different from that for beginning reading. A child may want to use a book, a dictionary, or an encyclopedia to learn about something; he may desire to read a story or a poem. When such a desire arises, he should be guided to read purposively and as efficiently as possible.

A teacher should note a child's progress toward each of the major objectives; in this appraisal, she will recognize that an activity planned for one objective often is valuable in working toward another, and that frequently two or more related objectives may be sought in the same reading assignment. For example, a child may be intensely interested in reading a story, but as he advances toward the objective of interest he will improve his mastery of skills, of word recognition, or correct phrasing. The purposes for reading of one type may help in building a desire for a second type.

*Recognition of the Major Phases of Reading Instruction*

In teaching reading to elementary school children, these phases of development have been identified generally by authorities:

1. Preparatory — preschool, kindergarten, first grade
2. Intial reading instruction — first grade and beginning second grade
3. Rapid progress in fundamental skills, habits, and attitudes — normally second, third, and fourth grades
4. Wide reading — generally fourth, fifth, and sixth grades
5. Refinement — seventh and eighth grades and above.

The essentials of these phases of reading development should be considered for every child as he comes into them. It should be understood that a pupil working in one of these stages may need instruction on another, below or above the phase in which he is exercising his major effort. It should be recognized that there is no clear line of demarcation leading from one phase to another. Some children may need to go back to one of the stages through which he has passed for review or remediation, while others may sail along without need for remedial work.

A class may include pupils working in two or three of these phases. In a third grade, for example, children differ sometimes as much as four or five grade levels in reading ability. In one sixth-grade class pupils read, according to scores on a nationally known reading test, on levels including second grade to eleventh grade. The teacher of this sixth grade had to guide pupils in improving skills, habits, and attitudes; in wide reading; and in refinement of reading abilities.

## PREPARATORY PHASE FOR READING

The purpose of the preparatory phase for reading instruction is principally to develop in the child a desire to read and a readiness for reading. The child in the normal home acquires an urge to read by talking and listening, by observing, by being read to, and through experiences. Before he comes to school, he talks to members of his family and people in the neighborhood, he listens to them, and he observes many things that interest him. He goes, for example, with his mother to the supermarket, with his father to the park, with his brother, sister, or aunt to the beach. He asks questions and listens to answers. Some homes provide colorful materials and guide him to look at picture books and handle them with care. Some parents talk to their children, tell them interesting stories, and engage them in conversation. Children from other homes do not have such rich advantages. Experience is an important basis for promoting reading; it motivates interest in objects, animals, and people — their actions and behavior. At first, a child may like to learn about things and scenes with which he is familiar. Later he desires to progress from the familiar to the strange and unknown.

## Appraisal of Each Child When He Comes to School

A teacher should become thoroughly acquainted with each child. She should understand insofar as possible his background, personality, interests, mental ability, and his social and emotional characteristics. She has the responsibility of determining as soon and as accurately as possible how ready each child is for reading.

## Readiness and Its Importance

When a child first enters school, he has many problems, one of which is that of "beginning" readiness for learning the various subjects and skills necessary to his education. A young learner benefits from an exposure or activity only if he commands properly functioning physiological mechanisms for responding to such stimuli, has a stock of experiences sufficient for perceiving and reacting to the stimuli, and if he possesses adequate energy and endurance to continue attention long enough to learn the lesson presented.[15] Without satisfactory development of bodily reactions, without the necessary preliminary experiences, and without sufficient energy to attend successfully to the stimuli, his readiness exercises will not benefit him.

Because many children fail to learn to read satisfactorily or learn only with difficulty, teachers must be concerned with the problems of developing an effective readiness. Teachers recognize the concept of reading readiness as a requisite not only for children entering school, but for those who arrive at various levels and encounter even more complex problems of reading. In this section, we shall be concerned particularly with the development of readiness for those who are unready to read upon entering school.

Tinker and McCullough reported conclusions of investigators which show that 25 percent or more of children who enter first grade are

---

[15] Gerald T. Kowitz, "Readiness: Its Three Phases," *The National Elementary Principal,* 43:22–25, February, 1964.

not ready to learn to read. To force reading upon them would no doubt cause difficulty in beginning instruction and perhaps in later life. Since there is no assurance that reading readiness will develop merely by the passing of time, it follows that a program to develop attitudes, habits, skills, and experiences should be planned and carried out.[16]

Among factors important for developing reading readiness are favorable background, challenging experiences, normal vision and well-being, mental age of about six years, fluency in talking, skill in listening, desirable personal relationships, ability to adjust socially, interest in pictures and books, and a desire to learn to read.[17] Children who lack one or more of these factors require careful attention and guidance before they can be expected to read with facility.

Readiness should be so developed that children will consider reading as a worthwhile and a happy experience. A child who is ready to learn to read and learns successfully will be generally a happy child. A child who is unready and is forced to go through the motions of reading usually will be unhappy about reading. Thorndike stated the law of readiness clearly. A paraphrasing of his statement suggests that for a child ready to read, to read is satisfying, and not to be permitted to read is annoying; but for a child unready to read, to be forced to read is annoying.[18] Readiness to read means that a child has achieved the physical and mental maturity, the interest, desire, and attitudes to begin the process of learning to read.

A program of readiness should be planned for those who need it. That program should not be prolonged unduly when the child comes to the point where he desires to read. When ready, he should read. This does not mean that readiness activities cease after he begins to read. Readiness for various types of reading will be necessary as the individual proceeds through the many phases of reading. Sometimes this readiness will be self-activated, but often it must be motivated by the teacher.

A readiness program should be devised to take care of those who are almost ready to read as well as those who are a month or two away from sufficient readiness for beginning reading. A total readiness program should consider: first, initial reading readiness; second,

[16] Miles A. Tinker and Constance M. McCullough, *Teaching Elementary Reading* (New York: Appleton-Century-Crofts, Inc., 1962), pp. 51–60.

[17] *Ibid.,* pp. 51–73.

[18] See Edward L. Thorndike, *The Psychology of Learning* (New York: Teachers College, Columbia University, 1926), pp. 1–2.

motivation concerning a particular type of reading; third, the acquisition of permanent interests and strong desires to read; fourth, the attainment of acceptable attitudes and effective habits of reading; fifth, the development of efficient skills for reading both recreational and vocational materials.[19] In this presentation, the purpose will concern initial readiness.

## Appraisal of Factors Relating to Readiness

In determining the readiness of a child for reading, mental maturity, physical development and health, social and emotional qualities, home, language, and background should be considered.

*Intelligence and mental maturity.* There seems to be a moderate correlation between intelligence and the ability to read. Several studies have shown that the correlation ranges from 0.50 or a little lower to about 0.65. Despite the negating of intelligence tests in some school systems, the mental maturity of a child should be noted. Studies of reading progress seem to indicate that children of high mental ages are generally likely to achieve more satisfactorily in beginning reading than those of low mental ages. Authorities have indicated that a mental age of perhaps six or six and a half years is one criterion for favorable consideration for beginning reading if other qualities are advantageous. A child who has a mental age of six may learn to read readily if he has a strong desire, good experience, and a proper language background. On the other hand, a child who has a mental age of seven may not make acceptable progress if he is uninterested or does not care to learn to read. To determine the mental age of the child, one of the following group tests of intelligence or a comparable one can be administered.

1. *Kuhlmann-Anderson Intelligence Tests,* Personnel Press, Inc., Princeton, New Jersey. A nonlanguage test at the first-grade level. Two forms for first grade. One form for grades above first.

2. *Detroit Beginning First Grade Intelligence Test,* Harcourt, Brace, and World, Inc., New York. A nonlanguage test suitable at the first-grade level. One form.

3. *Pintner-Cunningham Primary Test,* Harcourt, Brace, and World, Inc., New York. A nonlanguage test suitable for children in kindergarten through second grade. Three forms.

---

[19] Gertrude H. Williams, "What Does Research Tell Us About Readiness for Beginning Reading?" *The Reading Teacher,* 6:34, May, 1953.

4. *The SRA Primary Mental Abilities,* Science Research Associates, Chicago, Illinois. Measures verbal meaning, space, perceptual speed, reasoning, perception, and number. Suitable for first grade and above. Three batteries.

5. *California Test of Mental Maturity,* California Test Bureau, Los Angeles, California. Suitable for preprimary and primary grades, and elementary school. Three forms.

Manuals of directions generally accompany these tests, and information concerning administration and scoring is available.

When it is necessary to appraise the mental ability of a child with a language handicap, foreign background, or some other peculiarity, an individual intelligence test may be given. Several good tests are available but such tests should be administered by an expert. The *Wechsler Intelligence Scale for Children,*[20] the *Revised Stanford-Binet Intelligence Test,* Form L-M,[21] or the *Arthur Point Scale of Performance Test*[22] would be suitable. Since the MA and IQ scores derived from different tests vary, it is well to record the test used.

*Appraisal of physical development and health.* A teacher will note the chronological age of the child, his appearance, size, and alertness. She will read his health record, noting any deficiencies or abnormalities. Special attention should be given to vision, talking, hearing, and coordination. Does the child play energetically? How does he compare with others in size and weight? Does he eat and sleep properly? Is he overweight, normal, or underweight? Does he fatigue easily and require more rest than normal children of his age? These questions should be answered, and the answers used in determining the needs of the child.

1. *Vision.* The child who seems to have defective vision, whose eyes water or are inflamed, who squints, who holds his paper too close to his eyes or his eyes too close to his desk, should receive attention. There are several tests such as those of the Betts Telebinocular,[23] the Eames Eye Test,[24] the Snellen Chart,[25] and the American Medical Association Rating Reading Card[26] which are effectively employed for screening.

---

[20] Published by Psychological Corporation, New York.
[21] Published by Houghton Mifflin Company, Boston.
[22] Published by C. H. Stoelting Company, Chicago.
[23] Keystone View Company, Meadville, Pennsylvania.
[24] World Book Company, Yonkers, New York.
[25] National Society for the Prevention of Blindness, New York.
[26] American Medical Association, Chicago, Illinois.

When there is uncertainty about a child's vision, it is well to see that he is examined by an eye specialist. Some assertions have been made to the effect that beginning reading should be deferred because the child's eyes are too immature for reading at the age of school entrance. However, Dr. Eames, who conducted extensive research on the physical factors in learning, reported that five-year-old children were "found to have more accommodative power" than those at any older age. Accordingly the contention that reading should be deferred to a grade level after the first seems to be unwarranted.[27] Such a procedure would discourage many children, a great majority of whom are ready when they enter first grade or become ready to read during first grade.

2. *Hearing.* Hearing is particularly important in learning to read, and a child who has defective hearing should be identified. The child who has a pronounced hearing loss is quite easily known, but the one who has a less evident loss may be overlooked or misunderstood. It is important to screen out all those who have difficulty in hearing. There are several types of audiometer for measuring hearing.[28] With the Western Electric Company's 4C, it is possible to test a whole class at one time. Because the response is made by writing numbers, it will not suffice for young children.

If an audiometer is not available, a watch test may be given. A child with normal hearing should be able to hear a loud watch tick from forty to fifty inches.* A low whisper should be heard at fifteen inches, and a word enunciated with a low voice at a distance of twenty feet. When a child cannot hear at normal distances, the examiner may move up until hearing is established. In this way, it is possible to appraise roughly the degree of hearing handicap. In case of pronounced hearing deficiency, the child should be referred to a physician.[29]

Exercises which call for listening may be utilized to good advantage. Simple oral directions given in a normal voice will be responded to by the average child, but they may be ignored by a child with partial

---

[27] Thomas H. Eames, "Physical Factors in Reading," *The Reading Teacher,* 15:427–432, May, 1962.

[28] Among the companies manufacturing audiometers are: Greybar Electric Company; Aurex Corporation, Chicago; Sonotone Corporation, Elmsford, New York; Medical Acoustic Instrument Company, Minneapolis, Minnesota.

* An ordinary "testing" or old-fashioned pocket watch can be used for this test. The modern wristwatch is not adequate.

[29] Miles Tinker, *Teaching Elementary Reading* (New York: Appleton-Century-Crofts, 1952), pp. 48–50.

hearing deficiency. The teacher should be considerate of the child with a hearing loss by speaking distinctly and directly to him, by seating him advantageously, and by encouraging him to watch and listen to a speaker.[30]

3. *Other aspects of health.* A child's ability to learn depends in part upon other aspects of health such as nutrition, rest, and proper bodily functioning. A child who does not eat sufficient food, or eats the wrong food, or does not obtain proper rest or sufficient sleep may have difficulty in paying attention or in concentrating. All aspects of health should be scrutinized carefully in the appraisal of each child's readiness.

*Social, emotional, and environmental aspects.* A child's social and emotional life is closely associated with his environment. The community life in the neighborhood of the school may be healthy and stimulating, or it may be the reverse. But even in an excellent community, a child may be handicapped because of home conditions. For example, he may be "overprotected." He may not be guided to become independent. He may not be allowed to take responsibility of any kind and may not have any duties to perform. He may have everything done for him, and may grow up in the habit of depending upon his father, mother, brothers, or sisters. If this is the case, the teacher should encourage the child to develop confidence, independence, and self-reliance.

A child may show various kinds of social and emotional disturbances. He may not "get along well" with his father or his mother. He may become jealous of a brother or sister who is a superior student and is held up to him as a model. He may resent parental authority and develop either withdrawal or aggressive tendencies. Because of thoughtless statements made in the home or at school, he may develop feelings of insecurity or resentment. Because of these feelings, he may not be able to play happily with his fellows or work effectively with his classmates. One child may be made to feel inferior because of his mistakes; another may try to cover up inadequacies and mistakes he makes from day to day. He may develop a type of defense mechanism to brush aside embarrassment. Competition with other members of the group may be quite detrimental to the slow-learning pupil. To be labeled as thirtieth in a class of thirty,

---

[30] Kathleen B. Hester, *Teaching Every Child to Read* (New York: Harper and Brothers, Publishers, 1955), pp. 25–30.

time after time, is a disheartening occurrence for any individual.

Instruments are available for studying emotional and social characteristics of children. These may consider self-adjustment and social adjustment. By reacting to questions, an individual is supposed to indicate how he feels about himself and about others. One such test attempts to reveal evidence of the degree of self-reliance, his estimate of his personal worth, his sense of personal freedom, and nervous symptoms, if any. Furthermore, social relations are appraised, and antisocial tendencies, if any, are to some extent indicated.[31]

## Some Procedures for Determining Reading Readiness

Standard tests and teacher appraisal are valuable approaches for determining readiness.

*Using reading readiness tests.* Probably no one available test can measure validly all factors that indicate reading readiness. However such tests are helpful for a teacher in screening those who are ready to read from those who are unready. In cases where there is doubt, it may be helpful to use a second test. Among the tests of value are the following:

The *Lee-Clark Reading Readiness Test,* published by the California Test Bureau, is useful in kindergarten and first grade. This test measures child ability in visual discrimination, vocabulary, and following directions. Pictures, letters, and words are employed.

The *Gates Reading Readiness Tests,* revised edition, published by the Bureau of Publications, Teachers College, Columbia University, is useful principally in the kindergarten and first grade. There are five parts: picture directions, word matching, word-card matching, rhyming, and reading of letters and numbers. Capital and lowercase letters and digits are presented as needed. The tests are administered individually. Suggestions for developing readiness are presented.

The *Metropolitan Readiness Tests,* published by Harcourt, Brace, and World, may be used in the kindergarten and first grade. One purpose is to identify the pupils who need more work before attempting to read. These tests are designed to appraise ability in word meaning, sentences, information, matching, numbers, and copying in indicating the degree of readiness for reading. Mattick, who compared the predictive value of four tests for determining readiness to read in both

---

[31] *California Test of Personality,* California Test Bureau, Los Angeles, California.

kindergarten and first grade, concluded that the Metropolitan Readiness Tests are "highly useful in predicting early successes in the first grade."[32]

The *Murphy-Durrell Diagnostic Readiness Test,* published by Harcourt, Brace, and World, useful for the first grade, measures auditory discrimination, visual discrimination, and learning rate. Suggestions are given for instruction of children who evidence varying degrees of ability in reacting to the items.

The *Monroe Reading Aptitude Tests,* published by Houghton Mifflin Company, are valuable in kindergarten and first grade. They cover visual functioning, auditory discrimination, memory, motor control, articulation, and vocabulary.

Letters to the publishers will bring descriptions and details of these tests. If directions are followed, the scores should be reliable. Groups of from three to fifteen children (except in case of individual tests) may be tested, but when a child shows an exceptional peculiarity, he should be tested individually. It is obvious that a child cannot be expected to perform properly on a test if he cannot handle a pencil or if he has not achieved normal adjustment in the school. A well-adjusted child however can generally perform in such a way that his score on a test will be helpful in preparatory reading guidance.

*Using informal approaches to appraise readiness.* In order to read, a child must be able to think about the experiences that he has had and compare them with the expressions in books. He should be able to evaluate what he reads in the light of his background. In order to do these things, he should have ability in language — speaking and listening; he must be able to discriminate differences in objects, symbols, and numbers; he should have a degree of muscular control and coordination.

A teacher will be able to gain information about the child's facility for beginning reading by informal technics.

1. *Appraising experience.* Answers to questions such as the following are helpful. Does the child have a rich experience? Has he traveled? Has he gone, for example, to a circus? Has he visited a factory, a park, a farm, or a zoo? Have his parents provided him with a rich, mediocre, or meager background? What has his home life been like? If his experiences have been fruitful, he will be more likely to

---

[32] William E. Mattick, "Predicting Success in the First Grade," *Elementary School Journal,* 63:273–276, February, 1963.

be interested in beginning reading than if he has had few or no interesting experiences.

2. *Appraising listening and oral language.* Listening and talking factors are important in the appraisal of reading readiness. A child who speaks well and listens attentively is more ready for activity in another language art than one who does not speak or listen acceptably. A child who understands spoken words and uses them readily is quite likely to want to read such words. If a child takes part in conversations and discussions, if he listens to stories, if he asks questions, if he has developed pleasant speech and is able to articulate reasonably well, if he recognizes the necessity for listening and responding to the instructions of a teacher, he will be generally favorably disposed to reading.

Hildreth concluded after appraising several investigations of the relation between reading and other communication arts, that language is a basic factor in reading, that a strong relationship exists between reading comprehension and hearing comprehension, and that there is a possible connection between inferior language comprehension and reading difficulties.[33] Accordingly, a teacher should answer the following questions. Does the child talk fluently? Does he converse naturally? Does he listen attentively? Does he have a rich vocabulary? Does he use words meaningfully and correctly? If the answers to these questions are negative the chances are that the child will require preparatory instruction for reading.

Another phase of language concerns a child's ability to discriminate between sounds. Is he able to differentiate sounds of letters such as *p* and *b,* or *m* and *n?*

A teacher may have a child listen to similar sounds and to different sounds. She can ask him to say whether the articulated letters sound the same or different in these and similar pairs: *m, n; m, m; b, b; b, p.*

She may have the child listen to determine which words in a pair sound alike and which have different sounds.

Another type of exercise can be organized to determine whether the child can recognize a rhyming word. For example, a teacher may pronounce words and ask the child to pick the word that rhymes with the first word:

| | | | | | | |
|---|---|---|---|---|---|---|
| bone: | did, | pot, | lone | came: | run, | let, | name |
| come: | up, | all, | some | time: | boy, | see, | dime |

[33] Gertrude Hildreth, "Interrelationships Among the Language Arts," *Elementary School Journal,* 48:538–549, June, 1948.

Another ability in language is attentive purposive listening. Does a child listen attentively to a story or explanation? Does he understand a simple question? Can he repeat a short sentence, or tell in his own words the main points of a simple story?

A teacher may test responses and reactions. She can enunciate action words as the following and note the correctness of the response:

*a*) Sit        *b*) Stand        *c*) Walk        *d*) Jump

Listening is hearing with a purpose. A child, who listens to a direction, follows it, answers a simple question, retells a story, or repeats a sentence, is more likely to succeed in beginning reading than one who cannot do these things.

3. *Appraising visual discrimination and observation.* The ability to discriminate among different forms is most important. A child may be asked to match a circle with a circle when the second circle is presented with a square and a triangle. Can he tell what is lacking when a table is pictured with one leg missing? Can he see differences in word forms such as: *hit, sit, bit?* He may be asked to draw lines between the two words that are alike in squares as the following:

| dog | bed |
|-----|-----|
| do  | dog |

| line | time |
|------|------|
| fine | time |

| do | to |
|----|----|
| do | he |

| name | we  |
|------|-----|
| all  | all |

A child can be asked to determine how many people are in a picture, or how many houses there are. He may be tested to note discrepancies in a picture or in a succession of pictures. He may be asked to tell a story by viewing an arrangement of four or five pictures of: (*a*) a boy playing with a dog; (*b*) the boy throwing a stick; (*c*) the dog running after the stick; (*d*) the dog picking up the stick; (*e*) the dog bringing it back to the boy. Another approach to such a test is to place pictures in an incorrect order and direct the child to place them in proper sequence.

4. *Appraisal of interests and attitudes.* The child's interests may be determined frequently by observing what he likes to do. The child who is interested in books and in looking through them will want to know what they tell. An individual who handles books carefully, looks

at them, shows them to others, discusses them, and asks questions about them, is developing a healthy attitude toward books.

A checklist may be developed by any classroom teacher to determine likes and interests. Questions such as the following may be asked verbally:

*a*) What do you like best to do?
*b*) What games do you like?
*c*) What work do you like to do?
*d*) What do you want to do when you grow up?
*e*) For what do you wish most?
*f*) Who is your favorite hero?
*g*) Who is your favorite person?
*h*) What kind of pictures do you like most?
*i*) About what do you like to know or hear or read?

| | | | |
|---|---|---|---|
| 1) animals | 3) birds | 5) cars | 7) people |
| 2) adventure | 4) homes | 6) airplanes | 8) others |

*j*) What do you like to ride on best?

| | | | |
|---|---|---|---|
| 1) auto | 3) bicycle | 5) subway | 7) roller coaster |
| 2) pony | 4) boat | 6) airplane | 8) bus |

*k*) What sport do you like best?
*l*) What color do you like best?

The interests expressed may be used as clues to the kinds of books to provide for a group. The answers are helpful in selecting books for oral reading by the teacher and also for selecting materials for individuals to look at. A boy who is intensely interested in Indians, for example, will be eager to hear stories of them. One who is interested in jet airplanes will likely be excited about a picture book with various types of aircraft. The interests of each child should be considered in planning both the prereading and beginning reading program.

5. *Appraisal of a child's writing or attempted writing.* Does the child desire to write? Does he want to write his name? Does he attempt to write a letter or a message? Are his "writings" intelligible or partly intelligible? Does he try to express himself? Clymer suggested that the use of the "Copy a Sentence" Test, which has comparable reliability to some other readiness technics, is fairly economical of time and may be used as a predictor of reading success. The sentence used was, "The lazy fox jumped over the box."[34]

6. *Interview with parents.* The interview with a parent may reveal

[34] Theodore Clymer, "Report of 'Copy a Sentence' Test as a Predictor of Reading Success in Grades One and Two," Joint Meeting IRA — NCRE — AERA, Chicago, February 15, 1963.

many facts of importance concerning a child's readiness for reading. Among questions to which answers will be helpful are:

*a*) In what kind of activities does the child engage at home?
*b*) Does he or she enjoy playing with books or coloring pictures?
*c*) Does he enjoy playing with toys?
*d*) Does the child prefer to play actively with others, or alone?
*e*) Do the parents read to the child?
*f*) Does the child ask to have stories read to him?
*g*) Does a child ask to be taught to read?
*h*) Does the child ask to know the meaning of a word or of words in a story?
*i*) Is he interested in using paper and pencil?

7. *Appraisal of ability to follow directions.* The teacher may test the child to determine his ability to follow a simple set of directions, for example, getting started in running a race, as: (*a*) On your mark. (*b*) Get set. (*c*) Go. The boy or girl may be tested upon the ability to follow the sequence of chores preparatory to dismissal from school: (*a*) putting his things in his locker; (*b*) closing the locker; (*c*) discarding scrap paper in the wastebasket; (*d*) arranging things in his desk; (*e*) being alert for the dismissal signal; (*f*) going out of the room in an orderly manner.

*Teacher consideration and judgment.* In determining readiness for reading, the teacher plays a major role. Her observation from day to day, her informal notations about a child's behavior and activities, and her judgment are most helpful in determining the right time for beginning reading. She is the most important agent of appraisal. The well-trained teacher will find this type of interpretation a labor filled with meaning and portent for each child under her tutelage.

After a careful comparison of first-grade teachers' estimates of reading status of children entering the first grade with the results obtained by use of the Metropolitan Readiness Test battery, Kermoian concluded that teacher judgments were a valid and effective means of determining readiness.[35] The teacher knowing the facts arrives at her decision because she understands that readiness is, as Jersild stated, "the timeliness of what we wish to teach in the light of the child's ability to take it."[36]

---

[35] Samuel B. Kermoian, "Teacher Appraisal of First Grade Readiness," *Elementary English,* 39:196–201, March, 1962.

[36] Arthur Jersild and Associates, *Child Development and the Curriculum* (New York: Bureau of Publications, Teachers College, Columbia University), p. 31.

## Some Children Read When They Enter First Grade

Sometimes among the children who come to the first grade, there are those who know how to read. These should be identified. Durkin reported a longitudinal study of forty-nine children, who learned to read at home before entering first grade. Their homes ranged from low socioeconomic through the middle class. They possessed IQ's from 91 to 161, and read on levels from 1.5 to 4.6 based on a standard reading test. They were Caucasian, Negro, and Oriental youngsters who wanted to read. Their families were favorably disposed to reading, and at least one member of each family answered the child's questions and guided him in reading.[37] A second study by Durkin indicated that children who read before first grade came from varied backgrounds, that early reading is not necessarily harmful, and that school people could help parents to understand their function as teachers of preschool children.[38]

Plessas and Oakes studied twenty first-grade children with a mean IQ of 128, who scored above second-grade reading ability in December. These children were read to at home, and a majority were taught reading there. They were interested in books and learned the alphabet at early ages. They were able to write their own names, watched television, and were encouraged to participate in many communication activities.[39] Sutton reported a study of children who learned to read in kindergarten. Those who were interested, enjoyed reading to each other, and read one or more preprimers in a month. By the end of the year, the mean level was 1.78 — that is in the seventh month of the first grade. Many of these children enjoyed reading by brothers or sisters at home. Their socioeconomic background was good, and their parents were interested in school affairs.[40]

These studies emphasize the point that some children are ready to learn to read when they enter first grade and sometimes even when they are in kindergarten. To require them to spend time on readiness exercises which they do not need is poor methodology which may cause discontent and even irritation with school and reading. Accord-

[37] Dolores Durkin, "Children Who Read Before Grade One," *The Reading Teacher*, 14:163–166, January, 1961.

[38] Dolores Durkin, "Children Who Read Before Grade I: A Second Study," *Elementary School Journal*, 64:143–148, December, 1963.

[39] Gus P. Plessas and Clifton R. Oakes, "Prereading Experiences of Selected Early Readers," *The Reading Teacher*, 17:241–245, January, 1964.

[40] Marjorie Hunt Sutton, "Readiness for Reading at the Kindergarten Level," *The Reading Teacher*, 17:234–239, January, 1964.

Developing reading readiness

ingly, it is proper to direct such individuals to the reading level which will challenge them to learn.

## Developing Reading Readiness

*Purpose.* In a prereading program, the teacher's purpose is to determine which of the children, if any, are ready to read, which ones will be ready after a brief readiness program is carried out, and which ones will require extended preparatory instruction before a reading program can be inaugurated. After making these appraisals, it is necessary to plan programs of readiness that will fit the needs of individual children. A teacher is doing a great service for a child when she creates in him a desire to read. This she may do by her knowledge of children and of books, by discussions, by storytelling, by guiding growth in language, experience, interests, attitudes, skills, and understanding, and by developing confidence in ability to learn to read. A desirable attitude toward reading must be built up in every child.

*Approaches.* McBroom stated clearly the important approaches for developing greater readiness for reading in the prereading period as follows:

a. Increasing firsthand experiences in order to build up clearer basic concepts back of words and ideas

b. Building up and clarifying the child's speaking vocabulary

c. Giving the child some experience in expressing ideas in clear sentences

d. Accustoming the child to the fact that symbols stand for ideas

e. Acquainting the child with the physical make-up of a book, and with the left-to-right progression of symbols across the page

f. Giving some practise in seeing likenesses and differences in words

g. Accustoming the child to working with other children and to giving attention in a group

h. Clearing up any mispronunciations, poor enunciation, or false concepts of words

i. Giving the child who does not speak English some fluency in using the language

j. Stimulating a desire to read.[41]

*Some materials useful for a readiness program.* Many materials are available for a reading readiness program. The following have been employed beneficially:

1. Objects such as educational toys, blocks, models, playthings

2. Materials such as tagboard, papier-mâché, paints, brushes, crayola, clay, tin pie plates, cardboard for labels, signs, bulletins, posters, lumber, sand

3. Tools, blunt scissors, children's small hammers, shovels, buckets, rakes

4. Bulletin board, easel, flannel board, wall chart, wall pockets, practice cards, flash cards, chart holder, sand table, sandbox

5. Typewriter (large type), duplicating equipment, printing set

6. Housekeeping materials, miniature furniture, dishes

7. Simple science materials, plants, aquarium, collection of shells, fossils, rocks, pictures

[41] Maude McBroom, "Desirable Scope of the School Program in Reading," *Newer Practices in Reading in the Elementary School,* Seventeenth Yearbook of the National Elementary Principal, July, 1938, p. 238. By permission of the National Elementary Principal of the NEA.

8. Picture books, story books, Mother Goose rhymes, readiness books, simple picture dictionaries, child periodicals

9. Audio-visual aids such as simple pictures, charts, diagrams, drawings, projectors, lantern slides, filmstrips, tape recorders, record players and records, sound motion pictures, radio, and television.

The purposeful use of a few of the above should be of more value than an attempt to use all without proper planning.

*Some procedures for developing readiness.* The alert teacher develops important activities as they are required. Brief presentation of some of these follow:

1. *Experiencing.* One of the truly great learning procedures is experiencing in new and intensive situations. In a school in New York City, a first-grade girl stated that she had never seen a river although the mighty Hudson flowed not more than a half mile away. Her teacher remedied that lack of experience within a few weeks when a group visited the east bank of the great river, and the little girl looked in wonderment at the flowing water, the tugboats, and the large ocean liners. Trips or excursions can be made to one or more points of interest in the locality — a supermarket, a park, a zoo, a farm, a library, a botanical garden. Since the interests of the group will vary, no excursion or trip should be made without preplanning, carefully making the trip itself, and discussion after the return. When the children know what things they intend to look for in a fair, find them, and discuss them upon their return to school, they are purposing, exploring, thinking, organizing, and expressing. Such experiences are helpful in preparing for reading because they will stimulate the children to find out more about what they saw and will engender the desire to read.

2. *Enjoying listening experiences.* A child may enjoy hearing a train, an airplane, the howl of a wolf, or the roar of a rapids. He will listen to a band, a chorus, or a glee club. He will give close attention to a story told by the teacher, or enjoy the reading of a poem by the teacher. Listening ability can be enhanced by means of recordings, rhythms, music, radio, and TV programs. Exercises should be purposeful as well as enjoyable. A child should sometimes listen to a story with the purpose of retelling it. Hearing stories increases interest in them, and eventually leads to a desire to read them.

3. *Talking and discussing.* Talking about pets is interesting. Boys like to bring their pets to school to show them to classmates. Girls

sometimes bring their dolls for others to see. Objects such as a new dress, new shoes, or a hat may be the subject of conversation. A boy who has taken a trip to the mountains or seashore will describe his trip. Others may ask questions about it. Thus discussion is motivated, and a desire for information is developed. Pictures, charts, and books are used to find answers.

4. *Games and dramatic play.*    Play, more or less free at first, which becomes organized as the children mature is a useful readiness activity. Playing house brings out discussion and characterization of people. Playing school does this also and suggests the values and needs for books and reading. Games, set to music and utilizing rhythm, interest children and are useful in developing muscular control and coordination.

5. *Working together.*    Children enjoy building with blocks and construction materials, a little town, or street, or farm. Such projects are conducive to talking, listening, and cooperating, and lead to a desire to use books. The setting-up of a library corner or a science exhibit requires thinking, planning, cooperating, and searching for information. Pictures, too, can be "read." Conversation leads to further search through materials. The actual carrying out of a project and its evaluation are important in developing readiness for reading.

6. *Following spoken directions.*    Children who are viewing, listening, talking, and cooperating with each other and with the teacher are in situations in which they may be guided to follow directions. They can be directed to place their desks in order, put materials in the proper place on a shelf, and pick up used paper from the area around their desks. The teacher may suggest several things to do. For example, the teacher may say:

> "Bring me a pencil and a piece of paper, Mary."
> "Open the door of the birdcage, Arthur."
> "Point to the largest fish, Joseph."

7. *Making collections.*    Bringing in pictures of buildings, animals, parkways, or streets is worthwhile. A committee on buildings, for example, may cut materials from newspapers and other sources to exhibit. Collections of flowers, grains, seashells, or rocks lead to interest in picture books and picture reading. A shell or rock may be of such interest to a child that he will try to find out more about it and lead to the selection of a book that has pictures which are helpful to him. The children can be guided, because of their discussion of the things collected, to the pictures in a book, next to the captions, and finally to simple context.

8. *Viewing pictures.*   Looking at pictures in a prereading book will aid in developing interest in reading because the child "sees people, objects, things, places, and action." Pictures viewed at first should be simple with little detail. A pet, people, houses, and children playing are appropriate. Later, pictures with more detail may be gradually introduced.

Films, motion pictures, and other visual aids can be used. Filmstrips depicting children's favorite stories such as "Peter Rabbit," "The Three Bears," and "Little Red Riding Hood," may be shown advantageously. These bring forth questions that induce discussion.

9. *Looking at and enjoying books.*   Picture books can be displayed in a library corner. A kindergarten girl leafed through each of seven books with word and phrase captions that had been displayed on a little round table. After her inspection, she chose one, placed it on a chair, and rearranged the remaining six books artistically. She then went to her seat with the selected book and began "reading" it. The pictures were read and she began asking about the context: "What does this word mean? What does this sentence say?" She was evidencing readiness for reading.

10. *Placing labels by teacher and children.*   The teacher may place labels on several objects in the room: desk, chair, table, locker, book, clock, library corner, and chalkboard. If she prints the name of each child on a card, he can attach it to an item of his own.

11. *Ear training.*   When a child comes to school at six, he has heard many words and many sounds. He differentiates between a dog barking and a cat meowing. He is generally able to identify a whistle blowing, a horn honking, and a bell ringing. Exercises such as the selection of words that rhyme or words that sound alike or unlike are helpful in ear training. Exercises as those presented in the chapters on oral language and listening are valuable here. Simple exercises are useful. Have children listen to pronunciations of pairs of words to determine which are alike in sound and which differ:

| | | | | |
|---|---|---|---|---|
| *a*) sing | rain | | *d*) game | same |
| *b*) pan | pan | | *e*) keep | keep |
| *c*) hit | him | | *f*) when | then |

12. *Matching words and pictures.*   Toward the end of the readiness period some teachers have the child match words and pictures. Present several pictures with names under them as, *pig, cow, car, dog.* Give a child cards to match the pictures. He will learn to select a card and

place it below a designated picture with its word. A child finds a card with the word *cow,* for example, and places it under the picture of the cow.

13. *Seeing likenesses and differences in pictures, words, and symbols.* Visual discrimination may begin with the use of objects. A child may select from several two dolls that are identical. Next, pictures can be used, and later letters and words can be differentiated. Directions can be given to draw a line between two pictures that are alike in a series of pictures, or to point to drawings similar among a group of varying kinds.

A series of four or five pictures may be presented in which the child is directed to cross out the one that is different. He may be asked to cross out the letter that is different in the following:

|  |  |  |  |  |  |  |  |  |  |  |  |
|---|---|---|---|---|---|---|---|---|---|---|---|
| *a*) | S | S | S | C |  | *c*) | a | a | A | a | a |
| *b*) | n | n | a | n | n | *d*) | d | D | d | d | d |

He may be asked to cross out the words that do not belong in:

| with | with | go | go | in | in |
|---|---|---|---|---|---|
| with | when | go | did | it | in |

14. *Training and practice in left-to-right direction.* Training in left-to-right progression is aided if the child knows his left from his right hand. The teacher may ask the child: to lift his left hand first, and then his right one; to look at pictures from left to right which tell a story; to view a sentence on the board from left to right as she reads it. She can do the following: ask a child to trace a word from left to right which has been written in dots; write names on the board beginning at left and proceeding to the right; use a pointer in reading the title of a story or a caption of a picture.

15. *Arranging a book exhibit or library corner.* Book week is a good time to call attention to books. Walking into a kindergarten in which about twenty-five children were engaged in several types of activities relating to books, a visitor noticed in one corner an attractive exhibit of picture books and book jackets. "What are you doing?" a five-year-old was asked.

The little girl answered slowly, "This is book week. This is our exhibit of books."

A second question, "What do you learn about books?" was answered, "We learn how to open books, how to take care of them, and how to look through them at pictures. We want to learn to read about things that are in books. We hope to read soon."

In this library corner, there were two small tables with chairs around them. On each table were four or five books. Other books had been placed in a bookrack and on shelves of a bookcase. Five or six children were sitting at the tables looking at pictures in books. One of the children said, "We started this library corner only two months ago. We got books from the library, and we bought some books. These are very pretty, and we like them very much." A reading corner and a collection of bright colorful books are incentives to read.

16. *Reading to children.* Oral reading by parents or teachers is a most potent means for developing strong interests in reading. "Which book do you want me to read?" a teacher may ask. From several books on the reading table, one may be selected. The teacher may read the title of the book and the story. On another day if the teacher is asked to reread it, she can ask, "What story?" A child will give the title and the teacher will ask for the book. The child must "read the title" in order to select the book. Others will follow this example, and soon the titles of favorite books will be known, and childen will differentiate them. Reading stories to children is effective if the stories are well chosen and enthusiastically read. A well-illustrated story with some captions and a little context may be "read" sometimes by children in this preparatory stage.

17. *Using paper, pencil, and crayon.* Children are interested in and helped by using writing and drawing materials. They enjoy using color crayons to draw designs or to print letters of the alphabet. When they become successful in identifying colors, some, properly guided, will begin to read words — *red, blue, green,* and *yellow.*

*Résumé.* The following are some suggestions for developing rapport and reading readiness. An experienced teacher will add others to them.

1. Meet each child as he comes to school as considerately as possible and gain his confidence.

2. Learn to understand each child and his aptitudes, attitudes, interests, abilities, and needs.

3. Create an environment of books, love for reading, and a climate of expectancy for learning to read.

4. Develop a feeling of mutual security in the group.

5. Motivate boys and girls to listen attentively to directions and to listen appreciatively to stories.

6. Encourage each child to ask questions.

7. Motivate children to talk about their experiences, their pets, and their activities.

8. Tell and read stories, and have children retell, dramatize, and discuss them.

9. Display children's names and some labels of familiar objects, and display titles of books and jackets attractively.

10. Note the auditory and visual discrimination skills of each boy and girl, and guide learners to improve these skills.

11. Help children to become accustomed to *left-to-right* movement in looking at words and sentences.

12. Guide boys and girls to handle books properly.

13. Take advantage of their interest in paper and pencil activities.

14. Be enthusiastic in reading to them. Teacher enthusiasm is caught.

15. Begin reading instruction when a child is ready to read.

## SUMMARY

In the present day, everyone must learn to read — the more efficiently the better. Reading is a complex set of attitudes, abilities, skills, and habits needed in many situations and most vocations in life. A balanced program of reading instruction is necessary in order to guide a child to develop the required reading abilities necessary for leisure and work. Important objectives in teaching include making reading interesting and meaningful to children, developing word attack skills and habits, and stimulating appropriate attitudes toward reading for recreation and study.

In the preparatory stage, each child's mental maturity, physical development, and health factors should be appraised, as should his emotional and social qualities. His background, experience, language, interests, and attitudes should be evaluated by means of readiness tests and informal observation and interviews. Teacher consideration of all available facts is important in deciding when a child should begin to read. Materials useful for the prereading program should be collected and used as they are necessary. Procedures beneficial in developing readiness are: experiencing, listening, talking, enjoying games, dramatic play, and introduction to books. Children should learn to work together, to follow directions, to differentiate sounds, objects, pictures, letters, and word forms, and to practice left-to-right directional viewing. Among the activities in which a child may engage with profit are: looking at pictures, labeling objects, making collections of objects and pictures, and arranging a book exhibit and library corner.

## ACTIVITIES, PROBLEMS, QUESTIONS

1. Find in other books three definitions of reading. Compare and evaluate them.

2. List the needs you have for reading both in school and outside of school in the period of one week.

3. Explain the importance of the following in reading instruction: (a) experience; (b) interest; (c) attitudes; (d) habits; (e) skills.

4. What is the significance of the statement, "Teach when the child is ready to read."

5. Discuss each of the major phases of reading instruction.

6. Outline "The Preparatory Phase for Reading."

7. Why is it important to appraise each child when he is in the preparatory reading stage?

8. What are the factors which indicate that a child is ready to read?

9. Why are some children slow to achieve readiness for reading?

10. List the important procedures for determining a child's readiness for reading.

11. Compare the advantages and the disadvantages of the informal approaches to the appraisal of reading readiness with the more formal approaches.

12. List and be able to describe the most important activities for developing reading readiness.

## SELECTED REFERENCES

Baker, Augusta. *Stories: A List of Stories to Tell and Read Aloud.* New York: New York Public Library, 1960. 77 pp.

Betts, Emmett A. *Foundations of Reading Instruction.* New York: American Book, 1957. 757 pp.

*Development In and Through Reading.* Sixtieth Yearbook of the National Society for the Study of Education, Part I. Chicago: University of Chicago Press, 1961. 406 pp.

Dolch, Edward W. *Teaching Primary Reading.* 3rd ed. Champaign, Ill.: Garrard Press, 1960. 429 pp.

Gans, Roma. *Common Sense in Teaching Reading.* Indianapolis: Bobbs-Merrill, 1963. 416 pp.

Harrison, M. Lucile. *Reading Readiness.* Rev. ed. Boston: Houghton Mifflin, 1939. 255 pp.

Monroe, Marion. *Growing Into Reading.* Chicago: Scott, Foresman, 1951. 274 pp.

*Report of the National Committee on Reading.* Twenty-Fourth Yearbook of the National Society for the Study of Education, Part I. Bloomington, Ill.: Public School Publishing Company, 1925. 339 pp.

Russell, David H. *Children Learn to Read.* 2nd ed. Boston: Ginn, 1961. 612 pp.

Spache, George D. *Reading in the Elementary School.* Boston: Allyn and Bacon, 1964. 356 pp.

Tooze, Ruth. *Your Children Want to Read: A Guide for Teachers and Parents.* Englewood Cliffs, N. J.: Prentice-Hall, 1957. 222 pp.

See also references for Chapter V.

# Chapter V

# Beginning Reading: Word Attack — Phonics and Other Procedures

## PURPOSES IN BEGINNING READING INSTRUCTION

THE major aims of reading instruction are to guide the child to experience richly through reading, to achieve ever increasing interests and self motivation for reading, and to develop "desirable attitudes and economical and effective habits and skills" in reading. These cannot be accomplished perfectly in initial reading, but an encouraging beginning can be made if the purposes which should direct instruction are sought with considerate and dynamic effort.

In *beginning* reading a teacher should strive to guide the child to do the following:

1. Read to comprehend thought presented through printed symbols.
2. Read to enjoy experiences in real or imaginative simple stories.
3. Develop independence in identifying printed symbols — words, word parts, phrases, sentences.
4. Become adept in recognizing printed symbols — words, phrases, and sentences — previously identified.
5. Use reading in study activities.

When these purposes are being moderately accomplished, the learner becomes capable of making rapid progress in developing fundamental skills, helpful habits, and desirable attitudes, of expanding and intensifying his interests, and of refining his reading to meet modest study needs and some recreational aspirations.

The beginning reading stage must be experienced by all normal children at one time or another. It is fruitful when the child becomes interested in reading, recognizes the need for it in study and recreation, and wants, for example, to find out what books say. The goals of beginning reading are achieved early by some children and late by others — in grade one by some, and one, two, or three grades later by others — depending upon differences in ability to learn, background, and variations in teaching and teachers.

## INTEREST AND MOTIVATION

Interest is a most important motive for learning to read. A child who wants to read will try to read, but a child who is not interested in reading must be made ready to want to read. A teacher must ask, "What are this child's interests?" By means of interviews, discussions, and questioning, she can determine some of the dominant ones of each child. These interests generally include home and community, children and their activities, animals and flowers, work and recreation, building and constructing, excursions and exhibits. Children are interested in music, singing, stories, and current happenings.

The teacher must establish good rapport with each child she teaches and promote good personal relations among the children of her group. Motivation to read is enhanced by discussion of problems and sharing of activities. The interests that a child has when he comes to school are opportunities for beginning the program of readiness and initial reading, but other useful ones can be developed in the school.

Among the factors and activities which will motivate reading indirectly or directly are the following:

1. Teacher understanding of each member of the group — his background of experience, his readiness or nonreadiness, and his desires for reading

2. Teacher enthusiasm for and knowledge of child reading materials and methods

3. Reading of stories by the teacher and encouraging the boys and girls to talk about the characters in them

4. Enjoyment of interesting and attractive pictures and finding out what the context says about them

5. Talking about a story and how it proceeds and terminates

6. The presentation of words, phrases, or brief sentences with illustrative pictures — filmstrips or other means

7. Dramatizations planned and carried out under the guidance of the teacher

8. The use of audio-visual materials and technics to portray interesting scenes or episodes

9. Teacher reading about interesting current events

10. Talking about an activity such as airplane or space travel

11. A well-planned reading program to meet a variety of tastes and interests.

## MEANINGFUL BEGINNING READING

Reading instruction is begun most advantageously when children are able and willing to learn to read. An important objective to be kept always before the child is that of reading for meaning, which should be purposed because it is satisfying and becomes increasingly so as the child develops skills and abilities in comprehending context. Reading thoughtfully with success stimulates the desire for further reading.

There are several ways to make reading interesting and useful to the beginner who generally wants to read. In this section, six approaches to beginning reading — experience, the beginning book, activity-utility, writing, oral reading, and the integrating approach — are outlined, any one of which may be used under certain circumstances by teachers with different groups.

### Using Experiences in Beginning Reading

Although there has been criticism of the experience chart, experiences are basic to learning to read, and the chart can be used profitably. For example, first-grade boys and girls who lived in a town, went to visit a farm. None of them had ever lived on a farm, but some had seen farms while driving with their parents, and they liked what they saw. They arranged with a farmer, an uncle of one of them, to make the visit. They wanted to see many things, and at the suggestion of the teacher, they decided to form into several groups so that each group could bring back information about one aspect of farm life. One group decided to concentrate on chickens, ducks, and geese; another on the cows, and a third on pigs. A fourth group thought it would be nice to study the flowers and the shrubs, and a fifth decided to look at the beautiful fields of corn.

The farmer showed the children around the yards and through the buildings. They saw the pigs and chickens, and the calves; they looked at the corn and oats growing in the gently sloping fields. They observed the milking machine. They liked the calves, which were drinking milk from a trough and eating alfalfa. They thought that the pigs acted very hungry as they guzzled the feed the farmer placed in a trough. They gave out exclamations of wonder at the poultry — the little chickens, ducklings, and goslings. They liked the farmer who answered many questions, and the farmer's wife who treated them to cookies and milk.

On their way back to school they talked with interest and excitement about all they had seen. Each of the five groups discussed stories they could tell. In the following days each group dictated a story to the teacher who edited it and wrote it on oak tag paper. Two of the stories are reproduced below.

### The Little Pigs

We went to a farm.
We saw the little pigs.
They were in a pen.
They were hungry.
They ate corn.

Each group read with the teacher's help the story it created. The teacher asked one group, "What was your story about?" "The Little Pigs," the children answered. The teacher asked questions and the children replied by reading answers. For example, in reading "The Little Pigs," the teacher asked, "Where did we go?" She pointed to the first word in the top line and then to the other words one after another, and asked the children to read the thought silently. Again she asked, "Where did we go?" The children read, *We went to a farm.* The teacher continued, "What did we see?" When she pointed to the second line and let her pointer pass slowly from left to right, the children read first silently and then orally, *We saw the little pigs.*

The other sentences were read in like manner. There was a little difficulty with the word *hungry,* but one child said *hun — gry.* Another spoke up perhaps from memory of the word, and said, *They were hungry. The White Duck* was read similarly.

### The White Duck

We saw a duck.
It was on the bank.
It went into the lake.
It was white.
It put its head under the water.

At a class assembly, the committees read their stories about the Little Pigs, the White Duck, the Calves, the Flowers, and the Tall Corn. After each reading, there were questions about the story and about the experiences. Volunteers read the stories about their topics.

One objection made to this type of activity is that children read from memory. Admittedly they do use memory, but they associate the sentences with meanings which are helpful in reading, and they read silently and thoughtfully before reading orally.

A second objection to experience charts is that the vocabulary is not properly controlled. No attempt was made to control the vocabularies of these stories. Every word, however, except *pigs, pen, bank,* and *lake* are among the 644 words of the Integrating Basic Communication Vocabulary.[1]

A third criticism of experience charts is that they are not interesting. This was not true in the case of these made from the visit to the farm. If the chart is made from happenings that are not interesting, it is conceded that it could be boring and of little value. If however, the children's experiences are real and interesting, if they have discussed them enthusiastically, if the vocabulary is understandable, and the language simple, the reading will be valuable for beginners.

A fourth criticism is that some children do not know or care, for example, about such a topic as pigs which others enjoy. A normal child, nevertheless, has interests in life around him — on the street, in the store, or in the crowded city. The language and the vocabulary of the city child are different from those of the suburbanite or of the farm child. The story of the pigs is a farm story and town children were interested in it. The story of the duck although a farm story in this instance might be duplicated for city children who visit a park. Although more evidence would be needed concerning the vocabulary, language, and interests of underprivileged children, those who teach reading to them should appraise them in order to teach effectively.

*Some possible trips or excursions for the first grade.* Trips of first graders may be made to a city park, a zoo, the botanical gardens, a museum, an aquarium, a forest, a bank, a store, a newspaper office, a factory, or an air terminal. Other types of excursions which could be made the bases for stories follow: observing a game; seeing a play; a boat ride; an airplane ride; going to a fair; obtaining information about an event; attending a celebration. If the children are interested in seeing, hearing, talking, or doing, the chances are that what they see, hear, talk about, and do can be subjects of stories which may be told to the teacher and made into worthwhile experience records. Such stories may be printed in manuscript and read with satisfaction.

---

[1] James A. Fitzgerald, "An Integrating Basic Communication Vocabulary," *Elementary English,* 40:285–289, March, 1963. (The singular form *pig* is in this vocabulary.)

*Some criteria for experience charts.* The following may be useful in evaluating an experience chart:

1. The experience should be real and interesting.
2. The experience should motivate lively discussion among the children.
3. If the children want to tell a story, it can be used for reading.
4. The language should be simple and without difficulty.
5. The sentences in the beginning should be short enough to be presented on one line.
6. A large majority of the words written in the chart should be most useful for reading.
7. The story should be written in clear print or manuscript.

## Introducing Beginning Books

A teacher's manual provided with a basic reading series should be consulted for introducing the beginning reading book. Some systems of reading provide large pictures or picture books which contain materials similar to those in the beginning book. Such pictures are usually well within the experience of the children.

*Using individual books.* A teacher should demonstrate how books should be opened and handled. She may find it worthwhile to write in manuscript on the board the context of the first reading lesson and show how she reads a sentence from left to right. She may then repeat the reading from a book, and have the children read along with her. She should show them how to hold the book and how to turn a page so that the reading may be continued. Each child should learn about opening the book, finding the page, reading from left to right, and comprehending the meaning of the context.

Generally the teacher will group the class and teach first those who are ready to read. The materials in the preprimer are carefully prepared. The vocabulary load is light and generally only one or two new words are presented on any page. Usually a story is spread over three or four pages accompanied by pictures. A plan for reading should be made and followed. It should, however, be flexible. Some children will need much more help than others. Those who breeze through a lesson should not be held up. Those who require added instruction should be helped considerably.

The discussion will be so planned that the words of the story are identified by the children. The teacher often directs attention to the matching of oral statements with printed matter. She may ask questions which can be answered from the context. The reading of the printed story understandingly is the aim of the lesson. Rereading the story, if it has interest and appeal, is a valuable practice for some. However, rereading of the preprimer stories may become tiresome for others because of the lack of intrinsic interest in the materials themselves. Children in the beginning reading stage generally like repetition. A child, asked to read again a story that he read the day before, will strive under proper encouragement to improve his reading. He may wish to read a certain episode of the story — a part that gives him and the listeners pleasure; yet, the monotonous rereading of a story to determine whether the child knows a word is poor practice.[2] Other groups as they become able and ready should be introduced to the beginning book with consideration of their needs and abilities.

*Features of a preprimer and primer materials.* Essential features of a beginning book follow:

1. It should deal with meaningful experiences interesting to children.

2. The vocabulary should in general be words of frequent use in reading — such as those determined by Dolch,[3] Gates,[4] or Fitzgerald[5] — words that are used repeatedly through life.

3. The vocabulary load should be moderately light so that the child can succeed without difficulty.

4. The thought should be presented in simple and understandable language. Content should be appealing.

5. Appropriate colorful pictures and illustrations which assist in conveying thought and action should be provided.

6. The preprimer should be attractive, well bound, and durable; the paper, opaque and without gloss; the print of proper size; and the length of line and the leading between the lines appropriate for beginners.

7. An adequate well-organized teacher's manual provided with a set of preprimers should be studied by the teacher.

---

[2] Fay Adams, Lillian Gray, and Dora Reese, *Teaching Children to Read* (New York: The Ronald Press, 1949), pp. 249–251.

[3] Edward W. Dolch, *Methods in Reading* (Champaign, Illinois: The Garrard Press, 1955), pp. 373–374.

[4] Arthur I. Gates, *A Reading Vocabulary for the Primary Grades,* revised and enlarged (New York: Bureau of Publications, Teachers College, Columbia University, 1935), 29 pp.

[5] Fitzgerald, *loc. cit.*

8. A workbook of related exercises usually accompanies the pre-primers and should be utilized.[6]

*Some suggestions for beginning book reading.* It is well to have discussion of a picture or of pictures which generally parallel the context and at first dominate the story. The child should be helped to appreciate the action in the picture, "John plays." Have him identify the printed sentence by asking "Who plays?" and guide him to respond, *John plays.* Here the child recognizes the relationship of the action picture, the printed word *John,* and the oral word — *John.* In like manner, the relationships among the action in the picture, printed word *plays,* and the oral word are stressed. The teacher may ask, "What does John do?" A volunteer reads, *John plays.*

As the stories become longer, there is need of careful guidance and expert questioning. "What is this story about?" may be asked of a boy who is reading a three- or four-line episode of a man driving an automobile. "What is he driving?" "Read to find out where he is going." Response should be given to each question. The answers should be read: *He is driving a car. He is going to work.*

The setting for the story may be discussed, but the story should not be spoiled by giving the child the message. Ideally, he should get the meaning more and more through the contextual materials as he goes along to the end of the preprimer.

*Continuing readiness.* If children are ready to read and want to learn, good progress can be made. Boys and girls ready and prepared to read should read. Every story will be read more enthusiastically if the factor of readiness is promoted. Children, who begin to read with enthusiasm and success will be benefited by continuing readiness activities, and they will develop a readiness based in considerable part on success and enjoyment.

## The Activity-Utility Approach

Leading systematically from the readiness phase of reading, a teacher could begin with useful action or name words. Among many types, the following may be used successfully.

*Use object labels and names of children.* Have the youngsters read labels on the chalkboard, the desk, the table, chair, and so on. If boys and girls help the teacher place the labels on the respective

---

[6] Paul McKee, *The Teaching of Reading* (Boston: Houghton Mifflin Company, 1948), pp. 203–216.

objects, the learning becomes meaningful. They may easily recognize their own names and their neighbor's on each locker and on each desk.*

*Use action words.* Have the children perform a few meaningful acts from spoken commands as may have been done in the readiness period: *sit, jump, run, go, stand, come.* After determining that each child of the group understands the meaning of these words enunciated, print in manuscript on the board, for example, the word "stand." Ask for a volunteer to do what the word says. If a child reads the word correctly and stands, others may read the word and perform the act. It may be well to have the group say the word in unison. After another word *jump,* for example, has been read, the teacher may write a name before it — *Pat jump. Sally jump.* After several have acted out the direction, a child can be asked to read the sentence, *Stand and jump.* This process may be carried out with other words.

On another day, before any new word is introduced, the boys and girls are asked to react first to oral directions and then to visual ones, such as, *Sam stand. Bill jump.* After this, new action words may be introduced and learned. A game including the new words and the review words may be played. Children then read sentences using the vocabulary learned.

*Write directions.* The teacher prints on the board: *Get your books. Open your books. Find page 4. See the pictures on page 4. Say the name of the boy on page 4.* After the children have read the name, print on the board: *See page 5. Say the name of the girl on page 5.*

Other types of written commands in the form of a game may be written:

1. Put your books away.
2. Pick up the papers near your desk.
3. Open the window, Tom.
4. Water the plant, Jim.
5. Clean the board, Harry.
6. We will read stories now.
7. Read the story, Henry.

*An example: reading for safety.* An exercise may concern crossing the street:

The green light says, "Go."
The red light says, "Stop."
When we come to a red light, we stop.
When we come to a green light, we go.

---

* Use at first only the given names of the children — George, Tom, Harry, Jane, Julia, and Susan.

When the sign says "Walk" we cross the street.
We cross the street at street corners.
We watch out for cars.
We are careful.

These are a few examples which illustrate how reading may be used in activities of the curriculum. Reading can be taught effectively in many situations.

## Writing

The communication arts are interrelated. Learning one has a favorable effect on learning another. As good oral language and listening are advantageous in learning to read, so is writing helpful. Since the printed and manuscript alphabets are similar in form it is obvious that learning to read and learning to write should reinforce each other. Fernald[7] and Stauffer[8] have shown the value of writing in connection with the kinesthetic method in teaching reading to slow learners.

Young children want to write just as they want to read. Before entering school, they are interested in pencil and paper activities. They draw and write. Some print letters and their names. Hildreth suggested that because of the interrelationships between writing and reading processes there is advantage in teaching them concurrently.[9]

Writing is an active motor process. A child looks at a letter *b*, and copies it or prints it. He reads it, *b*. He sees a word below a picture, *ball* for example, and prints it. Then he reads it. Later he may write the sentence: *I have a ball*. Again he reads what he has printed. Reading and writing are coordinated because the child writes what he reads and reads what he writes.

Writing the letters of the alphabet strengthens the image of letters because the writer has produced them purposively and actively. His identification of the letter *s* for example is more complete after seeing and writing it than if he only saw it. Writing helps the learner to differentiate the words — *made* and *make*. The differences between *here* and *there* are clarified by writing. Writing the words strengthens the recognition process. Reading reversals such as *saw* for *was* may

---

[7] Grace M. Fernald, *Remedial Techniques in Basic School Subjects* (New York: McGraw-Hill Book Company, 1943), pp. 21–178.

[8] Russell G. Stauffer, "Certain Basic Concepts in Remedial Reading," *Elementary School Journal,* 51:334–342, February, 1951.

[9] Gertrude Hildreth, "Early Writing as an Aid to Reading," *Elementary English,* 40:15, January, 1963.

be corrected by writing. When writing words, the child selects letters to represent sounds successively such as *h* and *e* in *he*. He hears the likeness of the identical beginning sounds in *he, hear,* and *him,* and by reading the three words, he voices and learns to recognize the phoneme — the sound that the grapheme *h* stands for. Thus, writing aids phonics. The writing of basic words such as *all, are, at, I, could, mother,* and *together* as words and in sentences facilitates sound-letter relationships, promotes eye movement from left to right, and also strengthens symbol-sound relationships. Saying each part of a word as it is written is helpful to retention of the word.

The active use of words, involving writing or reading, or both, familiarizes the learner with them. Writing a letter or a story requires words which a child must consciously select, think about, use, spell, and place properly in a sentence. A little girl who wrote:

> Dear Daddy,
>    Thank you for the candy.
>        Love,
>        Joan

used considerable time and thought in composing her letter. She read it to her mother for her opinion.

Such reading requires a left-right eye movement. It gives practice in the use of words in communication. Thus written communication strengthens the visual reading process by adding motive and meaning to it.

The kinesthetic method has proved to be valuable with disabled readers. Boys and girls who require remedial reading procedures respond readily to instruction which encourages them to trace letters, words, and sentences as they say them. Writing words and stories stimulates meaningful reading. After learning a small basic vocabulary by tracing and writing, disabled readers gradually develop less laborious procedures of learning to read.[10]

To conclude, writing is a help in learning to read because it dynamically strengthens letter and word formation, identification, and recognition. In the process, children learn the letters, associate sounds and letters, and develop meanings of words and sentences. Reading what has been actively written is a successful procedure with slow-learning and foreign children; it can be advantageous with the beginning readers.

---

[10] Fernald, *loc. cit.,* Stauffer, *loc. cit.*

## Oral Reading

It should be noted that although meaningful silent reading has been emphasized in the approaches outlined in the preceding pages, oral reading has been used as a helpful technic. Acceptable oral reading is, however, an objective in reading instruction.

*Oral reading by the teacher.* The teacher will take advantage of opportunities to read to children. She may read preferred poems frequently because children love poetry, properly presented. She may read an exciting story or a crucial excerpt from a book taken up casually from the reading table. If she will then read the title of the book and the page from which she chose the passage, and place the book on the table, volunteer readers will be attracted. She may write the title and the page reference on the chalkboard. This procedure may be repeated with other books from time to time. If the teacher reads enthusiastically well-selected materials which she knows are favorites of children, they will want to read more widely and no doubt more intently.

*Silent reading necessary for oral reading.* In the primary grades, children should learn to read orally. If they are to achieve normal proficiency in oral reading, the important factor is silent reading. Reading is not just recognizing words; it is thought-getting and in the case of oral reading, it is thought communication also. To transmit thought effectively, a reader must comprehend the thought which he gets through silent reading. He will convey the thought not necessarily by sounding letters or by voicing words one after another. He can communicate thought effectively only if he comprehends it, and to comprehend the thought silent reading of sentences is necessary. The child must be taught to read silently to understand what he is to say verbally, and then to think how to convey the message clearly and with proper emphasis.

In beginning book reading, the teacher may show a child how to read a passage or line that answers a question. She may suggest that a child who reads haltingly, tell what the book says. She can have the child find the place on a page to answer a question. In reference to a story of a cat, she may ask for example, "Was it a black cat?" The child reads the answer and stresses *white* in the statement, *Tom was a white cat.* In early oral reading, meaning as well as facility in the skills of oral speech must be emphasized. Good oral readers will win attention, but poor readers will lose the interest of some individuals in the group.[11] Patience should be exercised. A very slow learner may read to the teacher or to one or two children in his group.

*Types of exercises.* Among the types of oral reading exercises in which a primary-grade child will be interested are:

1. A word, phrase, or sentence presented on a screen or card
2. The title of a story or poem on a particular page of a reader or other book
3. A sentence on a chart or in a book in answer to a question
4. The answer to such a question as, "How did Joan play with her doll?"
5. What the child who was lost saw and heard in the story
6. Simple directions for playing a game.

As the children's interests widen and become more intensified and as their skills improve, they may be guided to read parts of a story they like, a little verse or rhyme, or a riddle. Two children may read a dialogue. In such procedures, silent and oral reading are made correlative in achieving competency in comprehension and communication.

## Integrating Procedures in Initial Reading

*Evaluation of criticisms.* No one approach to initial reading is completely adequate. Integration of the procedures suggested and others can be useful. The experience approach has been criticized because it is said to be desultory, haphazard, and incidental. The basal series approach is currently under fire because it is accused of being slanted particularly to the middle-class children and because it does not provide for individual differences in interests, needs, and progress. Preprimers, primers, and readers have been severely castigated because stories and selections have been said to be "insipid and boring." They are criticized by some because vocabulary control is said to be too rigid and because of their limited vocabularies. They have been criticized for their lack of appeal to boys. The activity-utility approach is opportunistic and curtailed in scope. The reading of names, labels, announcements, and directions in their natural settings is limited.

Although no one method is wholly adequate for achieving all the aims of initial reading, it may be useful in integration with others. A multiple approach should be utilized. Instructional procedures should be em-

---

[11] See Mildred A. Dawson and Henry A. Bamman, *Fundamentals of Basic Reading Instruction* (New York: David McKay Company, Inc., 1963), pp. 199–202.

ployed as needed in guiding children to achieve the important goals in beginning reading. Methods should be adapted to the special needs of the groups and individuals who are being instructed.[12]

*Procedures in initial reading.* All legitimate materials and methods properly used have some value at one time or another for beginning reading. Experiencing is basic for learning to read and presents motivation for it. It is an excellent avenue to the understanding of the meaning of words. Names, labels, and action words have specific uses in beginning reading. Reading signs, "Keep off the grass," "Save," "Do not erase," "Stop," "Walk," and "Don't walk," are meaningful and practicable. Basal readers are helpful in presenting necessary skills. A simple preprimer, a primer, and successive readers, properly composed are valuable to most children, but each child should read a preprimer, a primer, or reader at his own rate and go on to other materials. Workbooks are useful in practicing and mastering word structure and phonic skills. Reading skills of varying kinds can be analyzed and practiced in them. Word and flash cards should be used purposefully as required. A child who likes a story in a supplementary or trade book may well select another which similarly interests or challenges him. Writing has value for most children in coordination with reading. The kinesthetic method sometimes has been found to benefit individuals with disabilities. Oral reading can be helpful to the readers and stimulating to the listeners.

An effective integrating approach in beginning reading uses methods which best promote progress and elicit success for each learner. It correlates experiences with obtaining meaning from written and printed materials. Word attack skills are developed and practiced when needed to make the individual independent. The integrating approach is intrinsic. It involves reading for information, thinking, and organization. It promotes appropriate reading abilities, skills, habits, and attitudes. It emphasizes meaning, interest, interpretation, writing, and use. It includes oral and silent reading of study and recreational types. It is concerned with learning to read, reading to learn, reading to enjoy, reading to know, reading to evaluate, reading to create. The intrinsic integrating procedures should begin in initial reading and continue through the successive levels of reading, instruction as individuals need them.

---

[12] *The Teaching of Reading: A Positional Paper* (Albany, New York: The University of the State of New York, The State Education Department, September, 1963), p. 12.

## DEVELOPING INDEPENDENCE IN
## WORD IDENTIFICATION AND RECOGNITION

Word identification and word recognition are necessary in the process of reading. In a real sense, identification concerns the study of a word so that when it appears subsequently to the learning of it, it is recognized. Word recognition, however, concerns the reidentification of a word in succeeding viewings of it after it has been learned. In order to read, new words must be identified, after which they should be recognized.

The following are useful in identifying and recognizing words for developing a meaningful vocabulary: oral language and listening, picture clues, contextual clues, configuration, communication core vocabulary, meaningful seat work, structural analysis, phonics, audio-visual technics, and the use of the dictionary.

### Language — Listening and Speaking

Oral language and listening are basic approaches to reading. Words used by children in speaking and heard by them in communication with parents and others are valuable for reading. The concepts with which a child is familiar, his experiences, his activities, and the happenings of everyday living are comparatively easily read because he understands them. All language is interrelated, and the wise instructor will plan the development of reading vocabulary through the language approach. Words and concepts understood in speaking and listening will be more easily learned in reading than unknown words.

In the beginning of reading instruction, the oral language approach is helpful. Children who have experience in fishing, for example, will be aided by that experience in reading about fishing; they will be helped additionally by discussion of fishing before reading a simple story about a man and a boy in a boat fishing. In a picture, the man and the boy are holding fish poles with lines and at the end of each line there seems to be a cork floating on the water. A discussion of the purpose of the fishermen brings out the idea of catching fish. The children are led to expect that fish will be caught. They may discuss the kind of fish and how they will be brought into the boat, and what the fishermen will do with them. The context may read simply, "Sam and his father are fishing." A second picture may show Sam pulling in a fish. The conversation may bring out the fact that Sam caught a fish. The story might read: "See Sam fish. See the fish he caught." Experience with boats and fishing helped children in this instance. They expected that fish would be caught. The discussion led them to relate the picture story to the printed sentences and to the comprehension of them. Seeing the picture, talking about the act of fishing, and listening to the discussion, all combined to give meaning to the simple sentences accompanying the fishing pictures.

## Picture Clues

A picture has been said to be worth a thousand words. Some pictures are indeed worth many words, particularly in the beginning of reading. Before a child reads, he is interested in looking at pictures. He sees a great deal in a picture, and learns to enjoy what he reads into it. A child generally enjoys pictures of animals, of cars, of boats, and of boys and girls playing. He will interpret the pictures at first in the light of his own experiences, but later, under guidance, he will look for details of interest to him. For example, in the picture of a soldier, he may note that the soldier stands very straight, that he is dressed differently from other people, that he has insignia of some kind on his shoulders or sleeves. A child may "read" through a preprimer or through part of it that does not contain one printed word and understand much about the story the pictures tell.

A picture may be used to introduce a word. A child may identify a picture of a boy with the spoken word *boy,* and another of a dog with the spoken word *dog.* He has heard the words many times and he has used them. He has seen boys and dogs. He will associate the written word *boy* and the picture of a boy if after looking at the picture his attention is directed to the word, *boy.* In like manner, the child may view the picture of the dog, note the word *dog* beneath the picture and associate the two. The child then may be asked to look at two word cards — *boy* and *dog* — and directed to match the pictures and words.

A picture may be used to introduce a thought. For example, a picture of a little girl setting the table can be used to help the child read the sentence: *Jean sets the table.* In addition to the first picture, others may be shown to illustrate other sentences, such as: *Mother cooks the dinner. Father comes home. They eat supper.* The pictures are helpful in guiding the child to the thought expressed in the three simple sentences. By "reading" them the child is helped to read the sentences and the story.

Preprimers and primers present stories with many pictures and few words, but as the child progresses from preprimer to first grade and onward, the pictures become fewer and the context more important.

## Context Clues

Context clues are a means for identifying words and meanings in reading. A child should be guided in looking for meaning in context. Staring helplessly at a word is a habit which makes reading frustrating, but searching for clues for analyzing the thought and the form of words makes reading a fascinating activity. For example, in the sentence: *On a clear day, the sky is blue,* the child may know all the words except *clear.* An analysis of the context will help him to figure out the word *clear.* He knows that when the sky is blue, the day must be bright, sunny, or clear. He knows *cl* from association with *clean* and *clock.* He combines *cl* with the word *ear* and voices the word *clear* in the sentence — *On a clear day, the sky is blue.* In his thinking he has used sounding in connection with context to identify *clear.* Another example might read: *He shot the rabbit with his bow and arrow.* A child who has played with bow and arrow, even though he has never seen the word *arrow* in print, should reason or reflect, "I played with a bow and arrow. The printed word is *arrow.*" This comes of experience and a context clue.

Meaning is determined by context. A word may be used to convey many meanings, and the meaning in any sentence will depend upon the context. The use of the word *set* is an example. Its possible meanings run into the hundreds. Note the following: We *set* a trap for the mouse. The explosion *set* the house on fire. Mary *set* the table for four. The sun *set* at six o'clock last evening. My uncle is *set* in his ways. Mother got a nice *set* of dishes for her birthday. We go with the younger *set* in school. I played a *set* of tennis before dinner. His jaw was *set* stubbornly. Paul *set* words to Jim's music. We *set* out at dawn yesterday.

Assuming that the child has not met the words in parentheses in the following sentences, he should be able to identify them from the context aided by experiences:

> Mary ate bread and (butter).
> Tom gave me his (baseball) bat.
> Lillian has a new set of (knives) and forks.
> She has cups and (saucers) too.

Other types of exercises follow:

1. The child is directed to select the right word to complete each of the sentences:

> John threw the —— over the fence. (*king, wagon, ball*)
> We will —— to the park. (*got, tell, go*)

2. The child is asked to select *one* word that will complete the three following sentences properly (*watch, look, clock, door*):

> The boys —— the fast trains go by.
> Tom can tell time on his ——.
> The —— kept a careful lookout for fires.

3. The pupil is asked to complete the sentences by making compound words from the following words (*mother, dry, run, grand, day, black, right, board*):

> Our —— will visit us next week.
> Julia wrote on the ——.

4. The child is asked to select the correct words for the blanks in the following sentences:

> There are —— cars in the yard. (*one, two*)
> Can you —— me? (*is, our, see*)

## Configuration

Words are identified in many ways, and for some words one method of identification may be better than another. The form of a word — its shape, length, and sequence of letters — may be helpful for some rather long words such as *elephant, Christmas, teacher,* and *children.* The word *elephant,* because of its distinctive configuration after one or two exposures has been found to be easily recognized by children. *Christmas* also, partly because it is distinctive, partly because it is long, and partly because of the capital *C,* is not difficult for children. These words are less likely to be confused with other words than such short words as *am, an, and, any, as,* and *at.* Individuals who have slight astigmatism may confuse *am* and *an* or *is* and *it,* but have less difficulty with distinctive longer words. A teacher will sometimes compose exercises to help a child to identify important words by their configurations. Such aids can involve a child's knowledge of one word with which he attacks a similar word with a different beginning letter such as *kind* and *find.* A child may know *five* and *from* its form and a knowledge of the sound of *d* use the word *dive* successfully in the sentence: *Henry and William dive into the water.* A child may know the words *told* and *cold* and from their common form identify the word *sold* in the sentence: *Father sold his car.* In his identification of *sold* he combines context, phonics, and configuration. A child learns to combine several word attack skills in identifying words. A configuration clue requires careful scrutinization of a word in the first identification, but it is a valuable aid for recognition thereafter and a valuable help in the development of rapid reading.

## Developing a Sight Vocabulary

Use of the child's background of experience, language facility, and interest in learning to read are bases for the development of a sight vocabulary. Well-selected vocabulary investigations are highly useful in this. Dolch's "A Basic Sight Vocabulary," which has been used quite generally, is composed of 220 most commonly used service words — verbs, adjectives, adverbs, prepositions, conjunctions, and pronouns — which are important in beginning reading.[13]

*Using an integrating communication core vocabulary.* A vocabulary which is basic to all the communication arts is most important in the teaching of reading because it presents most useful words which have already become familiar in listening and speaking. An integrating basic communication vocabulary[14] was developed. A comparison of the 500 commonest words of Madeline Horn's spoken vocabulary of children[15] and the 500 most common in the Gates vocabulary of primary reading,[16] revealed 340 common words.

When these were checked against the McKee-Fitzgerald vocabulary of children's letters[17] and the Rinsland vocabulary of elementary-school children's compositions,[18] 250 words were found to be common to the

---

[13] Edward W. Dolch, "A Basic Sight Vocabulary," *Psychology and Teaching of Reading* (Champaign, Illinois: The Garrard Press, 1951), pp. 507–508.

[14] James A. Fitzgerald, "An Integrating Basic Communication Vocabulary," *Elementary English*, 40:283–289, March, 1963.

[15] Madeline Darrough Horn, Chairman, *A Study of the Vocabulary of Children Before Entering the First Grade* (Washington, D. C.: The International Kindergarten Union, 1928), 36 pp.

[16] Arthur I. Gates, *A Reading Vocabulary for the Primary Grades,* revised and enlarged (New York City: Bureau of Publications, Teachers College, Columbia University, 1935), 29 pp.

[17] Paul McKee and James A. Fitzgerald, "Child Writing Vocabulary," unpublished, 576 pp. The data for this vocabulary were approximately 1,500,000 running words of letters written principally outside the school by elementary-school children.

[18] Henry D. Rinsland, *A Basic Vocabulary of Elementary-School Children* (New York: Macmillan Company, 1945), 636 pp. The data for this vocabulary comprised more than six million running words, principally of pupil school writing in grades one to eight.

most frequent 500 of children's listening, speaking, reading, and writing vocabularies.

These 250 words are printed in boldface in *A Basic Integrating Core Vocabulary* presented below. Because they are among the 500 commonest words of valid studies of children's listening and speaking, primary reading, and child writing, they are of highest value in teaching beginning reading. The remaining 90 are also of high frequency in child speaking, listening, reading, and writing.* In fact, the 340 are an integration instrument in the six language arts. They are also of very frequent use in adult reading and writing.

*Some ways of presenting sight words.* The development of a sight vocabulary is an important project, for without the ability to recognize some words at sight, reading would be tremendously laborious. Sight words are most useful. Those in *A Basic Integrating Core Vocabulary* are known by normal children in speaking and listening. Activities should be developed to make them familiar in reading. They can be learned in simple exercises and in beginning reading books in which they appear repeatedly. The procedure is generally from the known to the unknown — from listening and speaking to reading.

## A BASIC INTEGRATING CORE VOCABULARY

| | | | | |
|---|---|---|---|---|
| **a** | **back** | **boy** | **clean** | **dress** |
| **about** | **ball** | bread | coat | drink |
| **after** | barn | **bring** | **cold** | duck |
| **again** | **be** | **brother** | color | **eat** |
| **all** | bear | brown | **come** | egg |
| **always** | **because** | **but** | **corn** | **every** |
| **am** | **bed** | butter | **could** | face |
| **an** | **been** | **buy** | cow | fall |
| **and** | **before** | **by** | **cut** | **farm** |
| **another** | bell | cake | **daddy** | fast |
| **any** | **best** | **call** | **day** | **father** |
| anything | **better** | **came** | **did** | **feet** |
| apple | **big** | **can** | **do** | fell |
| **are** | bird | **candy** | **does** | **find** |
| **around** | **birthday** | **car** | **dog** | **fire** |
| **as** | **black** | carry | **doll** | **first** |
| ask | blue | cat | dolly | **fish** |
| **at** | boat | **chair** | **done** | **five** |
| ate | **book** | chicken | **don't** | flag |
| **away** | **both** | **children** | **door** | floor |
| **baby** | **box** | **Christmas** | **down** | flower |

___

* The 340 words and their repetitions comprise 70 percent of the running writing basic to Rinsland's comprehensive vocabulary. If an extension of this vocabulary is desired, an additional list of 304 words is presented in Chapter 13.

| | | | | |
|---|---|---|---|---|
| fly | ice | not | shall | time |
| for | if | now | she | to |
| found | I'll | of | shoe | today |
| four | I'm | off | show | together |
| from | in | oh | sing | told |
| funny | into | old | sister | too |
| game | is | on | sit | took |
| garden | it | once | six | top |
| gave | its | one | sky | town |
| get | it's | only | sleep | train |
| girl | jump | open | snow | tree |
| give | just | or | so | turn |
| go | keep | other | some | two |
| goes | kind | our | song | under |
| going | know | out | soon | up |
| good | leaves | over | squirrel | us |
| got | let | paint | stand | use |
| grass | like | paper | start | very |
| great | little | party | stay | walk |
| green | live | people | stick | want |
| ground | long | picture | stop | was |
| grow | look | pig | store | watch |
| guess | lunch | place | story | water |
| had | made | plant | street | way |
| hair | make | play | summer | we |
| hand | mamma | please | sun | went |
| hard | man | pretty | table | were |
| has | many | pull | take | when |
| hat | may | put | teacher | where |
| have | me | rabbit | tell | which |
| he | milk | rain | than | white |
| head | Miss | ran | thank | who |
| hear | money | ready | thanksgiving | why |
| help | morning | red | that | will |
| her | mother | ride | the | wind |
| here | Mrs. | right | their | window |
| hill | much | robin | them | winter |
| him | must | room | then | wish |
| his | my | round | there | with |
| hold | myself | said | these | wood |
| hole | name | Santa Claus | they | work |
| home | nest | saw | thing | would |
| horse | never | say | think | write |
| hot | new | school | this | yellow |
| house | next | scissors | those | yes |
| how | night | see | three | you |
| I | no | seven | tie | your |

1. *Using action words presented verbally.* Have the child act out such simple verbal commands as: *come, go, stop, stand, sit, walk, sing,* and *read.*

2. *Using action words presented visually.* Write the words in Exer-

cise 1 above in manuscript on the chalkboard. Have the child follow directions such as: *come, go, stop, stand, read, walk, sing, look.*

Another method of presentation is the use of action cards found in Dolch's word cards.[19] Let a child select a printed action word and have the others act it out.

3. *Matching names of animals with sounds.** A teacher may distribute word cards of animal names, such as *dog, cat, pig, cow, duck,* and *chicken.* She may then give the following words in her best animal imitation and have the children present a card to indicate the animal that makes the sound.

| | | |
|---|---|---|
| bowwow | meow, meow | oink, oink |
| quack, quack | moo, moo | cluck, cluck |

4. *Matching printed and spoken words.* The teacher may speak a word; the child then points to that word on the board or produces it from a group of word cards on his desk.

5. *Using labels and names.* The teacher may give the child a group of labels and ask him to match each with an object in the room. Common things such as *box, ball, coat, doll, floor, flower, book, chair,* and other nouns in the core vocabulary may be used. Signs or labels placed about the room by the children may be: *our coats, our books, the table, a window, the fish.*

6. *Matching words on cards with words in a story.* The teacher may give out cards with words used in a story, and have the boys and girls match them with words in the context.

7. *Matching phrase cards and pictures with phrases.* A teacher may show pictures with phrases:

| | | |
|---|---|---|
| a green tree | a red dress | the yellow house |
| the black horse | the blue sky | the white egg |
| | the brown rabbit | |

Cards with the above phrases may be distributed, and volunteers may then match the cards and the pictures with phrases — saying the phrase as a card is placed next to the picture.

8. *Matching phrase cards with pictures.** A teacher may have pictures of the following:

---

[19] Edward W. Dolch, *Methods in Reading* (Champaign, Ill.: The Garrard Press, 1955), p. 373 f.

* See *Webster's Third New International Dictionary* for pronunciations.

* The words used in Exercises 1 to 7 are selected principally from *A Basic Integrating Core Vocabulary.* In Exercises 8 to 15 some inflected forms and other simple words are included.

| one squirrel | two trees | two balls | three windows |
| four balls | five chickens | three sticks | six apples |
| an apple | seven sticks | a window | three chickens |

Distribute phrase cards to a group and have members match the pictures with the cards, saying each phrase as a match is made.

9. *Following printed directions.* The teacher may print a short direction on the board and write the name of a pupil at the right of the direction. The child named will read silently and perform the command. If one of the group thinks it is not carried out correctly he signals the teacher and is permitted to carry out the act as he thinks it should be done. Some examples of these directions follow:

Open the door.    George
Bring me your book.    Lillian
See if the plant needs water.    Tom
Give a book to each of us.    Dora
Open your books to page 10.    All
Bring the paper from the table.    Pat
Get water for the fish.    Marie
Feed the bird.    John

Such exercises can be well adapted for instruction of a group of five or six.

10. *Using books.* The children may be asked to find the page where:

The boy looks at the bear
The dog ran after the man.

The pupils may be directed to page 17, for example, and different children may be asked to read the line that tells:

Who is coming soon?
Where has father been?
How is father coming?
Which car did he take?
What is he bringing to Joe?

11. *Picture clues.* Picture clues have been referred to as useful in helping the child to recognize a word, phrase, or brief sentence. Such sentences as the following can be written on the board under respective pictures. These are to be read in reply to questions (see parentheses).

(What is Jip?) Jip is a black horse.
(Who ran away?) Jip ran away.
(Where did Jip run?) Jip ran up the hill.
(What does she like?) She likes corn to eat.
(Who rides Jip?) Tom rides Jip.

In all such exercises, meaning is crucial, but word recognition is necessary also.

12. *Solving riddles.* Have pictures of birds, animals, and objects available. Children give the solution of a riddle by pointing to a picture, by oral response, or by selecting a word as the teacher directs.

> He is yellow. He has two legs. He can sing. Who is he?
> (A canary bird)
> He has four legs. He says "meow." Who is he?
> (A cat or kitten)

13. *Finding words in a story.* Have children read a "story" in an experience chart or book. Write a list of words on the board, some of which are in the story and some not. Have the children identify those that are in the story.

14. *Identifying words that do not belong in a group.* Cross out the word in each group that does not belong.

| walk | jump | red | play |
|---|---|---|---|
| cat | chair | dog | horse |
| white | black | brown | barn |
| five | tell | four | three |
| chicken | duck | robin | squirrel |

15. *Word selection.* Children are directed to:

Pick out two words that begin alike. (*some, fat, boat, see*)
Pick out two words that rhyme. (*man, find, be, he*)
Pick out words that have the letter *a* in the middle of each. (*man, dog, feet, can, get, has*)
Pick out words that end alike. (*from, but, you, got, out, hard*)

Similar exercises and others may be devised by a teacher to assist children of a particular group in becoming familiar with frequently used words.

## Structural Analysis

The purpose of structural analysis is to identify words by studying their parts — roots, prefixes, suffixes, and syllables — in order to pronounce, understand, and use them. Structural analysis and phonetic analysis will be used by the child as he proceeds through the successive levels of learning to read. As Gray indicated, the two are often used in attacking a word.[20] There are four general avenues to structural analysis of words during the processes of beginning reading: roots and

---

[20] William S. Gray, *On Their Own in Reading* (Chicago: Scott, Foresman and Company, 1960).

their inflectional forms, derived forms, compounded words, and syllabication of words. A few suggestions for illustration are presented in this chapter concerning each of these approaches to identification of words.*

*Root forms with inflected endings.* The root gives meaning to the word. Useful inflectional forms are made up by adding *s, es, ed,* and *ing* to a root. Some common forms are the plurals such as the following:

| | | | | | |
|---|---|---|---|---|---|
| apple | apples | boy | boys | box | boxes |
| boat | boats | car | cars | fish | fishes |
| bird | birds | egg | eggs | watch | watches |

If these are approached in context, they become meaningful. If the inflected words are in the speaking and listening vocabularies of the child, their use in reading will be made easier. A normal child who can read with the help of a picture, *Tom has one apple,* will be able to read with the help of a second picture without much difficulty, *Dan has two apples,* if he has a sight vocabulary of the words in the first sentence and of the word *two.* In like manner, if he can read and understand with the aid of a picture, *Tom and Jenny play,* he will read with the aid of a picture, *Shep plays too.*

*Derived forms.* Derived forms are made by combining roots with prefixes, suffixes, or with both prefixes and suffixes. A child may meet occasionally such derived words as player (play er), reader (read er), return (re turn), and uncover (un cover). Each of these may be approached functionally in context, by picture, or through explanation. For example, the child who knows what "to cover a box" means, can understand without difficulty the sentence, "Ray, please *uncover* the box." Examples of other simple derived forms (roots and prefixes) follow: "Will you *return* my book, please?" "Please *admit* Bill to the classroom." "Julia was a happy girl." "Alex was an *unhappy* boy." Explanations and practice help in each case.

The use of suffixes to derive words is also interesting. The pupil who knows the meaning of "thank" will be able to understand by structural analysis and context clues the following sentence: "The boys were *thankful* for the ice cream." A child who knows "use" should be able to read meaning into this sentence: "The broken window is *useless.*"

A pupil will be helped by learning to recognize a root plus both prefix and suffix. For example, the word "tie" gives opportunity to guide youngsters to extend their efforts with structural analysis. If the

---

* See Chapter 13 for a more intensive and extensive consideration of roots, derivatives, compounds, and syllabication.

statement, "Each boy will *tie* his shoestrings," is meaningful, then "Each boy will *untie* his shoestrings" can become easily understandable. The use of the suffix *-ing* may be indicated in the sentence: "The boy scouts are *tying* knots."

Common prefixes such as, *re-, un-, dis-, im-,* and *in-,* and common suffixes, *-or, -er, -est, -ing, -ly,* and *-y* combined with familiar roots not only add to a child's vocabulary but increase his competency in reading. To know what it is "to agree" is helpful in unlocking the word *disagree.* To know that the prefix *un-* conveys the idea of *not* or *the opposite,* aids the learner to understand the words, *unhappy* or *unhappiness.* The normal child has little difficulty with *player* in the statement, "Jerry is a good *ballplayer,"* for he understands that *-er* is a suffix combined with *play* to build another word which gives a different meaning. Likewise, *talk* and *write* may be extended to *talking* and *writing* in the sentence: *"Talking* is used more than *writing."* A teacher will help the child to understand that the affix does not change the meaning of the root, but redirects or gives power to it.

*Compound words.* The compound words met in context may be considered. An understanding of one or both of the joined words will help children to unlock the meaning and to pronounce the compound word correctly. For example, children have in their listening and concept vocabulary the word *playground.* Assume that *playground* is used in a story and that children know *play* in reading and have used *ground* in talking. They can be guided to put the two words together when they realize that the long word in "We raced to the *playground"* is the word they have often used orally. In like manner, *basketball* is recognized because the children know *ball.* They have been able to read such a sentence as, "We throw the *ball* into the *basket."* By discussion of the two words, they are able to read: "We played *basketball* at noon today."

A few compound words that primary children meet incidentally in their reading are: *birthday, homerun, afternoon, baseball, football, everybody, myself, schoolhouse, outside, sometime,* and *thanksgiving.* Should one of these be needed the pupils may be helped to approach it in one or more of several ways — in context, through structural analysis, from knowledge of one of the connected words, or by use of a picture.

*Words of more than one syllable.* Although a sight vocabulary in the beginning generally contains principally one-syllable words, the child has used such words as: *many, after, carry,* and *baby.* He is not altogether unfamiliar with such syllables in talking and listening as *-ing,*

*-er, -y, a-, -ly, in-,* and *re-* in such words as *coming, player, needy, aloud, slowly, into,* and *return.* These may be made a nucleus for studying words of more than one syllable as he meets them in context.

The pupil can figure out the meaning and use of the suffix *-ing* in *writing* and of *-er* in *writer* when he reads:

| | |
|---|---|
| See May write. | May writes well. |
| She is *writing* a letter. | She is a good *writer.* |

The meaning of two-syllable derivatives comes from knowing the root or base word and associating the derivative with it. Experiences, remembering adult expressions containing the word, context, and configuration are used with structural analysis in understanding words of two syllables.

## Phonics

A good program of word analysis for reading utilizes both phonetic and structural analysis. In structural analysis, a child studies an unfamiliar word to see whether he can identify it from a root, prefix, or suffix. In phonetic analysis, a pupil learns to associate visual symbols with sounds in his search for meaning.

A group of twenty-seven reading experts working in a policy conference agreed that phonics is an essential skill in unlocking unknown words, and that "most children cannot become self-reliant, discriminating efficient readers without phonics."[21]

*Some definitions and understandings.* Phonetics is the science of speech sounds, considered as elements of language. By many, phonetics is considered to be the general theory of the nature and relations of speech sounds. Phonics may be considered as the application of phonetics to instruction in reading. The phonic method is useful in identifying and recognizing words. After a word has been once identified phonetically, it is possible to recognize it more readily when meeting it a second time, and it may be recognized quite easily by sight or in meaningful context in successive uses. Phonics should be thought of as one of the most important ways of word attack, but not the sole means of word recognition.

All individuals need phonics in reading; some seem to acquire phonetic skills very easily, and accordingly require very little teaching. Others require instruction in phonics in beginning reading and later, as

[21] Ralph C. Staiger, "Agreements About Phonics," *Elementary English,* 41: 204–206, 229, March, 1964.

they progress, in sounding words, analyzing them, and using the dictionary. Many children are benefited by carefully organized instruction in phonics throughout the primary grades. Phonics should be used to help the child become independent in identifying and recognizing words. However, it is a great mistake to force phonics instruction upon a child who does not need it. It is a mistake also not to give phonics guidance when a child does need it.

*Phonics procedures.* No issue in reading has been discussed more vehemently in this century than that of the use of phonics. Many attempts have been made throughout the years to develop practicable systems of phonics for beginners.[22] In some reading programs, an excessive amount of stress has been placed upon phonetic approaches with the result that beginning reading became a type of drill procedure, sometimes with almost complete neglect of meaning. However, other systems of reading were developed in which, because phonics was officially almost entirely avoided, bad habits of guessing at words and other inaccurate practices of word identification were developed. At present, the most thoughtful practitioners recognize the great value of phonics as one of the several means of word attack.

In a recent investigation, Grimes administered a battery of tests to 156 children who were selected randomly from a population of 1456 pupils on the third-grade level. He reported that the correlation between skill in phonics and achievement was greater than that between any other measure of intelligence, reading skill, or proficiency and emphasized the finding that skill in phonics was a most important factor in reading and scholastic success.[23]

Teachers should test their methods of guiding word attack and strive to answer the questions: Are my methods of teaching phonics best for pupils? Are my phonetic practices blocking reading interests and progress? Is phonics being neglected or impeded because of emphasis upon telling or memorization of sight words? Dolch proposed a reasonable and practicable principle for phonics as follows: "Learn what we can use and use what we learn."[24] Since children generally forget some of

---

[22] Emmett A. Betts, *Foundations of Reading Instruction* (New York: American Book Company, 1957), pp. 377–378.

[23] Jesse W. Grimes, "A Study of the Meaning of Phonics Skill in Its Relationship to Intelligence, Reading, and School Success," *Changing Concepts of Reading Instruction,* J. Allen Figurel, Editor, International Reading Association Conference Proceedings, Vol. 6, 1961, pp. 130–133.

[24] E. W. Dolch, "Am I Teaching Phonics Right?" *Elementary English,* 34:228, April, 1957.

what they memorize, since there are many nonphonetic common words in our language that require an attack different from that of phonics, and since children vary greatly in their ability to sound out words, it seems sensible to guide the approach to reading not by a rigid phonics procedure but by means of an intrinsic integrating process in which phonics, structural analysis, context clues, and other procedures are used as needed. A reading program while placing the main emphasis upon thought getting, should recognize phonics as a necessary word-attack instrument for making the reader independent.[25]

Dolch described three methods of teaching phonics in the first grade: (1) the total memorizing method, (2) the parallel method, and (3) the developmental or discovery method. He showed that the total memorizing of all phonics generalizations before beginning to read is impossible of achievement by first-grade children. He indicated the impracticability of the parallel method because in sounding his way through the reading of a simple first-grade story a child would require about all the principles of phonics that are known. No first-grade system of phonics can teach these principles so that an ordinary child can use them effectively.[26] Dolch favored the third system — the development or discovery procedure. Discovery of letter-sound relationships is generally a thrilling experience to a learner, and an active process which can be made to fit special and varying needs of individuals. In this procedure, a child should be guided to understand what his problems are in word identification, and be motivated to attack these problems under guidance and with satisfaction and success. This developmental discovery system promotes right attitudes on the part of the learner. By such practice, the individual can become independent and confident in reading.[27]

Some phonics reading systems, more or less rigid, have been promoted during the last decade or two, and some success has been claimed for them. Gates, however, reported an investigation of the effects of a rigid system of phonics teaching on pupils of grades three, four, and five in four schools in a community near New York City, and his findings indicated that the reading abilities produced in American schools in the last decade were equal to or superior to those of the more complex and rigid system.[28]

---

[25] *Ibid.,* pp. 227–234.

[26] E. W. Dolch, "Phonics in the First Grade," *Elementary English,* 32:514–518, December, 1955.

[27] *Ibid.,* p. 518.

[28] Arthur I. Gates, "Results of Teaching a System of Phonics," *The Reading Teacher,* 14:248–252, March, 1961.

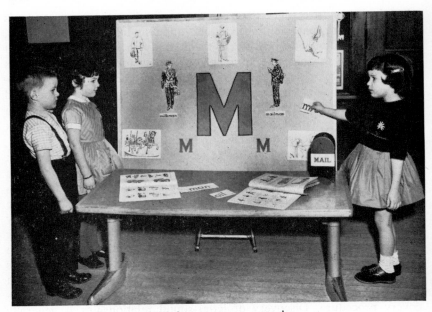

Initial consonant sounds

*Some essential phonetic elements.*  Most useful elements for word analysis are the consonants, blends, vowels, digraphs, dipthongs, and silent letters. Common examples of such elements are presented below. The effective application of these in word attack should aid a child to become more and more independent in reading.

The order of teaching these elements will depend upon the individual's needs and abilities, but consonants are generally presented before vowels. It is helpful to introduce an element as part of a known sight word. The sound represented by a letter should be practiced in pronunciation as, for example, of *l* in *let,* of *r* in *ride,* or *n* in *no.* The sounding of consonants in isolation may be confusing to the young learner. The pronunciation of the word *cab* is correct only when the word is pronounced as a single unit, not as three sounds of the letters *c, a,* and *b* (*c — a — b*).

1. *Initial consonant sounds in words.*  Words should be pronounced and sounds represented by beginning consonants identified. The pupil should note, for example, that the initial consonant sound is the same in *let, like, look,* and *last.* Further, he may be taught to substitute other consonants as *m, b,* and *f* for the *k* in *kind.* The words developed should

be pronounced. Many other exercises may be devised from the following common words:

| | |
|---|---|
| b — big, box, bat, be, but | n — no, not, now, new |
| c — can, came, cab, cut, come | p — pet, pull, putt, pick |
| d — do, dog, did, done, day | r — red, run, rat, ride, right |
| f — for, fat, fun, fall, find | s — sit, see, six, so, sing |
| g — get, got, give, go, gave | t — to, take, tell, table, time |
| h — had, has, him, he, home | v — very, vase, vine |
| j — jump, just, jet, jelly | w — we, was, well, wood |
| k — keep, kind, kite, kitten | y — you, yes, yellow |
| l — let, like, look, last | z — zoo, zero |
| m — man, my, me, made | |

2. *Some common initial consonant blends.* A consonant blend is a combination of two consonant sounds voiced together, with each keeping its identity. Consideration in the beginning of phonics instruction should be given to commonly used initial consonant blends. Examples are indicated:

| | |
|---|---|
| bl — black, blue | sc — score, scout |
| br — brown, bring | sl — slow, sled |
| cl — clean, climb | sm — smile, small |
| cr — crack, cry | sn — snow, snake |
| dr — dress, draw | sp — spell, spot |
| fl — fly, flower | st — stop, stand |
| fr — free, fruit | sw — swim, sweet |
| gl — glad, glass | tr — tree, trap |
| gr — green, grow | tw — twelve, twin |
| pl — play, please | sk — sky, skip |
| pr — price, pretty | |

Rapid learners may supply other words with beginning blends such as *bright, breeze, brought, brand* to go with *brown, bring,* and so on.

3. *Common vowel sounds.* Important vowel sounds for the beginning reader are the long and short sounds of *a, e, i, o,* and *u.* Sometimes the letter *y* is used as a vowel. Although the long sounds of vowels do not appear so frequently as the short sound of vowels, they are more easily remembered because they name the letters. Note sounds of vowels in *a* and *b* below:

### a) Long Sounds of Vowels

a — late, ate, gate, take, came, name
e — he, me, be
i — ice, kind, find, line, dine
o — no, go, so, old, hold
u — use, cube, tube
y — by, cry

**b) Short Sounds of Vowels**

*a* — at, cat, sat, can, fat
*e* — get, pen, send, well, set
*i* — it, sit, did, bring, is
*o* — top, on, not, hop, hot
*u* — cut, up, but, jump
*y* — needy, happy, handy

4. *Some common final consonant sounds in words.* Although the emphasis in teaching sounds should be placed first on initial sounds of words, the final consonant sounds should be considered also. Learners should note, for example, the final sounds in the following:

*b* — rob, cab, job, mob
*d* — did, sad, and, good
*g* — dog, hog, big, dig
*l* — all, call, tell, full

*n* — an, can, ran, ten
*p* — up, hop, stop, sleep
*t* — at, but, get, let
*ks* — box, ox, fox, ax, tax

5. *Final consonant blends.* The learner should identify the final consonant blends. In such words as *best* and *rest, st* should be recognized. Pupils may add other words ending with the sounds represented by *st, sk, rt, nt, nd,* and *ng:*

*st* — best, rest, guest, list
*sk* — risk, ask
*rt* — start, part, art
*nt* — want, went, ant
*nd* — kind, hand, find
*ng* — sing, ring, thing

Care must be given to the pronunciation of such words as *sing, ring,* and *thing* to properly voice the sound represented by *ng*.

6. *Some common consonant digraphs.* Digraphs are composed of two letters that represent one sound. Common ones are illustrated:

*ch* — child, church, chicken, much
*ch* — character, chorus
*ck* — pick, sick, duck
*ph* — phone, phonics
*sh* — show, shine

*th* — them, then, the
*th* — thin, with
*wh* — what, when
*wh* — who, whole

Some of these, the *th* digraph, for example, should be most carefully taught and practiced. Children who say *dere* for *there* and *den* for *then,* require help. Others need emphasis on the *wh*(hw) in *what, where, white,* and so on.

7. *Common vowel digraphs.* As in the case of consonants, two vowels may also represent one speech sound. Some fairly common examples in child reading and spelling follow:

Common consonant
digraphs

| | |
|---|---|
| *ea* — great, head, clean, hear | *ee* — been, green, keep |
| *ei* — eight, height, weigh | *ay* — bay, say, day |
| *ie* — pie, flies, piece | *oo* — balloon, broom, moon |
| *oa* — coal, boat, float | *oo* — look, book, cook |
| *ai* — again, pain, plain, main | *ow* — grow, show, know |

Although there is a statement in many books to the effect that "when two vowels go together the first is heard," this does not always hold true as is shown by examining the *ea, ei,* and *ai* vowel digraphs presented here. Often the second vowel is sounded as in *great* and *height*.

8. *Diphthongs.* A diphthong is made up of two vowel sounds enunciated in sequence (in one syllable) which seems to form one sound:

> *oi* — toil, coil, soil, oil, join
> *oy* — boy (boi), toy (toi), joy (joi)
> *ow* — how, howl, cow, fowl, bow (bou)
> *ou* — count, out, round, ground

9. *Some silent letters.* Pupils should note that the final *e* is not sounded in *take,* *k* and *w* in *know,* *b* in *lamb,* or *w* and *e* in *write*.

Phonics

Final *e* — take, come, gone, live, done, same
*gh* after a vowel — sight, right, fight, high
*b* after *m*   — limb, lamb, comb, climb
*b* before *t*  — debt, doubt
*k* before *n*  — kneel, knee, knot, knife
*l* before *k*  — walk, talk
*w* before *r*  — wrist, write, wring
*t* before *ch* — watch, witch

10. *Vowels followed by r.*  When the final letter *r* follows a vowel in a word, the vowel sound is generally modified. Some common examples are:

| | | | |
|---|---|---|---|
| car | fir | fur | jar |
| far | sir | war | bar |
| for | her | or | nor |

11. *The a before l (or w).*  When the letter *a* is followed by *l* or *w* the sound represented by the *a* is modified. It is neither long nor short. Examples of common words are:

| | | | |
|---|---|---|---|
| all | ball | call | wall |
| law | saw | paw | raw |

*Some suggestions for teaching phonics.*  The ideal time to present phonics instruction is at the moment when the child needs it and will use it. Pupils vary in the length of time and amount of instruction required to master a phonics skill. They should not be held for practice which they do not need because others require it, but practice should be carried on meaningfully when it enhances facility in word recognition.

Children generally cannot master all phonics needed in reading in one year or in one stage of reading. The study of phonics must be continued as the child progresses from one stage of reading to another, from one grade level to higher grades, as it is required.

Gray stated that the order of teaching phonics elements is important, and suggested that: (1) The teaching of consonant phonics should take precedence over the teaching of the sounds of vowels because most consonant letters stand for only one sound, and the vowels represent many sounds. (2) Teaching of vowel phonics should generally follow next. (3) Finally, accent phonics should be taught.[29]

Durrell and Murphy emphasized the importance of phonics in a reading program. They stressed early ear training in which the child moves from speech to print as highly valuable. Children who had such early training in recognizing sounds and were able to differentiate sounds made generally good progress in learning to read.[30] Accordingly, *in phonics teaching,* begin with the spoken word and work toward the printed word. It must be clear however that *in reading,* the reverse is true — the printed word is met and recognized or identified by phonics or other word attack procedures in order to determine meaning.

*Some specific suggestions.* Some basic elements have been presented which are useful in guiding children to identify and recognize words. In addition to suggestions made, the following may be helpful in guiding phonics learning.

1. The needs for phonics instruction of individuals of a group should be appraised and instruction directed to each child's requirements.

2. A small sight vocabulary developed from meaningful experiences, most useful words, and beginning reading, is an important base for phonics instruction.

3. Ear training should be taught and practiced early in word attack. Help the child to hear the sound of *m* in *man* and *me,* for example, and to differentiate consonant sounds represented by *m* in *mine, f* in *fine, l* in *line,* and so on.

---

[29] William S. Gray, *On Their Own in Reading* (Chicago: Scott Foresman Company, 1960), pp. 35–37.

[30] Donald D. Durrell and Helen A. Murphy, "Boston University Research in Elementary School Reading, 1933–1963," *Journal of Education,* 146:14–17, December, 1963.

4. The direction of procedure in analyzing a word is from left to right. Attention should be directed to the initial sound before medial or final sounds.

5. Children may make use of context, configuration, and other clues as they begin phonics training.

6. Teach children how to recognize familiar elements in a necessary word, how to translate them into sounds, and how to combine them in word pronunciation.

7. Substituting beginning letter sounds in words is a fruitful activity. From the word *can*, children may discover the words *man*, *pan*, and *fan*. In like manner, from the word *cold*, the words *bold*, *hold*, *gold*, and *fold* may be developed.

8. Matching sounds and visual symbols may be practiced. The teacher may pronounce the word *cap*, and the child may identify the written word among *map*, *nap*, *tap*, *cap*.

9. Pupils should identify phonograms as *and* in *hand* and *land*. They may combine blends and phonograms to build words such as *br* in *brown* and *ing* in *ring* to make *bring*.

10. Other activities should be developed concerning the use of consonant and vowel digraphs, diphthongs, silent letters, vowel sounds such as those affected by *l, r,* or *w*. Authorities in the field have developed appropriate exercises.[31]

11. Although reasonable generalization is to be used, memorizing rules without understanding is not desirable. Discovery of principles is important. A child may list many words of one syllable such as *hat, cat, bit, sit, red, bed, bug, dug, hot, cot*. He may note that in every case the vowel represents a short sound, and he will generalize that a single vowel in a syllable between two consonants (a closed syllable) is usually short. Such a generalization should be used with discretion for there are many exceptions, some of which should be made known to the learner.

12. In grade four generally, and earlier for rapid learners, some diacritical marks should be taught to indicate enunciation and accent

---

[31] See William S. Gray, *On Their Own in Reading* (Chicago: Scott Foresman Company, 1960), pp. 34–53, 66–90. See Emmett A. Betts, *Foundations of Reading Instruction* (New York: American Book Company, 1957), pp. 614–644. See Fay Adams, Lillian Gray, and Dora Reese, *Teaching Children to Read* (New York: Ronald Press, 1949), pp. 333–360. See John J. DeBoer and Martha Dallman, *The Teaching of Reading* (New York: Henry Holt and Company, 1960), pp. 23–26, 82–90, 104–109. See also Albert J. Harris, *Effective Teaching of Reading* (New York: David McKay Company, Inc., 1962), pp. 191–203, 357–372.

for pronunciation. The individual pupil should become aware of the accented and unaccented syllables as in a gain′ (*a* gĕn′), cho′ ral (kō′ răl) and learn how both types of syllables are pronounced. The dictionary should become a useful instrument at this level.

13. Two-syllable words are often made up of a root and a prefix or suffix. Early, the child hears and sees an additional syllable such as *–ing* added to *be* in *being,* *–er* added to *fight* in *fighter,* and *re–* added to *write* in *rewrite.*

14. Phonics development should continue throughout the period of beginning reading and on into succeeding stages of reading as it is needed.

15. Throughout instruction in word analysis, the learner should be encouraged to become independent in identifying and recognizing words. He should understand that the recognition of words helps him to obtain meaning through reading.[32]

16. The pupil will become enthusiastic when he discovers he can unlock new words with his phonics knowledge.[33]

*Words of warning.* As previously indicated, a child should not be "taught" phonics he already knows. He should not be forced to learn phonics for which he has no use. He should not be denied the phonics he needs for identifying and recognizing words. He should not be made to feel that phonics is of greater importance than comprehending.

A long section might be presented on the topic "How Not to Teach Phonics." Betts lists several common confusions such as: "Pronounce every letter in the word clearly. . . ." "The vowel sounds are *a e i o u.* . . ." "What letter do you hear at the end of jumped?"[34] These indicate confusion of the terms — letter and sound. A teacher should not confuse the child with a direction to listen for a silent letter such as *k* in *know* or *w* in *wrist.* It is confusing to ask a child to find a little word in another such as *own* in *brown* because the sound of *own* is different in the two words. Other examples of this confusion are *on* in *done,* *flow* in *flowers,* and *of* in *off.*[35]

*Phonics generalizations.* Phonics generalizations present many complex and unsolved problems. Difficulties have arisen in applying them because of the many exceptions to some which have been accepted

---

[32] Jeanette Veach, "The Materials and Diagnosis of Reading Problems," *The Reading Teacher,* 14:24, September, 1960.

[33] McKee, The Teaching of Reading, *op. cit.,* pp. 246–255.

[34] Betts, *op. cit.,* pp. 624–625.

[35] *Loc. cit.*

as rules without evidence of their value and disadvantages. Some investigations are reported recently which help practitioners to select the useful generalizations and omit those of no benefit.

Clymer reported that 121 different phonics generalizations were being presented in at least one of four widely used series of readers. One series presented 33 and another introduced 68. Of the 50 vowel statements, eleven only were common to the four series, but none was introduced at the same half-year level.

A vocabulary of about 2600 words — made up from the words of the four series of readers and the Gates Reading Vocabulary for the Primary Grades — was used to appraise 45 generalizations selected for study. Only 18 of the 45 were found to be acceptable according to the criteria applied: (1) that the composite word list must contain at least 20 words to which the generalization would apply, and (2) that the percent of its utility should be at least 75.[36] In other words, a generalization to which there are 25 percent of exceptions or that has a very few applications should be considered not acceptable for instruction or study. Some of the amazing results concerning generalizations follow.

Specific findings on the generalizations are presented in two sections. In *A. Questionable Generalizations,* data on 14 of the 26 rejected rules are presented. The number of words conforming to each statement and the number contrary to it with examples of a word which conforms and of one which is an exception to the rule are presented. In *B. Acceptable Generalizations,* data on 18 phonics principles which meet the criteria used by the investigator are reported, with illustrative data on numbers of words and examples.

### A. Questionable Generalizations

1. (1)* "When there are two vowels side by side, the long sound of the first one is heard and the second is usually silent." (309 words conform to the generalization — *bead* is an example; 377 words are exceptions — *chief* is an example.)

2. (2) "When a vowel is in the middle of a one-syllable word, the vowel is short." (408 conform — *dress;* 249 are exceptions — *scold.*)

3. (4) "When there are two vowels, one of which is final *e,* the first vowel is long and the *e* is silent." (180 conform — *bone;* 108 are exceptions — *done.*)

---

[36] Theodore Clymer, "The Utility of Phonic Generalizations in the Primary Grades," *The Reading Teacher,* 16:252–258, January, 1963.

* The numbers in parentheses are the numbers assigned to the statements in Dr. Clymer's original context.

4. (6) "The first vowel is usually long and the second silent in the digraphs *ai, ea, oa, ui.*" (179 conform — *nail;* 92 are exceptions — *said.*)

5. (7) "In the phonogram *ie,* the *i* is silent and the *e* has a long sound." (8 conform — *field;* 39 are exceptions — *friend.*)

6. (9) "When words end with silent *e,* the preceding *a* or *i* is long." (164 conform — *cake;* 108 are exceptions — *have.*)

7. (14) "The two letters *ow* make the long *o* sound." (50 conform — *own;* 35 are exceptions — *down.*)

8. (17) "When *y* is used as a vowel in words, it sometimes has the sound of long *i.*" (29 conform — *fly;* 170 are exceptions — *funny.*)

9. (18) "The letter *a* has the same sound (*ô*) when followed by *l, w,* and *u.*" (61 conform — *all;* 65 are exceptions — *canal.*)

10. (33) "One vowel letter in an accented syllable has its short sound." (547 conform — *city;* 356 are exceptions — *lady.*)

11. (34) "When *y* or *ey* is seen in the last syllable that is not accented, the long sound of *e* is heard." (None conforms; 157 are exceptions — *baby.*)

12. (38) "If the first sound in a word is followed by two consonants, the first syllable usually ends with the first of the two consonants." (404 conform — *bullet;* 159 are exceptions — *singer.*)

13. (39) "If the first vowel sound in a word is followed by a single consonant, that consonant usually begins the second syllable." (190 conform — *over;* 237 are exceptions — *oven.*)

14. (43) "When a word has only one vowel letter, the vowel sound is likely to be short." (433 conform — *hid;* 322 are exceptions — *kind.*)[37]

These findings reveal that the teaching of many generalizations as rules is highly questionable. The facts regarding phonics generalizations indicate that if they are to be taught, they must be appraised with exceeding care, and exceptions to them shown in order that children will not be confused.

On the basis of the criteria and evidence, the following 18 phonics generalizations presented by Clymer are valid. They can be introduced through discovery procedures. If they are learned through inductive processes, used properly, and if the exceptions are identified as they are met, these generalizations should be useful in reading instruction.

### B. Acceptable Generalizations

1. (5) "The *r* gives the preceding vowel a sound that is neither long nor short." (484 words conform to the generalization — *horn* is an example; 134 words are exceptions — *wire* is an example.)

---

[37] Clymer, *loc. cit.* Reprinted with permission of the International Reading Association and the author.

2. (8) "Words having double *e* usually have the long sound." (85 conform — *seem;* 2 are exceptions — *been.*)

3. (10) "In *ay* the *y* is silent and gives *a* its long sound." (36 conform — *play;* 10 are exceptions — *always.*)

4. (16) "When *y* is the final letter in a word, it usually has a vowel sound." (169 conform — *dry;* 32 are exceptions — *tray.*)

5. (20) "When *c* and *h* are next to each other, they make only one sound." (103 conform — peach; no exceptions.)

6. (21) "*Ch* is usually pronounced as it is in *kitchen, catch,* and *chair,* not like *sh.*" (99 conform — *catch;* 5 are exceptions — *machine.*)

7. (22) "When *c* is followed by *e* or *i,* the sound of *s* is likely to be heard." (66 conform — *cent;* 3 are exceptions — *ocean.*)

8. (23) "When the letter *c* is followed by *o* or *a,* the sound of *k* is likely to be heard." (143 conform — *camp;* no exceptions.)

9. (25) "When *ght* is seen in a word, *gh* is silent." (30 conform — *fight;* no exceptions.)

10. (28) "When two of the same consonants are side by side, only one is heard." (334 conform — *carry;* 3 are exceptions — *suggest.*)

11. (29) "When a word ends in *ck,* it has the same last sound as in *look.*" (46 conform — *brick;* no exceptions.)

12. (30) "In most two-syllable words, the first syllable is accented." (828 conform — *famous;* 143 are exceptions — *polite.*)

13. (31) "If *a, in, re, ex, de,* or *be* is the first syllable in a word, it is usually unaccented." (86 conform — *belong;* 13 are exceptions — *insect.*)

14. (32) "In most two-syllable words that end in a consonant followed by *y,* the first syllable is accented and the last is unaccented." (101 conform — *baby;* 4 are exceptions — *supply.*)

15. (40) "If the last syllable of a word ends in *le,* the consonant preceding the *le* usually begins the last syllable." (62 conform — *tumble;* 2 are exceptions — *buckle.*)

16. (41) "When the first vowel element in a word is followed by *th, ch,* or *sh,* these symbols are not broken when the word is divided into syllables and may go with either the first or second syllable." (30 conform — *dishes;* no exceptions.)

17. (44) "When there is one *e* in a word that ends in a consonant, the *e* usually has a short sound." (85 conform — *leg;* 27 are exceptions — *blew.*)

18. (45) "When the last syllable is [has] the sound *r,* it is unaccented." (188 conform — *butter;* 9 are exceptions — *appear.*)[38]

The findings of such investigations are challenging and somewhat disturbing. Through classroom experimentation, the use of these generalizations can be studied and improved. Publishers as well as teachers

---

[38] Clymer, *loc. cit.* By permission. See note 37.

should consider valid evidence carefully in planning and making use of phonics generalizations.

*Keeping a proper perspective.* It is necessary to keep a balanced perspective about phonics and reading. The objective is to teach a child who cannot read to read, or who cannot read well to improve his reading. Phonics is one of the important methods in the instructional program of reading. It should be taught from the beginning — not as tiresome drill or boring memorization of wordy generalizations, but as an inviting challenge to discover new ways of pronouncing, getting meaning through symbols, and using words for communication. It should be remembered that the child before coming to school learned thousands of words through listening and speaking with little direction and no drill. He discovered how to talk by listening to others and by speaking of his wants and needs as they arose. He improved his pronunciation, sentences, and communication as he talked and listened. He was challenged by need and aided by freedom to listen, think, and vocalize. Similarly, he must be challenged to read, for reading presents an opportunity to live richly and happily. Phonics is an important means to the achievement of proficiency in reading and independence in seeking information, knowledge, and culture.[39]

## The Initial Teaching Alphabet, i.t.a.

The initial teaching alphabet invented by Sir James Pitman has 44 symbols or combinations of letters, each of which represents one phoneme — a single sound of our language (see the accompanying chart). Twenty-four of the symbols are letters of the conventional alphabet. The other 20 are new characters or combinations, 14 of which resemble a digraph — two traditional letters joined.

No one is unaware of the inconsistencies of English spelling and its difficulties. Some sounds are spelled in many different ways, and some letters frequently represent several different sounds. There is evidence that a considerable percent of elementary school children have difficulty in learning to read, in part probably because of the complexity of letter-sound relationships. Millions of high school pupils and college students also are handicapped severely in reading.

The initial teaching alphabet is offered as an aid by which many

---

[39] *The Teaching of Reading: A Positional Paper* (Albany: The University of the State of New York, The State Education Department, September, 1963), pp. 13–15.

# CHART II.  THE INITIAL TEACHING ALPHABET

Words beneath the symbols illustrate the sounds represented.

| æ | b | c | d | ɑ |
|---|---|---|---|---|
| face | bed | cat | dog | key |

| f | g | h | ie | j | k |
|---|---|---|---|---|---|
| feet | leg | hat | fly | jug | key |

| l | m | n | œ | p | ɹ |
|---|---|---|---|---|---|
| letter | man | nest | over | pen | girl |

| r | s | t | ue | v | w |
|---|---|---|---|---|---|
| red | spoon | tree | use | voice | window |

| y | z | ʒ | wh | ch |
|---|---|---|---|---|
| yes | zebra | daisy | when | chair |

| th | th | ʃh | ʒ | ŋ |
|---|---|---|---|---|
| three | the | shop | television | ring |

| ɑ | au | a | e | i | o |
|---|---|---|---|---|---|
| father | ball | cap | egg | milk | box |

| u | ω | ⍵ | ou | oi |
|---|---|---|---|---|
| up | book | spoon | out | oil |

Initial Teaching Alphabet Publications, Inc.

reading difficulties can be avoided. The use of this alphabet requires approximately 90 visual patterns while the conventional alphabet requires more than 2000 such patterns. The approximate number of 90 rather than a smaller number is, according to Downing, a concession to the conventional alphabet in order to make the transition to it easier after i.t.a. has been mastered.[40]

Additional purported advantages of the i.t.a. are: (1) A symbol stands for one sound. There is excellent consistency in spelling phonemes. (2) Fewer word and letter representations are necessary because no capital letters are required. The i.t.a. symbols are enlarged to represent capitals. (3) The i.t.a. maintains a strict left to right direction in reading. For example, the conventional *gone* is spelled and pronounced *gon* in i.t.a. *One* and *tune* are spelled and articulated *wun* and *tu-en*.

Downing reported that children in general learn to read sooner in i.t.a. than with conventional methods, that a much larger percentage of children succeed in learning to read satisfactorily using the i.t.a. than with the traditional alphabet, and that they are able to transfer from the i.t.a. to the conventional reading without apparent difficulty.

It is reported that thousands of children in England have learned to read i.t.a. contextual materials with facility. After a year and a half of instruction, tentative results indicate that children transfer from it to the conventional and read better than those who used the conventional alphabet from the beginning.[41] Several experiments with the i.t.a. are being carried out in the United States; chief among them is the Bethlehem project — directed by Dr. Albert Mazurkiewicz — which has been reported as highly successful.

Several reading experts are cautious about accepting i.t.a. procedures without more evidence. Downing also cautions that evidence from further investigations should be evaluated before drawing final conclusions. Because of the need to solve serious problems of reading difficulties, the value of i.t.a. should be thoroughly investigated. If tentative findings are confirmed, it will become useful as an aid in beginning and also in remedial reading.

---

[40] John A. Downing, "Teaching Reading with i.t.a. in Britain," *Phi Delta Kappa,* 45:322–329, April, 1964. See also John A. Downing, *To Be or Not to Be: The New Augmented Roman Alphabet Explained and Illustrated* (London: Pitman Publishing Corporation, 1962), 123 pp. See also John A. Downing, "The Augmented Roman Alphabet for Learning to Read," *The Reading Teacher,* 16:325–336, March, 1963.

[41] Downing, "Teaching Reading with i.t.a. in Britain," *op. cit.*

## SUMMARY

Main purposes in initial reading are to teach the child: to read for meaning, to identify and recognize words in context, to build strong interests in reading, and to use reading in study and recreation. Meaningful beginning reading should utilize several types of methods — experience approaches, beginning book procedures, activity-utility exercises, writing and oral activities, and intrinsic integrative procedures.

In becoming independent in word identification and word recognition, a child is taught to utilize meanings from experiences. Language, picture clues, context clues, and configuration are helpful in developing independence in word attack. A sight vocabulary of most useful and serviceable words is beneficial as a basis for developing competency in reading. Structural analysis, highly valuable in word attack, assists the pupil to identify words by studying root forms, inflectional endings, affixes, simple derived forms, and compound words. Phonics is stressed as a most essential means of word attack. Developmental phonics in initial reading should be taught as children need it. Some children learn phonics easily, while others require prolonged instruction in specific phonics elements. Discovery is a most useful procedure in word analysis. Generalizations should be carefully analyzed and used only when they can be helpful without confusing the learner. The initial teaching alphabet has been suggested as an aid for developing greater facility in reading. Experiments are now being conducted to test its worth.

### ACTIVITIES, PROBLEMS, QUESTIONS

1. Appraise the five stated purposes to be sought in beginning reading.
2. How can interest in learning to read be stimulated?
3. Make a list of experiences which would motivate normal children to read.
4. Read a set of preprimers, primers, first readers, and the teachers' manuals. Make a list of the types of exercises which would be most helpful in beginning reading.
5. Explain several ways to use word cards, phrase cards, and flash cards.
6. What values have the following in teaching beginning reading: writing, oral reading?
7. Explain several procedures for teaching beginning reading. Rate them in order of their importance.
8. Show the difference between word identification and word recognition.
9. How important is oral language and listening in teaching reading?
10. List carefully the values of each in teaching word attack: (a) picture clues; (b) context clues; (c) configuration.
11. Should a sight vocabulary be developed in initial reading? If so, what vocabularies are most useful?

12. Devise five exercises which will be useful in developing a sight vocabulary.

13. Define structural analysis. Describe the use of each of the following in word attack: (*a*) roots; (*b*) derived forms; (*c*) prefixes; (*d*) suffixes; (*e*) compounding of words; (*f*) syllabication.

14. Define: phonics, phonetics. Why is phonics useful in teaching reading?

15. Compare the following methods of teaching phonics: total memorization, parallel, or discovery.

16. What should be the order of teaching phonics elements? Why?

17. Develop essential exercises for teaching phonics.

18. Make a critical evaluation of the use of phonics generalizations.

19. Select ten phonics generalizations which can be useful in teaching phonics.

20. Develop important principles for instruction of beginners in the use of phonics.

## SELECTED REFERENCES

Artley, Sterl A. *Your Child Learns to Read*. Chicago: Scott, Foresman, 1953. 255 pp.

Austin, Mary C., and Coleman Morrison. *The First R: The Harvard Report on Reading in Elementary Schools*. New York: Macmillan, 1963, 270 pp.

Austin, Mary C., *et al. The Torch Lighters, Tomorrow's Teachers of Reading*. Cambridge, Mass.: Harvard University Press, 1961. 191 pp.

Bond, Guy L., and Eva Wagner, *Teaching the Child to Read*. 3rd ed. New York: Macmillan, 1960, 416 pp.

Bond, Guy L., and Miles Tinker. *Reading Difficulties: Their Diagnosis and Correction*. New York: Appleton-Century-Crofts, 1957. 486 pp.

Downing, John A. *To Be or Not to Be: The Augmented Roman Alphabet Explained and Illustrated*. London: Cassell, 1962. 123 pp.

——— *The Initial Teaching Alphabet*. London: Cassell, 1963.

Durkin, Dolores. *Phonics and the Teaching of Reading*. New York: Teachers College, Columbia University Press, 1962. 75 pp.

Gates, Arthur I. *Teaching Reading*. What Research Says to the Teacher. No. 1. Washington, D. C.: DCT and AERA of the NEA, 1953. 33 pp.

Gray, Lillian. *Teaching Children to Read*. 3rd ed. New York: Ronald, 1963. 446 pp.

Gray, William S. *On Their Own in Reading*. Rev. ed. Chicago: Scott, Foresman, 1960. 248 pp.

Harris, Albert J. *Effective Teaching of Reading*. New York: David McKay, 1962. 387 pp.

Hildreth, Gertrude. *Teaching Reading: A Guide to Basic Principles and Modern Practices*. New York: Holt, 1958. 612 pp.

Mazurkiewicz, Albert, ed. *Controversial Issues in Reading*. Proceedings of the 10th. Annual Reading Conference, Lehigh University, January 31, 1961. Vol. 1. Bethlehem, Pa.: The Reading and Study Clinic, Department of Education, Lehigh University, 1961. 78 pp.

Pitman, Sir James. *Learning to Read: An Experiment*. Reprinted from the February 1961 Issue of the Journal of the Royal Society of Arts. Second Printing, July, 1962. 32 pp.

Smith, Nila Banton. *Reading Instruction for Today's Children*. Englewood Cliffs, N. J.: Prentice-Hall, 1963. 594 pp.

See also references for Chapters IV and VIII.

# Chapter VI

# A Developmental Reading Program

IN CHAPTER IV, the preparatory phase of reading was discussed. In Chapter V, important problems of beginning reading were considered. In this chapter, suggestions concerning a program for developing basic reading skills and furthering interests are set forth.

## DEVELOPMENTAL READING

A developmental reading program is essential. To foster the maximum reading ability of every child is a most important objective. Each pupil must receive instruction which he needs — not necessarily that which another requires. To accomplish this, many types of procedure must be carried out in group and through individualized teaching.[1]

Evidence from teachers in the field and from research indicates that a developmental program of reading should be planned and carried out in such a way that learners will be taught to read as their needs and potentialities require. Instruction in groups and classes is economical and beneficial, and individualized reading is valuable in guiding individuals of varying abilities and interests to accomplish objectives which differ from those of others in the class or group. As further research is reported and new materials become available, changes in methods will be promoted, which should stimulate individuals to greater accomplishments and higher success than present procedures promote.

If the child is able to use context in obtaining meanings from words, if he has developed an ample beginning sight vocabulary, and if he has learned to use structural and phonetic analysis effectively in at-

---

[1] See Paul A. Witty, "Individualized Reading: A Postscript," *Elementary English,* 41:211–217, March, 1964.

tacking new words, he should be able to progress rapidly in mastering the content of appropriate basal texts and supplementary materials.

In planning rapid development for independence, a program should be outlined in which each child is guided: (1) to read for the joy of reading; (2) to extend interests in reading about peoples, activities, and things; (3) to develop clear understanding of what he reads; (4) to improve his ability to analyze and interpret what he reads; (5) to increase his vocabulary and his skill in identification and recognition of words; (6) to step up generally, his speed of reading comprehension; (7) and to improve his oral reading skill.[2]

In purposing, planning, and carrying out a developmental reading program, a teacher will consider the interests of the child in the world about him as well as the skills to be developed. Hildreth presented helpful suggestions concerning environment of the classroom, skill improvement, variability, using printed materials, selecting books, readability, oral reading to children, dramatization, writing, comprehension, use of workbooks, recreational reading, children's literature, pupil oral reading, word recognition, picture dictionaries, increasing rate, providing for learners of varying abilities, and evaluation.[3]

## SOME MATERIALS AND ACTIVITIES

Among the materials of value in a program for teaching reading in a period of rapid progress are the following: a series of basic readers, a series of workbooks accompanying the readers, teachers' manuals, supplementary books including trade books and storybooks, a wide variety of library books, recordings of stories and dramatizations, dictionaries, reference books including encyclopedias, books on various areas of living (science, literature, history, social studies, communication, and transportation), word cards, "flash" cards, filmstrips, and children's newspapers and magazines. These materials will vary with the program, the school, and the teacher. In some programs, all may be utilized but in others only a few.

### An Important Issue

Some practitioners feel that a basal series is not required to teach

---

[2] William S. Gray, *The Teaching of Reading and Writing* (Chicago: UNESCO, Scott, Foresman and Company, 1961), pp. 137–138.

[3] Gertrude Hildreth, "Reading Programs in Grades II and III," *Reading in the Elementary School,* Forty-Eighth Yearbook of the National Society for the Study of Education, Part II, 1949, pp. 93–126.

reading effectively. They negate the value of basic texts and contend that each child should read individually what he wants to read, especially in grades above the initial reading period. The issue of whether to use basal texts or not may be stated in this fashion. Can children obtain values from a basic series that they would not otherwise obtain? The answer seems clear that most children need to learn how to read properly before they can read to learn independently. It may be that the gifted can learn to read without extensive or intensive guidance, but it seems certain that normal children can obtain a great deal of value from reading a basic series under teacher guidance. It is necessary to fit instruction to each child's needs, and this may be done economically in this stage generally in small groups, properly formed and flexibly maneuvered.

A good reading program provides not only a broad sampling of stories, selections, literature, science, biography, geographical concepts, historical episodes, and poetry, but it provides within the texts themselves and in the workbooks accompanying them, training in many kinds of activities and exercises which broaden abilities and extend and intensify skills. Such a program can be tailored to meet the requirements of many — perhaps most — of the children who are in elementary school. To relegate the teaching of the essential skills to incidental learning is a mistake. The basic books provide many worthwhile activities and exercises for reading. The teachers' manuals offer directions for using the texts and workbooks. If these are used, the reading progress in skills for a majority of children should be assured.[4]

## Using Basal Series

In some schools, two or more basal series and supplementary materials are available for the reading program. In others, in addition to one series, a few copies of two or three reading texts are used. In the more typical programs, one basal series is used in which a textbook on one level is followed by the textbook on the next level. Sometimes, there are two or more groups using different books on different levels as they are required.

A well-planned series with workbooks and manuals contains stories and selections designed to accommodate the reading development of youngsters. The exercises and activities are planned to meet the accumulating sequential needs of skill development. A second important

---

[4] Fay Adams, Lillian Gray, and Dora Reese, *Teaching Children to Read* (New York: The Ronald Press Company, 1949), pp. 223–226.

reason for using a basal series is vocabulary control, which is so planned that only a small number of new words — in the early grades, one or two — are presented on a page, with ample distributed repetition to assure the recognition of each word in various types of context.[5] The vocabulary of one book of a series is a basis for the succeeding book, and so on. The slow learner with proper guidance can succeed if he is paced according to his ability. The rapid learner and the normal pupil also may proceed according to their needs and enrich their reading in other books. The basal books are generally supplemented by trade books, library books, current literature, and reference materials. An important objective for children in the early stages of rapid progress is reading widely for enjoyment and information. Readers and supplementary sources should supply appealing literature and other selections. Reading must not be made an exercise to be endured, but rather an activity to be sought, enjoyed, and used with satisfaction.

## Planning

The work that a child does in the stage of rapid progress should be based upon the goals achieved in the stage of initial reading. As a child progresses from first grade to second and then to third, he should continually maintain and improve the reading skills and abilities learned at each level. Since every child progresses at his own individual rate, his problems and progress must be considered in every lesson. Accordingly, every lesson should be planned, carried out, and evaluated. Gray suggested four stages for preprimer reading: (1) "preparing for reading," (2) "interpreting the story," (3) "extending skills and abilities," (4) "extending interests."[6] Adams, Gray, and Reese presented a five-step plan for beginning reading which includes: preparation, guiding the reading, interpreting the thought, building skills, and enrichment.[7]

Some considerations for purposing, planning, teaching, and evaluating a reading lesson at this level should be helpful.

1. *The objectives.* What are the teacher's aims? What are the children's purposes? Not only must the teacher be clear about her aims, she must also be sure that pupils understand their purposes.

---

[5] Miles A. Tinker, *Teaching Elementary Reading* (New York: Appleton-Century-Crofts, 1952), pp. 118–119.

[6] Gray, *op. cit.*, p. 133.

[7] Adams, Gray, and Reese, *op. cit.*, p. 185.

2. *The approach.*   How should the lesson be introduced? What motivation is necessary to interest the learners? What incentives are helpful in making children aware of the importance of reading? Teacher awareness of the pupils' interests, her knowledge of selections, and her enthusiasm in stimulating reading are highly valuable in approaching any reading activity.

3. *Subject matter and materials.*   Appropriate books should be available. What story is to be read? What is the title of the story or the topic of the selection? What is the book and page reference? References to workbooks or other supplementary materials should be made. Other essential sources should be at hand for study, enrichment, and extension of interests.

4. *Some suggestions for method.*   Preparation, reading, activities, appraisal, and remediation are important points of method.

*a*) What specific preparation should be made for the reading of a story? Reference to an event or a character may be motivating. Difficult words, if any, can be written on the board, pronounced, and pertinent meanings presented. A desire to enjoy or to learn should be developed.

*b*) How should pupils read? The teacher may plan different types of reading lessons. If a silent reading lesson on a story of eight or ten pages is planned, it is advantageous if the children of a group finish about the same time and are ready for discussion without individual waste of time.

*c*) What activities shall be inaugurated? A discussion may follow the reading. If a controversy arises on a particular point, children may skim rapidly to find the right answer. One child may read the answer to the question, and the answer may be verified by others.

*d*) How shall testing and appraisal be carried out? A teacher may ask questions about the characters of a story, or about its forward movement. Responses will indicate the degree of understanding and enjoyment. Discussion by pupils should be evaluated. If the assignment is a selection (not a story) the teacher may have prepared a short mimeographed test — multiple choice, completion, true-false, or matching — for checking comprehension and retention. After the tests have been completed, responses may be checked with the teacher, corrected by the pupils, and discussed.

*e*) What remediation should be applied? Children who scored high on the test may go on to other work. Those who did poorly should be guided to correct their mistakes and to improve their understanding, interpretation, and evaluation. Causes for lack of success should be determined and remediation provided.

5. *Outcomes.* What outcomes are achieved? Recognition should be made of the interests developed or the lack of interest, by one or more members of the group. Comments made to the effect that this was one of the best stories ever read should be noted. A culmination in the form of a dramatization may indicate an increased interest in reading. A request for rereading should be considered. A request for another story "as good as this one" should be responded to with a story similarly interesting. On the other hand, expressions of dislike for, or an obvious lack of interest in a story should be recognized in selecting stories for future assignments.

6. *Enrichment, extension, application.* The enrichment that comes from a well-chosen selection, whether an adventure story or a description of a new type of rocket can be extended and intensified by additional reading. References to other materials should be available for those who desire to study further along the lines of the class reading. An interest born in a class reading may be extended even into a life activity. A pupil can be guided to use facts developed from reading in panel discussions or class assemblies, and be stimulated to use phonics and structural analysis in attacking new words in other areas. The outcomes of a reading lesson should be used as a basis for further assignments.

## Using Workbooks

Workbooks which accompany basic texts are generally helpful in improving skills. Properly utilized, workbooks are valuable in developing understanding of new words. They are particularly useful in presenting meaning, word attack exercises, and in stimulating pronunciation and syllabication activities. Among the types of practices presented in a workbook are those that enhance the locational, comprehensional, evaluative, interpretive, and organizational skills. Exercises are also presented to develop the ability of children to note detail and to follow directions.

Workbooks motivate activity in the study of useful skills. They are valuable because they can be worked at individually by the pupils in study periods. They permit flexibility. A pupil may work at his own speed without being pushed forward or held back by the rate of work of others, and he may study when he has a strong desire to learn. Workbook exercises should have definite purposes, and should

Workbook aids

be studied when and if they are needed by a child, but they should never be given as "busy work." Such use is generally detrimental to the pupil's progress in reading.

A benefit of workbooks is the development in the child of the ability to check and correct his work. A child who is able to find his mistakes can be motivated to correct them by rereading, by thinking about the context, and by comparing his answers with his experiences. Although the teacher should appraise a child's answers in exercises he completes, it is well for her to place the responsibility upon the learner for checking answers and for correcting mistakes.[8]

---

[8] See Tinker, *op. cit.*, pp. 229–230. See Gray, *op. cit.*, p. 261.

## Word Cards, Phrase Cards, Flash Cards

Word cards may be prepared by the teacher or procured commercially. These cards may be used in games such as Lotto or Wordo. They are of value to help develop word recognition by comparison with pictures or in practice exercises. Phrase cards are helpful in guiding the learner to see a whole phrase rather than just one word in a fixation. The criticism of word and phrase cards should be directed to some of the uses to which they are put rather than to the cards themselves. Cards containing words, phrases, and sentences from a basic communication core vocabulary,[9] or the 220 basic sight words[10] are of value in preparing remediation exercises.

One of the fruitful ways to use flash cards is to present questions about materials which the child is studying. These questions can be flashed and the child can read each one silently as it is shown, but instead of vocalizing the question he is guided to give the answer orally.[11]

## Filmstrips

Visual aids very helpful in reading instruction are filmstrips and slides. The filmstrip is used in presenting prepared supplementary reading exercises of many types. The showing may be easily controlled by the teacher and visibility can be made almost perfect for all individuals in a group. Children generally like the use of the machine and accordingly give attention to the filmstrip activities. Some excellent references to sources for filmstrips and other audio-visual materials are presented by DeBoer and Dallmann.[12]

## Current Reading

Reading must be interesting. In addition to basal books, other materials are desirable not only for development of interests but also for the improvement of skills. The use of newspapers and maga-

---

[9] James A. Fitzgerald, "An Integrating Basic Communication Vocabulary," *Elementary English,* 40:283–289, March, 1963.

[10] Edward W. Dolch, *The Basic Sight Vocabulary Cards* (Champaign, Ill.: The Garrard Press). See also Edward W. Dolch, *Picture Word Cards* (Champaign, Ill.: The Garrard Press).

[11] See Emmett A. Betts, *Foundations of Reading Instruction* (New York: American Book Company, 1957), for values and pitfalls of flash cards, pp. 522–523.

[12] See John J. DeBoer and Martha Dallmann, *The Teaching of Reading,* revised edition (New York: Henry Holt and Company, 1964), pp. 276–278.

zines on the child's level is motivating. Horn listed periodicals for children and youth which may be considered by anyone interested.[13] Widely read is *My Weekly Reader* in several editions. The advantage of such a paper is that editions can be selected to fit the reading levels of the individuals. Instead of ordering thirty copies of the Third Edition for a third-grade class, a teacher could order editions to fit requirements of the class, for example, five copies of the Second Edition, twenty-one copies of the Third Edition, and four copies of the Fourth Edition, so that each child would be able to read on his own level the current news.

*Class use of "My Weekly Reader."* By means of standard reading tests, informal tests, and observation, a teacher knows the reading ability of each child. Sometimes children may read an article on the same topic in different editions. After the reading, a discussion will bring out important considerations and cause some pupils to want to read further about an event. In the remaining time of the period, each pupil may read in his edition whatever he wishes to read. A three- or four-minute conference at the end of the session will give opportunities for comment on different articles. These are valuable to the one who talks and to those who listen and receive information.

*Group use of "My Weekly Reader."* A teacher who has grouped her class on the basis of ability to read can meet each group at different times during the reading period. Before class, she may have written on the board an assignment of two articles on "Jets" and "Air Travel" for the group using the Fourth Edition. The attention of the children in this group should be directed to the written assignment and they may begin to read. The Third Edition group may be directed similarly to read an article for example on "Rockets." They also can begin work immediately. A group of slow learners reading the Second Edition may be directed verbally to read a selection, for example, about the uses of corn. The teacher will help those who need help and after they have read the article, questions and discussion may well follow. If there is a question which the children are unable to answer, they are guided to read at the proper place, or one child finds and reads the answer.

After helping the slow group, a conference may be held with the Third Edition children. Questionable statements and inferences can be checked by reference to the article, and misconceptions if any,

---

[13] Thomas D. Horn, "Periodicals for Children and Youth," *Elementary English,* 36:342–344, May, 1959.

corrected. These pupils may then choose other items to read. While the other groups are reading independently, a conference should be carried on with the Fourth Edition group. Each pupil in this group and in the other ones, may be asked to list the most interesting point in the article of his choice.

*Independent reading of current events.* Pupils may want to read individually the editions provided for them. At a meeting of the class a brief discussion about current topics will often arise. Some children may be stimulated to read other periodicals at this time, such as *American Childhood, The Catholic Messenger,* or *Child Life,* in order to obtain further information about a topic.

## UNDIFFERENTIATED (WHOLE CLASS) INSTRUCTION

The question, which type of organization for instruction should be used — the undifferentiated (whole class), group, or individualized — is important. The real issue, however, concerns not only which of these three types of procedure should be employed but also when each should be utilized in instructing children in reading. It is likely that a teacher uses the three types at different times in order to best achieve the goals of reading. Certain kinds of instruction may be given most economically to the whole class. Vicarious experiences, for example, may be enjoyed enthusiastically by an entire class. However, there are skills for which only a small group is ready, and there are items that only one individual requires at a specific time.[14]

### Some Values of Undifferentiated Instruction

Instruction of the entire class will be most economical when it presents something that all pupils of the class can learn beneficially at one time. Among the situations which could be considered are:

1. The approach to a unit of study or experience so that all will understand the purpose of the unit, its significance, the reason for undertaking it, and the goals to be sought

2. The approach, definition, and limitation of a problem in order to bring about most effectively the understanding of its scope and importance by those who will engage in its study

3. The discussion of a project, such as a class assembly, before

---

[14] Josephine B. Wolf, "How Can I Help Every Child With Thirty or More in the Classroom?" *Reading Teacher,* 6:13–16, September, 1952.

groups or committees can be properly appointed to do more detailed work

4. The basic instruction about the care and handling of books as well as directions for the use of dictionaries and encyclopedias

5. Instruction on the library. This may include a showing by a librarian of filmstrips explaining different types of index cards in the card catalog — author, subject, and title

6. The preparation, reading for, carrying out, and evaluating of an exhibit

7. The presentation of a motion picture showing effective reading practices, and in some instances the viewing of filmstrips, slides, graphs, maps, or charts

8. Discussion about improving the school newspaper

9. A culminating activity, for example, the result of a unit on pioneers or patriots.

Choral reading by the entire class — involving search for appropriate selections and determination of procedures for staging the reading — lends itself to this type of organization. Oral reading by a librarian, a teacher, or a gifted reader may be presented. An entire class may enjoy a poetry festival in which everyone in the class participates.

It is obvious that there are many types of reading in which the entire class should participate. One of the outstanding values of whole class instruction is the sense of belonging to the class which it provides for every child.

## Disadvantages of Whole Class Instruction

Whole class or undifferentiated instruction will not meet the needs of some pupils. It can be too difficult (or too rapid) for the slow learners and too simple (or slow moving) for rapid learners. In beginning reading, the average child requires generally careful instruction in sight vocabulary, in phonics, in structural analysis, and in other basic skills for which the slow learners are not ready and which the rapid learners may not need. To teach all these pupils together may serve the extremes in the class poorly. The rapid learners are bored and lose interest when listening to explanations that are unnecessary for them. The slow learners are confused by instruction which is not wholly comprehensible to them. It is therefore obvious that to present children who differ one, two, or more grade levels with the same instruction and materials is not correct procedure.

## GROUPING FOR READING INSTRUCTION

The literature contains many opinions about grouping for the teaching of reading, some favorable and some unfavorable. Gray reviewed the evidence on reading instruction and, noting the problems of a teacher because of the individual differences in the ordinary reading class, concluded that some form of grouping, in the class itself or among classes, was more favorable to guiding children to efficient reading than the undifferentiated instructional program.[15] Most school programs utilize some kinds of grouping in the teaching of reading, but there are difficulties which concern teachers and often handicap pupils when groups are not carefully formed and properly taught. Unquestionably, grouping has advantages when it is properly controlled. Boyer indicated the importance of pupils working together congenially for a common purpose and the naturalness of individuals contributing to group projects. Purpose must determine the bases for grouping because the grouping that may be important in one type of activity may be without value in another.[16]

### Bases for Grouping

A quite practical basis for grouping is that of the equality of the instructional reading levels of children. If a class contains pupils who represent several different grade levels of reading as measured by standardized tests, grouping for instruction can be useful. Furthermore, at any particular level, the needs of readers rated equal may be somewhat different. Some may need help in a phonics skill that a second group has mastered, and the second may require help in reading to obtain proficiency in noting specific details, which the first group has mastered. These two groups, on approximately equal levels, ought to be helped to master the skills required. A third basis for grouping is interest. Children who love country life may work together on rural interests, while another group curious about urban living may study the aspects of living in a city. Another important basis for grouping is that of purpose. Purposes change but while they are dominant, they should be recognized in grouping youngsters for read-

---

[15] William S. Gray, "Reading," *Encyclopedia of Educational Research,* third edition, 1960, p. 1118.

[16] Philip A. Boyer, "The Administration of Learning Groups in Elementary Schools," *The Grouping of Pupils,* Thirty-Fifth Yearbook of the National Society for the Study of Education, Part I, 1936, pp. 191–193.

Our new blends and hyphenated
words :—

scramble scratch screw-
scream scrape Scranton

skit-blue, gay-colored
dark-eyed

Ability grouping

ing.[17] Individuals who have like purposes may be grouped together while accomplishing them.

## Procedures for Appraising and Testing for Grouping

Among the procedures used for appraising and testing for grouping are the following: using tests of mental ability; appraising personality traits; inventorying interests; using knowledge of background and experience; testing with standard achievement batteries; evaluating the performance on standard reading tests; making notes of achievement on informal teacher-made tests; studying anecdotal records; evaluating the results of a sociogram; using a record of progress; observing the child read and do other work; interviewing the child. The recorded results of such procedures are helpful in forming groups for work-type and recreational reading. In addition, a teacher should note the

[17] Emmett A. Betts, "Adjusting Instruction to Individual Needs," *Reading in the Elementary School,* Forty-Eighth Yearbook of the National Society for the Study of Education, Part II, 1949, pp. 276–277.

changes in a child's attitudes, interests, and performances. Even a small change may be of great importance. On the basis of information — determined, recorded, and interpreted — lessons or units may be planned. Because of their more common needs or interests, pupils in small groups generally may be directed more definitely to worthwhile work than would be possible if the whole class was taught in an undifferentiated program.

## Grouping Within the Classroom

Grouping is a means by which instruction may be facilitated. Some teachers try to group homogeneously, but the term is confusing because there is no possibility of absolute homogeneity. Some systems group according to ability on the basis of one criterion, but such grouping is likely to be ineffective. When children are grouped on the basis of intelligence scores, for example, the variation in reading range of that group will be from 80 to 90 percent of the heterogeneous group.

*Inflexible grouping.* A rigid pattern for grouping has developed in some school systems. Frequently, three groups are formed sometimes on the bases of one or two abilities — regardless of the changing needs, growing interests, and the developing powers of children. Fixed reading groups — inflexible and permanent — for a semester or a year are difficult to justify. Children in a lower group are sometimes wrongfully stigmatized as "slow" or "dumb." Inflexible grouping is often unjust to the "late bloomer." Although fixed groups are often organized because they are said to be homogeneous, the practice is questionable and often unfair. The instruction tends to separate the groups more and more, and the longer the rigid grouping lasts the more unlikely it is that children in a lower group will be able to advance to a higher one. The move to a lower group is questionable also because a child moved to that group will often be thought of as a failure.[18]

*Flexible grouping.* If grouping is a correct practice and if inflexible grouping has more disadvantages than values, it follows that some type of flexible grouping should be utilized within the classroom or among the classes. A majority of authorities approve of flexible grouping if it is used to meet the needs and abilities of youngsters. Because children in a group progress at varying rates, it is evident that there

---

[18] Guy L. Bond and Miles A. Tinker, *Reading Difficulties: Their Diagnosis and Correction* (New York: Appleton-Century-Crofts, Inc., 1957), p. 59.

are some who will "outdistance" others.[19] Grouping should be carried out generally only after careful testing and consideration of the problems and characteristics of the pupils. The similar purposes espoused by several children may be a reason for grouping them together. Pupils may be teamed up because of their similar experiences. The deficiencies made clear by testing, observing, or interviewing will suggest the need for corrective work on a skill or a cluster of skills. Four or five children may require, for example, aid in recognizing the importance of identifying the root words in such derivatives as *transmit* and *remit* or need instruction on the prefix *de–* in *depart, deport, depend,* or *deposit.* Another group of nine or ten may need help, which others do not need, on certain initial consonant blends such as *bl, gl,* and *fl* in *black* and *blue, glass* and *glad,* and *fly* and *flower.* To neglect to instruct them on the blends they need when they need them would be to handicap them, but to insist that all other children of the class sustain instruction which they do not require would be wasting time and effort.

The interest level is important. Some children do not like certain types of reading but they are fascinated with other types. To require primary-grade boys to read a story about dolls would be poor practice though girls frequently revel in such activity. To stimulate children to select topics and titles from the library under the guidance of a librarian would appeal to them and indicate the importance of reading because of the enjoyment and value obtained. Because interests change, the use of the inventory and the informal but careful appraisal of pupils by a teacher from day to day should be helpful in selecting materials which meet children's interests on appropriate levels.

One caution should be clear. By flexible grouping, it is not meant that children should "jump" from one group to another haphazardly, for to do so would probably be detrimental to purposeful learning. Betts warned that the change from one group to another should be made only after deliberate and considerate appraisal of the child's purposes, needs, interests, and progress. The transfer from one group to another requires guidance by the teacher and a new adjustment by the pupil to the individuals of the group into which he enters. A move of this kind should be made in such a manner that the pupil will be accepted by the new group without friction or embarrassment.[20]

---

[19] Betts, *op. cit.,* p. 178.
[20] Betts, *loc. cit.*

Bond and Tinker suggested that children requiring help in a specific skill, although they may ordinarily be from different basic groups, can be instructed in a temporary group.[21] It seems sensible that when a temporary group is formed for a purpose, it should be disbanded when the purpose is accomplished. It is possible also that when flexible grouping is practiced, the whole class should frequently meet as a class in order to achieve certain goals. This practice is particularly helpful when pupils of different groups are reading about the same topic although on different reading levels. When the groups meet in class occasionally and are treated as members of the class rather than as members of a subgroup, the pupils have a feeling of belonging to the class. Sometimes when the whole class is organized in such a manner that all contribute to a unit of work, committees may be formed to include some of the best readers and some of the slowest particularly when such readers have a common interest or purpose.

## Related Interclassroom Grouping

Related interclassroom grouping concerns the teaching of reading to children of equivalent reading ability from different grade levels and different rooms. For years related grouping has been used successfully particularly in remedial instruction. Floyd reported excellent success in related grouping at Joplin, Missouri. Pupils of grades four, five, and six who ranged from first grade to ninth grade in reading abilities were instructed for fifty minutes a day in nine groups formed according to reading ability. After the reading sessions in which they worked at their approximate reading levels, they returned to their homerooms to work in their regular classes and to read individually.[22]

Nephew reported a highly successful reading program for fourth, fifth, and sixth grades in the Palmdale School District, Los Angeles County, California, in which flexible groups were formed on the basis of actual reading ability. After careful testing and appraisal programs, pupils were assigned to groups for reading above, at, or below their homeroom levels. For example, good fourth-grade readers were grouped with some fifth-grade, or even sixth-grade pupils in the reading period. On the other hand, sixth-grade pupils who read on a third-grade level were grouped with fourth- or fifth-grade children having similar difficulties but reading on third-grade level. Ap-

---

[21] Bond and Tinker, *op. cit.*, p. 60.
[22] Cecil Floyd, "Meeting Children's Reading Needs in the Middle Grades," *Elementary School Journal,* 55:99–103, October, 1954.

propriate materials — basic readers, workbooks, supplementary books, trade books, and current literature — were provided for nine different levels from the preprimer to the seventh grade. Various kinds of reading were practiced. Basic skills were emphasized. Library reading was promoted. Pupils evaluated their own work. Teachers appraised the improvement. Pupils making sufficient progress were permitted to move from one group to another.[23]

In order to achieve success in such a program, a core of teachers under the guidance of a supervising principal or a reading coordinator must understand the total program of reading — its objectives, requirements, processes, appraisal technics, and the importance of successful outcomes. Continuous measure of every child's efforts and achievement is necessary. A basic reading program with careful attention to individual needs is mandatory. Suitable books and materials are highly desirable. Important also is consideration of personalities and personal problems. Learners must be directed considerately; never should they be made to feel in any way that they are failures. Their confidence should be developed, bolstered, and sustained.

## Teaching Groups

A variety of lessons should be planned for the group. Whether they are within the classroom itself or drawn from two or more classrooms, they should be taught so that they will endeavor to improve their reading. Several types of reading lessons are enumerated:

1. *Recreational silent reading.* Each child reads silently an interesting story selected for him. After each has completed his story, he may tell the group about it and how he liked it.

2. *Study-type silent reading.* Each child reads for information and understanding about some project or activity such as fishing, hunting, farming, mining, or one of a hundred other types of work in which people engage. Questions may lead to discussion and frequently to further research and reporting.

3. *Library reading.* Every child can be interested in the library and in the books and magazines to be found there. If there is a central library in the school building, groups may be sent to it on schedule to learn about library technics and to browse in books selected for the program.

---

[23] Ervin Nephew, "We Organized the Reading Program Around Actual Reading Ability," *The Instructor,* 69:75–76, 87, March, 1960.

4. *Recreational oral reading.* The children will listen to the librarian or teacher read a story or a poem. A group can plan a reading period in which each one is responsible for reading his best-liked selection. It may be well to plan this type of activity on a day following the free reading in the library when a pupil has had an opportunity to select an item for his oral presentation.

5. *Poetry.* If a teacher loves poetry, obtains several appropriate compilations, and reads poems of interest to the group, she will find pupils looking through them and poring over choices. Among the useful anthologies are: *Time for Poetry* by May Hill Arbuthnot (Scott, Foresman), which presents seven hundred poems grouped in appropriate categories; Helen Ferris's *Favorite Poems Old and New* (Doubleday), which contains seven hundred poems also grouped appropriately; and *Sung Under the Silver Umbrella* by the Association for Childhood Education (Macmillan), which offers two hundred poems for young children. Among the well-known and well-loved specialized selections are: Maud and Miska Petersham's *The Rooster Crows* (Macmillan), Rachel Field's *Poems* (Macmillan), and A. A. Milne's *The World of Christopher Robin* (Dutton).[24]

6. *Current Reading.* Children should be guided to know the important periodicals and newspapers which meet their needs and engage their interests. It is possible to have a current reading lesson such as the one described previously in this chapter.

7. *Skills improvement.* A group may need instruction in finding materials in the library, topics in encyclopedias, or words in a dictionary. Such skills should be explained one at a time by a teacher and practiced by the pupils. Outlining a chapter, making notes for a report, preparing an outline of readings also may require attention.

8. *Mechanics.* The mechanics — phonics, sounding of digraphs or diphthongs, recognition of root words and derivatives, learning how to make use of punctuation — call for attention, and children should be helped with them when necessary.

## Some Questionable Practices Concerning Grouping

Among questionable practices are the following:

1. Grouping a class rigidly into three or other number of groups and not permitting appropriate relations with the whole class or other groups

---

[24] See Leland B. Jacobs, "Poetry Books for Poetry Reading," *The Reading Teacher,* 13:45–47, October, 1959.

2. Not grouping when there is need for grouping to help those who require assistance

3. Formulating different programs for the groups, in such a manner that the class never works as a whole

4. Teaching all individuals in a group the same concepts, processes, and skills in the same way

5. Neglecting to teach individuals within a group as they require instruction

6. Showing varying attitudes to the pupils of different groups.

Each group should be taught and each individual of a group should be guided to learn the skills and habits necessary to progress in reading.[25]

*Résumé.* Grouping is economical when the members of a group have common problems and tasks that others in the class do not have. Flexible grouping may be carried out on the bases of needs, interests, and achievement. Grouping is productive in both work-type and recreational reading, but it must be purposeful, and instruction should be applied as needed to individuals or to small subgroups within a group when necessary. Grouping from two or more grade levels may be utilized profitably for instruction in reading. However, grouping should not overshadow the class organization or class procedure.[26]

## INDIVIDUALIZED APPROACH TO READING

Approaches to the teaching of reading vary considerably in different programs. Basal series and other materials are used in an undifferentiated approach. Grouping is practiced; sometimes two groups, often three, and occasionally four or more are organized in a classroom. Frequently mentioned in the literature of reading at the present time is the individual approach to reading instruction.[27]

### Some Considerations of Authorities

Lazar, one of the most enthusiastic proponents of the individualized instruction program in reading, suggested that it is as much an atti-

[25] Tinker, *op. cit.,* pp. 204–205.

[26] David Russell, *Children Learn to Read* (Boston: Ginn and Company, 1949), pp. 332–333.

[27] Margaret McKim, "Reading in the Primary Grades," *Development In and Through Reading,* Sixtieth Yearbook of the National Society for the Study of Education, Part I, 1961, p. 276.

Individual reading instruction

tude as a procedure, and provides a positive consideration for the differences of individuals in society. Her emphatic contention was that schools should cultivate individual interests, aptitudes, and talents rather than ignore or equalize them.[28] Veatch indicated that the individualized reading program is characterized by the concepts of *seeking, self-selection,* and *pacing.* Each child seeks stimulating materials, chooses reading which is conducive to his development, and reads at his own rate in achieving his purposes.[29]

Groff reported that the individualized program emphasizes reasons for reading and makes reading more realistic. He maintained that the individualized approach strengthens concentration, stresses problem solving, encourages thinking, and makes possible opportunities for creativity.[30] Many reading authorities recognize the desirable features of individualized reading. For example, Gates set forth the therapeutic values of the properly conducted individual conferences for slow learners. In such conferences, a teacher obtains insight concerning a child's difficulties and needs. Furthermore, Gates approved in the individualized program the tendency to read without being required to read.[31] Many authorities affirm that individualized reading has a place along with basal reading, undifferentiated teaching, and instruction in flexible groups. To contend, as some do, that a teacher must use one of these programs to the exclusion of others seems unwarranted. To use the individualized program when it best fits the needs of the readers is a most tenable proposition. Some basic lessons should be taught in the whole class. Other skills and abilities are most economically taught in a group in which individuals require the same skills or have the same purposes. An individualized reading program also at times is certainly most effective in meeting individual purposes and requirements in many work-type and recreational situations. Only one child of a group may be interested in doing research on insects or in studying the account of "flying dragons" and reptiles in the Mesozoic era. Only two or three may do extensive reading about the Crusades. These and others should follow their interests and read both intensively and extensively.

[28] May Lazar, *Individualization of Instruction in Reading* (New York City: Board of Education, 1941), p. 1.

[29] Jeanette Veatch, "Individualized Reading — For Success in the Classroom," *The Educational Trend* (Washington: Arthur C. Croft Publications, 1954).

[30] Patrick J. Groff, "Getting Started With the Individualized Reading," *Elementary English,* 37:105, February, 1960.

[31] Arthur I. Gates, "Improvement in Reading Possible in the Near Future," *The Reading Teacher,* 12:85–86, December, 1958.

*Agencies, Sources, and Materials for an Individualized Program*

The most important agency in promoting individualized reading is an enthusiastic teacher who knows and loves children and books. A trained librarian also is invaluable to the program.

Groff reported that teachers frequently state that they do not have a sufficient number of books for individualized programs, and that they do not know the books in their collections sufficiently well. If an individualized program is to be properly carried out, it follows that adequate collections should be made available and teachers ought to be given time to familiarize themselves with a wide variety of books and authors.[32] Books, books, and more books of many types and levels, are necessary to meet the varying interests and the recreational and study needs of children of a class. They are useful also in the correction of definite difficulties of each child.

Where may books be procured? How many books are necessary? School and public libraries are sources. Class libraries may be built up. A teacher may start with twenty books, fifty books, one hundred books, and plan to make her collection rich and varied. Although second-hand stores, attics, and storerooms have been suggested, they should be used only with the greatest consideration of the child's purposes and needs. Just any "old book" will not suffice. The books should be carefully selected upon the advice of a trained librarian or teacher. Book lists, such as *Adventuring with Books* (published by the National Council of Teachers of English), *The Children's Catalog* (H. W. Wilson Company), *Graded Lists of Books for Children* (American Library Association), Margaret Clark's *Keeping Up with Children and Books* (Scott, Foresman and Company), and Clara Kircher's *Character Formation Through Books: A Bibliography* (Catholic University of American Press), are excellent references. They and other lists should be studied systematically in order to select worthwhile books for varied tastes of children. The "Weekly Reader Children's Book Club" membership supplies six books during a membership year, and appeals to pupils from eight to twelve years. The "Teen Age Book Club" has over a million members. Books from such sources should be carefully appraised.

Of all the books that have been written, only a comparatively few can be read by any ordinary individual in his childhood or even in

---

[32] Patrick J. Groff, "A Check on Individualized Reading," *Education,* 84:397–401, March, 1964.

his lifetime. Accordingly, book selection is of great importance. Only the best of literature should be presented for children to read. The Lewis Carroll Shelf Award is conferred upon books which, like *Alice's Adventures in Wonderland,* possess imagination and originality, genuine emotion, consistent characters, plausible events, and a logical and gently unfolding plot.[33] Among the many books that have received the award are the following: *And to Think That I Saw It on Mulberry Street* by Dr. Seuss; *Blue Willow* by Doris Gates; *Caddie Woodlawn* by Carol Brink; *Five Chinese Brothers* by Claire Bishop; *Hitty Her First Hundred Years* by Rachel Field; *Jungle Books* by Rudyard Kipling; *Millions of Cats* by Wanda Gag; *Pecos Bill* by James Bowman; *The Tale of Peter Rabbit* by Beatrix Potter; and *Wind in the Willows* by Kenneth Grahame. Such books and hundreds of others appraised in *Fifty Years of Children's Books* by Dora V. Smith offer excellent materials for almost every taste.[34] If children can be guided to read good books in childhood, they will thirst after them in adulthood.

### Procedures to Stimulate Individualized Reading

A teacher uses group or class instruction to develop individual interests and to motivate individual reading. She may pick up a book and make a comment about it to a class. She may read an interesting story or an exciting poem. She may have pupils report on books they have read. She can plan a reading period in the library in which each pupil is permitted to read what he wants to read. In such a period, she must stand ready to help those who need help in book selection. She may be asked to explain the background of a poem or dramatization, or to answer questions about rockets, satellites, or space ships. It is possible that she might be called upon to help a child understand the tremendous importance of Einstein's great formula: $E = MC^2$. She must be alert to help the child find a pertinent source in which information can be obtained.

The outcomes of a free reading period in the library are: self-selection, spontaneity, intensity, and variety. One child may read about ships and boats, a second about airplanes, a third about electronics, a fourth about the pioneers, a fifth about cave men, a sixth a fascinating

---

[33] David C. Davis, "A Tool for the Selection of Children's Books: The Lewis Carroll Shelf Awards," *Elementary English,* 38:549–552, December, 1961.

[34] Dora V. Smith, *Fifty Years of Children's Books: 1910–1960 Trends, Backgrounds, Influences* (Champaign, Ill.: The National Council of Teachers of English, 1963), p. 149.

fairy tale, a seventh about King Arthur and His Noble Knights, an eighth about flowers above the Artic Circle, a ninth about oceanography, and so on. A few minutes before the period is over, a brief conference in which each child comments in perhaps a sentence or two about the wonders of his reading will serve for appraisal of the interest and effort of the reader and also as a motivation to other pupils to extend their reading to some of the books mentioned or reported.

Although most elementary school children are attracted to the comics, the normal and gifted tend to replace them sooner or later with more vital reading materials. Those who guide children should, realizing the importance of their preferences, supply books which satisy them. Cowboy and Indian stories are liked very much by boys, but young girls often prefer fairy and funny stories. Stories about great men and animal stories appeal to boys and girls.[35] Pupils soon find out what kinds of reading are available and read what they like best.

Interests and preferences are promoted by a combination of teacher's personality, enthusiasm, and integration of literature with other activities in the curriculum. A word about a prominent statesman, gifted writer, or a successful inventor may be the cue for self-searching in sources by a pupil. Desire to read must be properly planted, adequately culti- vated, and successfully expanded and intensified from the beginning through the succeeding stages by the presentation of desirable and valuable materials in cultural and vocational areas. Guidance for some children may come from an inspiring word; for others it may be developed through careful and patient direction. Individual guidance functions best when the child in the primary grades and the pupil in the middle and upper grades learn what is of worth and develop a desire to read it.

## Teacher Responsibility in the Individualization of Reading

When only one of a group requires assistance of a particular kind, the teacher should guide that child to materials for his purpose. She may schedule interviews with an individual for the purpose of listen- ing to him read. She can then give him the help he needs, for example, in phrasing or in enunciation. She may assist another child in sounding or in word identification. It may happen also, that a pupil from the rapid reading group needs help in locating materials for a creative project, a specific need which others do not and may never require.

[35] Vera Slover, "Comic Books *vs.* Story Books," *Elementary English,* 36:319– 322, May, 1959.

In a social study period a teacher may find it necessary to give instruction for making a critical evaluation of a statement by a writer. Help may be given to an individual, to two pupils, or to several. It is obvious that individualized instruction should be used in a group or in a whole class as it is considered helpful.[36]

## Encouraging Self-Teaching

Self-teaching should be encouraged in preparation for the time when a child will guide himself in the reading necessary and beneficial to his vocation in life. Individualized reading can be excellent preparation for this. After receiving instruction in groups and guidance in individual conferences with the teacher, the pupil must become proficient in reading for many purposes. He may wish to assemble a model boat, for example, which requires reading to comprehend the blueprint, to note the details of the model, and to follow directions in putting the model together. Another pupil may wish to find a poem for an assembly. He consults the card catalog in the library and skims through books of poetry in search of a poem which he likes. A project may require the reading of the poem creditably, so he practices in a vacant classroom and finds that he cannot pronounce several words and that he does not understand a specific passage. He uses the dictionary to study meanings and pronunciations; he finds an explanation in a footnote that helps him. He thinks about the passage, studies it, and practices reading the poem again in order to convey the emotion expressed by the author. His practice and preparation pay off.

## Some Suggestions for Integrating Individualized Reading With Group and Whole Class Instruction

Class and group participation affords enrichment to the individual in discussion, communication, and sharing; conversely, the individual adds to group and class activity. Individualized instruction has great values when a child advances at a rate different from any other in the group. It is highly valuable when an individual has purposes and interests different from any other in the group. Furthermore, it becomes more and more self-impelled by the reader himself. A competent reader reads to achieve objectives, to understand a process, to enjoy an adventure, or to satisfy other needs. He is not forced to read a particular book. He reads enthusiastically to comprehend new concepts, to experience new scenes, to feel new emotions. These, he can report to

---

[36] Russell, *op. cit.,* p. 339.

the class as his offering for he feels that they are his to communicate. In reporting them, he is sharing with others what he has discovered. Individual reading takes its place in the totality of reading, and it should be undertaken by each child when he is able to derive value from it.

The following suggestions should be of value in planning an individualized reading program for children of a class or group.

1. Know the class, and study the interests and needs of every child in it.

2. Equip a library shelf or corner with an adequate supply of books of varying types and interests on the levels necessary.

3. Describe books enthusiastically so that readers will desire to know more about them and want to read them.

4. Guide each child to select the right book — appropriate in difficulty level, interest, and need.

5. If possible, arrange for free reading in the library and instruct children about the way to find books, periodicals, and reference materials.

6. Keep in a cumulative record folder for each child a notation of needs, interests, assignments, achievements, progress, degree of success, and outcomes.

7. Evaluate the reading of each child in each period. Note changes in interests and improvements from day to day and month to month.

8. Guide the child in seeking, self-selection, pacing, and in responsibility for extending and intensifying his reading in realms which interest him.

9. Motivate each reader to compete with his own record and to strive for the degree of excellence which he seeks and can attain.

10. Have individuals appraise their progress, and recognize the importance of success in reading.[37]

## ORAL READING

Reading is silent and oral. Silent reading can range from the fascinatingly recreational type to that of a most intensive work-study nature. Oral reading may also be recreational or work-type. Effective oral reading without silent reading is obviously impossible, but in the begin-

---

[37] See Gertrude Hildreth, "Reading Programs in Grades II and III," *Reading in the Elementary School,* Forty-Eighth Yearbook of the National Society for the Study of Education, Part II, 1949, pp. 121–122.

ning stage oral reading is an approach to silent reading. Children read orally for fun and enjoyment and sometimes to show how well they can read. To read well, however, each must gain meaning by interpreting symbols in the light of his experiences and background. A good oral reader reads silently — scouts several words or phrases in advance of his vocal communication of thought. Oral reading, thus, involves acquiring thought and feeling through printed or written symbols, thoroughly interpreting them, and communicating them to the listeners.

## Needs and Values

The following illustrate the types of needs for and values of oral reading in situations in and out of school.

1. Reading a story or poem to a class or audience
2. Reading a letter from a friend or acquaintance to a class
3. Reading a report to a committee, to a class, or to members of a club
4. Reading the minutes of a meeting, a financial statement, or a log
5. Reading an announcement about the excursion which a class has planned
6. Reading directions for planning an exhibit of books collected for book week
7. Reading a part of a play with others
8. Reading aloud for practice in preparation of a program for a PTA meeting
9. Choral reading.[38]

## Audience Reading

Instruction in oral reading is closely allied with speaking and with silent reading. A reader must comprehend thought before he can express it orally, and he should be able to enunciate it in a clear, pleasant voice in communicating confidently to others. Oral reading should be enjoyable to the reader and pleasing to the listeners. It should convey meaning or interpret feeling.

A slow or retarded learner should read to a small group. Three or four children may read in their own little group after preparation. A really limited reader should not be called upon to read to an entire

---

[38] See Ernest Horn and James F. Curtis, "Improvement of Oral Reading," *Reading in the Elementary School,* Forty-Eighth Yearbook of the National Society for the Study of Education, Part II, 1949, pp. 255–256. See also DeBoer and Dallmann, *op. cit.,* pp. 227–248.

Oral reading

class. A child who "freezes" in front of a small group should read to the teacher who can give him individual attention.

*Reading a play.* An appealing activity in the middle or upper grades is the reading of a play. Each pupil should have a copy and each should prepare to read his assigned part. Reading parts to an audience can be satisfying to the readers and rewarding to the listeners.

*Group story reading.* In achieving her aim — to motivate interesting audience reading — a teacher obtained two copies of a suitable story cut from an old reading series (two copies were necessary because the story was printed on both sides of the pages). These were divided into sections of appropriate length and each section was pasted on a card. The cards were numbered consecutively, and distributed to members of the group who were to read. The teacher had provided a brief synopsis of the story to the group. Each pupil prepared his section — read the context, checked pronunciation of difficult words, and studied the meaning so that he might read with enthusiasm and clarity. The readers were seated in front of the room in order to have good visual contact with the class.

The listeners — the remainder of the class — who knew nothing of the story, listened attentively to the novel presentation. A discussion period followed, in which there were questions, answers, and comments by pupils and teacher.

*Children's choices.* In another type of oral reading, each child chooses a story, poem, or selection, and prepares to read it. Each reads to communicate and to share joyously with others. A class assembly may be arranged. Pupils may be seated in a circle or semicircle to read their favorite selections or passages from books. Applause often is spontaneous for well-delivered presentations. After each reading, a reader should be prepared to answer questions. Comments can be made about the content or characters. Constructive criticism is permissible. When a reading is interesting, the pupils often ask about the book and where it may be obtained. In this way, wide reading is motivated for many children.

## Some Instructional Exercises

No one can face an audience confidently without competency in the mechanics of expression, and such competency can be best achieved through instruction on the part of the teacher and study and practice by the pupil. Children need to learn the value of the dictionary for the study of pronunciations and meanings. They must also practice the correct use of words in expression. The teacher will find it necessary, frequently, to point out errors and guide a learner to work intensively for improvement. A most important responsibility, however, is to motivate him to develop self-criticism and independence in remediation. Another phase of training in oral reading concerns the utilization of effective silent reading. A pupil should learn sooner or later — and the sooner the better — that he must comprehend silently before giving thought orally. In good oral reading, the eye will see in advance of the functioning of the voice in order that the message will be perceived, comprehended, interpreted, and effectively communicated. Audience reading such as the following should be planned and practiced to coordinate silent and oral reading in verbal communication:

1. Reading a sentence or brief paragraph from a source to support a statement made

2. Skimming rapidly for an important point of information, and reading it effectively to support a proposition made in a committee meeting

3. Finding and reading to a group an exciting passage in an adventure story

4. Reading a dramatic excerpt of a biography of a famous person

5. Reading a plan for construction, for example, of a baseball diamond

6. Each pupil reading his ending to a story, part of which the teacher read to the class

7. Reading to teammates how to execute a new play in basketball

8. Reading into a tape recorder and listening to the playback to determine deficiencies to correct

9. After remediation exercises, reading again into the recorder to determine progress.[39]

### Appraisal of Oral Reading

Appraisal is important before, during, and after teaching. The teacher will note voice control, articulation, enunciation, pronunciation, phrasing, presentation, and audience acceptance. She will recognize tension and lack of facility in expression. The type of corrective work will depend in a large measure on her diagnosis of deficiencies and difficulties.

A helpful instrument is the *Gates Reading Diagnostic Tests* by which vocabulary, omissions, additions, repetitions, mispronunciations, and reversals are identified. This instrument, which is part of a more comprehensive diagnostic program, is valuable for determining measures for correcting oral reading mechanics.[40]

The *Gray Oral Reading Tests,* edited by Helen Robinson, offer four comparable forms — of thirteen passages each — which accommodate individuals from the preprimer to college and adult levels. These are valuable in diagnosing oral reading difficulties and word perception. By use of the multiple forms, it is possible to determine pupil progress from time to time in order to better adapt instruction to changing needs.[41]

### Some Criteria for Oral Reading

Questions which should be asked about the oral reading of a pupil follow:

1. Has the reader prepared properly to read the selection?

---

[39] Lillian Gray, *Teaching Children to Read,* third edition (New York: The Ronald Press, 1963), pp. 274–278.

[40] Published by Bureau of Publications, Teachers College, Columbia University, New York.

[41] Published by the Bobbs-Merrill Company, Inc., Indianapolis, Indiana.

2. Does he understand what he is reading and interpret it properly?

3. Does the reader react courteously, considerately, and responsibly to his audience, and does the audience react favorably to him?

4. Does he read purposefully to communicate a message?

5. Is the reader well poised and confident?

6. Does he read distinctly, with enthusiasm and with ease?

7. Does he vary his delivery to meet the conditions of the environment and audience?

8. Are his pronunciation, articulation, and phrasing correct and natural?

9. Can he be heard by all without difficulty?

It is not expected that the normal elementary school pupil can achieve perfection in oral reading, but he can develop considerable reading power and facility. Because there is a need today for a high degree of excellence in oral reading and language, the criteria stated above should be satisfied to the highest degree of a pupil's capability.

## SUMMARY

A developmental reading program should be carried out efficiently. A well-selected series of basic readers — with workbooks and manuals — word cards, flash cards, filmstrips, and children's literature are valuable so that every child will learn to read with facility and confidence.

Undifferentiated, group, and individualized reading are important in the developmental program for children of an ordinary class. Undifferentiated instruction has many values. All members of a class may share richly in the reading and study of a unit. All may profit in preparing and presenting an assembly program. Skills and abilities which all need at the same time may be taught effectively and economically to a whole class.

Grouping is necessary frequently because of the differences in readiness, ability, interests, and backgrounds of pupils. Inflexible grouping is generally undesirable, but flexible grouping is workable with children in a single room or from different rooms. Groups formed on the bases of purpose, ability, interests, attitudes, and background work well in both recreational and work-type reading.

The individualized approach to reading has received strong impetus recently. A teacher may use individualized instruction to guide every pupil to read what is essential in his study, what he likes to read for enjoyment, and what he requires to overcome his deficiencies. Individualized reading should be integrated into the total reading program. It will be helpful in the whole class and in large or small groups.

Because oral reading has value in many situations in and out of school, activities which develop it should be planned and carried out.

## ACTIVITIES, PROBLEMS, QUESTIONS

1. Make a list of essential materials for teaching reading in one grade (choose a grade level).
2. How would you employ the interests of each child in a reading program?
3. Formulate a lesson plan for teaching reading to children at a selected grade level of your choice.
4. Explain carefully the value of workbooks in a developmental reading program.
5. State the values of whole class or undifferentiated instruction. Give the difficulties also.
6. Set up a plan for grouping which you think will work effectively in teaching reading to third-grade children.
7. Enumerate several types of lessons for teaching groups, and explain how each can be employed.
8. Describe individualized approaches to instruction in reading. Prepare a table setting forth the advantages and a second one showing the difficulties. Compare the two tables.
9. List the names of five authorities who approve of individualized instruction. State reasons each presents for such procedure.
10. Plan a program for reading showing how you can effectively integrate class, group, and individualized instruction.
11. Show the relationships between oral and silent reading.
12. Outline a program for teaching and reading. List the kinds of situations you would use in teaching: (*a*) oral recreational reading; (*b*) oral work-type reading.

## SELECTED REFERENCES

Burton, William H. *Reading in Child Development.* Indianapolis: Bobbs-Merrill, 1956. 608 pp.

Carter, H., and Dorothy McGinnis. *Teaching Individuals to Read.* Boston: Heath, 1962. 229 pp.

Crosby, Muriel, and Beatrice David Hurley. *Adventuring with Books: A Reading List for the Elementary Grades.* Champaign, Ill.: National Council of Teachers of English, 1960. 189 pp.

Darrow, Helen Fisher, and Virgil M. Hawes. *Approaches to Individualized Reading Instruction.* New York: Appleton-Century-Crofts, 1960. 102 pp.

Draper, Marcella K., and Louise H. Schwietert. *A Practical Guide to Individualized Reading for Teachers and Supervisors in the Elementary School.* New York: Bureau of Educational Research, Publication No. 40, Board of Education of the City of New York, 1960. 158 pp.

Figurel, J. Allen, ed. *Changing Concepts of Reading Instruction.* International Reading Association Conference Proceedings. New York: Scholastic Magazines, 1961. 292 pp.

*The Grouping of Pupils.* Thirty-Fifth Yearbook of the National Society for the Study of Education, Part I. Chicago: University of Chicago Press, 1936. 319 pp.

Hughes, Rosalind. *Let's Enjoy Poetry: An Anthology of Children's Verse for Grades 4, 5, and 6 with Suggestions for Teaching.* Boston: Houghton Mifflin, 1961. 298 pp.

*Individualizing Instruction.* Sixty-First Yearbook of the National Society for the Study of Education, Part I. Chicago: University of Chicago Press, 1962. 337 pp.

McKim, Margaret G., and Helen Caskey. *Guiding Growth in Reading in the Modern Elementary School.* New York: Macmillan, 1963, 454 pp.

Miel, Alice. *Individualizing Reading Practices.* New York: Teachers College, Columbia University Press, 1958. 92 pp.

Strang, Ruth, Constance M. McCullough, and Arthur E. Traxler. *The Improvement of Reading.* 3rd ed. New York: McGraw-Hill, 1961. 480 pp.

*The Teaching of Reading.* Thirty-Sixth Yearbook of the National Society for the Study of Education, Part I. Chicago: University of Chicago Press, 1937. 442 pp.

Veach, Jeannette. *Individualizing Your Reading Program.* New York: Putnam, 1959. 242 pp.

See also references for Chapters V and VIII.

# Chapter VII

# Reading: Fundamental Thoughtful Processes

## ORIENTATION

READING is a basic tool of learning in the school and in life outside the school. If an individual can read adequately, he can solve many problems of language and living.

### Reading Related to Other Language Arts

Reading is related to all the areas of the language arts — to speech, listening, writing, spelling, and handwriting. To a great extent, the quality of reading depends upon these interrelationships. In general, silent reading is an intaking or receptive art in which the reader strives to experience vicariously or to comprehend the ideas which the author wished to express. In such reading, an individual achieves understanding through symbols which have been written to tell a story, describe an episode, or depict an event. If the writing is clear, reading is carried on effectively, provided of course that the individual has learned to read competently. Reading, on the other hand, contributes to the effectiveness of other language arts particularly to oral and written language.

### Reading Opens Up a Rich Store of Knowledge

"Reading maketh a full man . . ." because reading opens up to the individual who reads purposively and proficiently the whole study of mankind — the struggles, the history, the literature, the science, the art, and the religions of the races as they evolved from ancient times. Reading connotes the attainment of meaning by comprehending, interpreting, and critically evaluating nonoral communication conveyed through words, letters, and numerals which appear in context of books, papers, periodicals, and other materials.

## Complexities and Difficulties in Reading

English is a rich language. One of the unabridged English dictionaries presents more than 600,000 different entries with definitions, derivations, and pronunciations. English is a conglomerate of many languages — Greek, Latin, Arabic, Germanic, Anglo-Saxon, French, and others. Its very richness, resulting from various roots and derivations, adds to the complexity of pronunciation, spelling, and writing, and requires comprehension, interpretation, evaluation, and organization processes of a high order to bring about satisfaction and enjoyment in reading. Difficulty is indicated by the fact that some vowels are sounded in many different ways, and some sounds are spelled in many ways also. The long sound of *o,* for example, is conveyed in at least fourteen different ways.[1] Horn reported that, although the short sounds of vowels are more consistently spelled than other vowels sounds, the short sound of *i* as in *pin, in,* or *bin* is spelled nearly half the time in other ways than with the single letter *i.* The schwa sound, he found, "is spelled in more than thirty ways in common words."[2] There are, for example, words spelled alike that have different pronunciations and convey varying meanings, and words spelled differently that are pronounced identically. Meanings of most words vary according to use in context. Some words, for example, are used as nouns, verbs, and adjectives.

These statements merely suggest the complexity and some difficulties of learning to read English and also imply the satisfactions in reading a language so rich and challenging.

## Purpose of This Presentation

The purpose of this chapter is to consider reading as an integrating cluster of thoughtful processes — comprehension, location, evaluation, organization, and retention — which are important in recreation and study.

### READING TO COMPREHEND

Comprehension is a crucial basic factor in reading, for it is necessary in all reading processes and skills. There is no understanding, organizing, evaluating, or, for that matter, location or worthwhile retention without it.

---

[1] Gertrude Hildreth, *Teaching Spelling* (New York: Henry Holt and Company, 1955), p. 3.

[2] Ernest Horn, "Phonics and Spelling," *Journal of Education,* 136:233–234, May, 1954.

## Some General Considerations

Since the child reads by perceiving words and their relationships with other words, it is important to consider the acquisition of word meanings, activities for developing comprehension, and skills related to comprehension.

*The acquisition of meanings of words.* A young child finds that by saying a word, he can receive service. At an early age, he learns, for example, that by saying the word *water,* he can obtain a drink of water. His repeated experience with this word gives him an understanding of its value. He realizes that the request *water* (please?) brings a response from his mother of a cup of cool colorless liquid which quenches his thirst. Gradually he increases meanings of the word *water:* quenches thirst; a clear liquid; wet. Other meanings develop as his needs grow. By the time he recognizes the word *water* in print, he will associate it with the concepts that he built earlier. As he grows, he meets other situations which make it important for him to use the word *water* with both noun and verb meanings such as: bath *water, water* in the bath tub or wash basin; *water* in the river, pond, lake, or ocean; to *water* the lawn, the shrubs, or the flowers; rain *water* or well *water;* eyes *water* when you cry; to *water* — weaken by adding water; the ice cream makes the child's mouth *water.* In addition there are many uses in connection with nouns, such as: *water* buffalo, *water* clock, *water*fall, *water* lily, *water* front, *water* line, *water* main, *water*shed, *water*mellon, *water* level, *water*spout, *water*tight, *water*way, *water* wheel.

The significance of the above is the variety of meanings which a child has gained. An individual who has had meager experiences has not derived some of these; one who has had extensive experiences may have developed these and others. Some children with limited backgrounds require further study of the word. The teacher in addition to discussions and readings, may use still pictures of a *water*fall, motion pictures, or filmstrips to extend the concept of *water.*

The meaning which a child obtains when he reads a familiar word depends upon his past experiences, his mind-set, and the context. In reading a familiar word in a sentence the child will generally obtain an idea similar to the one he would derive if the word were spoken to him in the same or similar type of sentence.

The problem is not so simple when the word a child reads is not a familiar one. In such a situation he has several avenues for obtaining meaning: he may try to get understanding from the context, from a picture which accompanies the text, by asking the teacher or someone else what the word means, by finding the word in a dictionary, or by studying the structure of the word — its root and its affixes. The procedure to which a child will turn to determine the meaning of a word will depend to a great extent upon his training, experience, and personal qualities. For example, in a football story, Bill may read, "John returned the kick twenty yards." Two words in the sentence may cause concern to a reader without knowledge of football language. How can a boy return a kick? That is the question. What does "returned" mean? By use of structural analysis, he can see that *turn* is the root word meaning "change direction," *re* is a prefix meaning "back," and *ed* connotes past time, so he thinks *brought back* or *carried back*. Now the question arises: Carried back what? One who has not played football or has not observed it, may be baffled, but he can "put two and two together" and realize that the writer meant by the word *kick* the thing kicked and that would be the ball. Were there a picture of the play, the meaning would probably be clear. To a boy in the intermediate grades who plays football and understands the terms used in the game, the sentence should give no difficulty. In his case, he understands the sentence without study of the context, structural analysis, or use of a dictionary.[3]

There are particularly two points to note in the above: (1) The reader must have had real or vicarious experience by means of activities, or through pictures, discussion, study, or thinking about the context. (2) He must be able to associate the symbols he reads with concepts or processes he has developed.

*Activities to develop comprehension.* The approach to meaning must be active. No individual can experience directly everything he reads. He must have other avenues for comprehension. It is impossible here to discuss all the active approaches to achievement of meaning. A few will be illustrative of what can be done.

1. *The project.* Several kinds of projects may be used. As an example, a primary group initiated a trip to a botanical garden.[4] The children talked about flowers and although they had little experience with them they were interested in several types — roses, tulips, lilies, and violets. They set up their purposes and planned their trip. Committees were formed to study the various flowers. They read supplementary books and looked at pictures of flowers they hoped to see. The

[3] Arthur I. Gates, *The Improvement of Reading,* third edition (New York: Macmillan Company, 1947), pp. 180–185.
[4] The only part of the project reported is that relating to flowers.

preproject discussion alerted them concerning what to expect, and how to learn a great deal on their trip. During the visit to the garden, the committees looked at the flowers selected as well as other kinds. They attended a talk on flowers arranged by their teacher with the superintendent of the garden.

When they returned to school the next day, there were interesting discussions about flowers — their beauty, their colors, and their fragrance. Pictures were looked at in the literature collected. Simple books were withdrawn from the library and "read." Pictures were drawn of some of the flowers. The children's interests were enhanced in seeing flowers and by reading about them.

2. *The unit approach to comprehension.* One of the most satisfying types of study on any level of learning is the unit. A unit is "a comprehensive and significant aspect" of experience, of an art, of science, or of conduct which causes a change in personality.[5] The work on a unit is a purposeful, active, and integrating enterprise which crosses subject-matter lines and is directed to objectives formulated by a group or an individual. A good plan for a unit comprises:

*a*) The approach or approaches
*b*) Tentative objectives
*c*) Appraisal and testing
*d*) Teacher and pupil procedures
*e*) Bibliographies — teacher, pupil
*f*) Selected materials and data
*g*) Child activities including problems and projects
*h*) Integration and correlation
*i*) Outcomes, understandings, and products
*j*) Culminating activities
*k*) Evaluative procedures
*l*) Use of skills and abilities developed.

A group perhaps two or three years more advanced than the one which conducted the project described above, wanted to study about newspapers to determine whether they should publish one in their school. Following the steps suggested, they brought in newspapers of various kinds — weeklies, dailies, foreign, school, college, and community papers — and placed them on the reading table. They read these papers and noted the important sections: news, editorial, sports, society, travel, and so on. They obtained books in the library about school news-

[5] See Henry C. Morrison, *The Practice of Teaching in the Secondary School,* revised edition (Chicago: University of Chicago Press, 1931), pp. 24–25.

papers. They noted from the samples they collected and from the books they read the kinds of papers schools produced. They studied, discussed, read, evaluated, and planned, but most of all they learned a great deal about various kinds of newspapers. They comprehended the kind of news that was published, the advertising that was presented, and the different formats. They learned about the many types of newspaper work — writing news articles, writing editorials, soliciting advertising, proofreading, meeting deadlines, and distributing the papers — from their reading, from interviews with newspaper people, and through discussions about the various phases of the unit. These activities motivated reading of various types.[6]

3. *Other types of related activity approaches to comprehension.* Among the other important approaches to comprehension are various types of integrating activities: historical reading, literary reading, organizations, practical mechanics, arts and crafts, science, sports, vocations, humor, storytelling, and current events. Problem solving is important to understanding, and reading is vital to the solving of many problems and the answering of many questions. Understanding is enhanced by reading, studying, interviewing, observing, viewing, discussing, questioning, and answering. In attempting to comprehend, learners may study nature — mountains, rivers, oceans, lakes, plateaus, canyons, and other formations either directly or indirectly. They view construction of houses, office buildings, stadiums, and fairgrounds. They use maps, charts, tables, recordings, radio, television, and motion pictures. These can be made incentives to reading. Some require reading. None need detract from reading. All may be made means for understanding and evaluation.[7]

*The skills approach to reading comprehension.* The skills approach may not be necessary for rapid learners, but it can be advantageous to them. This approach seems to be of high value to those who may consider reading, for one reason or another, less enthusiastically than the best readers of the class. In other words, skills exercises should be provided for the average and the slow learners who need them. In providing such exercises for the slow learners, care should be taken not to force upon the rapid learners activities of no value to them. The abilities

    [6] James A. Fitzgerald and Patricia G. Fitzgerald, *Methods and Curricula in Elementary Education* (Milwaukee: The Bruce Publishing Company, 1955), pp. 276–313.

    [7] See Donald D. Durrell, "Development of Comprehension and Interpretation," *Reading in the Elementary School,* Forty-Eighth Yearbook of the National Society for the Study of Education, Part II, 1949, pp. 193–198.

of children who require skill training should be appraised and materials and activities should be provided to meet their needs. Youngsters should be "paced" in such a way that simple basic exercises will be presented first; gradually, as they become successful in using these items, the complexity of the exercises may be increased.[8]

Motivation is an important process in the teaching of comprehension skills. Stimulating the child to want to read, first for a single purpose and subsequently for other purposes, is important. A variety of materials selected to develop skills in reading should be provided. Those necessary to help a child overcome a difficulty or to eradicate a deficiency are desirable. Those that provide information about a topic in which a child is interested will be read with enthusiasm.

A record should be kept of the specific skill exercises and of the scores in comprehension and performance on various levels. Satisfaction by each child in having improved his record from one week to another or during a semester may be achieved by the use of a progress chart. An old dictum, "Success succeeds," is true for almost all children. Unless a child can succeed in improving his efficiency, he is likely to lose interest in the effort and the work. If a child is not improving in his performance, the teacher should determine the reason. If the materials are unattractive or uninviting, interesting ones should be procured. If the exercises are failed because they are too difficult, less difficult ones, with which he can succeed must be provided. The child should begin where he can work effectively and successfully. When he has mastered a skill, he should not be kept too long working on exercises designed to improve this skill, except as he may need review for maintenance of it; other skills which require his attention should be studied.

## Some Specific Suggestions for Comprehension Activities

Many types of activities may be considered for developing comprehension in reading. Exercises in workbooks should be used and others may be initiated by the teacher. Among them, the following have been employed effectively:

*Developing vocabulary comprehension.*    Simple exercises are used to increase vocabulary comprehension.

1. *The Fireman.*    First-grade children dictated the following story to the teacher who wrote it on the chalkboard. They read it and discussed it.

---

[8] Durrell, *op. cit.,* pp. 198–204. Kathleen B. Hester, *Teaching Every Child to Read* (New York: Harper Brothers, 1955), pp. 194–225.

> The fireman came to school.
> The fireman is our friend.
> He told us how to be safe from fire.
> He helps children.

The teacher wrote the following questions on the board and discussed the answers suggested for the blanks. She gave each child a mimeographed copy of the questions. Each wrote answers in the blanks; the answers were checked and the papers returned to the children for further study.

> What did the fireman do? He —— to school.
> Whose friend is the fireman? He is —— friend.
> What did he tell us about? How to be safe from ——.
> Who helps us to be safe from fire? The ——.

2. *Metals.*   After reading a story about metals, children of a fourth grade may be challenged to strike out the words that are not metals.

| | | | |
|---|---|---|---|
| silver | copper | dirt | stone |
| gold | coal | steel | iron |

3. *Others.*   Pupils can also be guided to find words in a paragraph which mean the same as given words: say (tell), wide (broad), pole (stick), raise (lift). Similarly, they may be directed to find antonyms of given words.

*Understanding the main idea of a selection.*   Many children who can read words have difficulty in getting the main idea of a paragraph or the general significance of a report or story. Practice in putting the paragraph into one's own words is advisable. A pupil who reads a paragraph should be able to state the topic. He may improve his understanding of the main idea by picking out the topic sentence. Gates and Peardon have developed excellent *Practice Exercises in Reading* on levels approximately from grade three to six to help pupils to read to appreciate the general significance of a paragraph. Using such exercises, a child may obtain practice in selecting the best title, recognizing the significance of a story, and understanding meanings. He can find his mistakes and learn to correct them.[9] The workbooks accompanying basic readers also supply excellent exercises for improving this skill.

Poetry may be used to test the ability of boys and girls to understand the general significance and to critically evaluate the title. The poem *Washing* by John Drinkwater may be read aloud to them without

---

[9] Arthur I. Gates and Celeste Comegys Peardon, *Practice Exercises in Reading: Type A. Reading to Appreciate the General Significance of a Selection* (Bureau of Publications, Teachers College, Columbia University, New York).

Reading for comprehension skills

divulging the title. Each can indicate what he thinks would be a good title. The children may also recognize the distinct sense of humor which is so well brought out. Many other poems lend themselves to the enjoyment of humor and give pupils an opportunity to indicate the main idea conveyed. *Presents* by Marchette Chute, *The Swing* by Robert Louis Stevenson, and *Troubles* by Dorothy Aldis are useful in achieving such an objective.

*Determining the main points in an article.* Comprehending organization is a problem in reading from primary school through college and university. In the primary grades, children can be asked to tell the number of paragraphs in a selection, and to indicate what each paragraph is about.

In the intermediate grades, it is appropriate to have pupils read longer selections and to note the essential points involved. From the level of determining the two or three points in a brief selection, the pupils may be guided to the stage of determining the basic divisions of a chapter of several pages. The outlining of a selection which consists of two or three principal sections and noting the subpoints in each should be taught.

*Reading to note details.* The purpose of reading to note details is to obtain the essential facts in a selection. The retention of many details is necessary in study of science or health. Gates and Peardon have presented practice exercises in which a list of questions follows an explanation or a description. *The White Pine Tree,* for example, is a "description" of the growth and use of the white pine. This is followed by several questions in the form of multiple-choice exercises to which the reader reacts by checking the correct answer to each question.[10]

*Reading to find specific facts.* Reading to find specific facts should be a simple exercise at first, in which a child searches through a paragraph for factual answers to two or three questions, or it may be a more complex assignment in which a student searches in a library for information needed to solve a problem. A pupil who has been assigned several questions to be answered in a unit for which there is a textbook and a set of junior encyclopedias has a relatively simple project. He should learn how to proceed on such a project by using all aids available to him. He can use the table of contents of the text and note the chapter titles. He should learn to read the main headings and subheadings of a chapter in an effort to find a fact. He should learn how to use the index. He should read the lists of tables and charts to find one which presents evidence for which he is searching. The pupil should be taught also how to use an encyclopedia. Using the index, he may determine two or three headings in which possible data concerning a question may be found. If, for example, he wishes to answer a question about Forests, he may find a reference in the alphabetic presentation in the Volume labled *F*. In this, he reads the headings: Forest Protects Water Sources. Life Struggle of the Forest. Fire the Greatest Enemy. The Men Who Fight Fires. Other Enemies of the Forest. Good Forestry Today. Farm Forestry. The World Extent of Forests. If he is unable to locate what he desires in one of these headings, he may turn to a Fact Index in which other materials such as areas of National and State Forestry in the United States are presented.[11]

*Determining the correct sequence of sentences in a paragraph.* Practice in comprehending sequence should begin in kindergarten and con-

---

[10] Gates and Peardon, *Practice Exercises in Reading:* Type D. Reading to Note Details, *op. cit.*

[11] See *Compton's Pictured Encyclopedia.* The *World Book Encyclopedia* and *Brittanica Junior* are equally helpful.

tinue through the elementary school years. The ability to recognize first things as coming before others is a valuable asset in living and in reading.

If a child in the primary grades is asked to repeat a report he has heard, he often presents an inexact sequence of points or episodes. An exercise such as the following helps in sequence arrangement.

The teacher may write on the chalkboard the three sentences in wrong sequence:

> Come again some other day.
> Little Tommy wants to play.
> Rain, rain, go away.

After discussion, the children will rearrange these sentences to show the correct order.

> Rain, rain go away.
> Come again some other day.
> Little Tommy wants to play.

*Comprehending the correct sequence of events in a story.* Primary children who listened to the *Story of the Three Bears* should relate the points of the story in proper order.

A mimeographed test may be arranged in which there are some facts out of sequence. The problem is to renumber the facts in the correct order. The following illustrates this type of test:

——— Goldilocks went to the house of the Bears.
——— The Bears made their porridge.
——— "Somebody has been lying in my bed," said the Big Bear.
——— "Somebody has been sitting in my chair and has sat the bottom through," said the Little Bear.
——— "Somebody has been at my porridge," said the Middle-Sized Bear.
——— Goldilocks ran and tumbled herself out of the window.

*Recognizing the sequence of historical events.* Reading cannot be taught effectively in isolation in a reading class only. It should be considered in all areas of the curriculum. For example, in studying the colonial period of American History, it is necessary for the learner to obtain a correct perspective of events to understand the various movements important in the development of the country. Discoveries, explorations, westward movements, establishing settlements, fighting for life and sustenance, building homes in the forests and prairies, living in various types of communities, problems of health, the beginning of schools, government in the town meetings, moral training — all should become parts of a unified and sequential understanding of the readers.

As pupils read and study, they develop sequence sense and understand for example, that America was discovered first, next explored, and then settled.

*Developing time and space concepts.* In reading history, a pupil should learn the significance of geography, and recognize the importance of space and time. Ten years and one hundred years may seem to be about the same to a young pupil because he cannot comprehend the duration of either. Integration of geography, history, science, arithmetic, reading, and the many areas of language is accordingly helpful in laying the foundation for clarifying time concepts. The use of a time line would indicate that a period of thirty years which a parent has lived is three times as long as that of ten years a child has lived and only one-half as long as that of a grandmother who has lived sixty years.

The child's space concepts are also undeveloped, as incorrect sometimes as the Long Island woman's idea of distance, who affirmed emphatically that she could drive her automobile from New York to California in a day and a half. Map reading and interpretation are important. A child who rides ten miles and then one hundred miles in an auto and is shown the route on a road map begins to understand the concept of distance in miles. Required instruction on units of time and space aids in placing events of history in proper perspective.[12] Understanding of space and time concepts assists learners to comprehend the impact of change upon our civilization. For example, they will gradually realize that trips which required months in pioneer times are now completed in hours because air travel has replaced the foot and horse locomotion of earlier times. Such knowledge is the basis for understanding that improvements in communications and transportation have modified living in our country.

*Reading to follow directions.* A most practical kind of reading is that which guides a child to learn how to follow directions accurately and precisely, for in one way or another he will be striving to follow directions throughout his entire life. Nurses must follow directions in administering to the sick. Doctors, electricians, farmers, teachers, housewives, and many others have need to read and follow directions in their vocations. Inability to do this often causes frustration, failure, and sometimes disaster. Informal tests may be designed to appraise a child's ability to follow precise directions. With consideration concerning the performance on tests and knowledge gained by observation and inter-

[12] See Kathleen B. Hester, *Teaching Every Child to Read* (New York: Harper Brothers, 1955), pp. 215–220.

view, a pupil may be given exercises which fit his level of ability in following directions. A simple type of exercise follows:

1. Draw two squares at the right just like this one □ about one inch apart.

2. Draw circles the same size as this one ○ about one inch below the squares.

3. Draw a line from the middle of the first square to the middle of the last circle. Draw another line from the middle of the last square to the middle of the first circle.

4. Do these lines cross each other? ——

Another helpful procedure is to print directions on the chalkboard. These should be directed to individuals of a group so that the ones who are to carry out the directions will be alerted by silent reading to the project assigned. A simple direction about a paper may be set forth as follows for an elementary group.

### Directions for Committee A on Creative Writing

1. Members of Committee A will meet at the front table at 10:00 a.m., Wednesday.
2. Each member should bring his notes for the story he will write.
3. Each member should bring writing paper and two sharpened pencils.
4. Each member should write the title of his story on the top line of a page.
5. Each should write his name on the second line in the upper left-hand corner.
6. Each should write the date on the second line in the upper right-hand corner.

Such directions should be read silently by each child and carried out individually.

Many opportunities for similar directions present themselves to the teacher of the elementary school groups. The following are a few types:

1. Directions for making boat or airplane models
2. Directions for constructing an aquarium or a terrarium
3. Directions for performing experiments in science
4. Directions for forming a reading club
5. Directions for planting a flower bed
6. Directions for Arbor Day tree planting
7. Directions for playing a game
8. Directions for planning an oral reading program.

*Reading to perceive relationships and make comparisons.* If reading is not related in some way to experience it is likely to be without much

value. Elementary school children enjoy reading about things that have
some connection with their experiences. If a boy has a dog, it is probable
that he will be interested in a "boy and dog" story. His thinking as he
reads will concern his own dog and the dog in the story. He will enjoy
making comparisons between himself and the boy he is reading about.
He will note the relationships of boy and dog in the story. Perhaps
he will learn how to care for his dog in a more appropriate way because of the narrative. He may feel that the boy in the story should
have treated his dog differently.

*Reading to predict outcomes and draw inferences.* A most valuable skill which should be taught and practiced throughout elementary
school is that of drawing inferences from facts. An appealing exercise
is to have children read, or the teacher may read to them, a part of a
story and have them complete it orally or in writing. This type of exercise is sometimes called reading to predict outcomes. It assists children
to use imagination and develop creativity.

A situation can be set up indicating there is drought, hot winds, and
high temperatures which scorch the vegetation and the land. Reasoning
from these facts will indicate that poor crops result, and inference can
be made to the effect that people do not have sufficient food.

Another example might concern a situation in which some small
towns were built in a deep narrow valley which ran down from a gently
sloping plateau in the mountains to a river below. On the occasion of
a terrific rain storm over the plateau in the mountains, the rain water
flowed through the narrow valley causing deep rushing floods in many
places. Inferences can be drawn from the situation and the circumstances. Among them, pupils might infer the following:

1. Many buildings were destroyed.
2. Farm animals died in the floods.
3. Trees and other vegetation were uprooted.
4. People, because only a little advance notice was given, were unable
   to withdraw from the valley.
5. Some people were trapped on the roofs of the buildings.
6. Some people climbed trees to avoid the swirling waters.
7. Some people were drowned.
8. The Federal Government sent in relief through the Army.
9. The Red Cross set up shelters and served food to the homeless.
10. The Federal Government declared the towns a disaster area.

Scores of opportunities occur in social studies, science, history,
and geography for drawing inferences and for evaluating them. The
validity of inferences and evaluations depends upon comprehension and
interpretation of facts comprehended.

*Formulating basic questions.* One of the most neglected skills in reading in the elementary school is that of guiding pupils to raise basic questions through reading. We are enthused when a bright student asks thought-provoking questions even if our best response is to suggest sources where he may find answers. The skill of formulating important questions can be taught in the middle grades and often earlier by having pupils write questions about materials in a paragraph, in a section of a chapter, or in a short article. After an article has been read, each individual can write what he thinks are the important questions. A discusison by the group will help to clarify the thinking of individuals. Skills may be developed also by incorporating in a unit examination on colonization the question: What were the most pressing problems or questions which confronted the American colonists? Pupils of an intermediate class, putting themselves in the place of the colonists, after some study of the unit, raised such questions as the following:

1. How can we (the colonists) feed ourselves?
2. How can we obtain clothing for our families?
3. How can we grow corn, potatoes, and other vegetables?
4. How can we protect ourselves from weather, wild animals, insects, and unfriendly Indians?
5. Which Indians are friendly and why are they so?
6. Why are some of the Indians unfriendly?

These questions, not all of which were answered completely in the unit, became topics for discussion and investigation.

*Reading to comprehend figurative language.* Thoughtlessly we often assign a selection which contains figurative language which may not be intelligible to a group because of use of the simile, metaphor, hyperbole, or other figures of speech. For example, consider such expressions as those in italics in the following sentences.

He is a *deadbeat.* He stood up like the *Rock of Gibraltar.* Keep your *chin up.* The child said, "I saw a *million* bumblebees."

Pupils should be guided to understand the meanings of such figures of speech, each of which conveys something other than what it seems to say. If a man is said to be a *deadbeat,* he is thought of as one not financially responsible, one who has a tendency to "sponge" on another, or who avoids paying his debts. If, however, a boy is said to be *dead beat,* the speaker would probably mean that the boy is tired out, almost exhausted from exertion — a meaning quite different from that of *deadbeat* in the previous example. All reading is accordingly a striving for understanding, and in such striving, context clues, experience, and active use of the dictionary are important aids.

In summary, to teach comprehension, a teacher must continually challenge learners with materials that are interesting and useful in promoting the thinking required in the various areas of elementary school curriculum. Thoughtful reading is needed in arithmetic to understand problems. Directions must be followed precisely in science to perform experiments. Situations must be interpreted intelligently in social studies to promote justice and freedom in a democratic society. Word power and use must be construed properly by the reader in assimilating thought and feeling of writers.

## LOCATING INFORMATION

It is obvious that one cannot read a book, a chapter of a book, or a sentence in a book until he locates and obtains the book. One may have access to the finest library, but if he does not know how to find information in that library in books, periodicals, monographs, and other reference materials, it will be of little value to him.

### A General Statement

Every person should learn how to locate what he needs for the purposes that arise in and out of school. When an individual is confronted with a problem, he must define it, limit it, and determine what he knows and what he does not know about it. Having determined what he needs to learn, he must use location skills to obtain the information. If, in the elementary school, a pupil can learn these skills, he has developed a cluster group of tools which will enhance his ability to meet the problems of reading and study. Ways of locating information in books, periodicals, and other sources are presented by Butler who described technics of instruction and procedures for use of the library.[13] In the present-day curriculums, the library is not just a supplementary instrument of instruction; it is essential to the development of education of the individuals who must meet the complex problems of life. The purpose in the following section is to suggest some of the simple skills which a pupil needs in reading — skills that are basic to finding information of value. The explanation will be confined insofar as possible to locational technics.

### Developing Some Specific Location Skills

Location skills are interrelated with comprehension, evaluation organ-

---

[13] George E. Butler, "Using the Elementary School Library," *Education*, 84: 213–216, December, 1963.

ization, and retention skills. One is of value in teaching another. It is recognized that in order to find materials, a learner must comprehend the kinds he needs. To use the encyclopedia, for example, he must know the value of such aids as the alphabet, the index, cross references, bibliographies, and so on.

*Locating a word or words.* Frequently, location of information depends upon the finding of a word — sometimes a key word, a name of a person, a thing, or a title. Simple exercises can be used to help the child in such procedures. For example, a reader who is asked to find the word in a paragraph that tells how John felt when he saw a big bear following him in the woods, will discover the word "scared." A child who is directed to find the word in a sentence that rhymes with *ring,* locates the word *sing.* In another type of exercise, children will read to note the names of plants mentioned in an article. Such an exercise could be used to help the child read rapidly for one specific purpose.

*Locating a sentence or a thought.* A location exercise, which is comprehensional as well, might concern the finding of a sentence which tells a fact. This should be useful in grade one, or it can be planned for the intermediate grades. For example, children might be asked to find the sentence, "Bob was frightened" in the paragraph:

> Bob was a beautiful horse. When he was young, he played in the pasture and ran with other horses. When he was three years old, he was led into the barn for the first time, and tied to a manger. Bob was frightened. He kicked the door and the sides of the stall. The farmer tried to pet him but Bob was afraid. At last the farmer and Bob became good friends.

Children were asked to determine what Bob did when he was frightened. They could be asked to find out how the farmer finally got along with Bob.

*Learning to use the alphabet.* The alphabet is a timesaving device. Some children come to school knowing most of the letters of the alphabet. Others are slow to learn them. Dictionaries, encyclopedias, telephone directories, catalogs, and libraries make use of the alphabet. Children should know the alphabet thoroughly in order to use books efficiently. Beginnings can be made in the lower primary levels. The names of children on a committee or the names of the class members may be written by the teacher on the chalkboard in alphabetical order. A list of objects, plants, or animals could be written in the same way.

Individual picture dictionaries may be set up and hard word lists recorded in alphabetical order.

By the time the child has completed the third grade, he should be well aware of the values of alphabetical sequence in reading and writing, and should be able to use the alphabet to advantage in locating information in books. During the fourth grade, a normal pupil will have need for the alphabet from *a* to *z*. He should also know the letters which precede and follow a letter. Exercises to establish these skills are easily developed and many workbooks have such exercises. A worthwhile skill which facilitates the use of a dictionary is to know without hesitation the part — first, second, third, or fourth — in which words beginning with a specific letter appear. A pupil in the fourth grade, for example, should learn that words beginning with the letter *c* are in the first fourth of the dictionary, that words beginning with the letter *g* are in the second fourth, ones beginning with *o* are in the third part, and those beginning with *t* are in the fourth part. Pupils should be taught to arrange several words in alphabetical order. A second exercise could be to arrange several words beginning with the same letter in this order. A quite similar and valuable exercise would direct pupils to alphabetize words beginning with the same two letters.

*Learning to use the dictionary.* A knowledge of the alphabet is basic to the location of words in the dictionary.

1. *Using guide words.* Pupils should understand the value of guide words in finding words rapidly. Practice in their use should be carried on. A game which suggests the finding perhaps of three or four words as quickly as possible adds zest to the study.

2. *Finding the spelling of words.* Finding a word in the dictionary, when the first letter but not the second is known, is a valuable skill. The pupil may be certain that the first letter, for example, of *legitimate* is *l,* but is uncertain whether the second is *i* or *e*. Rather than search randomly, he should look through the words beginning with *l* that have *e* as a second letter, and achieve success. In case of another word, he may not be successful using *e* and so resorts to *i* in order to find it. Other location problems in finding words should be considered.

3. *Finding the correct pronunciation of a word.* Among the skills to be learned are: (*a*) locating the word; (*b*) noting its syllabication; (*c*) studying the respelling for pronunciation; (*d*) using properly the key to pronunciation and interpreting diacritical marks in enunciating the correct sounds of letters in the word; (*e*) using the primary

and secondary accent marks for proper pronunciation of the word. These require practice to achieve desirable proficiency.

4. *Locating the correct definition of the word.* Among the many definitions of a word often presented in a dictionary, there is usually one that is more meaningful in a specific context than the others. By means of evaluation and comparison, the right choice can be made.

5. *Finding and selecting appropriate synonyms and antonyms.* Good writing requires careful reading in the dictionary or in a thesaurus. After meaningful instruction, practice should develop skill and facility in location, evaluation, and selection of proper synonyms and antonyms.

*Locating information in an encyclopedia.* A child should become aware of the many values of an encyclopedia. He should know when it is necessary to use it. After recognizing a specific problem, and the need for information, he must select the key word or words to look for. Suppose he wants to learn more about the Declaration of Independence than his text tells him. He can select *Declaration* as the key word and in the volume which contains the entries beginning with the letter *D* find an excellent article on the Declaration of Independence. In this article, he may become interested in the desire of the colonists for independence. He may locate some pictures such as those of Jefferson, Adams, and Franklin discussing the draft prepared by Jefferson. Perhaps the reader would like to learn more about the men who signed the Declaration, particularly those who were prominent in planning and sponsoring it — Jefferson, Adams, Franklin, Hancock.

By locating the volume that contains the entries beginning with *J*, Jefferson's life and works may be studied. Jefferson's work on the Declaration, as President of the United States, in behalf of the Statute of Virginia for Religious Freedom, and his devotion to education may be located. Cross references and bibliographies are available in either the article on Declaration of Independence or on Thomas Jefferson. Sources suggested may be used to find further information about other men and facts.

*Using books for locating information.* The pupil should know the kind of information found in a textbook, catalog, or the *World Almanac*. A study of the introductions in these assist him to understand their use. The introduction and the preface usually clarify objectives. In the table of contents in a textbook, chapter titles generally and section titles frequently, are found. An index reveals many locational facts about major and minor topics covered. When center headings and subheadings are included in the context, they can be scanned rapidly to find the desired information. Lists of tables, charts, and figures may indicate the kind of knowledge for which a reader is looking. Some books contain maps, photographs, and drawings which offer useful information.

*Skimming.* Skimming is a type of rapid but efficient reading in which one skips irrelevant facts and obtains pertinent information. The purpose of skimming may be to locate a fact, a name, a title, or the answer to a specific question. A pupil should be taught to skim to locate a word, a sentence, a thought, or a paragraph desirable for a purpose.

Especially in some books which do not have tables of contents or indexes, skimming is the most efficient way in which specific information can be located. Training in this type of reading should begin with simple exercises and lead into more complex types. The skimming of a short selection to find the page where "John meets Sammy, the white rabbit" is relatively an easy assignment. Skimming is practiced, for example, when a learner reads rapidly through a book or article on animals to determine the types that live in the polar regions. An article on plants may be skimmed to find the kinds most useful in the United States for making bread. Skimming a book to determine the many improvements made in aviation is a more complex type of reading.[14]

*Locating materials in a library.* Using the library effectively is becoming more and more important in elementary education. Accordingly, locational technics and facilities must be studied, practiced, and utilized. The librarian and her assistants are highly efficient in helping a child.

The common reference books should be pointed out to children and instruction given in their use. Among these are: Junior encyclopedias, *Who's Who in America, American Men of Science, Who Was Who,* the *Book Catalog, The Reader's Guide to Current Literature, The Index to Poetry,* atlases, almanacs, and abstracts.

Among the most valuable and most used location devices is the card catalog. Pupils are interested when they are aware of its importance and its arrangement whether the Dewey Decimal or the Library of Congress system is followed. The importance particularly of the author card, the title card, and the subject card should be emphasized. Instruction in using the card catalog to locate books related to a topic or problem is very valuable. The writing of withdrawal slips neatly and accurately should be practiced.[15]

---

[14] Miles A. Tinker, *Teaching Elementary Reading* (New York: Appleton-Century-Crofts, Inc., 1952), pp. 183–185.

[15] Butler, *op. cit.*

*Using bibliographies, cross references, and footnotes.* The bibliography is important because it is economical. Pupils soon recognize that a bibliography at the end of a chapter is generally pointed to the theme of the chapter and is worth using in further study. They also soon realize that footnotes in an article or chapter of a book are similarly useful. Cross references in encyclopedias, dictionaries, and particularly in the card catalog present leads which if followed are fruitful. The use of these should be understood and practiced.

*Locating information on maps.* Everyone who drives a car locates information on a map — generally on a road map, but sometimes on the map of a city, state, or country. Orientation should be taught; learners must be able to use the map to decide whether to travel in one direction or another. The distance from town to town may be determined, the child learns, by using the scale of miles in the legend. Children have need to read maps in atlases, geographies, history texts, science books, and weather bulletins. The information supplied is different from one map to another. On a map in geography, one can ascertain the largest cities and capitals of states; on a physical geography map, one can determine altitudes as well as divides, lowlands, and highlands. On weather maps, "highs," "lows," and "fronts" can be located. It has been shown that instruction in map reading can be beneficial to pupils on levels beginning in the primary grades.[16]

*Locating and using graphs, charts, diagrams, tabular and pictorial materials.* A child, who records his progress in spelling on a progress chart, studies the chart to see how well he has done, to find out whether he has improved from week to week, and to determine the change in achievement from the first week of the semester to the final week. Progress in other areas may be recorded and studied similarly. A diagram is a drawing or a sketch which presents information. It may be a plan of a house or a presentation of a mechanical device. The pupil can locate information on a plot for example of a basketball court. He can find the size of the area and the distance from the "free throw line" to the basket. The coach may diagram plays and the players will read them to obtain information about how to implement them.

A graph may be a line, sometimes laid off on grid or squared paper. Such a graph may indicate for example the population growth of the United States from colonial times to the present. The location of information on this type of graph is not difficult for the elementary school

[16] Haig A. Rushdoony, "Achievement in Map-Reading: An Experimental Study," *Elementary School Journal*, 64:70–75, November, 1963.

child instructed in its use. Tables generally present quantitative or statistical information on subjects such as health, social studies, science, and mathematics. Reading of tables about population, production, consumption, or transportation is a skill to be understood and practiced. Pictorial materials — photographs and drawings — are useful. An old maxim suggests that "a picture is worth a thousand words." By viewing of pictures, a reader may sometimes recognize relationships and locate more detailed information than that which he finds in accompanying context. After effective instruction on graphs, charts, diagrams, and other types of symbolic materials, adequate practice on their use should be planned and carried out.

*Locating questions and answers to questions.* One of the most important study and reading skills is that of the location of questions and the answers to them. Study questions are frequently found at the end of a chapter. Questions and answers to them are located often by study of a unit, after careful reading of materials in texts and supplementary sources. The determination of *the* important question to be answered in a debate or discussion may be the difference between success or failure.

*Finding materials for a problem, a project, or an activity.* All the skills suggested above — locating words and sentences, using the alphabetic organization of dictionaries, encyclopedias, card catalogs, tables of content, and symbolic designs are very important in reading. Using cross references, bibliographies, and footnotes adds immeasurably to a pupil's locational skills. Location and comprehension of information on maps, charts, graphs, and other pictorial materials facilitate reading. Finally, locating important questions and ferreting out adequate answers enhance skills and abilities for solving problems, executing projects, and carrying on activities in almost every field.

## EVALUATING ACCURATELY AND CRITICALLY

A reader today is exposed to many kinds of published materials — contextual, pictorial, and graphic. In school, a pupil should be guided to evaluate these critically and accurately. Whether he is reading a published report in a newspaper, an article on moon shots in a magazine, or advertising, he should ascertain what is true and what is false, what is relevant to the topic at hand and what is irrelevant, what is fact and what is opinion, what is emotive and what is logical, what is authoritative and what is propaganda. He should be able to determine the degree of authenticity of sources and to differentiate reasonable inferences from those improperly drawn. He must learn to distinguish between conclusions based upon adequate evidence and those based upon insufficient facts.

## Appraising Ideas in the Light of Experience and Knowledge

A pupil must compare what he reads with facts which he possesses. If he has insufficient facts or experiences for making a judgment, he should search for information and keep an open and an inquiring mind to determine whether what he reads is corroborated by evidence.

Suppose, for example, that a child wrote a story about a fight between a dog and a racoon in which the racoon scratched the dog, ran high into the tree, and the dog followed to force the racoon down from his perch. One or more of the pupils who read this story will question the statement about the dog going high into a tree.

One child might say, "We have a bulldog and he cannot climb a tree." Another may agree with this statement. After discussion, the children talk to their parents and to others about the dog's ability to climb trees. They are prompted to read about dogs. In these ways they check this statement with their experience, with the experience of others, and in sources concerning dogs.

## Differentiating Essential Materials From the Nonessential

In a situation in which a group is making a booklet about the domestic animals of the United States, a pupil may read a report of the bear and deer of mountainous areas. His materials are questioned by members of the class because these two animals are not classified as domestic. He argues the point, and recourse is made to encyclopedias and other sources. After several children have brought in reports, the issue is cleared up by defining what is meant by "domestic" animals, and the bear and deer are ruled out as not domestic. The pupil who reported the information about bear and deer may affirm that his information is true, but he should be helped to understand that, though true, it is not essential in meeting the purpose of the class project. Pupils sooner or later must recognize the importance of purpose in reading, learn to select materials which are pertinent, and to discard those which are not.

## Checking Validity of Statements

Throughout a person's life, he must continually consider the truth or

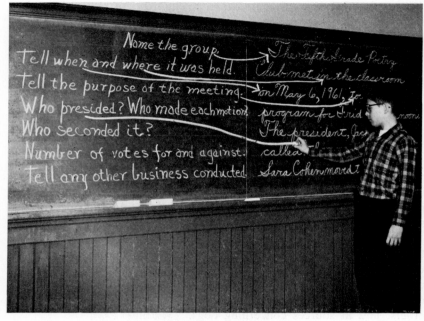

Exercises in logic

falsity of statements and reports. There are many superstitions such as the following:

It is bad luck to walk under a ladder.
It is bad luck for three people to light cigarettes on one match.
If a groundhog sees his shadow on February 2, there will be six weeks of hard winter.
Potatoes and corn should be planted in the light of the moon.

These and other statements may be questioned and investigated. For example, the statement about the groundhog can be considered in a science course. Wide-awake pupils will ask questions. How does a groundhog know that February 2 comes on a certain day? Is it true that there will be six weeks of hard winter if he sees his shadow? The weather reports for six weeks following February 2 are available for many years. For the pupils who are interested, there is great satisfaction in showing that such a statement is not a valid one.[17] In like

[17] Glenn O. Blough, Julius Schwartz, and Albert J. Huggett, *Elementary School Science and How to Teach It,* revised edition (New York: Henry Holt and Company, Inc., 1958), p. 283.

manner the idea that certain seeds grow better if planted in the "light" of the moon may be appraised. A careful search for facts about how plants grow and their requirements — water, temperature, and fertilizer — will help pupils to refute such a statement. An interesting project on superstitions and their falsity can be carried on with value in an intermediate class.

Another approach to checking the validity of statements is to read the advertisements in many of the magazines and newspapers. A teacher can present a few statements and ask children what they think of them. A little research will refute the statement: "This product holds relief for everyone." Pupils may appraise claims such as: "X car is the most economical car on the market." "Y is the richest most complete motor oil in the world." Investigations of slogans as, "The Biggest Little City in the State," and "The Finest State to Live In" may be carried on. Pupils can become aware of the types of writers, the purpose of their writing, and the characteristics of the periodicals in which they write. In evaluation, it is important that pupils appraise a writer's motive for writing a slogan or advertisement. A careful consideration of the language used helps the child to recognize the possibility that the writing may have some merit and that, although it may be true in some situations, it is not so in all instances. Sometimes there is a conflict in statements. It is advisable then to consider the validity of the sources. An encyclopedia, for example, is more authentic than a popular periodical. A physician would be more likely to be a reliable authority than an ordinary magazine writer on a problem in medicine. If a problem concerned science, it is highly likely that a scientist would be a better authority than a mechanic. An expert on European history would be a more authentic source of information about the Crimean War than an expert on American history. If a problem of religious tenets arose, a theologian would be a more reliable consultant than a layman.

There may be a conflict in textbooks of science concerning scientific accomplishments or a conflict in geographies about the borders between countries. Sometimes a reader can settle such a contradiction himself by noting the date of printing or the copyright. A science book or a geography book with a copyright date of twenty years ago is outmoded because of the rapid changes in science and in geography. A young reader should learn the necessity for understanding that the validity of a statement may be affected by the author, the source, the purpose, and the date of publication.

## Distinguishing Facts From Untruths and Opinions

An evaluative activity may be begun with a simple exercise similar to the following:

*Directions.* Place a *T* after a true statement, an *F* after a false one, and an *O* after one that is an opinion.

1. A tomato is a vegetable. . . . . . . . . . . . . . .  F
2. The principal food factory of the common plant is the leaf. . .  T
3. Warblers will eat their own weight of food in a day. . . .  T
4. A cat is the nicest of all pets. . . . . . . . . . .  O
5. Sitting in an automobile is generally unsafe in a thunderstorm.  F
6. The pulley is a more important simple machine than the lever.  O

Those who do not agree on the appraisal of one or more of these statements may be directed to reading which will help in determining which are facts, which are opinions, and which are false.

Another simple type of evaluative exercise is the multiple-choice test which may be used to guide reading or to test knowledge gained from reading. The following is illustrative of items used in science:

*Directions.* In the blank at the right, write the letter which indicates the best answer.

1. Of the different kinds of animals, which percent are vetebrates?
   (A) 5; (B) 10; (C) 15; (D) 20. . . . . . . . . . .  —
2. If there are ten seconds between a lightning flash and its thunder clap, the distance of the lightning is approximately:
   (A) 1.5; (B) 2; (C) 2.5; (D) 3 miles. . . . . . . . .  —
3. The most abundant part of the air is:
   (A) hydrogen; (B) oxygen; (C) nitrogen; (D) helium. . .  —
4. The most used refrigerant is:
   (A) alcohol; (B) methyl chloride; (C) gasoline; (D) dry ice.  —

If there is uncertainty about items, pupils may read to find the correct answers.

The elementary school pupil should learn to seek facts to support his purposes and to attest to them by reference to sources. Sources from which a statement is quoted should be shown to be authentic. Facts should be set forth; untruths should be rejected; opinions should be identified for what they are — unproved hypotheses or speculations.

## Differentiating Facts From Emotive Writing

Another consideration is the differentiation of factual and emotive writing. Scientists and historians present findings of research and state the conclusions drawn from their studies. A poet and other literary writers frequently color their expressions by emotive words and phrases.

Some poets use "poetic license" and youngsters must be taught to understand the different purposes and procedures of literary and factual writers.[18] Literary writers use figures of speech to give an impression or to paint a beautiful picture. A name is sometimes changed to rhyme with a word in a poem, or a metaphor or simile is employed to present an effect. A scientist must state the facts, the limitations, and the tested results of his investigation. The poet's purpose is often beauty or effect, but the scientist's is always truth; the former expresses thoughts with feeling, the latter states findings objectively. The pupil must learn to recognize the value of each in its proper place or sphere.

## Comparing Truth and Propaganda

If all the people of the world were well educated, there would be little reason to direct attention to the importance of this comparison because people would be able to distinguish the truth from propaganda which is sometimes intentional or malicious. For example, such statements as those indicating that the Soviet system of rule is a people's republic is propaganda, for the common people have very little to say about this type and method of government. Never has there been so much effort and money given over to propaganda as there is by Communist regimes concerning the "advantages of their systems." So emphatic and so persistent is this propaganda that many people are impressed even though the record of cruelty and tyranny is obvious to anyone who can and will read critically. The trouble is that many in some countries cannot read and many others who can read are permitted to read only what a controlled press publishes. Accordingly, the ability to read, and a free and honest press are highly important in promoting truth. Unfortunately in America there are some who fail to evaluate propaganda. This is in part the fault of poor teaching of reading. Therefore, it is necessary to teach each reader to evaluate written and printed statements as well as spoken expressions to determine truth.

## Assessing and Interpreting Data Required for Making a Report

When a reader wishes to make a report, he must state the purpose of his investigation, define the limits of his study, collect necessary facts, and express his findings accurately and clearly. He will need valid sources, such as those in encyclopedias, statistical abstracts, and

---

[18] Paul McKee, *The Teaching of Reading in the Elementary School* (Boston: Houghton Mifflin Company, 1948), pp. 392–396.

research materials. He must read understandingly and interpret statements accurately. He will require organizational and evaluative thinking to differentiate the relevant from the irrelevant, and the essential from the nonessential. He must determine what is necessary, record it, and report it.

## Critically Evaluating Evidence Upon Which a Generalization Is Based

Elementary school children are not too young to begin to appraise data upon which a generalization is based. A reader should consider all facts before drawing a conclusion. Principles should be based upon relevant, essential, and complete data. If there are specifics contrary to the principle, the statement should be made in such a way that exceptions may be expected. There are scores of generalizations stated wrongly as absolute truths. For example, a so-called phonetic principle often taught to children affirms that when a one-syllable word contains two vowels, one of which is final silent *e,* the other vowel has a long sound. As was shown in Chapter V, there are many exceptions to this rule. If children find that a large majority of cases do conform to a generalization, they may wish to add the word *generally* or *usually* to the statement. The discovery of an affirmation with exceptions and recognizing them as such are challenging activities for learners. If there are too many exceptions, the use of the proposition may be valueless as a principle. Skill in testing generalizations and the habit of testing them are greatly to be desired.

## READING TO ORGANIZE

In work-type reading, a pupil must understand organization. He must search out the design of an article, the outline of a chapter, or the framework of a book. A young reader should be trained from the primary grades to recognize relationships. Furthermore, he must be guided to organize his reading of several selections on a topic into a unified pattern which will be effective for understanding and retention.

## Recognizing Relationships

When a child reads a paragraph and understands the relationship of one sentence to another he is beginning to understand organization. When he can pick out the topic sentence of the paragraph, he has comprehended thought and relationships of parts to the whole. When he recognizes that the paragraph is a unified whole written about the thought expressed in a topic sentence he has begun to structure his reading.

## Studying the Organization of a Selection

Pupils should note that a selection is quite often divided into an introduction, a discussion, and a summary. After they recognize these main divisions, they should see the arrangement within each of the divisions. In the discussion, which is the principal part of a selection, they will generally find main points and subtopics under each important heading.

As learners recognize the organization of a selection and understand its value, they can begin to make outlines. These may be discussed in class and revisions made to perfect them. While it is not essential that every child turn out identically worded main and subheadings, it is important that a standard type of outline be presented — similar to the ones below. In the one on "Ships and Boats" lower case letters may be added, if necessary, following the Arabic numerals. For example, if submarines were discussed at greater length, three divisions might be set up: (a) nuclear-powered submarines, (b) Polaris-carrying submarines, (c) conventional submarines.

## Reading to Comprehend the Organization of a Chapter

In chapters of many books, outlines are quite clear because the authors have arranged the contexts under main and subheadings. In other books, the organization is not so readily recognized. It is good practice to have pupils, when reading a chapter from such a book, look for the frame or outline, critically evaluate it, indicate a deficiency in relationship if any, and make suggestions for improvement of the structure.

If a pupil wishes to understand a chapter and comprehend its organization with all that is in it, three activities are helpful. First, he may skim through the chapter — noting the purpose and the main points. Second, he may read the chapter carefully noting not only the main and the subpoints but also details and relationships among them. Third, he may make notes on the content following the outline of the writer. Such a procedure will not only enhance the comprehension and clarify organization but will aid in retention which is discussed in the following section.

## Organizing and Outlining Readings

A child who is interested in boats will read articles and books about boats. In selecting them, he locates materials, and as he reads he comprehends their content and organizes it into a configuration or whole. Perhaps from a few sources, but sometimes from many, a pupil builds the concept "boats." He makes notes and an outline of his concept. He then evaluates the outline and understands that he has not included several types of boats. He may realize further, that some subpoints are not properly related to the main headings as he has placed them. By careful evaluation, he finds them more properly related to another main head. Accordingly he will read further to enhance, correct, and enlarge his outline to present a more perfect concept. His purpose is to organize knowledge. After reading one or two selections the child may make an outline as follows:

**Boats**
I. Riverboats
    A. Canoes
    B. Rowboats
    C. Motor Boats
    D. Excursion Boats
II. Oceangoing Boats
    A. Passenger Liners
    B. Freighters

If he reports his findings to the class, someone is likely to tell him he has omitted the whole class of warships. Another pupil may indicate that he has not listed tugs and ferry boats. Other criticisms will be made. However, if the pupil continues to read, he may set forth an expanded outline as follows:

**Ships and Boats**
I. Oceangoing Boats
    A. Commercial Ships
        1. Passenger Liners
        2. Freighters
        3. Fishing Boats
    B. Warships
        1. Airplane Carriers
        2. Cruisers
        3. Submarines
        4. Torpedo Boats

II. Inland Water Boats on Lakes and Rivers
    A. Small Boats
        1. Canoes and Rowboats

       2. Motor and Speed Boats
       3. Yachts or Sailing Boats
  B. Larger Boats
       1. Passenger and Excursion Boats
       2. Fishing Boats
       3. Ferries
       4. Tugboats

Although this is a more comprehensive outline than his first, there will be criticism. A classmate may say, "You have neglected the boats of the past, the history of boats." Another is likely to say, "You have nothing about barges." He may be challenged with the statement, "You have nothing about the boats of the future." Other probable criticisms could be, "Yachts sail the ocean." "Some yachts are power-driven." The pupil's reading has been good and his progressive construction has been excellent, but there is still much that can be done by way of comprehension, location, evaluation, and organization. He has selected a topic about which he read profitably, but he realizes that he can learn much more by further study.

Organizing based upon location and comprehension goes hand in hand with evaluation for one must evaluate in organizing and organize to evaluate effectively.

## Learning to Summarize

The principal idea in summarizing is to express the substance of a selection tersely. In the beginning, an acceptable project for summarization would be, for example, to guide children who made a trip to the zoo to tell about the animals they saw. The teacher may write them on the chalkboard. Similarly, after reading a selection in the first reader, a child can report the important points for the teacher to write on the board. Others may add items omitted.

A summary is easily made after comprehending the organization of a chapter or a section. A pupil may give a brief review of an article by stating the main points. He can write a paragraph which presents the substance of a chapter or selection. It is possible to recall the interesting things that a character in a story did. The important battles of the Revolutionary War can be enumerated. Similarly, the causes of soil depletion may be set forth. After doing one of these things, a pupil should evaluate his work to determine whether the summary is complete, and if he has omitted important points they should be entered in their proper places in the sequence.

## READING TO REMEMBER

Reading to remember depends to a great extent upon the degree of comprehension, the adequacy of evaluation, and the recognition of the organization of the content. If a child tries to remember a paragraph or selection by learning it verbatim, without proper comprehension, his task is difficult. If he does not carefully evaluate or organize what he reads, he will probably achieve unsatisfactory retention. The interest a child develops in a topic, the understanding of relationships of sections or components in it, and the recognition of the values of the materials are basic to recall.

### The Relation of Purpose to Retention

If a reader has an evident purpose to retain what he reads, he will be more successful in remembering than if he reads without this objective. When a child formulates such a purpose, his chances for success are greatly enhanced. Generally, one cannot remember everything after a first reading of a selection. It may be necessary to read a second time to retain the main points.

### Situations and Needs for Retention

Some situations in which a reader desires to remember follow:

1. Reading to remember the gist of a paragraph
2. Reading to remember the main points in a story
3. Reading to remember the important ideas of a selection
4. Reading to remember the details of an explanation
5. Reading to remember directions to be followed in carrying out an exercise
6. Reading to remember the main points of criticism of a book
7. Reading to remember the correct sequence of events in a period — such as World War II
8. Reading to remember causes and effects of a disaster at sea
9. Reading to obtain questions for a discussion
10. Reading to remember a selection which is to be reported in class
11. Reading to make a report of an experiment in science
12. Reading to remember a poem to be presented in assembly
13. Reading to prepare for a test or an examination.

## Remembering What Is Read

Attention should be given to remembering the content of various kinds of selections. A good reader in the primary grades will remember the main episodes and the general forward movement of an interesting story. A pupil may read something that is useful to him. If it is something in which he is vitally interested, his concentration generally will be so pronounced that he will retain a great deal.

Interest is important in retention. If reading about an exciting event — a fight or a game — is what a pupil desires, his retention normally will be good. A discussion about what he has read will assist him. If he does not recall some important point, he may read again in the section containing the incident. The desire to learn is one of the greatest incentives to remembering. Sometimes the direction to read carefully and think about the materials read is fruitful. If a pupil will read and compare what he reads with his previous knowledge, he will generally improve retention. Another aid to memory is to try to think of the content read in one's own way. If a pupil can think about his reading and reproduce thoughts in his own words, better comprehension and recall seem assured.

Research has shown that readers retain generally less than 40 percent of materials in a first reading. Rereading, particularly of sections where memory fails, aids recall. A good reader checks by trying to reproduce to himself what he has read. When he finds that retention is deficient, he should read again and check once more. If he finds by this second checking that retention has improved but is still lacking in one important item, he should make note of it, see its relationship to items before and following it, read the section containing that item, and make a special effort to remember it in relation to the whole.

A reader should attempt to see the whole presentation — its beginning, discussion, and ending. He may outline the selection, note the logical arrangement of its parts, and recognize their relationships one with another, and with the whole. If he does not write an outline, he may be able to see the organization in the context, notice the headings, and use them as keys to sequential and orderly reporting. Well-formulated study questions to which answers may be found are helpful. A learner who finds the answers to such questions will remember them for a test, but he may not remember so well materials that were not included in the study questions and answers.[19]

---

[19] See McKee, *The Teaching of Reading, op. cit.,* pp. 531–552. See Hester, *op. cit.,* pp. 234–237.

## Appraising Retention

Retention may be evaluated in several ways. A discussion after reading should reflect important points remembered. Oral questions directed to the members of a class are conducive to appraisal of memory. A written quiz — either essay or objective — is helpful. One of the best checks is usage. A pupil who reads purposefully to locate information on the "Whale" for example, for a science report, reads to learn and to retain the information correctly because he has use for it. Materials that a reader finds beneficial in a project are of themselves incentives. Success in retention becomes evident in expanded and intensified interests in reading.

## SUMMARY

Efficient reading requires comprehension, location, evaluation, organization, and retention. Comprehension is the focal point of the reading process. Learning to comprehend involves: relating vocabulary to experience; understanding ideas, concepts, and processes; recognizing relationships; making comparisons; drawing inferences; reflecting and interpreting; and reading between the lines.

A reader must locate what he intends to read: words, sentences, books, and other sources. Among the elements to be considered in making location practical and fruitful are: the alphabet, dictionary, encyclopedia, bibliographies, and the library. A reader must learn how to skim, and to use maps and charts in his quest to locate information about problems, projects, and activities.

Critical evaluation of ideas and materials is important in modern life. In reading, essentials must be distinguished from nonessentials. Validity of assertions must be appraised; opinion must not be confused with facts; truth and falsehood must be differentiated; generalizations must be carefully evaluated to determine whether they are valid.

Learning to organize in reading involves recognizing relationships and understanding of the framework of paragraphs, selections, chapters, and books. Organization motivates clarity of summarization and assists a reader to construct an outline as a basis for recognizing interrelationships in reading and study.

Retention of what is read is important for the use that can be made of it. In remembering efficiently, an individual requires purpose to retain and interest in the content read. Measuring of retention may be done through discussion, by questions, listening, and testing.

Reading involves, then, comprehension, location, evaluation, organization, and retention — each integrating with the others in the totality of the process. If all functions efficiently, reading becomes satisfying and fruitful in study and recreation.

## ACTIVITIES, PROBLEMS, QUESTIONS

1. Explain the interrelationships among: comprehension, location, evaluation, organization, and retention in reading.
2. Why do meanings of many words vary according to use? Illustrate the many uses of a word such as *set* or *bank*.
3. Show how the value of a word may be increased for communication as an individual develops reading skills and abilities.
4. Plan several simple exercises for developing vocabulary comprehension in reading.
5. Find some examples of figurative language in your recreational reading. How can figurative language affect reading comprehension?
6. If you wished to study the history of Pennsylvania (or any other state), what important sources would you try to locate? How would you find them?
7. Make a list of the needs you have had for alphabet skills during the past week.
8. Describe the uses you have made of graphs, charts, diagrams, tables, and pictorial materials during the past year.
9. Compare evaluation and organization in reading and study. How are they correlative?
10. Formulate several statements showing uses of effective evaluation.
11. Compare the writings of scientists and poets. Contrast the criteria for appraisal of the writings of each.
12. What are the purposes of teaching organization skills to an elementary school pupil?
13. Indicate in several brief statements the dependence of retention upon comprehension, evaluation, organization, and location in reading.
14. How can a person learn to remember what he has read?

## SELECTED REFERENCES

Dawson, Mildred A., and Henry A. Bamman. *Fundamentals of Basic Reading Instruction.* New York: Longmans, Green, 1959. 304 pp.
DeBoer, John J., and Martha Dallmann. *The Teaching of Reading.* Rev. ed. New York: Holt, Rinehart & Winston, 1964. 422 pp.
Durrell, Donald D. *Improving Reading Instruction.* Yonkers-on-Hudson: World Book, 1956. 402 pp.
Gates, Arthur I. *The Improvement of Reading.* 3rd ed. New York: Macmillan, 1947. 657 pp.
Harris, Albert J. *How to Increase Reading Ability.* 4th ed. New York: Longmans, Green, 1961. 624 pp.
McKee, Paul. *The Teaching of Reading in the Elementary School.* Boston: Houghton Mifflin, 1948, 622 pp.
*Reading in the Elementary School.* Forty-Eighth Yearbook of the National Society for the Study of Education, Part II. Chicago: University of Chicago Press, 1949. 343 pp.

Robinson, Helen M., ed. *Materials of Reading*. Chicago: University of Chicago Press, 1958. 231 pp.

*The Teaching of Reading*. Albany: The New York State Education Department, 1963. 129 pp.

Tinker, Miles A., and Constance M. McCullough. *Teaching Elementary Reading*. 2nd ed. New York: Appleton-Century-Crofts, 1962. 615 pp.

See also references for Chapter V.

# Chapter VIII

# Recreational and Work-Type Reading: Using Books and the Library

## INTRODUCTION

"LEARNING to read" and "reading to learn" are complementary. Yet, many adults who have learned to read do not take advantage of it either in their vocations or in their leisure. A large proportion of college graduates read neither extensively nor intensively.[1] Nearly half the people of our country leave school during or after completing the tenth grade; their lives could be greatly enriched if they would read worthwhile materials. This situation is a challenge to the elementary and secondary schools. An ample reading program, as Witty indicated, must recognize a wide range of needs, interests, and purposes, utilize experiences and activities, and be integrated into the other facets of the language arts.[2]

After a pupil has learned to read simple context and has developed a fairly efficient word attack, he should undertake reading independently. Of necessity, he needs guidance. Teachers in the elementary school, who do not develop in boys and girls "strong motives for and permanent interests" in reading, fail to achieve one of the major objectives of reading.

Gates indicated because we have made reading the slave of other activities in the school curriculum, many pupils have a tendency to avoid it. They look upon it as work and the work from which they desire relief when they leave school.[3] Some think of reading as drudgery.

---

[1] Paul Witty, "Purpose and Scope of the Yearbook," *Development In and Through Reading,* Sixtieth Yearbook of the National Society for the Study of Education, Part I (Chicago: The University of Chicago Press, 1961), p. 3.

[2] *Ibid.,* pp. 1–2.

[3] Arthur I. Gates, "Improvement of Reading Possible in the Near Future," *The Reading Teacher,* 12:86–87, December, 1958.

One of the important aims of teaching reading is to develop right attitudes toward it. Permanent interests and right attitudes are not present in some individuals. According to evidence shown by Betts and Preston, America is not the reading nation it should be. Our people do not read comparatively as much as people in many other nations. The United States ranks fifteenth in the number of bookshops per capita, and twenty-sixth in terms of the number of titles produced per capita.[4] The right kind of reading can make people great, the wrong kind can harm character and deplete strength. The teachers of reading must not only motivate pupils to read, but they must interest them in books of worth.

## THE ELEMENTARY SCHOOL LIBRARY

### The Individual Needs a Library

It is the responsibility of the elementary school to teach the value of books which the library contains. After leaving school, most people would be greatly helped by knowledge of library offerings. Fortunately, in elementary schools there is a trend from studying one book or a few books to the use of many. A child must know how to study a textbook, but it is important that he learn to investigate other sources also.

The training for efficient library usage is generally challenging. Children enjoy libraries. From a study of 546 responses of elementary school children, Stewart reported that they prefer many books to one, and that they like to find materials themselves.[5] Individualized instruction requires many books to fit individual needs and tastes, and the most effective agency for selection and distribution of books to pupils is the school library. In order that pupils will use it to the best advantage, they need informative and dynamic teaching of its use. The elementary school has failed in one of its most important objectives if pupils leave school without desire for and habits of library reading and study.[6]

A well-balanced collection of books for boys and girls of different

---

[4] Emmett A. Betts and Ralph C. Preston, "The Role of the Community," *Development In and Through Reading,* Sixtieth Yearbook of the National Society for the Study of Education, Part I (Chicago: The University of Chicago Press, 1961), p. 101.

[5] Dorothy H. Stewart, "Children's Preferences in Types of Assignments," *Elementary School Journal,* 47:97, October, 1946.

[6] William W. Brickman, "Reading Instruction and Improvement," *School and Society,* 65:231–232, March 29, 1947.

reading levels and of varying tastes should be acquired and used. Research shows that many books and poems popular in one grade are often quite popular in others. Books worth rereading should be available to those who love them so much that they enjoy them a second or third time. Maps, charts, newspapers, magazines, and clippings should be displayed for use in the various activities of the curriculum.

A school library may be thought of as a collection of books, periodicals, and source materials located in an appropriate room in a school, administered by a qualified librarian or teacher-librarian who guides reading, supervises location of materials, instructs children in effective use of materials, and enlists their help in book distribution.[7] At present, less than 40 percent of elementary schools have central libraries in their buildings, but the schools are continually striving to provide books and materials. The time should not be too far away when every elementary school will have an elementary school library.

## The Purposes and Values of the Elementary School Library

The library provides opportunities for reading and when its selection is well balanced, it offers a fountain of information and inspiration. A well-run library offers instruction for discovery of knowledge and guidance in investigation and study. The curriculum in an elementary school is enhanced by the library which fits not only into the program of reading but also into the programs of the other language arts, the social studies, science, mathematics, art, and music. Reading, writing, thinking, and other types of activity are guided and improved by library technics.

As the center and heart of the school, the library offers many advantages. Properly organized, it fosters some highly important values especially in connection with reading.

1. It enriches and expands experiences and activities.
2. It develops motives for and interests in reading.
3. In it and through it, thoughtful location, comprehension, evaluation, organization, and retention technics are enhanced.
4. The child is guided to materials and information in areas of elementary school curricula.

---

[7] Mary V. Caver, "The New Elementary Library Standards," *The Instructor,* 70:77, November, 1960.

5. Correct attitudes toward determining truth by reading and study are initiated and fostered.

6. Through it, the pupil is assisted to form appropriate habits of using the results of reading and study in constructive and creative work — habits that will serve him well in life after he leaves school.

7. A school library offers opportunity for interpretation and use of materials which assist in the development of thinking, construction, and creativity.[8]

An individual who frequents a library to study reference materials necessary to his work, to select and read good books for pleasure and information, and to utilize these materials for improving living has developed a technic which will be of increasing importance as he faces the problems of vocation and leisure. The individual who develops library skills and habits becomes self-reliant and independent in problem-solving.

## Organizing an Elementary School Library

Because the library is so necessary to instruction, teachers, principals, supervisors, the superintendent of schools, the board of education, and the community should cooperate in its development. The advice of a trained librarian is needed in planning for equipment, in guiding the selection of books and other materials, and in organizing the program. If no librarian is available, a teacher-librarian should be appointed to supervise the work. In a new building, a library room with proper facilities and equipment will be provided, but in an old building it will be necessary to select a room with ample space for stacks and reading. The room should be well lighted and favorable to reading and study. The Department of Public Instruction, Bureau of Curriculum Development, Commonwealth of Pennsylvania, suggests a minimum of 1050 square feet as size of the reading room for a school enrollment of 350 or less, 1275 square feet for enrollment of 350–499, and 2250 square feet for an enrollment of 500–999. A half-time certified librarian is suggested for an enrollment of 350 or less and a full-time certified librarian for an enrollment from 350 to 999. A floor space of 30 square feet per reader is suggested. A workroom area of 150–200 square feet is recommended.[9] Ten volumes

---

[8] James A. Fitzgerald, "The Elementary School Library," *The Catholic School Journal,* 61:39, February, 1961.

[9] *School Library Standards,* Department of Public Instruction (Harrisburg: Bureau of Curriculum Development, Commonwealth of Pennsylvania).

properly selected for balance should be sought for each pupil within a three-year period for ordinary service, and 20 carefully selected books per pupil are recommended for superior service. A school of 350 or less should have two encyclopedias, and a school of from 500–999 should have four. The standard recommended for periodicals is as follows: 10 for enrollment of 350 or less, 15 for an enrollment of 350–499, and 20 for enrollment of 500–999. A library, according to the Pennsylvania standard, should contain a primary, intermediate, junior, and an unabridged dictionary in good condition. A daily newspaper ought to be available. The book selection sources recommended are Wilson's Children's Catalog and the American Library Association Basic Book Collection for Elementary Grades. The library may be classified according to the Dewey Decimal System. The shelf list, card catalog, loan system, and information files should be kept up to date. An inventory should be taken once a year; soiled books should be cleaned or replaced.[10]

*Book selection.* A school library should be equipped with study materials essential for classroom and laboratory work and with books for recreational and general reading. These books should be selected only after careful evaluation. The following types of materials are useful:

1. General reference books, such as the *Britannica Junior Encyclopedia, Compton's Pictured Encyclopedia, World Book Encyclopedia,* a general encyclopedia, an unabridged dictionary, other dictionaries including pictured dictionaries, atlases, style books, book catalogs, indexes, and so on

2. Books and materials for special reference in areas such as history, literature, social studies, geography, biography, travel, science, mathematics, music, art, invention, electronics, transportation, and communication

3. Recreational books, drama, poetry, fiction, children's plays, fairy tales, folktales, anthologies, and other child literature

4. Periodicals, children's magazines, and newspapers

5. Miscellaneous source materials, such as the *World Almanac,* books of quotations, standard catalogs, a periodical index, *Junior Book of Authors, Who's Who in America,* maps, globes, charts, and audiovisual aids.[11]

---

[10] *Ibid.*

[11] See the following: *A Basic Book Collection for Elementary Grades,* Seventh Edition, American Library Association, Chicago, 1960. *Adventuring With Books,*

In selecting books for children, there must be understanding of the nature of the child, the total school program, and the wide variety of interests, reading abilities, and background. Books of value and good books of interest are desired by all concerned with the development of young Americans. The selection of a book for a children's library should be made upon the basis of its own particular qualities rather than upon its inclusion in a particular list. Each book should be read by a member of the school staff and reported upon favorably to a selection committee or to the librarian before being placed on a list for use by a class. The librarian will consider the advisability of ordering duplicate copies of books that have been requested by more than one teacher or that may have appeal or importance in any area.[12]

*Evaluation and appraisal of books.* Although a librarian, an expert on books, is looked to for aid and advice in book selection, she cannot be expected to read all the books in a library. Accordingly, a cooperative plan for book appraisal may be organized. McCormick suggested a plan in which each teacher in a department agreed to read and appraise a book a week. A card (5 by 8 inches) with a rating of each book was filed for use by teachers in selecting books for various purposes.[13] Questions as the following are useful in making an evaluation of a book:

1. Is the book worthwhile? Does it have developmental value?
2. Is the book appropriate in plot and content?
3. Does the book have literary quality? Is it suitable for the purpose desired?
4. At what reading level is the book suitable?
5. What appeal has the book? Will it be liked better by boys or girls?
6. In what area — literature, science, art, biography — is the book useful?
7. Is the physical makeup of the book durable? Is the book hygienic?
8. Is the book attractive? Are the illustrations adequate and well placed?
9. Is the book readable? Are print and mechanics satisfactory?

National Council of Teachers of English, Champaign, Illinois, 1960. *Children's Catalog,* last edition, H. W. Wilson Company, New York, *Graded Lists of Books for Children,* American Library Association, Chicago. *Inexpensive Books for Boys and Girls,* American Library Association, Chicago. *Children's Books and Materials for Classroom Use,* Thirtieth Yearbook of the National Elementary Principal, September, 1951, pp. 294–308. *Good Books for Children,* compiled by Mary E. Eakin, University of Chicago Press, 1959. "Recent Books for Classroom and Library," *The Catholic School Journal,* published yearly in a spring issue. *Reading for Fun,* edited by Eloise Ramsey, National Council of Teachers of English, Champaign, Illinois.

[12] Fitzgerald, "The Elementary School Library," *op. cit.,* p. 40.

[13] Alice McCormick, "Our Library — Present and Future," *Elementary English Review,* 23:255–261, October, 1946.

If teachers have an opportunity to discuss the books read, the co-operative effort will be rewarding.

*Magazines and newspapers.* One of the most important avenues to the understanding of society is current reading. Local and daily newspapers should be available in addition to the children's newspapers discussed elsewhere in this book. The Bureau of Elementary Curriculum Development, New York State Education Department recommended magazines listed below because of their merit and appeal to children, with the admonition that because the quality and character of periodicals change quickly, teachers should be alert to add or delete titles as conditions require revision.

> *American Girl* (Ages 11–18)
> *Boy's Life* (Ages 10–18)
> *Child Life* (Up to 12)
> *Children's Digest* (Ages 9 and up)
> *Humpty Dumpty's Magazine* (Ages 3 and up)
> *Jack and Jill* (Ages under 10)
> *Junior Natural History Magazine* (Ages 11 and up)
> *Model Airplane News* (Ages 12 and up)
> *National Geographic Magazine* (Ages 9 and up)
> *Natural History* incorporating *Nature Magazine* (Ages 9 and up)
> *Popular Mechanics Magazine* (Ages 12 and up)
> *Popular Science* (Ages 12 and up).[14]

Horn presented a list of periodicals for children and youth which should be known to teachers of reading.[15]

## Operating the Library

In a large school, the librarian will have no difficulty in operating the library with the proper number of experienced and trained assistants, but in a small school library functioning may be more difficult because of the lack of trained personnel.

*Some general activities.* A trained librarian understands the organizational and operational requirements. The following suggested activities may be helpful to a teacher-librarian who has been assigned the task of organizing and operating the library in a small elementary school:

1. The classification of books should be made in accord with a

---

[14] *The Elementary School Library* (Albany: Bureau of Elementary Curriculum Development, New York State Education Department, 1957), pp. 20–21.

[15] Thomas D. Horn, "Periodicals for Children and Youth," *Elementary English,* 36:342–344, May, 1959.

system such as that of the Dewey Decimal Classification or the Library of Congress.

2. Books may be accessioned and prepared for borrowing with the assistance of advanced pupils.

3. An adequate simple record of purchases and accessions should be kept.

4. A card catalog which includes author, title, and subject cards should be prepared.

5. Dictionary stands, shelves, magazine racks, reading tables, and chairs may be procured, or built by boys in the shop.

6. Student-librarians may be trained to check books in and out, assess and collect fines, and keep records.

7. Student assistants may be encouraged to visit a public library to note procedures.

8. Instruction in the use of books and other materials may be given to groups or classes of children.

9. Reading lists should be supplied for units or activities for classwork.

10. Library week may be observed with activities designed to develop interest and use of books.

*Cooperation of the public library.*    Advice and assistance are usually available from a public library staff. Public librarians are very cooperative in supplying schools with books and materials for class projects, and in guiding teachers and pupils.

*Managing a library.*    In many comparatively small schools, where a full-time or half-time librarian is not available, the teacher-librarian will require assistance in "running the library." Able pupils may be appointed as assistant librarians for a period of time — a month or a semester. These pupils work according to plan and keep the library open at certain periods of the day to lend and reclaim books and make necessary records of withdrawals and returns.

Committees may be appointed for various purposes: (1) improvement of the library, (2) library fund for new books, (3) Book Week, (4) exhibiting new books, (5) interesting pupils in reading, (6) promoting library or reading clubs, (7) preparing study lists, (8) maintenance. Reading or study clubs may be organized in a cooperative integrating activity. Through such clubs, many of the real objectives of reading are developed. Pupils who engage in an activity as the running of the library serve the school, motivate interests in books and reading, and reap rich benefits themselves.[16]

*Some situations for using the library.*    Children will use the library if they understand the benefits to be obtained from it. The following should be indicative of the purposes in situations which call for library reading and study:

1. To find answers to questions
2. To obtain information about a topic
3. To develop a solution to a problem
4. To satisfy a desire to learn about an event
5. To get information on how to plan and carry out a project
6. To determine how to make a design or product
7. To find an appropriate poem or story for a program
8. To read and appreciate poems of various poets
9. To determine correct etiquette for a social situation
10. To ascertain the proper procedures for interviewing people
11. To study the best forms for addressing people in written correspondence
12. To make sure how to write possessive forms of proper names of persons — Williams, Burns, John, Moses
13. To learn the story of Columbus, Lief Ericson, or Ivan the Terrible
14. To learn of the relationships among the pioneers and various tribes of American Indians
15. To read about the Revolutionary, Civil, or World Wars
16. To contrast the ways people live in a democracy and in a totalitarian society
17. To study molecular attraction
18. To survey the new books in the library
19. To make a bibliography for a unit
20. To find current materials for a social study unit on transportation
21. To spend an hour in pleasurable reading of periodicals
22. To browse through books.

In such types of situations, the librarian is able to guide the individual or a group of pupils to read for pleasure or information, to

---

[16] See Lucile F. Fargo, *The Library in the School* (Chicago: American Library Association, 1939), p. 552.

A free reading period

find facts, to solve a problem, or to critically evaluate assertions made in books.

## Library Guidance and Instruction

Teachers and librarians must excite in the child a real desire to use the library. Not only should the pupil learn the common library technics, he must develop interests in the offerings that are available for his purposes. Library instruction should guide the child to guide himself.

*The library period.* Library periods differ. In a library period, pupils are free to work on their problems, or instruction is given which should range from whole class teaching to individualized guidance. Arrangements are often made with the librarian for instruction to be presented to a class or a group in library technics, such as in methods of using the card catalog to find materials. The various kinds of cards — author, subject, and title — can be shown and the value of each demonstrated. The book catalogs, indexes, and guides should be explained and their use developed.

*Some specific library activities.*   In preparing a free reading lesson in the library, a teacher of a fifth-grade class of thirty youngsters reading from third-grade to eighth-grade levels should review the cumulative record folder of each child. With consideration of the mental ability, the reading level, the absorbing interests, the attitudes, and the weaknesses, each individual can be helped to select a book. The teacher observes the class and offers assistance to anyone who needs it. The reaction of a pupil to the story he is reading should be noted. Perhaps another type of reading should be suggested to him. If a pupil indicates that a book is too difficult, a simpler book should be chosen. On the other hand, a pupil may like very much the story he has selected, and want to withdraw the book from the library.

A few minutes before the close of the period, members of the group can be assembled for discussion and comment. A remark by one child about a book may cause another to read it. A sentence or two written on a form which contains blanks for the pupil's name and the title of the book may be filed in the cumulative record folder and used for further guidance.

It is the experience of teachers and librarians that pupils who go to the library for successive free reading periods frequently desire to complete books they have begun, and when they have finished them, select others of similar nature or possibly one that was commented upon favorably by a classmate.

*Reports motivate reading.*   A sixth-grade teacher had motivated her pupils to obtain books from the public library to supplement the offerings of the school. Pupils having read their books, made reports about them to their classmates. One report is most memorable. Homer, a rather chubby but highly intelligent boy, with thick blond straight hair that seemed to stand on end to a distance of about two inches from his head told about *Michael Strogoff* excitedly in a rather high-pitched voice. As he talked very animatedly about the story, he began to find his own words inadequate for his purpose. In some confusion but with effectiveness, he opened the book and read rapidly two or three brief paragraphs in a most stirring manner which evidently thrilled his listeners. Two hours later, an observer stepped into the public library on his way home from the school and asked that the book be reserved for him. The assistant librarian smiled and asked, "What happened in school today? Twenty-two pupils have asked to withdraw *Michael Strogoff* in the period of the last two hours." This is the kind of incentive that is frequently achieved from an individual report to a group. If the reading had been carried on without comment, many of the group might never have heard of the book. Following this procedure, an individual motivates others in a group and shares in the richness of the readings of others.

*Some problems.* Fourth-grade pupils raised some questions about city life and decided to find answers for them. They divided the work of obtaining materials and information into twelve questions:

1. Why are cities where they are?
2. How do cities get food?
3. How do cities obtain water?
4. What kind of houses do city people live in?
5. How do people travel in the cities?
6. How are cities kept clean?
7. How are lives and property protected?
8. How are people in cities kept safe from fire?
9. How are people in cities protected from disease?
10. What kind of business places are there in a city?
11. What do people do for a living in cities?
12. What recreation is provided for people in cities?

Committees were formed to study these problems. The librarian was consulted. The pupils used the card catalog and reference materials to locate information. Articles in encyclopedias, books, and other sources were read. Notes were made. Materials were withdrawn for additional study in the classroom. Pupils found materials of value and improved their skill in using the library. By organizing their readings, each committee developed its report and a chairman presented it to the whole class. Members of the class discussed each report, and shared information. Reading is not completely mastered until the use of the library is made a habit of the pupil. Location, evaluation, interpretation, and organization are enhanced and perfected by using the library.

## RECREATIONAL READING FOR
## ELEMENTARY SCHOOL CHILDREN

### Orientation

If children in the elementary school are to develop a permanent interest in reading, they must become acquainted with the excellent prose and poetry which have accumulated in our literature. The teacher must know our heritage of stories, tales, poems, and other materials. She must know the reading interests of children. She should understand also the preferences of boys and girls at various ages and possess a means for assessing the individual choices of the members of her class. She must be able to convey to the children the great importance of reading good literature. She should not permit reading to become a boresome chore, but should individualize it to fit each pupil of the class.[17] Knowing that a child will read generally what he wants to read, a teacher must cause him to want to read by providing the opportunity for him to select the right books at the right time, and to read them for fun or for whatever other purpose he may have.

Furness emphasized the importance of proper instruction in literature, particularly in prose, to give children a broad and deep appreciation of themselves and of human beings in general. In her excellent discussion she describes values and methods of teaching the following types of prose: picture books, animal stories, myths, folktales, biography, science books, mystery stories, and periodicals. Her suggestions are useful in promoting both interest and experience through worthwhile reading.[18]

## Some Research on Preferences

The findings of investigations over nearly forty years should help a teacher in book selection. Jordan reported in 1921 a survey of reading interests of more than 3500 sixth-grade pupils in which he found that boys preferred adventure and girls fiction. Boys of 10 to 12 were interested in scouting, school, sports, and adventure. At the same levels, girls' major interests seemed to be principally in home, school, and fairy stories. His findings showed that a small amount of travel, history, biography, poetry, and science were being read by children of this age level.[19] Terman and Lima, in 1931, indicated that the reading interests of children change as they grow in experience, and reported interest trends for successive age groups. Young children liked nursery rhymes, fairy tales, myths, and talking-beast stories. Children two or three years older read factual materials, legends, stories of other lands, and lives of famous people. Boys at ten began reading about inventions, mechanics, aviation, and exploration. Girls in the middle and upper

[17] Arthur I. Gates and Frank G. Jennings, "The Role of Motivation," *Development in and Through Reading,* Sixtieth Yearbook of the National Society for the Study of Education, Part I (Chicago: The University of Chicago Press, 1961), pp. 109–126.

[18] Edna Lue Furness, "Pupils, Pedagogues, and Prose," *Education,* 84:402–410, March, 1964.

[19] A. M. Jordan, *Children's Interests in Reading,* Teachers College Contributions to Education, No. 107 (New York: Bureau of Publications, Teachers College, Columbia University, 1921), p. 143.

grades liked materials about home. Boys enjoyed vigorous action and adventure; girls delighted in poetry, fiction, and fairy tales. Terman and Lima stated that gifted children read more science, history, biography, travel, folktales, drama, poetry, and informal fiction but less of emotional fiction than unselected children.[20] Lazar, in 1945, reported that large print, gay colors, easy stories, action, and adventure books were liked by children. Girls enjoyed stories about people, and boys, those about activities. Special projects, children's comments, teacher enthusiasm were found to be important in book selection. Children did not care for books that preached or lectured them.[21] Norvell, in 1958, reported the results of a study of the opinions of more than 24,000 boys and girls in grades three through six. Boys preferred books depicting adventure, physical struggle, animals, humor, courage, heroism, and patriotism. They were unfavorably disposed to description, sentiment, romantic love, fairies, preaching, and physical weakness in male characters. They were unfavorably impressed with female leading characters. Girls at the same levels were pleased with stories of home and school life, domestic animals and pets, sentiment, romantic love, adventure, mystery, patriotism, and the supernatural. Elements disapproved by girls were violent action, description, preaching, fierce animals, and boys and girls younger than themselves (not including babies).[22]

The findings from these studies indicate that boys and girls in elementary school have distinct likings for books that present certain types of action, and a dislike for some types of books, topics, characters, and subjects. Insofar as it is possible, boys and girls should be encouraged to select books that they like from a good library offering. As they read, their interests should widen and also intensify in such a way that reading will become more satisfying and valuable to them.

There has been an impression that some children particularly boys, do not like poetry, but this seems unwarranted, especially when poetry is properly selected and presented. However, it might be fairer to say that children prefer some poems more than others. Poems preferred

---

[20] Lewis M. Terman and Margaret Lima, *Children's Reading,* second edition (New York: D. Appleton-Century, 1931), pp. 31–45.

[21] May Lazar, *Guiding the Growth of Reading Interests,* Educational Research Bulletin of the Bureau of Reference, Research, and Statistics, No. 8 (New York: Board of Education, May, 1945), p. 3.

[22] George W. Norvell, *What Boys and Girls Like to Read* (Englewood Cliffs, New Jersey: Silver Burdett, 1958).

in grade five, for example, are likely to be popular in grade six. Mackintosh reported the preferences of several hundred children in grades three, four, five, and six, made on a five-point scale. Teachers also read and made ratings of the same poems, but there was a pronounced lack of agreement between teacher and pupil ratings. In addition to the excellent findings on the preferences and dislikes of children for specific poems, Mackintosh formulated rightly the implication that children's choices were of value in poem selection for teaching.[23]

Avegno read 130 "old poems" and 120 "new poems" to 1200 fourth-, fifth-, and sixth-grade boys and girls in New York City public schools. Thirty old poems and 30 new ones made up the highest quarter — the best-liked poems. Twenty-eight new poems and 35 old poems made up the lowest quarter — the least-liked poems. Boys and girls agreed pretty well on the poems they preferred and on those they did not like. There was a high correlation of preferences and dislikes among children of the three grades. Fifty-five poems were common to the Mackintosh study mentioned above and to this study, and Avegno concluded after careful statistical treatment that "children of today generally preferred poems that the children of a generation ago liked, although they did not award them quite so high a rating."[24] Some preferences for poetry were expressed repeatedly. Avegno reported the implications for poem preferment by these public-school pupils as follows:

1) Children enjoy poetry that rhymes, produces a sense of melodious rhythm, makes common everyday experiences vibrant, or tells a story.

2) They like poetry that tells about animals, tells about nature, brings laughter to them, or sounds as though someone is talking to them.

3) They enjoy poetry that sounds soft and sweet like a lullaby, makes them feel happy, makes them feel sad, or shows strong feeling.

4) Children like poetry that is scary and spooky, teaches them a lesson, is filled with action, or tells about holidays.

5) They enjoy poetry in which they experience an exciting adventure, poetry that is real, that is different, or is filled with imagination.

6) Children enjoy poetry that contains the truth and brings God to them.[25]

---

[23] Helen K. Mackintosh, *A Critical Study of Children's Choices of Poetry,* University of Iowa Studies in Education, Vol. 7, No. 4 (Iowa City: University of Iowa, 1932), p. 128.

[24] Sylvia Avegno, "Intermediate-Grade Children's Choices of Poetry," (unpublished doctor's dissertation, Fordham University, New York, 1955), p. 223.

[25] *Ibid.,* p. 186. by permission of Dr. Avegno.

Among the factors which these pupils gave for disliking poetry were: failure to understand it, "no rhyme, no story, no action, extremes in length — too long or too short, boring, babyish, not interesting, silly, no expression of feeling, not true, and too repetitious."[26]

These findings from investigators of prose and poetry preferences over a period of nearly forty years indicate that the pupils of today have strong likes and some pronounced dislikes which were expressed quite clearly by pupils of more than a generation ago. These data should be helpful to teachers and supervisors who are striving to develop strong incentives and permanent habits of reading in pupils.

## Some Suggestions for Literary Reading

Progress in the reading of literature is gradual if the motivation is continuous and effective from one reading level to the following. Interest leads to activity in reading, but it is not quite correct to say that each child should follow his own spontaneous interests. Obviously a child's interests must be developed. If left to his own devices, they may be only accidental. A pupil may be fascinated with the comics or another limiting kind of reading which curtails his activity to one or two types, and so never learns about the great variety of materials available. A pupil should know about the scores of important types of appealing materials which are available to him as he develops from the kindergarten through the grades. Burton and Larrick suggested that books should brighten and expand the outlook of boys and girls, acquaint them with their literary heritage, and enhance skills for reading and understanding.[27]

*Stories with pictures for young children.* Stories with accompanying pictures are important in the primary grades. A good picture fascinates a child and is an approach to the context. Stories such as *The Three Billy Goats Gruff, Cinderella, Snow White and the Seven Dwarfs, The Gingerbread Boy,* and *The Ugly Duckling* appeal partly because the pictures aid the children to begin reading. Children enjoy laughing and laughter. They are thrilled with a simple exciting episode. Such a story as Lois Lenski's *Cowboy Small* may be enjoyed in grade one, two, and three and by some pupils in later grades.

*Stories about life and activities.* Children enjoy stories about city

---

[26] *Ibid.,* pp. 184–185.

[27] Dwight L. Burton and Nancy Larrick, "Literature for Children and Youth," *Development In and Through Reading,* Sixtieth Yearbook of the National Society for the Study of Education, Part I (Chicago: The University of Chicago Press, 1961), pp. 207–208.

and country life, about trains, planes, boats, and engines. In the kindergarten and early grades they like *The Little Engine That Could* by Piper. Stories of people and animals are appealing to these children also. Margaret Brown's *Big Red Barn* is a charming story with beautiful pictures depicting animal life. Munro Leaf's *Story of Ferdinand,* the sweet-tempered genial bull, is enjoyed by children throughout the grades. *Mother Goose* is cleverly utilized by some of the greatest writers for young children. Eleanor Farjeon's *A Prayer for Little Things* and Rachel Field's *Prayer for a Child* contribute to the literary and personal development of children. These child prayers ask favors and show thankfulness to benefactors for favors received. Such books are generally beautifully illustrated in color.

Among the desirable characteristics of stories well illustrated with drawings or accompanied with pictures are the following: (1) a simple plot; (2) a mood of one type — fancy, romance, adventure, or realism; (3) use of conversation; (4) forward movement; (5) simple, and natural climax; (6) one main character, or several that operate together; (7) a child hero is generally acceptable; (8) vivid easily remembered language — words, phrases, or sentences.

Jacobs made some excellent suggestions concerning illustrations. Harmony should be achieved between context and picture. The theme of the illustration should match the story. The mood and feeling of the story should be caught. Illustrations should depict activity. Photography, drawing, or other illustration types should promote the spirit of the story. Necessary detail is acceptable, but too much detail is likely to detract from the story.[28]

*Folklore, tables, and legends.* Folktales are enjoyable because they have a simple style and are forward moving. A folktale has an introduction, a body, and a conclusion. The themes are strong. In the smallest number of words, the introduction is sketched and the story is begun. The scene is portrayed in simple understandable language. The plot is developed without unnecessary verbiage. The heroes act swiftly and dynamically. They are winners and the good is perpetuated. In the conclusion, the victory is won. The hero is rewarded, and the villian is punished.[29] Malory's *Boy's King Arthur,* beautifully illustrated, is interesting ordinarily to sixth-grade pupils. Pyle's *Story of*

---

[28] Leland B. Jacobs, "Children's Experiences in Literature," *Children and the Language Arts* (Englewood Cliffs: Prentice-Hall, Inc., 1955), pp. 198–199.

[29] May Hill Arbuthnot, *Children and Books* (Chicago: Scott, Foresman and Company, 1947), pp. 225–230.

*King Arthur and His Knights* provides excellent tales for the upper grades. *Paul Bunyan and His Great Blue Ox* by Wallace Wadsworth is illustrative of American folklore. These are about on the level of sixth-grade reading or perhaps fitted to gifted readers of an earlier grade. The *Fables of Aesop* and Hans Christian Andersen's *Fairy Tales* are amusing to fourth-, fifth-, and sixth-grade pupils. Whitman emphasized the value of folksongs for elementary school pupils, and his bibliography is of aid to teachers.[30]

*Stories in the United States.*    Every child should be introduced early to the stories of his country. Hundreds of books of varied nature are available for those who are properly motivated and become interested. Books about the geography of the United States, our resources, the constitution, heroic deeds, and traditions should be supplied for the young learner. Books about Indians, about colonization, concerning pioneer times, and stories of the nineteenth century are available. *Our Country's Story* by Frances Cavanah, *Pinto's Journey* by Wilfrid Bronson, *Johnny Tremain* by Esther Forbes, Mary Jane Carr's *Children of the Covered Wagon,* and Louisa M. Alcott's *Little Women* are representative of these stories.

*Literature about other countries.*    Pupils gradually become aware of the other countries of the world and of their peoples, particularly of those related to us in background, proximity, and history. The explorations from Ericson to Dewey, the world-changing voyages of Columbus, Magellan, and others should be experienced. The neighbors to the south — Mexico and other Latin-American countries — and Canada to the north should become part of the store of knowledge of pupils in elementary school. *The Canadian Story* by May McNeer and Jim Breetveld's *Getting to Know Brazil* are effective in introducing the peoples of these countries to youngsters in the sixth grade. The stories of peoples and nations of Europe, Asia, and other continents are portrayed by scores of books such as Jean Kennedy's *Here is India,* Dola DeJong's *The Picture Story of Holland,* and Grace Hogarth's *Australia, the Island Continent.*

*Stories for everyone.*    Fanciful stories are good fun for anyone who likes them. The *Just So Stories* by Rudyard Kipling are nonsensical tales that many fourth and fifth graders love. A. A. Milne's *The World of Christopher Robin* and *Winnie-the-Pooh* are enjoyed by children in the primary grades. Among other books, children of fourth

---

[30] Robert S. Whitman, "Folksongs for Elementary School Children," *Elementary English,* 40:724–728, November, 1963.

and fifth grades, especially boys, like Mary Bonner's *Out to Win*. Clyde Bulla's *Riding the Pony Express* is enjoyed by third and fourth graders. Daniel Defoe's *Robinson Crusoe* and Mark Twain's *Adventures of Tom Sawyer* have thrilled millions and should not be missed by pupils of the elementary school. Rudyard Kipling's *Jungle Book* and Eleanor Clymer's *Sociable Toby* are illustrative of the animal stories which interest children.

Witty reported that the favorite books of boys in grades three through six were *Black Beauty, Davy Crockett, Daniel Boone, Robin Hood, Thirty Seconds Over Tokyo,* and *Custer's Last Stand*. Girls selected as their favorites *Little Women, Cinderella, Snow White, Heidi,* and *Black Beauty*.[31]

*Biography.* One of the richest approaches to knowledge of human relationships and to history is biography. *Abraham Lincoln* by Ingri and Edgar d'Aulaire, written for second-, third-, and fourth-grade levels, tells the story of Lincoln's boyhood and his work as president in the Civil War. These authors have enriched the literature with biographies of George Washington and other famous people. *Daniel Boone* by James Daugherty, *Dr. George Washington Carver* by Shirley Graham and George Lipscomb, and *Andrew Jackson* by Frances Wright are popular examples of biographies suitable for avid readers of the upper elementary grades and junior high school levels.

*Poetry.* Robert Browning's *The Pied Piper of Hamlin* is fascinating to pupils on levels three to six. Walter de la Mare's *Peacock Pie* appeals to children from second to sixth levels because of the imagery and liveliness about children, fairies, magic, and nature. *Eleanor Farjeon's Poems for Children* is a collection of beautiful poems for children in kindergarten to sixth grade. Rachel Field's *Poems* is a collection enjoyable on levels two to four. Rose Fyleman's *Fairies and Chimneys* contains well-liked poems for third-, fourth-, and fifth-grade pupils. A. A. Milne's *When We Were Very Young* is a collection delightful in rhythm and suitable to young children from the kindergarten to grade four. One cannot omit in the briefest consideration of verse, the delightful *Sing-Song* by Christina Rossetti, and the much loved *A Child's Garden of Verses* by Robert Louis Stevenson, for children of the kindergarten and primary grades. Among the scores of anthologies, *Silver Pennies* compiled by Blanche Thompson includes some of the most loved poems for children on grade levels two to five. Louis

---

[31] Paul A. Witty, "Pupil Interests in the Elementary Grades," *Education,* 83:451–462, April, 1963.

Untermeyer compiled *This Singing World* which contains hundreds of poems of gifted writers that appeal to fifth and sixth graders. Closely allied to poetry books are the many collections of game and dance presentations, such as Durlacher's *Play Party Book* with such favorites as "Skip-to-my-Lou" and "Farmer-in-the-Dell," which appeal to children in grades two to six. Of interest is Hendrik Van Loon's *Songs We Sing,* a picture book of favorites as "Hickory Dickory Dock," "London Bridge," and "Sleep, Baby, Sleep," exciting to those in kindergarten and the following grades.

*Holidays.* Stories about holidays bring to children joy because of their experiences at Christmas, Thanksgiving, and Halloween and also because of their anticipation of holiday parties, feasts, and gifts. The Association for Childhood Education Literature Committee's *Told Under the Christmas Tree* contains a variety of stories liked by children of grades one to six. Eleanor Farjeon's *Come Christmas* containing lullabies, carols, and other verse suitable for Christmas and New Year is appropriate for children in elementary school. Elizabeth Sechrist's *Heigh-Ho for Halloween* presents a collection of games, plays, poems, and stories on the fourth- to sixth-grade levels. *Heydays and Holidays* by Laura Harris is a colored picture book of Jewish and Christian selections for holidays which charm children of grades two to four.

*Animals.* Animals appeal to pupils in primary and intermediate elementary school. Boys particularly love various types of animal life. Boys in rural sections of the country and girls also have interests in farm animals. All children love the circus from the elephant to the monkey. Frank Buck's *Jungle Animals* has value in grades three through five because of appropriate illustrations and accounts of animals found in the zoo. Jerome S. Meyer's *The Picture Book of the Sea* appeals particularly in grades three to eight. George Mason's *Animal Homes,* which presents accounts of the ways animals live, is interesting to pupils in grades four to six. Addison Webb has authored *Birds in Their Homes* for pupils on levels three to six, which shows how birds build their homes, live, and bring up their young.[32]

---

[32] *Adventuring With Books,* the 1950 edition, and *Adventuring With Books,* the 1960 edition, prepared by capable committees of the National Council of Teachers of English — the former under the Chairmanship of Margaret Mary Clark and the latter with the leadership of cochairmen Muriel Crosby and Beatrice Davis Hurley — were consulted for age and grade range limits. These two sources of approximately three thousand titles most of them annotated are an invaluable source of reference for children's literature in many fields.

*New books, current publications.* In the selection of books for elementary school children's reading there is a tendency to disregard the old for the new, a tendency which should be practiced only when the new is better than the old. Many of the old favorites of children cannot be replaced by new books. Yet, an alert teacher will consider the new as it is described in the current indexes and lists of the American Library Association, the National Council of Teachers of English, and those of the H. W. Wilson Company. Every year some periodicals publish a children's book section. The *New York Times* reported in 1960 in the order of number of sales, the sixteen best sellers of children's books compiled from leading booksellers in twenty-nine cities as follows: (1) *Love is a Special Way of Feeling,* Anglund; (2) *One Fish Two Fish Red Fish Blue Fish,* Seuss; (3) *Happy Birthday to You!* Seuss; (4) *Green Eggs and Ham,* Seuss; (5) *The Human Body,* Wilson; (6) *Onion John,* Krumgold; (7) *America Grows Up,* Johnson; (8) *The Answer Book,* Elting; (9) *The Black Stallion and Flame,* Farley; (10) *Little Bear's Friend,* Minarik; (11) *Walt Disney's People and Places,* Watson; (12) *The Golden Treasury of Poetry,* Untermeyer; (13) *Two Flags Flying,* Sobol; (14) *You Come Too,* Frost; (15) *The Junior Illustrated Encyclopedia of Sports,* Mullin and Kamm; (16) *America and Its Presidents,* Miers.[33]

In 1963, the list of children's best sellers based on reports of sales from 125 bookstores in 64 communities in the United States was as follows: (1) *Hop on Pop,* Seuss; (2) *Spring Is a New Beginning,* Anglund; (3) *Nutshell Library,* Sendak; (4) *Happiness is a Warm Puppy,* Schulz; (5) *Rascal: A Memoir of a Better Era,* North; (6) *A Snowy Day,* Keats; (7) *Security Is a Thumb and a Blanket,* Schulz; (8) *Dr. Seuss's ABC;* (9) *Prayers From the Ark,* de Gasztold, translated by Rumer Godden; (10) *The Secret Garden,* Burnett.[34]

Based on reports from bookstores from 64 communities of the nation, children's best sellers up to about May 1, are listed as follows with the years of publication: (1) *Where the Wild Things Are,* Sendak, 1963; (2) *A Friend Is Someone Who Likes You,* Anglund, 1958; (3) *A Pocketful of Proverbs,* Anglund, 1964; (4) *Charlotte's Web,* White, 1952; (5) *Love Is a Special Way of Feeling,* Anglund, 1960; (6) *Stormy: Misty's Foal,* Henry, 1963; (7) *It's Like This, Cat,* Neville,

[33] Children's Book Section, *New York Times Book Review,* Section 7, Part II, November 13, 1960, p. 62.

[34] Children's Book Section, *New York Times Book Review,* Section 7, Part II, November 10, 1963, p. 60.

1963; (8) *The Wolves of Willoughby Chase*, Aiken, 1963; (9) *Hop on Pop*, Seuss, 1963; (10) *A Wrinkle in Time*, L'Engle, 1962.[35]

Among these ten are two Newbery Medal Books, Emily Neville's *It's Like This, Cat*, 1963, and Madeleine L'Engle's *A Wrinkle in Time*, 1962, and one Caldecott medal winner, *Where the Wild Things Are* by Maurice Sendak, 1963. The Newbery award is given for most distinguished contribution to American literature for children. The Caldecott award is made for the most distinguished picture book of the year.

It should be clear that these were listed because of sales. Each should be read carefully by a teacher or librarian or rated in some valid way before selection for child reading.

## The Role of the Teacher in Storytelling and Oral Reading

A teacher's comprehensive background of knowledge — of poetry, prose, stories of various kinds, books about many lands and eras, books of different types of content, books about men and women who lived richly, books about animals, things, activities, and events — is very helpful in the motivation and guidance of pupils in reading. A discerning appreciation of the sayings, conversations, wit, and humor of characters of a story or play is advantageous for presentation to and reception by a child audience.

*Personality.* A teacher should be a vibrant, active, healthy personality with ability to visualize a whole situation at a glance and with the auding capacity to hear everything that a good listener must hear in teaching oral reading. An oral reading teacher should love the old gems but keep abreast of the new. She should be alert to the precious tales of childhood and the accomplishments of adulthood. It is helpful to be familiar through reading with all kinds of creatures from the mighty whale and ancient dinosaur to the smallest humming bird or lowliest insect. A teacher must be a person who can tell stories to a class in an enthusiastic manner, yet listen with extreme patience to the beginning efforts of a shy, nervous pupil. A very fine story can be spoiled by inept telling, but a simple story may be entertaining because a teacher knows it perfectly, has prepared adequately to tell or read it, and presents it with the right tone in a pleasant and considerate manner.

*Telling the story.* A storyteller must realize that a good story has

---

[35] Children's Book Section, *New York Times Book Review*, Section 7, Part II, May 10, 1964, p. 38.

a beginning, a development, and an ending. She must consider just the right way to begin. In wordiness she may lose the audience. The beginning should lead to the development as expeditiously as possible.

The development of the body of the story should be thoroughly understood. The expression should be original, informal, and appealing. The wording of a timely phrase or sentence may be given verbatim. Characters may be portrayed by word, manner, or perhaps by facial expression to give tone to each and to indicate relationship that exists among them.[36] If the story is shortened, it should be done without a break so that it will be understood as a whole.

The ending of the story is most delicate for a beginner. It should be given as perfectly as possible. It must be carefully prepared and delivered. The omission of a word, or the addition of a phrase may spoil the effect. When the "punch line" has been given, it is generally time to stop.

*Qualities and technics in storytelling.*   Among the qualities of a good storyteller are enthusiasm for the story, consideration for an audience, and alertness for a change of mood or feeling. If a story is worth telling it should be related with the proper spirit. Voice control is important in communication. A monotonous or strained voice will not be conducive to effective reception by children. A well-modulated voice connotes freedom and power.[37] It will be listened to because it is productive, pleasant, and appealing.

A storyteller should be well poised and natural in appearance, alert in mind and body, and attentive to the audience. Naturalness does not mean leaning against the wall or sprawling across a desk. It does not mean walking up and down from one side of the room to another, nor does it mean standing tensely as if glued to one place. The storyteller communicates her story to the audience. Gestures of the showy, sweeping type are questionable. If gestures are used, they should be simple and natural. In telling a story, timing is important. A good storyteller will vary her voice with the requirement of action and event. A judicious pause is often far more dramatic than excited volume. A low spoken word or phrase or sentence may be more effective than a shout.

*Reading orally.*   Oral reading has much in common with story-

---

[36] Marie L. Shedlock, *The Art of the Story-Teller* (Dover Publications, Inc., 1951), pp. 31–39.

[37] Ruth Sawyer, *The Way of the Storyteller* (New York: Viking Press, 1942), p. 137.

telling. Poetry or prose may be recited or read orally. In fact, when a teacher reads from a book, she should be so well acquainted with the context that she can have eye-to-eye communication with the children. Since it is obvious that one can memorize only a small part of the materials used, she should master the art of oral reading.

A teacher should be a good psychologist, as well as a master reader. She must demonstrate to children how to read well orally. At first, she may read to the children and perform for them. Gradually however, she should make herself superfluous — that is, give way to the children's growing interest in and desire for oral reading and storytelling. A teacher who reads well orally from the best authors and poets will so motivate pupils to read that the time will come when all the pupils of a class will desire to read. From that point guidance should be given, as it is required, to pupils who can be helped. Then pupils will develop the art of oral reading and storytelling quite independently.

## THE UNIT APPROACH TO READING

If the "reading interests with which children come to school are our opportunities and those with which they leave are our responsibilities," we teachers in the elementary school have a solemn accounting to make. Among objectives, we must teach children to want to read and we must interest them in reading of value. Reading must be conceived not as drudgery, but as a happy and useful way of experiencing and enjoying the thought and action of other people. Through appropriate reading, a pupil can delight in the lives and works of great men and women and enjoy stories, adventures, actions, and events that are pleasant, useful, stimulating, and uplifting.

### Unit Motivation of Reading

The unit motivates reading because it is a purposeful, significant, comprehensive, and meaningful phase of learning and study which integrates reading, writing, speaking, thinking, and experiencing. The unit shifts emphasis in reading from teaching the child by telling him what to do, to guiding the child to purpose, plan, organize, evaluate, and use materials. In the unit, properly initiated and guided, children develop objectives, solve problems, carry out projects, engage in activities, and accomplish their goals through reading materials which they locate in books, periodicals, encyclopedias, and other library sources.[38] In a unit, they do not complain of being coerced; their attitude is that reading and study are necessary to learn and to create. The unit therefore is an excellent way of motivating meaningful reading.

### The Place of Reading in the Unit

In the unit, reading is a natural and inviting way to learn what the pupil requires in achieving his goals. Reading does not seem difficult because it leads to desired knowledge and understanding. In the topic assignment, the child often goes "as a slave scourged to his dungeon," but in a properly motivated unit, he progresses freely and happily to inviting and challenging materials.

Reading in a unit is a basis for identifying new problems, forming opinions, verifying facts, satisfying purposes, and making judgments. It is bound up with other communication skills — writing notes, making outlines, and talking. It is frequently the basis for discussion and it is often directed by the result of discussion. It is correlated with listening, handwriting, spelling. It is related to experiencing; in fact, it is experiencing.

Reading in unit activities may include: (1) work-type silent reading; (2) work-type oral reading; (3) recreational silent reading; and (4) recreational oral reading. Work-type silent reading requires in the unit: location, comprehension, evaluation, organization, retention, and use of materials in construction and creativity. Work-type oral reading is useful in reporting, making announcements, and giving directions. In many units, recreational silent reading is delightful, inviting, and stimulating. Reading of the oral recreational type, often involved in a unit, includes the reading of stories, plays, poems, recording a dramatic or creative selection, and choral presentations. Reading operates to a varying extent in every type of unit.

### A Unit: Enrichment Through Reading Biography

*Introduction.* Among the units that may be undertaken by a class for the reading of literature are: Fairy Tales, Fantasy, and Folktales; Poetry in the Lives of Primary Grade Children; Reading Historical Literature; Literature about Other Lands; Biographical Literature; and Bibliotherapy. Each of these units can be fruitful. Space permits the outlining of one unit, Biographical Literature.

---

[38] Arthur I. Gates, "Improvement of Reading Possible in the Near Future," *The Reading Teacher,* 12:86–87, December, 1958.

This unit can be developed satisfactorily in grade levels four to six. Such a unit should motivate every child in the class to read about his favorite heroes and heroines, and to hear from others in the class about other great and important men and women.

In preparing for such a unit, many biographies should be provided in several fields — art, music, history, geography, science, exploration, health, communication, transportation, and invention. Biographies should be available on hundreds of people and two or more biographies on persons such as Lincoln and Washington are useful on different reading levels to accommodate individual differences.

*Suggestions for approaches.* Several approaches are available to interest pupils in this type of unit. (1) Questions may be used. What was Washington's role at Fort Necessity? Why was Edison thought of as slow in school? (2) A discussion about the poem "The Swing" by Robert Louis Stevenson could bring about the desire to read more about Stevenson and other poets and writers. (3) A talk about the telephone might interest pupils in Alexander Graham Bell. (4) Boys studying Indians might read about Crazy Horse or Red Cloud. (5) Approaches such as an exhibit of art prints of Michelangelo, the reading of a poem as the "Skyscrapers" by Rachel Field, a recording as "Johnny Appleseed," an address as "The Gettysburg Speech," and stories of Israel Putnam or Clara Barton may awaken a desire to know about great people and their works.

*Objectives.* The objectives are reading — silent and oral reading — skimming, wide reading, thoughtful studious reading, curious reading, evaluative reading, organized reading, retentive reading, useful reading. The teacher must have clearly in mind what she intends to accomplish: extension of interest in famous people; appreciation of traits such as courage, excellence, and patience of great men and women in various fields; the encouragement of cooperative and creative work; appreciation and interpretation of biographical literature by the pupils.

The pupils should have an objective in the beginning and develop and recognize other objectives as they go along. Initially they may want to read about the life and work of a great person. Later, some may desire to find out why certain people became great; others may wish to know what qualities are found in leaders in various fields — painting, music, science, history, writing, and so on.

*Teacher procedures.* By means of testing, observation, interview, and the inventory, the teacher determines the ability levels of children and their preferences. She may read to the children and listen to them. She will have them read for enjoyment and also for knowledge and information. Teacher praise of successes, commendation of enthusiasm for reading, and encouragement of new interests are useful.

*Some selected materials.* In addition to biographies in various fields, audio-visual materials — filmstrips, films, and recordings — are important. Filmstrips such as those about George Washington, Abraham Lincoln, Christopher Columbus, the American Indian, those on authors, heroes, and patriots motivate biographical study. Films on invention, transportation, agriculture, and medicine that portray leaders in the fields excite interest. Recordings based upon stories such as those of Grant and Lee at Appomattox, Robert Fulton's first steamboat, and the Wright Brothers' exploits guide young seekers for knowledge. Recordings of marches, symphonies, waltzes, and concertos cause questions and research about the composers and masters.

*Possible pupil activities.* Among the projects initiated by pupils are: making a scrapbook of famous people, about their deeds and sayings; making a reading plan; organizing a readers' club; conducting puppet shows; dressing dolls to represent people; making posters and bookmarks; painting murals; and constructing models of inventions.

Among the writing and speaking activities, the following are often carried on: making book lists; publishing a paper or magazine; writing and reading brief book reviews; writing and reading original stories; reading silently favorite book selections; reading orally favorite prose or poetry selections to a group; writing imaginary letters to or from favorite people; singing songs of composers; dramatization of experiences of heroes of health or science; making sketches of heroes and reading them to find whether others in the group can guess the identities of the famous people.

Among the observing and listening activities, the following are more or less common: viewing films; seeing art pictures; listening to records; interviewing authors and publishers; listening to selected radio programs; viewing appropriate television programs; taking trips to art museums; listening to storytelling by teachers, librarians, and other pupils.

Many questions and problems develop from the projects and activities in such a unit, among them the following are examples: What qualities and opportunities made Washington, Lincoln, Columbus, and

Pasteur great? Who were the leaders of our country in statesmanship, exploration, pioneering, science, invention, engineering, music, oratory, writing?

Exhibits may be organized to display favorite books, pictures, and art, and to show old or rare books. An assembly may be held to present readings of poetry and to review books of pupil preferences. A book fair may be conducted to promote interest in reading.

*Integration.* Several types of integration are generally practiced in a unit. Subject-matter lines are crossed and recrossed. A unit on the lives of great people frequently makes use of all the skills of the language arts — reading, speaking, listening, writing, spelling, and handwriting. History, geography, social studies are integrated in considering the lives and exploits of leaders and pioneers in various fields of endeavor. Science, health, and medicine are considered naturally in the life of a man such as Louis Pasteur or Edward Jenner. Art and music activities are recognized to be part of the lives of many writers. Mathematics is seen to be important in the behavior of scientists, geographers, and inventors. As youngsters become interested in great lives, they recognize the many sides to living. They become aware of the fact that George Washington was a soldier, a statesman, a president, a farmer, a surveyor, and that in performing the activities involved in his many duties he used a wide variety of skills and knowledges to accomplish his goals.

*Outcomes.* A unit on biography acquaints pupils with great people and reveals their qualities in facing problems and carrying out projects. Appreciative attitudes toward greatness are developed by recognizing the sacrifices of heroes. Understanding of leaders' contributions to the progress of society is achieved. Enjoyment of wide and extensive reading is not the least of the outcomes. There generally is improvement in the thoughtful processes — location, comprehension, organization, evaluation, and retention. Vocabulary is enhanced by rich vicarious experiencing and through word study of many types. Increased abilities in interpretation and use of reading result.

*Culminating activities.* Among the most interesting and rewarding phases of any unit, especially to the participants, are the culminating activities. For a biographical unit these may include one or more of the following: a play, an exhibit, a recounting of items, stories, verses, anecdotes, or exploits of people in a field. In an assembly, pupils may present, for example, a program on the adventures of pioneers in the development of our country, or a panel on the great inventions of leaders in transportation. The compilation of a bibliography of leaders in a special field could be one of the individual accomplishments of a pupil. A trip made by a group or class to the Hall of Fame for Great Americans would be a never-to-be-forgotten activity. Quotations, anecdotes, and stories could be assembled and placed on the reading table.

*Bibliographies.* A teacher who directed such a unit listed a bibliography of hundreds of books, many of which pupils reported from their reading, in the following fields: (1) Early Americans, (2) Famous Explorers, (3) Noted Inventors and Scientists, (4) American Presidents, (5) Leaders in Religion, (6) Authors, (7) Indians, (8) Leaders in Other Lands, (9) Famed Musicians, (10) Distinguished Artists, (11) Men and Women Renowned in Medicine and Health. As the unit developed, individual pupils discovered books in these fields and located sources about leaders in electronics, space exploration, oceanography, animal husbandry, plant cultivation, rocketry, and other areas.[39]

*Evaluation.* Was the work worthwhile? Was the reading enlightening? Were the activities engaged in and the projects carried out useful to the pupils in extending their study about the great characters of history, literature, science, invention, art, or music? Have the children gained power in reading? Have the various abilities in language improved? Have the pupils improved their skills in library usage? Have the pupils learned to appreciate the traits of famous people? Have the children widened their interests in literature? Have they become aware of new fields and vistas through books? By means of informal questions, observation, individual records of readings, evidence of growth in discussion, written and oral comments, a teacher can answer such questions quite well for each child in her class. If progress has been made in extending and intensifying interests in the readings selected, pupils will carry the results of such a unit into other units and into the reading activities in the subject fields in school and into living after school.

## SUMMARY

Reading to satisfy recreational and work-type needs is of the greatest importance to the individual.

Ideally the elementary school library should contain books and other materials to fit every taste in acceptable recreational reading

---

[39] Credit is given to Dr. Theresa Sabellico Kelly for planning the unit from which this report was written.

and every study need of the pupils. Book and periodical selection should be carried out under the guidance of a trained librarian and experienced teachers. Children in the elementary school should become aware of the values of library reading and study.

A teacher should know the preferences of boys and girls on all levels. Among the types of reading which appeal to children at one or more levels are: picture stories, folklore, books about our country and peoples of other lands, biographies, poetry, animals, science, industry, arts, crafts, and hobbies. A teacher should know the new books, but should not discard the old favorites — those books that have proved to be worthwhile and popular for generations. The role of the teacher in oral reading and storytelling is important in developing pupil interests and desires for reading. The teacher must be for many an inspiration and a guide.

To promote interest in reading, units may be organized on literary topics — poetry in lives of children, literature of other places or periods, biography — or on work-type topics as boats, airplanes, communication, travel, farming, or safety. "The Indians of North America," "The Pioneers," "Our North American Neighbors" are examples of units that will motivate reading.

## ACTIVITIES, PROBLEMS, QUESTIONS

1. Compare and contrast: "learning to read" and "reading to learn."
2. How can the use of a library be made effective by a teacher in the elementary school?
3. Make a list of books and other references which should be available to intermediate pupils in the library.
4. Appraise the list of periodicals suggested by the New York State Education Department. Make up a supplementary list which you think would be important for your class.
5. Compile standards for the selection of periodicals for children's reading.
6. Guide pupils to make up a bibliography on a selected topic. What type of cards — author, title, or subject — would you have them use? How should they be arranged?
7. Describe a well-organized plan for stimulating pupils to read good literature.
8. Read the review of research on preferences and formulate several principles of book selection based on children's likes and dislikes in reading.
9. State the values of the following in children's literature: pictures, action, plot, conversation, legends, animals, biography, poetry.
10. See the reference to Witty's report on favorite books in grades three through six.
 a) Why do boys like *Black Beauty, Davy Crockett, Robin Hood,* and *Custer's Last Stand?*

*b*) Why do girls prefer *Little Women, Cinderella, Heidi,* and *Black Beauty?*

11. Describe the role of the teacher in storytelling.

12. Analyze the unit approach to reading, and study the plan of the unit on biography. What are the values attained by the group?

13. Plan a unit to meet the needs of pupils in a particular grade on one: folktales, historical literature, poetry, literature of other lands, or other titles. How can you best enlist the pupils' interest in the unit?

## SELECTED REFERENCES

*Arbuthnot Anthology of Children's Literature, The.* Chicago: Scott, Foresman, 1954. 418 pp.

Arbuthnot, May Hill. *Children and Books.* 3rd ed. Chicago: Scott, Foresman, 1964. 688 pp.

*A Basic Book Collection for Elementary Grades.* Chicago: American Library Association, 1960. 144 pp.

*Children's Catalog.* 10th ed. New York: H. W. Wilson, 1961. 951 pp. Annual supplements.

Eakin, Mary K., compiler. *Good Books for Children: A Selection of Outstanding Children's Books Published 1948–1961.* Rev. ed. Chicago: University of Chicago Press, 1962. 362 pp.

Eakin, Mary K. *Subject Index to Books for Intermediate Grades.* 3rd ed. Chicago: American Library Association, 1963. 320 pp.

Eaton, Anne Thaxter. *Treasure for the Taking.* "A Book List for Boys and Girls." Rev. ed. New York: Viking, 1957. 322 pp.

*Elementary School Libraries Today.* Thirtieth Yearbook of the National Elementary Principal. Washington, D. C.: NEA, 1951. 415 pp.

Fargo, Lucile F. *The Library in the School.* 4th ed. Chicago: American Library Association, 1947. 405 pp.

Haywood, Charles. *Bibliography of North American Folklore and Folkways.* New York: Greenberg, 1951. 1292 pp.

Johnson, Edna, Evelyn Sickels, and Clark Sayers. *Anthology of Children's Literature.* 3rd ed. Boston: Houghton Mifflin, 1959. 1239 pp.

Kennon, Mary F., and Leila A. Doyle. *Planning School Library Development.* Chicago: American Library Association, 1962. 89 pp.

Mahony, Bertha E. *Newbery Medal Books: 1922–1955.* Boston: Horn Book, 1955. 458 pp.

Mahony, Bertha E., and Elinor W. Field. *Caldecott Medal Books: 1938–1957.* Boston: Horn Book, 1957. 329 pp.

Norvell, George W. *Reading Interests of Young People.* Boston: Heath, 1950. 262 pp.

Smith, Dora V. *Fifty Years of Children's Books.* Champaign: National Council of Teachers of English, 1963. 149 pp.

See references for Chapters IV and V.

# Chapter IX

# Social and Creative Writing

## INTRODUCTION

CREATIVE writing, as thought of in this chapter, may be defined as original expression in prose or verse — the friendly letter, story, poetry, drama, or other types — which the writer creates by his own initiative and effort.

In the wonderful realm of childhood before entering school, the child expresses himself in many original and creative ways. When he does not have an audience, he talks to himself about the things in his real and unreal world. Strange imaginative tales are "lived" by young boys and girls. Before coming to school, many have fancied make-believe stories of caves and mountains, of creatures and people, of giants and dwarfs, unknown in reality. To understand the child, the teacher must strive to unlock the door of his impressions by exciting in him a desire to express. He has much to say if he can find a considerate listener, and he will begin to communicate if he finds a favorable environment. At first, his communication is vocal; later if properly stimulated, he begins to put his thoughts in writing. Creative writing cannot be taught so systematically as handwriting or spelling, but it can be exciting and challenging. A story, a letter, or a play may be produced to satisfy an urge to describe a pet, to tell about an experience, or to dramatize an adventure.[1]

Writing is a necessary and useful art. Bacon suggested that "Reading maketh a full man, conference a ready man, and writing an exact man." Reading and writing are reciprocal as are speaking and listening. Learning to write is a major language objective. Important in the teaching of writing is the guidance of the child to express his feelings. Too often we who teach fail to impress pupils with the idea that

---

[1] Rose Miller, "Children Open the Door," unpublished paper, 1962.

self-expression through writing is a valuable ability even more important than conforming meticulously to correct mechanics.

Research on composition has not sufficiently answered many questions which teachers of writing raise. Shane's review indicates a paucity of research in the field, but makes helpful suggestions concerning creative expression.[2] Wolf reported results of a survey which indicated that the typical teacher considered creativity as a characteristic which improved personal and social adjustment of boys and girls.[3]

## Freedom to Express

A sense of freedom in talking is conducive to creative writing. A child will in a sense portray himself in his original expression when he reconstructs experiences or activities which interest him. When such activities are purposively engaged in, he is setting forth ideas which for him are original.[4] There are important relationships among the activities of thinking, listening, speaking, reading, and writing. They should not be isolated — one from the other. For example, writing is frequently initiated by oral language, and oral language is often enhanced by writing.

Writing benefits from freedom to think, to experience, and to imagine. The first grade in Miss Miller's classroom had been learning a song about spring. It began, "The bees are telling every flower." One morning, a shy little boy of a rather underprivileged background came into the room in a very excited manner and said, "Teacher, I saw the bees telling the flowers, 'Spring is here.'"

A fourth-grade child who lived in a barren country wrote a beautiful letter to a friend of hers in a town a hundred miles away, a part of which follows:

> My little bunny is sure growing. He just loves his milk and alfalfa. He likes to sit at the door and look out and when he sees the dog he sure does scamper. His sides go in and out and his nose goes up and down. It is a lot of fun to watch him.

This letter indicates experiencing, close observation, and free, clear

---

[2] Harold G. Shane, *Research Helps in Teaching the Language Arts* (Washington, D. C.: Association for Supervision and Curriculum Development, 1955), pp. 44–47.

[3] William C. Wolf, "Creativity: The Concept of a Hot Tin Roof," *The National Elementary Principal,* 40:5–9, April, 1961.

[4] Harry A. Greene and Walter T. Petty, *Developing Language Skills in the Elementary Schools* (Boston: Allyn and Bacon, Inc., 1959), p. 130.

expression by a child without great concern about the mechanics of writing.

## An Expanding Background Creates an Urge to Write

Experiencing and thinking about events are important approaches to expression. Real experiences are the bases for most letter writing, which may be quite as original as storytelling, poetry, or dramatics. These may be supplemented and reinforced by vicarious experiencing, which comes about through reading and through audio-visual presentations. As a pupil views a picture, reads a story, or listens to a poem, he may develop a wish to write something. A plan may flash through his mind; perhaps he may have had a desire to write a story but was not sure of the approach. Now the experience or the activity gives him an idea for his own composition. This may be expressed first verbally and then in writing.

The urge to write cannot be taught formally. It must be caught and felt. A teacher who would engender such a purpose would do well to create an environment of art and literature appropriate for the pupils she is teaching. The class climate should be pleasant and stimulating. Poems may be shared with the class — read by the teacher and by members of the group. Stories will be enjoyed together. Plays can be presented, and books supplied for reading and study. Children require freedom for expression after they have begun to enjoy the environment and acquire the rapport aroused in such a classroom.

It was thought a few decades ago that only those who showed promise should be instructed in creative writing. At present there is a more desirable philosophy about original expression. It is realized now that although comparatively few individuals will write great books or beautiful poetry, it is certain that many people will write friendly letters and other communications which call for skill, originality, and considerateness.

Formal study and drill upon the mechanics of writing will not endear creative writing to children. The main approach is not through grammar; it must come from having something to communicate and from a desire to write it. In arriving at a procedure to induce children to write creatively, the interrelationships of the language arts should be clarified. Experience leads to oral language and oral communication to written language. Listening to people, talking to them, looking at pictures and scenes from real life, reading about animals and people, discussing poetry and stories, critically evaluating what has been read or spoken, and thinking about what has been learned in class and out of class — all contribute to a background from which originality and creativity germinate and develop.

## The Child Can Write Creatively

A child generally can write if he wants to write, and perhaps the most important duty of the teacher in written language is to *cause him to want to write*. The situations which call for writing must be made desirable to the child.

Children have freedom of will. They have native intelligence which differs greatly and experiences which vary widely from one to another. The experiences of one can be and usually are shared vicariously with others of the class. Fortunately, the background is added to from day to day. Outside the school, the child takes part in and enjoys home and community life; in school, activities are actuated and cultivated, many of them real and many vicarious. All of these should make writing richer and more meaningful. The alert child, stimulated properly, views these experiences with keen appraisal and reacts in his own way. He uses language for expression, and develops vocabulary as he talks, listens, reads, studies, and thinks. He has imagination which he must learn to develop and control as he wills to select the worthwhile for dynamic expression. He can write and he will improve his writing by making use of opportunities which guidance indicates. He will communicate as the need arises and as situations require. He can and he will write letters, articles, stories, editorials, compositions, plays, and even poetry, if he goes to a school in which the curriculum is permeated with good materials, interesting activities, and an acceptable climate.

## Kindling the Creative Spirit

The teacher is a primary agent for inspiring the pupil to write. If she can cause the learner to taste the thrills of creative expression, the way is opened to pupil efforts and development. The learner needs guidance to worthwhile literary materials in accord with his level of ability, his likes, and his interests. Mearns suggested, the dynamic creativeness inherent in children should not be stifled in a school situation.[5] Inspiration and freedom to write are important in pro-

---

[5] Hughes Mearns, "The Creative Spirit and Its Significance for Education," *Creative Expression,* second edition (Milwaukee: E. M. Hale and Company, 1939), p. 13.

A puppet show

ducing worthwhile products as are planning, concentrated thinking, and painstaking application. Creative writing requires effort, for it does not just happen without work; certainly, it must be planned. It requires thinking, study, evaluation, and often revision and rewriting. The teacher who guides the child must not bury creativity in a morass of mechanics. This does not mean that mechanics are not desirable. They should come, however, in their proper place in the whole scheme of writing.

An important approach to creative expression is through materials — books that a child enjoys and is capable of reading with ease and for pleasure. Let the young learner enjoy literature; let him browse and relax in a library or reading room. Pupils will describe and advertise favorite selections — poems or prose of various types — to their schoolmates.

A poetry club, a story club, a drama club, or a literary society is a powerful stimulation for speaking, reading, and writing. The enjoyment of plays may be a real steppingstone to writing one. At first, plays may be written by groups, but later individuals may "try their hands" at creating them. A play discussed in a club may be the incentive for a group to devise a plot for a school presentation. A radio program may encourage a child to plan an original skit. The projects in a unit or the activities in a group enterprise are often conducive to originality in speech and writing. The "give and take" of evaluative discussion and the critical appraisal of the work on an assembly program may lead individuals to create various types of expressional products. Interesting stories may be the motivating agency in inciting an individual to write a story of his own.

Purpose is primary in learning and teaching. In addition to a rich atmosphere of books and an environment for enjoying them, the teacher will promote purpose for working in challenging situations so that the pupil will build confidence in his ability to write and will develop a feeling of power in expression and a zest for originality. Challenge to investigate, to communicate, to express, to share experiences, and to improve output should be utilized to the fullest. A purpose clarified and defined by the pupil is a stimulant for original writing.

## Some Considerations for Creativity

Creativity should be promoted and not impeded. The following suggestions and comments indicate phases of creativity:

1. Creative writing concerns life and is closely related to other language arts — particularly reading, listening, and oral communication.

2. The child will develop the creative spirit through experiencing beauty, nature, scenery, and activities around him — sports, play, music, art, work.

3. The pupil will benefit from social relationships and activities of home, school, and community.

4. He will react favorably to wholesome stimuli in worthy programs of radio, television, and other media as he becomes able to understand and appreciate them.

5. He should immerse himself in reading fascinating aspects of our heritage and culture.

6. He should delight in literature — poetry, drama, stories, and other writings of his choice.

7. Sensitivity to his accumulated background of knowledge and experience will develop a desire to respond creatively.

8. From these responses — appreciations and understandings — the seeds of inspiration are often sown and cultivated.

9. Inspiration to express, developed by intensive stimuli, prompts the individual to communicate orally and in writing.

10. A creative product begun in a favorable moment is consummated and tested to meet an individual's developing standards of judgment.

11. Creativity in writing stimulates personality development beyond that which can be attained only by mastery and practice of skills and mechanics of writing.

12. Creative writings enthusiastically read and received by others, encourage further creative writing. To improve his writing, a child must write.[6]

## SOCIAL LETTER WRITING

Letter writing is important in the life of everyone, and friendly letters may be listed properly under the heading of creative writing. The fact that some are poorly written does not mean that letter writing should not be well planned, dynamically taught, and creatively developed in elementary school. Better instruction and the improvement of learning conditions and technics will enhance this type of communication.

### Some Research Findings in Child Letter Writing

*Situations in which letters were written.* Children from all sections of the United States of grades four, five, and six wrote 3184 friendly letters comprising approximately 460,000 running words. These letters were composed in real situations, principally in life outside the school. Children wrote most frequently about experiences, activities, and events of life. Often they wrote about school, objects, animals, and weather. Infrequently they wrote letters of congratulation, greeting, or condolence. Seldom were words of encouragement found in their letters. Seldom were there expressions of apology or explanation. Quite frequently, however, there were expressions of thanks, requests for materials or favors, invitations, and acceptances of them. The ordinary letter contained an average of less than three types and more than two types of content. For example, one rather typical letter told about an activity, asked for information, and discussed the weather; another quite as typical described a new dress and stated the essentials of work in school.

---

[6] See Wilhelmina Hill, Helen K. Mackintosh, and Arne Randall, *How Children Can Be Creative,* U. S. Department of Health, Education, and Welfare, Bulletin 1954, No. 12, 24 pp. See also Gardner Murphy, "The Process of Creative Thinking," *Educational Leadership,* 14:11–12, October, 1956.

These letters were written most often to *friends*. Second in rank of recipients were *cousins*. *Former teachers* received the third largest number of letters; fourth in rank of recipients were *sisters* or *brothers* of the writers; fifth were *uncles* or *aunts;* and sixth were *schoolmates* or *former schoolmates*. *Fathers* or *mothers* were seventh and *grandparents* were eighth. Some letters were addressed quite infrequently to *other relatives, folks,* and a very few to *others.*[7]

*The attitudes evident in these letters.* An analysis of these letters indicated the need for careful evaluation of the attitudes toward letter writing. A lack of courtesy and a type of impoliteness indicated, perhaps, an ignorance of etiquette and the manner of writing a letter rather than a willful purpose to be discourteous. For example, one girl wrote as follows, no doubt in an attempt at congratulation:

> Well, I hear you won. I supposed you would because you got so much help. It's sure fine to be teacher's pet. Glad you won, though.

Another girl penned the following message:

> Say, send me that doll I left at your place. It's my favorite one and I want it. Send it right away will you? (This was followed by a paragraph of news items and the letter ended with a postscript which stated, "Don't forget the doll. I'll thank you much to send it.")

Again, it is evident that the difficulty here is the lack of understanding of the way to write a request appropriately.

There was in these letters a tendency especially among the city boys to offer advice to their correspondents. Often the advice was based upon the merest conjecture but sometimes an unusual experience or activity was made the basis for the suggestions. One boy wrote:

> We have just finished decimals. They're not hard if you get a good start. Take my advice and when you have decimals get your lesson every day, if you don't you'll never get through them.

Another boy composed the following about the expense of "going out":

> I took Isabell to the show and bought her some candy. She sure is expensive. Boy, listen to me — don't ever fall for an expensive woman.

Another's advice for obtaining work is quoted:

> . . . I worked there three months. The best way to get a job is to walk right up and tell the boss you're good and what you want. I did.

[7] James A. Fitzgerald, *Letters Written Outside the School by Children of the Fourth, Fifth, and Sixth Grades: A Study of Vocabulary, Spelling Errors, and Situations.* University of Iowa Studies in Education, Vol. IX, No. 1 (Iowa City: State University of Iowa, 1934), pp. 3–50.

I told him what was what about me and that I wanted a job. It sure worked all right.

These types of letters were duplicated many times. The ideas contained in them often implied greater perspicuity than nicety of expression or considerateness of the recipient.

Many of the letters indicated that the child writers had problems, and that some had assumed responsibilities heavy for their years. All indicated that the youngsters had many things to write about, but lacked appropriate methods of expressing their thoughts and feelings. Many of the letters indicated insecurity and frustration. Although some of them reported poverty and distress, the most outstanding characteristics were those of confidence in the future, enthusiasm for activities, joy about improvements in home furnishings, happiness because of newly acquired possessions or skills, and the buoyancy of youth in "doing, going, and living."

*Generalizations about letters.* In general, from the letters of this investigation and from those of another similar study on third-grade life letters[8] the following implications were drawn.

Modern instructional practices have made it quite clear that children can learn to write acceptable letters, and they will do so if they understand the purpose and need for writing them. They will come to realize that the satisfaction and joy of receiving letters are the results of writing appropriately. With practice, children develop skill in organization and ability to write properly. In time, they acquire originality, considerateness, courtesy, and an acceptable style in communicating with their friends.

## Need and Function of Friendly Letters

Every child during his life will write letters about the many important activities and events which concern him and those to whom he writes; he will write about the little things of life, the "doings" and the "goings on" of his family and his friends. These communications will be desirable to his readers in the degree to which he is able to recreate the situations, describe the events, and tell the stories of his experiences.

*Values of letter writing.* Letter writing is pleasurable; it may serve as a record of activities; it may be mentally hygienic in producing good will and understanding. Writing to a person may unload a heavy

---

[8] James A. Fitzgerald, "The Vocabulary and Spelling Errors of Third-Grade Children's Life Letters," *Elementary School Journal,* 38:358–370, January, 1934.

burden from the writer's shoulders. Joy in reading what a friend has communicated truthfully and sincerely may be boundless. The satisfaction of writing letters is only a little less than that of receiving them, for the culmination of communication is experienced by both correspondents who truly enjoy each other's messages. A sincere letter, received or written, buoys one up and causes him frequently to glow with a warmth of understanding. Living is enhanced by corresponding with friends and members of one's family.

The pleasure which comes from receiving letters, of which the child should be made aware, was indicated by a woman speaking of her son's letter which came usually on Monday morning: "When the letter comes the work becomes so light and easy and my heart is so glad, but when the letter does not come . . . how heavy the work seems all day."

*The importance of instruction.* McKee stated that letter writing is the most important instructional job in written composition.[9] Children should be guided to write the letters that are needed and those that will give pleasure in the situations which confront them in their lives. Children have a right to expect instruction in social letter writing, which has purpose and in addition offers the lure of originality.

The letters of many children and those of many adults do not always present a true picture of life because they are cramped by misunderstanding and restricted by lack of expressional abilities. The deficiencies of the ordinary letters of children should cause teachers to recognize the need for instruction which will make letter writing the art that it should be. Children should be encouraged to write the original thoughts and the happiest feelings of their beings, as did the little Indian girl who penned the following:

Dear Mamma, I love you. Mano.

Unmeasured and unmeasurable satisfaction was given by the little girl who wrote:

Dear Papa, I love you and I pray for you every night.
Your Best Girl.

These letters were treasured because of the sincerity of the writers in conveying their love for the readers.[10]

---

[9] Paul McKee, *Language in the Elementary School,* revised edition (Boston: Houghton Mifflin Company, 1939), pp. 166–167.

[10] Frances Bennett Callaway, *Charm and Courtesy in Letter Writing* (New York: Dodd, Mead, and Company, 1895), p. 45.

## Occasions and Situations for Letter Writing

A correct approach to letter writing such as using a real situation for writing or taking advantage of occasions that call for writing, should be sought. Too often teachers have insisted that children write a letter or a theme or a report in which they were not interested and for which they saw no need. There are many occasions appropriate for writing: Easter, Christmas, Thanksgiving, birthdays, anniversaries, sickness, and death.

*Some examples of school situations for writing.* To attempt to set up a separate list of situations for each grade seems unnecessary because the situations in one grade are often quite helpful in another and because there are extreme individual writing differences in children's interests and abilities from grade to grade. The following types of situations are representative of those found useful in school writing at one or more levels:

1. Writing a letter to Santa Claus
2. Inviting the second grade to attend an assembly by the first grade
3. An acceptance by the second grade of the invitation
4. Writing parents for permission to go on an excursion with the class
5. Asking a mother to visit the classroom to view a film on Sweden
6. Writing a letter of congratulation to a graduate who has received an honor or an appointment
7. Writing a letter of gratitude to a speaker for his interesting talk on art at the assembly
8. Writing a "get well" letter to a classmate
9. Writing letters — group or individual — to children of a school in a foreign country
10. Writing a letter of thanks to a donor of books for the school library
11. Writing a note of thanks to the librarian for aid given
12. Writing a letter telling about the new school newspaper
13. Writing a letter of apology to a neighbor for running across his lawn and garden to retrieve a baseball
14. Writing letters of appreciation to a newspaper for publishing a story about a third-grade science exhibit.

The school promotes scores of activities about which to write, but many good situations for writing are ignored. For example, when a group writes a note to invite another group to visit an assembly, the opportunity for the second group to respond in writing is often disregarded. Such a real situation may well be used for instruction.

*Some examples of life situations for writing.* In life, there are many writing situations for individuals as the following indicate:

1. A letter to a father away on a business trip
2. A letter to a mother sick in the hospital
3. A letter to a brother in the armed services
4. A letter to a former schoolmate who lives in another city
5. An acceptance of an invitation to a party
6. A letter to a cousin recounting the accomplishments on a fishing trip
7. A letter to an aunt relating family activities and problems
8. A letter to a friend describing a championship baseball game
9. A letter to last year's teacher acquainting her with this year's school activities
10. A letter of congratulations to a cousin who has won an essay contest
11. A letter of thanks to an uncle for a gift
12. A letter describing a home garden
13. A letter of condolence to a friend on the occasion of the death of his brother
14. A letter to an uncle and aunt thanking them for their hospitality
15. A letter describing a science experiment
16. A letter telling about a surprise party
17. A letter about an Independence Day celebration
18. A letter to a class describing an airplane ride.

## Beginning Letter Writing

The first letters are generally group letters dictated to the teacher. As the youngsters think about the purpose of their letter, members in turn express themselves about the best way to write what is to be said. Each sentence is written on the board by the teacher, and revised if necessary after appraisal or criticism has been made by the group. The letter may consist of only two or three sentences. After reading and thinking about the letter, the construction and the sequence of the sentences may be changed until the members are satisfied with the whole.

In the very beginning, a letter may consist of only one sentence. One beginning letter was dictated early in the first semester of the first grade by a comparatively slow group.

"Dear Mother: Come to our play on Friday afternoon."

The letter was duplicated and each child signed his copy and carried it home. The mothers came, and the children who had written the letter enjoyed their presence. These youngsters had achieved important objectives: (1) they fulfilled a purpose in a real situation; (2) they received enjoyment and satisfaction from their effort; (3) they found that letter writing was a means of communication; and (4) they liked it because it brought results.

Later in the first grade and in the beginning of the second grade more group instruction and some group writing are helpful. However, in the second grade some children want to write their own letters. When the children ask to do this, individual instruction begins. The child becomes aware of the need for a purpose for writing to someone. Children in the second grade wanted to write to a friend sick in the hospital. After deciding what should go into a letter of sympathy, each child wrote his own letter and asked the teacher to look at it. After suggestions had been accepted and revisions made, each copied his letter in his best possible manuscript. The letters were read to the class before they were sent. (Some children may not wish to read their letters, and their wishes should be respected.) The letters were mailed. One of them read as follows:

March 21, 19—

Dear Bill,
    We are sorry you are sick. Do you hurt much? Get well soon. Tell us about the hospital.

Jim

Bill enjoyed the letters, and his mother sent a note thanking the children. In it, she said Bill would write too, and that he hoped to be back in school very soon. The reply was pleasing to the class.

A class of deprived fourth-grade children was visited by the teacher's wife. The next morning one child wrote:

Dear Mrs. W——
    You are a nice lady. You are so pretty you gleam. Your husband is a millionaire. I wish he was my father.

Your friend,
M——

P.S. Ask Mr. W—— who I am.

## Letter Writing in the Intermediate and Upper Grades

As the child grows from the primary grades into the intermediate grades, his outlook is developing and his experiences are expanding. Gradually he is confronted with letter-writing situations and develops more adequate methods for expressing himself and more effective technics for writing. Even in these grades, he should be guided to write simply — using correctly the abilities and skills acquired in the earlier years. He writes longer letters and realizes that he must keep his communications considerate and in good taste. He generally is confronted with problems of form, style, vocabulary, punctuation, and capitalization. As he needs them, he should learn to use the proper salutation, spacing and margins, closing, and signature. Practice on these should improve facility in their use.

A sixth-grade group who presented a playlet to a graduate class sent the following letter to the instructor:

> Dear Dr. F——
> We would like to extend our sincere thanks to you for having us over to give our play. We were all excited over it. Everybody agreed this would be a fine oppor- tunity to give our play before an elderly group.
> Sincerely,
> J—— P——
> For Grade Six

The following letter was an outgrowth of readings in a history project:

> 79 B.C.
> Rome, Italy
> Dear Julius,
> I hope that you can come to the party at Atlantis on August 23. There will be chariot races, gladiator fights, sea battles, and three movies "Ben-Hur," "Sparticus," and "King of Kings" and to top it off is "Demetreus and the Gladiators."
> Julius, do you remember that big enemy who almost cut your head off? What do you want me to do with him? For suggestions you could put him in gladiator school, a torture chamber, make a galley slave out of him, or you could cut *his* head off.
> Yours truly,
> Julius Caesar Jr.

If the situation for letter writing is real, there will develop a pur- pose for writing, and the learner should consider how to achieve it. If it is to inform a friend about experiences in the community, the pupil must first think about what has happened which is interesting and important. Next, he must plan how to describe and narrate the happenings. If a discussion is possible, letters of such nature may be profitably talked over and evaluated.

Children need guidance about sentence formation, punctuation, and paragraphing. They should feel free to ask the teacher's advice about the best way to describe an event. It is possible that several children may write letters to friends about the assembly to celebrate Washington's Birthday. Although the writing is individual, some of the pupils may like to hear what the others have written. Reading of the letters by some members of the group should be highly beneficial. Sometimes children, who are slow to remember interesting activities, are helped by knowing what others have observed and recalled. The manner of narrating by one pupil may stimulate his classmates. One pupil may learn an important thing from another, and make a statement which will help others. Writing first drafts and making revisions can be made interesting and profitable.

## Form, Procedure, Mechanics

The form of letters — although considered secondary by some authorities — is important. Good form will be developed gradually. Form should be studied. A group letter dictated by children can be written on the chalkboard properly. Copies may be made by each child, and these passed around from one to another. Letter models of accepted practice in arrangement of the heading, salutation, close, signature, and margins should be shown. Folding the letter, enclosing it in an envelope, addressing the envelope, writing the return address, buying the stamp at the post office, placing the stamp on the envelope, and mailing the letter appeal to young children.

Guidance in punctuation should be given. Gradually a child will learn to place a period at the end of a declarative sentence, and an interrogation mark after a question. As the other punctuation marks are needed, they may be introduced.

Instruction on capitalizing the first word of a sentence is necessary. In the early grades a child learns to begin a proper name with a capital. Other capitalization skills can be presented as the child needs them. To permit children to write without learning the importance of correct capitalization or punctuation is accepting a genial mediocrity, not conducive to the achievement of the excellence which many children are capable of and which our society needs.

Proofreading should be practiced in order that the message will contain what the writer intends. The pupil should learn that a communication must be legible in order that it can be read. He should learn that to write a good letter he must have a purpose, plan what he wants to tell, and express it in meaningful sentences.

## Some Suggestions for Motivating Letter Writing

Because faulty communication is a great handicap in normal living, pupils should be guided to understand the value and the joy of communicating by letter. Among the more or less specific activities for motivating and teaching letter writing a teacher may do the following:

1. Show children the joys of reading real letters received in life.
2. Help children to see need for writing letters to others who are away.
3. Help them to understand the necessity for writing to those at home when they themselves are away.
4. Show them the value of courtesy and appropriate language in writing letters.
5. Have pupils understand and enumerate the situations in which letters (*a*) *may* be written, and (*b*) *should* be written.
6. Develop a pupil's interest in writing greetings on such occasions as Christmas, New Year, birthdays, or upon an achievement such as graduation.
7. Explain the needs for notes of sympathy or condolence on occasions of illness, accident, or death in a friend's family.
8. Plan lessons on various types of letter writing — social or friendly and business communications of various kinds.
9. Teach acceptable forms for letter writing.

## Evaluation of Letter Writing

Schools usually formulate standards for letter writing. These should concern not only the situations, but also the content and form of the letter. One of the most hoped for objectives in letter writing is careful self-appraisal. Every pupil should ask questions such as the following:

1. Do I write letters in situations in which they are necessary?
2. Are my letters clearly written and readable?
3. Are my letters friendly and courteous?
4. Do my letters begin and end properly?
5. Are my sentences grammatical?
6. Is my spelling correct?

7. Are punctuation and capitalization acceptable?
8. Are the heading, salutation, and close in good taste?
9. Are the margins satisfactory?
10. Are my letters answered by those to whom I write?

Such questions or others appropriate to the instructional level may be made a part of the letter-writing appraisal technic.

## WRITING STORIES, ARTICLES, ESSAYS

Nothing was more boresome in the traditional school than writing essays or compositions principally because they "had to be written." The creative approach when rightly utilized avoids the punishment of having to write and brings forth the joy of expressing experiences, thoughts, feelings, fancy, and fantasies.

Originality is fostered by teacher motivation in a wholesome room climate, by children's interacting in a situation which enriches living and thinking, and by experiences that call for expression. Although a teacher usually will provide motivation for a project or an activity, incentive comes frequently because of a challenging environment which encourages discovery, thinking, and expression.

### Some Occasions and Situations for Creative Writing

Creativity reveals itself in many ways. Since the dim past, men have continually planned, designed, produced, originated, and created new processes in science, in expression, and in literature. They have written about the experiences, activities, and events of the peoples and the races of the world. People have need to create in many situations today, but concern here is with writing. Pupils will write articles, editorials, news items, and stories for a school newspaper, but they must have a definite purpose for writing. Creative expression will grow in experiencing, reading, playing, or working from which ideas are often stated in original ways.

Occasions and situations which promote written expression can be developed in the following: special days — Flag Day, Mother's Day, Thanksgiving, Christmas, Easter; projects — assembly programs, original plays, writing logs, making a book; cooperating activities — keeping a bulletin board, running a library, a literary society.

In a proper environment, under guidance, and in order to solve a problem or meet a deadline, pupils will work with enthusiasm individually or in groups. They will cooperate in writing a story, a play, a yearbook, or a newspaper. The creative product is not necessarily

Motivating creative writing

related to the absurd, the bizarre, or the ridiculous; it is often concerned with the commonplace, the lifelike, and most usual considerations and activities of life. Creative writing is not always produced by the most intelligent; often it is expressed by the individual of normal intelligence who has learned to think, to use imagination, and to work.[11]

## Some Ways of Motivating Creative Writing

An instructor should take advantage of the creative urges and desires of a class. The work of a boy, who is not perhaps the best student in the class, but who has talent for portraying scenes with a brush or pencil — picturing animals, making sketches of people at a picnic, or designing posters — can be an incentive to creativity. Such pictures and drawings excite the imagination of others, who perhaps, although they cannot draw or paint, can write about scenes and experiences. A girl who talks enthusiastically about a trip incites

[11] Frank Barron, "Creativity," *NEA Journal,* 50:17–19, March, 1961.

some members of her class to recall incidents or excites the imaginations of others who will bring forth ideas from their own activities.

The teacher may relate stories to children who will discuss the beginning, the ending, and the connecting events. At first, a child will enjoy a story vicariously; later he will appraise it critically — noting its form, plot, and climax.

If a teacher reads a part of a story — the beginning and some of the medial episodes that lead the hero or heroine into difficulties — pupils will begin to ask questions and to make comments. The teacher may ask: "How do you think the story ended? How do you think the hero got out of the difficulties? What would you have done in this situation?" A discussion concerning the problems, difficulties, and imagined experiences of the characters will follow. Individuals may complete the story.

The first drafts of the story endings may be read by volunteers. Although a pupil should not be compelled to reveal his creative efforts of this nature, it is likely that most children will enjoy reading their work. Discussions of the efforts will be satisfying and instructive. They will cause some who were not interested to begin to work and to write. Values for some involve pleasure, enjoyment, widening of experiences, thinking about plot, and evaluating the methods of writing.

The sources of inspiration for writing are legion. As one author pointed out, creative writing is where you find it. Pictures, trips, music, and observation inspire writing. The stars, the ocean, trees, flowers, the sunrise, clouds, rain, snow, birds, animals, and fish provide incentives for writing. God's universe, the constellations, the vastness of space, the minuteness and the power of the atom, although they are not understood completely by children or men, inspire thinking, imagination, and writing.

Writing, slow and difficult at first, is itself a motivation. Ferebee emphasized the importance of joy and practice in the process of developing creative writing.[12] "Success succeeds." The winning of an award for an essay, story, or article in a contest generally motivates and encourages the writer to write more and better products. If a pupil is to succeed in creative writing, he must accept the responsibility for purposing, planning, writing, revising, and perfecting his work.

Although a child should choose his own topic for writing, and will generally select one from his experience, one or more of the fol-

---

[12] June D. Ferebee, "Gaining Power Through Writing," *Elementary English Review,* 19:282, December, 1942.

lowing may stimulate him to think of or imagine a story or an article which he may want to communicate, or express.

1. *A Friendly Person.* A child will wish to choose a title to suit his taste such as: "My Best Friend," "My Favorite Aunt," "My Favorite Uncle," "The Most Courteous Person I Ever Met," "The Most Interesting Person That I Ever Knew." The *Reader's Digest* presents each month "My Most Unforgettable Character." Children can also write about their own most unforgettable characters. Such titles and such writing concern real people — a storekeeper, a salesman, a gardener, a cook. They are interesting and may be highly exciting.

2. *A Great Personality.* This title could bring out fascinating and interesting people from books. Scientists, inventors, heroes of health, and literary figures are alluring. The explorers, generals, statesmen, presidents, senators, and congressmen have appeal, and writing about them gives a child the opportunity to investigate their lives in library sources. Examples of other titles that might be appropriate for pupils are: "The Greatest General," "The Wisest King," "My Favorite Saint."

3. *Living in a Foreign Land.* Children may choose one such as the following: "Living in Communist Russia," "Living in Norway," "Living in Peru," "Living in Japan," "Living in the Congo," "Living in Mexico." Such a topic would not only create an urge to write, but it would challenge the young writer to read in order to present a real description of people.

4. *The American Indian.* A little study and some thinking about the life of the Indian could give the child opportunity to describe the way Indians lived and worked and fought. Titles might be: "The Sioux," "The Navajo," "The Iroquois," "The Cherokee," or "The Yankton." In place of these titles, others could be selected such as: "The Indian Warrior," "The Indian Woman," "The Indian Boy," "The Indian Girl," or "The Papoose." A pupil may select a title of his own which would suit his talents and his interest better than any of these.

5. *Science Adventure.* Other topics might be: "Orbiting the Earth," "My Adventures on the Moon," "My Experience as a Space Man," "My Ride in a Nuclear Submarine," "My Ride in a Rocket Plane at 10,000 Miles an Hour," "My Travels to the South Pole," "Some Strange Scenes in Oceanography."

6. *Historical Literature.* Titles which might interest children are: "My Life With the Maoris," "I Was a Survivor of Thermopylae," "I

Nearly Lost My Scalp in the Little Bighorn," "I Survived the Alamo," "To the Pacific With Lewis and Clark," "I Was the Last One to Be Picked Up in the *Titanic* Disaster," "With DeSoto to the Mississippi," "Down the Amazon in the Rainy Season," "Before the Mast in Revolutionary Times."

7. *A Favorite Possession.*   Titles could be: "My Dream Car," "The Book I Like Best," "My Talking Doll."

8. *A Pet.*   "My Pig, Jules"; "My Pony, Cinder"; "Our Chow Is a Chum"; "How We Raised an Elephant"; "Hercules, Our Buffalo"; "Our Tame Prairie Chicken"; "Our Parrot, Socrates."

These are a few suggestions, comparatively very few, for there are titles for almost every taste. Pupils properly stimulated develop great resource abilities and they think of the most original topics. Problems in mathematics, topics in social studies, projects in science, and reading activities aid them and sharpen their imaginations. They will think and write about their real and vicarious experiences. Their writing will progress slowly in the beginning, but it will expand and become intensified.

## Some Examples of Creative Writing

### Skating

I went ice skating
I fell down
My feet got cold
So I went home.
Maurice
Grade 1

### A New Baby Doll

I have a new doll.
She is pretty.
I got her at Christmas.
I love her and she loves me.

I let my little friend
play with it.
My friend likes to play
with it.
And I like to play with it too.
Jane
Grade 2

### Dinosaurs

My name is Mr. Giant.
I am 11000 feet big —
bigger than King Lizard.

and Thunder Lizard
and Armored Lizard. —
And Boy are they big —
But i'm still biger.
Why if he trys to
eat me I'll give it to him —
I culd kill ol dinosaurs.
the end
M. L.
Grade 2

**My Christmas Present**
I wanted a Book nameed
Old Yeller for Christmas
I wanted my mother
to get me that Book.
At first my mother
said no. But then
When Christmas came,
I went downstairs
and opened my presents.
The first present I opened
was that Book I was
very happy.
John
Grade 2

**Why I Am Thankful**
I am thankful that I have a good home to live in. Other people in
different countries aren't fortunate like I am. They just manage to keep
a decent home.
One of the reasons I am grateful is for all the freedoms I have. I have
the freedom of speech, worship, and other freedoms. Other people aren't
as lucky as I. They have to go to a certain church or synagogue.
Another reason to be appreciative is that I have an education.
I am thankful for my parents and relatives. Some other boys and
girls don't have parents. They're orphans.
I am grateful that I have clothes.
Another reason that I am thankful is that I exist. For what would
the world do without me!
B. G.
Grade 5

**My Favorite Person**
My favorite person is my mother. My mother is my favorite person
because if it wasn't for her I wouldn't be here. My mother gives me
food, a home, clothes, and most of all love. I give my mother back all
the love she gives me. My mother and I bake together, work together,
play together, and pray together. My mother and I are the best of
friends. Nobody has ever had such a good and kind mother. I give her
all my love.
B. C.
Grade 5

Production of the class newspaper

## Sharing and Publication of Creative Products

The school newspaper is an excellent organ for publication of the creative efforts of children. Since it is impossible to publish all the materials that are written by a class, it follows that only the best, the most interesting, and the most creative can be published *in toto.* It may be possible to publish in the paper, a résumé of the creative writings that have made the honor roll, or at least a list of them. Children like to see their work in print and enjoy reading and showing the articles or stories they have written.

Another means which may be used for sharing is the compilation of a book of creative materials written by members of the class. This book could be divided into sections which would comprise such headings as: stories, articles, essays, plays, anecdotes, and letters. Such a book may be bound or clamped together in covers and placed upon the reading table. Each child in the room may read and enjoy the writings produced by his classmates.

In addition to originality there can and should be tentative standards to be met before accepting any piece of writing for the book. Such standards might include: proper title headings, good alignment of margins, correct spelling, acceptable punctuation and capitalization, legible handwriting, and neat format. Rules concerning length of articles and signatures should be developed by the class. A committee of children may read the materials for interest as well as to check the mechanics. The judgment of the committee should presumably be guided by the teacher or moderator in selecting writing of any kind for inclusion in the book. The standards to be required would necessarily depend upon the developmental level of the children of a class. Writings in the primary grades should be judged by a less strict set of standards than those of the intermediate or higher grade levels.

## Suggestions for Class Activities and Procedures

Approaches to the problem of guiding children to write creatively vary with their experience and background. In general, each child may be given freedom to write in his own way what he has experienced, what he knows, what he thinks, and what he feels. Ideas and concepts should be considered primary, and the mechanics secondary. Grammar, spelling, capitalization, and punctuation, although important, should not stifle expression in the first draft. The important objective is to express thoughts and feelings as dynamically as possible. Some adults use shorthand; others use speed writing, a type of short spelling which permits facile note-taking. The child uses the only rapid writing he knows, writing without worry about spelling or language in order to express thoughts. After the first draft, corrections and revisions may be made by the writer. As the child writes, he will recognize the importance of clear expression, correct spelling and punctuation, and appropriate sentence structure. Guidance and practice will aid him to improve the vividness and clarity of expression. The special needs of each child should be considered. One child may be helped with a comment on a synonym of a word; another may be grateful for a question about the desirability of stating a thought in a different way. Some children need help in planning; others require probing to bring forth recollections of experiences important to the work at hand. Whatever a child needs, a teacher's judgment and consideration will generally arrange in one way or another.

Problems, units, projects, and activities which require thinking, planning, executing, solving, and evaluating are conducive to creative expression. Some children who despise themes of the traditional types become imbued with the idea of writing advertising and news items for a school paper. Those who may resent the required class composition, narrate the story of a game or track meet with vividness. They produce, under guidance and with practice, creative materials which are acceptable to the teacher and enjoyable to readers.

## Appraisal

Continuous appraisal by teacher and pupil is important in creative writing. Appraisal, certainly self-appraisal, is necessary in the beginning, during, and at the conclusion of a project in writing. Careful consideration of the beginning of a story and the ending cannot be properly put off until the writing is completed. To do so would be wasteful of time and effort and would probably foster mediocre production. The pupil must learn to evaluate the materials which are available for writing and the new data which he finds. Pertinent materials should be selected and used; the irrelevant must be discarded. Appraisal is an important function of a teacher's procedure in teaching, and a component of every child's activity in learning. Dynamic communication must replace the vague and the trite. Evaluation, which may be teacher guided in the beginning of creativity should, more and more, become the province and the responsibility of the pupil. His confidence in his ability to purpose and plan, to write and appraise, must be developed. In this process, teacher guidance must gradually but surely give way to pupil initiative, execution, and independence.

## MOTIVATION OF A POETRY CLIMATE

### Definition and Range of Subject

Poetry is the expression of thought or feeling in ideal ways. In a poem, a writer reveals in his original way a concept, a picture, a story, or a contemplation. He uses appropriate words and arranges them to paint a picture, to narrate a story, to describe a scene, to convey an emotion. Peaceful countrysides, sleepy villages, rugged mountains, terrible battles, heroic exploits, imaginative thoughts, satisfying activities, and productive work are only a few of the many topics that have been treated by poets. Love, hate, fear, horror, courage, anger, contempt, and other emotions have been portrayed.

Poets write about the most common things sometimes, and about the most unheard of things at other times. Robert Louis Stevenson's *My Shadow* and his *Where Go the Boats?* illustrate the rather common type, and Edgar Allen Poe's *The Raven,* the unusual. Examples of poems that are informative, descriptive, graphic, picturesque, epic, or biographical can be presented to pupils. A teacher who would guide children to write poetry should read and love poetry, and know how to introduce it enthusiastically.

## Building an Environment for Poetry

A teacher may promote a love for poetry by creating an environment permeated with it. She should read appropriate poems to the children, and select a number of suitable books for the classroom.

Many girls and some young boys enjoy a teacher's reading of Rose Fyleman's *The Fairies:*

> There are fairies at the bottom of our garden!

Scores of other poems about the fairies and elves by Walter de la Mare, Rachel Lyman Field, William Allingham, John Kendrick Bangs, and others interest children greatly.

An area which appeals to children is that of animals. Among the short poems in this category are Annette Wynne's *The House Cat,* Elizabeth Coatsworth's *The Kangaroo,* Kaye Starbird's *Speaking of Cows,* and Edward Lear's *The Owl and the Pussy-Cat.* Some young children like Tennyson's poem:

> What does little birdie say,
> In her nest at peep of day?

Because of its simplicity and beauty, it may lead an active young mind to write.

A theme which delights the young is that of children and their activities. *Blue Shoes* by Kate Greenaway, *Dancing* by Eleanor Farjeon, and *Mumps* by Elizabeth Madox Roberts assist them to think about the scenes, episodes, and experiences which they may portray, describe, or narrate. Many boys and girls, and adults also, have enjoyed listening to Eugene Field's *Little Boy Blue:*

> The little toy dog is covered with dust,
> But sturdy and staunch he stands.

Another category which gives pleasure is that of nonsense. Examples are: *The Height of the Ridiculous* by Oliver Wendell Holmes, *Mrs. Snipkin and Mrs. Wobblechin* by Laura E. Richards, *A Nautical Ballad* by Charles Edward Carryl, and William Brighty Rands' *Godfrey Gordon Gustavus Gore.*

Poems such as *Trees* by Joyce Kilmer call forth appreciation of nature and of God. *The Falling Star* by Sara Teasdale presents a glimpse of the universe. A patriotic theme is exciting and rewarding. Children love their country and the stories of those who settled it, fought for its independence, and gave their lives for its preservation. Poems read by teachers to intermediate-grade children may depict the discovery of America, the settlement of the country, the work of the people, the adventures, and the beauty of our land. Joaquin Miller has delighted millions in his poem *Columbus*. *America the Beautiful* by Katharine Lee Bates and the *Battle Hymn of the Republic* by Julia Ward Howe rouse not only feelings of pride and love of country but excite thought and emotion. Walt Whitman's poem *Pioneers! O Pioneers!* causes young Americans to consider the settlers who led the way through the prairies and the mountains in early days as they developed our country. Ralph Waldo Emerson's exciting words of the *Concord Hymn* have inspired thousands because of its lines commemorating the beginning of the War for Independence.

If these poems and hundreds of others which provide vicarious experiences — exciting, fascinating, alive with emotion — are read to youngsters at the proper levels, pupils generally will develop a love for poetry.

## Some Stimuli for Writing Poetry

In the above section it was suggested that children become acquainted with poetry through listening, reading, and browsing. In this section some further means for promoting poetry writing are set forth.

*Excursions or trips.* For children who have lived in an environment of poetry, an excursion to observe nature's richness is worthwhile. Stimulation of the desire to write a poem may come from: flowers or trees, the grandeur of mountains, the beauty of hills and valleys, rivers with rapids or waterfalls, boats on a lake, or ships on the ocean. A visit to a national park may open to view a herd of buffalo, elk, or deer.

Children become excited about animals at a zoo, fishes in an aquarium, or the alligator in a reptile farm. Children love to watch rabbits, squirrels, and other animals; these often motivate expression — oral or written.

*Pictures.* Paintings, photographs, motion pictures have presented far distant scenes or dramas which stimulate the imagination of prospective poets. Visual aids, films, and slides used properly are incentives to expression.

*Objects.* Trains, airplanes, mines, plants, factories, cities, roads, and buildings have appeal. A forest, a museum piece, a rock, a monument, or a fossil kindles interest. A visit to a great battlefield such as that of Gettysburg will stir the emotions and excite expression — most often oral but sometimes written.

*Notebooks and poetry books.* Individual notebooks are kept by pupils in which they record various types of language aids — new and interesting words, stories, and other original expressions.

Some classrooms have a poetry book kept in a special place on the reading table. This book contains the best poems that have been written by members of the class. Pupils who read and enjoy these poems are stimulated to write.

*The newspaper, an incentive.* The school newspaper is generally a cooperative enterprise to communicate the activities of the school and to provide expressional outlets for various kinds of writing including poetry.

## Some Examples and Excerpts of Children's Products

### Going to the Fair

If I were going to the fair
I'd be happier there than anywhere.
At the fair are many things to see,
At the fair is where I want to be.

R. M.
Grade 3

### The Spring Time

I like spring time best of all
When the grass grows green and tall.
I know summer soon will come
Then we will have lots of fun.

L. C.
Grade 4

### Houses

On my way to school each day
I see houses along the way.
Big and small, wide and tall
There are houses for us all.

A. N.
Grade 4

### A Surprise

I woke up in the morning and heard
a robin sing.
Right then and there I knew that it
was spring.

D. H.
Grade 4

The following was a fourth-grade class project with lines suggested by the pupils:

### How Thanksgiving Began

Thanksgiving is a holiday.
It started in a different way.
We'll tell you how it all began
It is of interest to every man.

In 1620, so they say,
Pilgrims were starving every day.
Squanto saved them when he came
Bringing corn and trapping game.

Next fall, when harvest was complete,
There was enough for all to eat.
They gave their thanks to God in praise.
We still do it now-a-days.

An original poem
by Grade Four
Harford School

The following poem was written by a fifth-grade pupil to a student teacher who was just completing his practice teaching.

You leave on Monday as you know;
We're sorry we must see you go.
Please take this gift; don't make a fuss,
For we want you to remember us.
We hope this gift will last quite long
We hope that nothing ever goes wrong.

R. M.
Grade 5

A sixth-grade class while studying Canada in social studies decided to write a poem correlating creative writing with the unit. A recording secretary wrote contributions on the blackboard. Lines were written, revised, and rewritten before the following group poem was evolved.

### Canada

Canada is a scenic place;
It covers a great deal of space.
From coast to coast its beauty shows,
A mountain, a valley, a stream that flows.

Its heritage is hard to trace;
Forefathers came from many a race.
Canada continually grows;
Its democracy and freedom glows.

The following verses were written by seventh-grade pupils in a class exercise for a student teacher.

### My Dog

My dog is a little pest
And never tries to do his best.
He bites things and tears them up
But after all, he's just a pup!

L. R.
Grade 7

### Fishing

Fishing is a lot of fun,
Hour after hour in the sun,
Waiting for a catch all day,
Sitting, standing, by the bay.

D. G.
Grade 7

The examples presented in this section are far from perfect in expression and mechanics. Pupils who wrote them were free to write what they thought and felt. Mechanics were not made barriers to progress. Improved expression of ideas will come about only to pupils who continue to write and are properly encouraged.

## SUMMARY

Normal children have original tendencies to communicate. If teachers stimulate them to think about interesting experiences and events, they will express themselves for they have an urge to talk, and when motivated properly, a desire to write. Letters to friends will be written about experiences, activities, and events of living. The joy of reading letters from friends and relatives goes hand in hand with the satisfaction of writing them. If a child recognizes the situations in which letters and other written communications are necessary, he will want to write. When he becomes sensitive to his correspondent, learns the importance of considerate and appropriate content, and recognizes the need for acceptable sentence structure, clarity, legibility, and form, he will strive to write correctly.

The writing of stories and essays may be positively stimulated by experiencing. Purpose in writing is important. Pupils who complain that they do not know what to write about when a composition is assigned will discover many activities and stories to write for a school newspaper. A celebration, a new car, a race, or a game will excite a story. The excitement of holidays will bring forth expression.

Before poetry can be written, it must be "lived." Creative writing requires inspiration, but to become adept in any of its forms, a pupil must experience, study, and evaluate, purpose, plan, and write, in the beginning with encouragement and guidance, and later with a strong independent desire to achieve.

## ACTIVITIES, PROBLEMS, QUESTIONS

1. Analyze Bacon's statement, "Reading maketh a full man, conference a ready man, and writing an exact man."
2. Evaluate the statement, "The child can write creatively."
3. State several ways and means to stimulate creative writing.
4. List types of situations in which one should write a letter.
5. What occasions may be used for teaching letter writing in school?
6. Contrast theme writing of the traditional school with creative writing of the modern school.
7. Collect and analyze some specimens of creative writing in your school.
8. How can sharing of creative products be best effected? What are the important values of sharing them?
9. State several ways for building an environment for poetry writing. Describe each.
10. Compare and contrast communication and mechanics in developing social and creative writing.

## SELECTED REFERENCES

Applegate, Mauree. *Helping Children Write.* Scranton, Pa.: International Textbook, 1949. 173 pp.

Arnstein, Flora J. *Poetry in the Elementary Classroom.* New York: Appleton-Century-Crofts, 1962. 124 pp.

Austin, Mary C., and Queenie B. Mills. *The Sound of Poetry.* Boston: Allyn and Bacon, 1963. 420 pp.

Burrows, Alvina T., *et al. They All Want to Write.* Rev. ed. New York: Prentice-Hall, 1952. 240 pp.

Fisher, Aileen. *Plays About Our Nation's Songs.* Boston: Plays Incorporated, 1962, 188 pp.

Hartman, Gertrude, and Ann Schumaker, eds. *Creative Expression.* Eau Claire, Wis.: Hale, 1939. 350 pp.

Irwin, Keith G. *The Romance of Writing, from Egyptian Hieroglyphics to Modern Letters, Numbers, and Signs.* New York: Viking, 1956. 160 pp.

*Language Arts, A Handbook for Teachers in Elementary Schools, The.* Kindergarten, Grades 1–6. Albany, N. Y.: The New York State Education Department, 1957. 262 pp.

Marksberry, Mary Lee. *Foundations of Creativity.* New York: Harper and Row, 1963. 178 pp.

Stevenson, Robert Louis. *Learning to Write; Suggestions and Counsel.* New York: Scribner's, 1920. 225 pp.

Strickland, Ruth C. *Language Arts in the Elementary School.* 2nd ed. Boston: Heath, 1957. 464 pp.

Walter, Nina Willis. *Let Them Write Poetry.* New York: Holt, Rinehart & Winston, 1962. 179 pp.

Wilt, Miriam E. *Creativity in the Elementary School.* New York: Appleton-Century-Crofts, 1959. 72 pp.

Zirbes, Laura. *Spurs to Creative Teaching.* New York: Putnam, 1959. 354 pp.

See also references for Chapter XII.

# Chapter X

## Learning to Spell

### ORIENTATION

SPELLING is a necessary part of life for everyone — the businessman, the farmer, the professional man, the housewife, and for the learner in elementary, secondary, and higher education. It is an integral part of the language arts — used in creative writing, keeping records, and making notes.

In order to carry on a successful program of spelling instruction, it is necessary for the teacher to know the place of spelling in life and the basic problems in teaching and learning spelling. She must know the objectives of spelling, how to plan the curriculum, the words most useful for a spelling curriculum, how to satisfy individual requirements, and how to use the most effective testing and teaching practices. The teacher should also be aware of the causes for difficulties in learning to spell and the best means of motivating learners to study the words they need. She should be able to guide the individual learner to develop independence in spelling correctly the words he needs in writing.

### Causes for Poor Spelling

Evidence on the causes of poor spelling is available both in spelling research and in investigations of writing done in and out of school. A summary of causes is presented.

In the first place, the objectives for spelling are not always purposed by the teacher or children. Frequently, children do not understand the values of spelling in school or in life outside school. They do not recognize spelling as an integral part of language. They do not study the right words. Often they waste time on unnecessary words or they study words that they already know how to spell. Words are not presented at the right time nor in the proper grade. Inefficient methods of teaching and learning are employed. Wasteful methods of testing, study, and review make spelling a monotonous exercise rather than a dynamic activity. Some technics used in learning to spell a word are ineffective. Many children do not use the dictionary efficiently, nor do they write legibly. Spelling is not integrated properly into the work of the other language areas. The varying needs, interests, and abilities of children are not taken into consideration sufficiently. A clear conception of the correct use of words is not emphasized.[1]

In the second place, English spelling is inconsistent because the English language is a conglomerate or composite of many languages. One letter may represent many sounds, and one sound may be represented by different letters or combinations of letters. The conflict of phonetic and etymological principles has not been resolved.[2] Changes in spelling over the years have added to the confusion of learners.

Thirdly, available research results are not utilized. For example, there is a tendency in many schools to use the old study-test plan in teaching a weekly unit of spelling, despite the findings of the Gates comprehensive study which showed that the test-study was superior to the study-test in the second half of grade three and in grades four through six.[3] Shubik in a carefully controlled experiment showed conclusively that for the third grade the test-study was superior to the study-test plan of teaching spelling.[4] Thomas Horn reported that recent surveys of spelling texts and workbooks indicate the acceptance and use of instructional procedures which have been shown to be inferior.[5]

A fourth probable cause of poor spelling is a misuse and an overemphasis on the so-called phonic method. There is a confusion between the phonics of reading and that of spelling. Phonics of reading requires

---

[1] James A. Fitzgerald, *The Teaching of Spelling* (Milwaukee: The Bruce Publishing Company, 1951), pp. 1–2.

[2] Ernest Horn, "Spelling," *Encyclopedia of Educational Research,* revised edition, 1950, pp. 1247–1248.

[3] Arthur I. Gates, "An Experimental Comparison of the Study-Test and the Test-Study Methods in Spelling," *Journal of Educational Psychology,* 22:1–19, January, 1931.

[4] Helen Maria Shubik, "An Experimental Comparison of the Test-Study and the Study-Test Methods of Teaching Spelling in the Third Grade" (unpublished master's thesis, Fordham University, New York, 1951).

[5] Thomas D. Horn, "Research in Spelling," *Elementary English,* 37:175, March, 1960.

letter-to-sound relationships, while that of spelling is concerned with sound-to-letter relationships which should be taught with consideration of both the consistencies and the inconsistencies of spelling. There are, for example, at least fourteen ways of spelling the long sound of *a* (as in *ate, main, day, great, veil, they, weigh, feign, aye, eh, matinee, fiance, gauge, bouquet*). Other long vowel sounds are spelled approximately as varyingly. Horn has shown that the short sound of *i* as in *pin* is spelled with *i* only a little more than half the time.[6] Hildreth has well exemplified the incongruities and inconsistencies of English, and most of the trouble she attributes to the nonphonetic character of common words such as *trouble, straight,* and *laugh.*[7] Less than 200 of the 350 most fundamental words for writing can be written as they sound. More than 150 of these common words such as *again, always, before, cousin, game, like, near, people, rain, third, where, who,* and *write* are not spelled as they sound.[8] There are 26 letters in our alphabet, three of which — *c, q,* and *x* — are in a sense duplicates of others. The 23 necessary letters represent 44 sounds. Consonant sounds as well as vowel sounds are spelled differently. Note the differences in spelling of the *f* sound in *four* and *phone,* the *k* sound in *car* and *kite,* the *j* sound in *gem* and *join,* and the *s* sound in *cite* and *set.* A learner could not be sure which letters to use from the sounds of the pairs of words. Accordingly, phonic presentation alone is not sufficient for acceptable spelling; other procedures are necessary.

## Some Basic Problems in Spelling

The problems which are important in the teaching of spelling may be stated as follows:

1. What are the objectives in teaching and learning spelling?
2. What basic consideration should be given to the curriculum in spelling?
3. How should the words for a spelling curriculum be selected?
4. What consideration should be given to the placement of words in grades?
5. What consideration should be given to incidental learning?
6. How should a child learn to spell a word?

---

[6] Ernest Horn, Teaching Spelling (Washington, D. C.: National Education Association, 1954), pp. 22–24.

[7] Gertrude Hildreth, *Teaching Spelling* (New York: Henry Holt and Company, 1955), p. 3.

[8] Fitzgerald, *op. cit.,* pp. 15–18.

7. How shall an efficient plan of procedure be organized for the teaching and learning of spelling?

8. How may testing be best organized and utilized?

9. What attention should be given to phonics?

10. How can generalizations be handled?

11. How should reviews be best conducted?

12. How should diagnostic and remedial work be organized?

## AIMS AND OBJECTIVES IN SPELLING

The aims and objectives in spelling should be most carefully formulated. The chief aim in spelling instruction is to teach the child to learn to spell the words he needs in his written communication. The Curriculum Committee on Spelling presented in effect the following aims: (1) to spell the words needed for written expression; (2) to develop meaning and use of words to be spelled; (3) to develop a spelling consciousness; (4) to develop a spelling conscience; (5) to develop a technique for study of spelling.[9]

Assuming that a valid core of words has been selected, the child under the guidance of the teacher should:

1. Learn to spell the words in this valid core and other words necessary for his individual work.

2. Learn to use correctly these and other words needed in writing.

3. Develop a desire to spell with 100 percent accuracy.

4. Develop an effective judgment as to the correctness of spelling in written work.

5. Acquire methods for learning additional words necessary for writing in school and in life outside the school.[10]

Since each child's needs, interests, and difficulties differ from those of other children, provision must be made to guide each individually in achieving correct spelling.

## THE CURRICULUM AND SPELLING

An elementary school curriculum must be a dynamic succession of carefully selected experience units, activities, problems, and projects which integrate the skills, areas, and fields of study basic to educa-

---

[9] "The Nation at Work on the Public School Curriculum," *Fourth Yearbook of the Department of Superintendence*, 1926, pp. 126–127.

[10] Fitzgerald, *op. cit.*, pp. 24–25.

tion. Spelling is one of those skills — a language art — essential to the achievement of the objectives of education. Spelling is necessary for writing in such solid subject areas as reading, composition, science, arithmetic, social studies, and so on. It is important in making notes and outlines in every field of study. It is of significance in communication activities such as the school paper and logs.

## Overlap of Core Vocabularies

Every child learns to spell in many ways in many areas. The child learns to spell in reading because he meets countless words in the various fields of his interests and needs. There is a high overlap between the core vocabularies of spelling and reading. In fact 180 of Dolch's *A Basic Sight Vocabulary* of 220 words are present in the Fitzgerald list of *350 Most Useful Spelling Words.* Dolch's list has a high cruciality in reading and speech, and the Fitzgerald list makes up a very high proportion of the words used in writing by children.[11] There is an important overlap of common vocabulary in speaking, spelling, reading, and writing. Four hundred and forty-three of the words in the speech of young children[12] before entering the first grade are among the 472 *Words Fundamental in Reading, Writing, Speaking, and Spelling.*[13] Approximately 75 percent, 1353 of the 1811 words in the basic reading vocabulary for the primary grades by Gates,[14] are present in the 2650 basic life spelling vocabulary.[15] Accordingly, a core of words useful for spelling, reading, speech, and writing is easily identified.[16]

## The Overlap of Child and Adult Needs in Writing

The activities of childhood are interrelated in home, school, and community. Language needs are overlapping for the child and the

---

[11] James A. Fitzgerald and Patricia G. Fitzgerald, *Methods and Curricula in Elementary Education* (Milwaukee: The Bruce Publishing Company, 1955), pp. 411–415.

[12] Child Study Committee of the International Kindergarten Union, *A Study of the Vocabulary of Children Before Entering the First Grade* (Washington, D. C.: The International Kindergarten Union, 1928), 36 pp.

[13] Fitzgerald and Fitzgerald, *loc. cit.*

[14] Arthur I. Gates, *A Reading Vocabulary for the Primary Grades,* revised and enlarged (New York: Bureau of Publications, Teachers College, Columbia University, 1935), 29 pp.

[15] James A. Fitzgerald, *A Basic Life Spelling Vocabulary* (Milwaukee: The Bruce Publishing Company, 1951), 161 pp.

[16] James A. Fitzgerald, "An Integrating Basic Communication Vocabulary," *Elementary English,* 40:283–289, March, 1963.

adult. As the learner grows through adolescence to adulthood his needs become progressively more and more like those of the adult. A comparison of the rankings of the 100 most common words of adult writing, high school writing, and child writing indicated a high concordance among the three vocabularies; "the greater similarity between adolescent and adult vocabularies than between elementary and adult vocabularies indicates that growth in years and experience is accompanied by growth in writing vocabulary as well."[17]

## Spelling in Curriculum Functioning

Spelling is required in language activities, and must be taught not as a skill apart but as an integrating instrument. However, in order that it may not be neglected, there should be specific periods during the week for most learners in which the aims and activities of spelling are emphasized. An excellent core of words and a most efficient method for learning to spell a word are necessary, but these are not the whole of learning to spell. Spelling to be effective must be made to function as a part of living and of working in and out of school. A learner has not mastered the spelling of a lesson when he can spell the words in a test. The only valid test of mastery is the correct use of words in necessary writing.

## The Effect of Child Differences Upon the Curriculum

The curriculum of one child in a class is necessarily different from that of every other child. Some of these child differences are small but others are great. Classes have been surveyed in which there were spelling differences of as much as ten years among children in one grade. Some children in a class may know how to spell all or nearly all the words selected for a semester's work, and others may be able to spell none or only a small proportion of them. The needs and difficulties of each pupil must be considered. No child should be forced to study what he has already mastered. The slow learner should not be swamped with work that he is incapable of accomplishing. The gifted or normal pupil should be guided to learn words which he requires for his individual projects — writing an editorial or a class play perhaps. The slow-learning child, who may never need any but a small core of words, should not be overburdened with the task of trying to learn to spell words that he will never use. The work of

---

[17] James A. Fitzgerald, "The Overlap of Child and Adult Writing Vocabularies," *Journal of Experimental Education,* 4:364–367, June, 1936.

learning and using the important basic core of words varies from child to child, as does the mastery of supplementary words. Each child will require guidance in his efforts to become independent in spelling.

## Learning to Spell — A Pleasant and Rewarding Process

The curriculum in spelling is today very different from that of four or five decades ago. Then, only a few learners benefited appreciably from the rather tiresome drill upon long and poorly selected lists of words. The majority of children profited little because many of the words studied were not used in writing. The spelling classes were isolated drill periods set apart without coordination with other subjects. During the past three or four decades, significant changes have been made. Research has indicated the words that should be taught. Improvements have come about in the placement of words in grades. Attractive books and other materials have been produced which suggest integrating activities based upon generally worthwhile vocabulary. In some well-designed books, but not in all, the results of vocabulary research and the findings of investigations on method have been utilized in order to make the learning of spelling a rewarding activity. The curriculum generally functions so that the pupil understands his problems, uses effective methods in working, and appreciates the results he achieves. In well-directed programs, the learner determines what he needs to do by testing and appraisal, does it with efficient procedure, and uses his learnings in writing both in and out of school. Awareness of success attained is pleasant and motivating.

## THE SELECTION OF WORDS FOR SPELLING

The selection of the basic core of words for a spelling curriculum should be made only after a careful consideration of the research on adult writing, child writing, and spelling errors in writing.

### General Sources

Authoritative statements in the three editions of the *Encyclopedia of Educational Research,* the yearbooks of the *National Society for the Study of Education,* those of the *Department of Superintendence,* the three-year summaries of research in spelling of the *Review of Educational Research,* and educational periodicals and publications are helpful in guiding the selection of the most useful words for a spelling curriculum.

## Adult Writing

Horn presented an excellent analysis of procedures and methods for determining the most useful words for adult writing. His *A Basic Writing Vocabulary* of 10,000 useful words for adult writing is invaluable as a major base for word selection in spelling.[18]

## Child Writing in Life Outside the School

Fitzgerald tabulated 7587 different words from a study of 470,046 running words in 3505 fourth-, fifth-, and sixth-grade letters written outside the school and 2928 different words from 100,480 running words in 1256 third-grade life letters.[19] The McKee-Fitzgerald unpublished list of words based upon approximately 1,500,000 running words of writing — the result of several studies — is highly valuable as a base for the selection of words for spelling.[20]

## Child Writing in School

Jones studied 75,000 elementary school themes and selected for spelling 4532 words from 15 million running words of child writing. Rinsland made a most detailed and valuable study of school writing which comprised compositions and other matter collected from 48 states in the union and published a list of 14,571 words. These studies and many others were reviewed for evidence on word selection.[21]

## Studies of Errors

Jones's famous *100 Spelling Demons* have been taught for half a century. The *222 Spelling Demons* selected from third-, fourth-, fifth-, and sixth-grade children's writing outside the school and from the second-grade children's writing in school are a most crucial list of spelling words.[22]

---

[18] Ernest Horn, *A Basic Writing Vocabulary* (University of Iowa Monographs in Education, First Series, No. 4, Iowa City, Iowa: University of Iowa, 1926), 225 pp.

[19] James A. Fitzgerald, "The Vocabulary, Spelling Errors, and Situations of Fourth, Fifth, and Sixth Grade Children's Letters Written in Life Outside the School" (unpublished doctor's dissertation, State University of Iowa, Iowa City, Iowa, 1931), 516 pp.; and James A. Fitzgerald, "The Vocabulary and Spelling Errors of Third-Grade Life Letters," *Elementary School Journal,* 38:518–527, March, 1938.

[20] See Fitzgerald, *A Basic Life Spelling Vocabulary, op. cit.,* pp. 18–19.

[21] *Ibid.,* pp. 13–18.

[22] *Ibid.,* pp. 141–152.

## A Basic Life Spelling Vocabulary

A vocabulary of 2650 words was compiled from the important lists of adult writing, child writing in life outside the school, and child writing in school.[23] These words were appraised, and it was found that they and their repetitions comprise 93.54 percent (approximately 5,624,000 of the 6,012,359) of running words basic to the extensive Rinsland list.[24] These and their repetitions made up approximately 95 percent of the running words basic to the unpublished McKee-Fitzgerald list. Several lists of words may be selected from this vocabulary. Among the most important are 473 words derived by adding s, d, ed, or ing to base words, and 449 words, most commonly used.

This list of 2650 words is most useful as a basic core for spelling. The typical child who masters this list has approximately 94 or 95 percent of the running words he will write in school and outside the school.

## Most Useful Spelling Words

The 350 Most Useful Spelling Words are presented below.[25] Everyone of these words is included in the McKee-Fitzgerald child vocabulary, in the Rinsland basic vocabulary, in Fitzgerald's vocabulary of fourth-, fifth-, and sixth-grade letters. All except the word Santa Claus are found in Horn's A Basic Writing Vocabulary. Nearly all of these are found in four other important vocabularies. These 350 words and their repetitions comprise 79 percent of the running words basic to Fitzgerald's child writing vocabulary and 74 percent of the running words from which Rinsland tabulated his extensive A Basic Vocabulary of Elementary School Children. Accordingly they are a most important list of spelling words for beginners, and highly useful for handwriting instruction because they will be written repeatedly in all kinds of writing.

### 350 MOST USEFUL SPELLING WORDS

| a | after | all | am | another |
|---|---|---|---|---|
| about | afternoon | along | an | any |
| across | again | always | and | are |

---

[23] See ibid., pp. 5–55 for a complete description of the methods used and the appraisal of the words of the list. See also pp. 56–127 for the list.

[24] Henry D. Rinsland, A Basic Vocabulary of Elementary School Children (New York: The Macmillan Company, 1945), 636 pp.

[25] Fitzgerald, The Teaching of Spelling, op. cit., pp. 16–18.

| | | | | |
|---|---|---|---|---|
| arithmetic | days | got | make | put |
| around | dear | grade | making | rain |
| as | did | ground | man | read |
| at | didn't | had | many | reading |
| aunt | dinner | hair | may | red |
| away | do | hand | me | remember |
| baby | does | happy | men | ride |
| back | dog | hard | might | right |
| bad | doll | has | milk | room |
| ball | done | have | miss | run |
| be | don't | he | money | said |
| because | door | head | more | Santa Claus |
| bed | down | heard | morning | saw |
| been | dress | help | most | say |
| before | each | her | mother | school |
| best | eat | here | much | second |
| better | eggs | high | my | see |
| big | end | him | name | seen |
| black | enjoyed | his | near | set |
| blue | every | home | never | she |
| book | far | hope | new | shoes |
| books | father | horse | next | should |
| both | feet | horses | nice | show |
| box | fifth | house | night | sister |
| boy | find | how | no | six |
| boys | fine | hurt | not | small |
| bring | fire | I | now | snow |
| brother | first | ice | o'clock | so |
| brought | fish | if | of | some |
| but | five | I'm | off | something |
| buy | flowers | in | oh | sometimes |
| by | food | interesting | old | soon |
| call | for | into | on | spelling |
| came | found | is | once | spring |
| can | four | it | one | started |
| candy | friend | just | or | stay |
| car | friends | keep | other | stayed |
| children | from | kind | our | store |
| Christmas | front | know | out | story |
| class | funny | last | over | street |
| clean | game | left | pair | summer |
| clothes | games | let | paper | Sunday |
| cold | gave | letter | party | supper |
| come | get | like | people | sure |
| comes | getting | liked | picture | table |
| coming | girl | little | pictures | take |
| corn | girls | live | place | teacher |
| could | give | long | play | teacher's |
| couldn't | glad | look | played | tell |
| country | go | lot | playing | ten |
| cousin | goes | lots | please | thank |
| daddy | going | love | pretty | that |
| day | good | made | program | the |

| their | to | us | well | with |
|-------|------|--------|--------|----------|
| them | today | use | went | won't |
| then | together | used | were | work |
| there | told | very | what | would |
| these | too | visit | when | write |
| they | took | walk | where | writing |
| thing | town | want | which | written |
| things | tree | wanted | while | year |
| think | trees | wants | white | years |
| third | two | was | who | yes |
| this | under | wash | why | yesterday |
| three | until | water | will | yet |
| through | up | way | winter | you |
| time | upon | we | wish | your |

## Number of Words Necessary in a Basic Spelling List

Data from three valid sources indicate that a comparatively small number of different words and their repetitions make up a great portion of running writing. Horn's data based upon a sampling of a million running words showed that the three commonest words and their repetitions made up about 10 percent of running writing; 100 words and their repetitions made up about 59 percent; 1000 words and their repetitions made up about 90 percent; 2000 words and their repetitions made up 95.3 percent; 3000 words and their repetitions made up 97.6 percent; 4000 words and their repetitions made up 98.7 percent; 5000 words and their repetitions made up 99.2 percent of the running writing of the million word sample.[26] Data from other studies give quite comparable results.

Since 3000 well-chosen words and their repetitions comprise 97.6 percent of the running writing and 4000 commonest words make up about 98.7 percent of the running writing, the fourth thousand adds less than 1.2 percent of the running words to be written. These data seem to warrant the assumption that the basic core of spelling words should include between 3000 and 4000, and the mastery of these should be supplemented with careful word study and word usage built upon this core.

## The Supplementary List, an Individual Project

A single suppplementary list of words to be assigned to the whole class in addition to the basic core is of questionable value because

---

[26] Ernest Horn, "The Curriculum for the Gifted: Some Principles and an Illustration," *The Education of the Gifted,* Twenty-Third Yearbook of the National Society for the Study of Education, Part I, 1924, pp. 73–89.

of the pronounced individual differences in needs and abilities in the class. Spelling words beyond the common core, needed by some children, will not be required by others. It may be possible that in certain peculiar situations, a group of children will be aided by a common supplementary list because of geographic location, types of occupation, or an exigency such as war. If necessary, such a list might be compiled by supervisor or teacher.

In general, however, it is expedient that each child keep his own supplementary list of words. This list should include words of special appeal to him, words of use in the type of writing in which he is active, difficult words for him, names, addresses, and particularly interesting new words. It is quite likely that a child will meet several words in a social studies unit, for example, that he will learn easily. Such incidental learning should be encouraged, but the strange words in the ordinary subject matter unit should not be assigned to the class as a supplementary spelling list, for many children will never be called upon to write them again. Aural, oral, visual, and conceptual study of new words will be very valuable, but the writing of these new words may not be useful and their spelling mastery may be an unnecessary burden for many.

### The Validity of the Spelling Words Selected for Study

The teacher will recognize the importance of presenting a valid list of words for spelling. The validity of the 350 useful spelling words listed on the preceding pages has been demonstrated. The selection of other words for spelling should be made with care. The following criteria for word appraisal — frequency of use, geographical distribution, spread in types of writing, permanence, quality, cruciality, and difficulty — have been suggested by Horn and others.[27] The teacher or supervisor who selects materials for spelling can be guided by the following questions about the words of a list:

1. How often is a word used in child and adult writing?

2. How widely is the word used throughout the states and cities of the United States? The basic data for Horn's adult list, for Rinsland's schoolchildren's writing list, and for the Fitzgerald child-writing list came from every section of the United States.

3. Is the word used in both social and business writing?

---

[27] Ernest Horn, "Spelling," *Encyclopedia of Educational Research,* third edition, 1960, pp. 1339–1340. See also Fitzgerald, *A Basic Life Spelling Vocabulary, op. cit.,* pp. 40–44.

4. Is the word a permanent word — not a trade name or an impermanent expression — in the language?

5. Is the word of good quality (rather than a slang expression)?

6. Is the word crucial — a word which if misspelled would penalize the writer excessively?

7. How persistently difficult is the word? Many useful words are so likely to be misspelled that they may be rightly presented at successive grade levels.

## Grade Placement of Words

Some consideration has been given to the selection of the core of words for spelling instruction. Of many criteria that have been presented by authorities two seem particularly important for grade placement in the curriculum: (1) the need for the word by children in writing both in and out of school; (2) the persistency of difficulty of the word in successive grades.[28]

Words needed for spelling should be placed in the grade generally where they will be first used for writing. It is obvious that the words which have been mastered in a previous grade need not be studied. For example, from 200 to 250 of the 350 basic words listed earlier in this chapter, should be presented systematically in the second grade. (Some of these words will probably have been learned incidentally in the first grade.) The remainder should be placed in the third grade. Additional words from *A Basic Life Spelling Vocabulary*[29] or other valid sources should be presented as they are required in successive grades.

The persistence of difficulty — not to be confused with the difficulty of a word — is a second most important criterion for the grade placement. One of the criteria of years ago was that of difficulty. A difficult word was not presented in an early grade because it was considered "too hard" for children of that grade level. That theory of placement has been proven faulty; a word which is needed frequently by children for example in the third grade should be presented at that level notwithstanding its difficulty, for it is better to master such a hard word at the expense of considerable effort than to misspell it repeatedly and form a persistent habit of incorrect spelling.

Consider the word *received,* among the 300 most used words of third-grade children's spontaneous writing. Only 205 words were

---

[28] See Fitzgerald, *The Teaching of Spelling,* op. cit., pp. 128–152.
[29] Fitzgerald, *A Basic Life Spelling Vocabulary,* op. cit.

used more often. Only 32 words were misspelled more frequently than *received* by third-grade children. Yet the average grade placement for *received* in 25 spelling series was in fifth grade. The word is beginning to be written by third graders and gives them difficulty. It is a demon in grades three to six inclusive. To permit children to write it incorrectly even though it may be difficult to learn, does not seem to be good psychology or methodology. It appears therefore that this word should be placed in the third grade. Since it continues to be spelled incorrectly in grades below the seventh, it should be tested in a review list in grades three through six. Those pupils who have mastered it need not study it, but those who misspell it should study it with an efficient method of learning to spell a word. Examples of words that give persistent trouble in grades two through six are: *because, don't, friend, our, their, too.* These and other demons should be presented in test exercises, successively from grade to grade after the grade of first presentation, and studied by those who misspell them.[30]

## METHODS OF LEARNING AND TEACHING SPELLING

*Readiness for Spelling*

Before a child can be taught to spell, he must become ready for spelling instruction. A child who has something about which to write — who wants to tell about his dog, who expresses a desire to compose a letter, or who wants to place his name on his notebook — has a degree of readiness for learning to spell. Generally a child who reads well and converses easily with other children or with adults will sooner or later express a desire to write. When he wishes to write and when he tries to write, he will be in a state of readiness to learn to spell. It is evident to the teacher that the child's readiness is an integration of the desire to write, to spell, and to make symbols — either manuscript or cursive. One of these desires aids the total readiness for an expansion and intensification of language. Naturally there will be differences in the readiness of members of a class. Some will be ready sooner than others. Those who are ready should be guided to write and spell. Those who are not ready should not be forced to do these things. Their education will be better served if they are permitted to engage a little while longer in social activities, listening, oral language, singing, music, observation, excursions, con-

---

[30] *Ibid.,* pp. 132–150.

struction, and reading. Any one of these or a combination of two or three of them will sooner or later bring about the desire to write. When the child is ready to write he will have an obvious purpose for learning the sequence of letters in words and to write them so they can be read. He will enjoy writing his message and reading it to his classmates, and hearing or reading what his classmates have written. Accordingly, spelling readiness grows as reading and communication abilities are increased.

## Incidental Learning: A Basis for Systematic Spelling

It has been shown that an individual learns to spell from many activities — reading, observing a teacher writing, looking at films, and going on trips. The learning that he accumulates from these incidental sources are valuable. A well-planned procedure in the teaching of spelling appraises by pretesting the spelling learned by various individuals. Such tests help the child to understand that he will not be forced to study what he has already learned. He appreciates the fact that he is being tested to determine what he needs to study. He therefore recognizes the value of incidental learning of spelling in his reading and in other types of study. In effect, the systematic learning of spelling should take up where incidental learning leaves off.

## Motivation

Interest is one of the most obvious incentives to learning. Creating interest in writing can cause the child to want to learn to spell. The learner should know the place of spelling in writing and the penalties for misspelling. He should know that the words which are presented in the spelling class are the words that he must have in order to write. He will appreciate the fact that the method he uses helps him to determine what he knows and what he does not know. When he sees that the method is efficient in achieving results, he will build up an enthusiasm for studying spelling.

Opportunities may be presented for writing. When real situations are recognized and accepted by the learner, spelling will become an activity of importance to him. Self-appraisal by a pupil of his difficulties and his progress will be helpful in guiding him. If self-evaluation and self-motivation are practiced, improvement in learning to spell should be assured.

## Plans of Instruction for Teaching Spelling

There are two general plans for teaching spelling — the test-study and the study-test. In brief, the test-study plan tests to determine the spelling proficiency of the individual members of the class in order to induce study on words of the assignment which each cannot spell. After study, a test is given to determine achievement and progress. The study-test plan reverses the procedure and directs study by the class and the members of the class first on the assignment of words and second provides a test to determine achievement and progress. Several investigations have been made to determine the merits of the two procedures. While there seems to be some variance in the results, the majority of investigators found evidence favoring the test-study procedure, in third through eighth grades. Opinion and practice vary concerning the comparative procedures at the second-grade level. A review of the research results supports the conclusion that the test-study method is superior generally for the normal and the gifted, and the study-test may have advantages for the backward or the slow learner. It is possible that a foreign group may be helped more in the beginning by the study-test procedure than by the test-study, but as individuals improve in English, the time comes when a change to the test-study procedure seems to be advantageous.[31]

## Selecting the Plan of Study to Be Used

By means of a preliminary term test on a sampling of the words for the term, a teacher can determine the approximate spelling level of the class and to some degree the achievement level of individuals of the class. A simple way to construct such a test is to select one word from each of the weekly lessons of the term for the primary grades and two words from each of the lessons for the intermediate and upper grades. The words may be dictated to the class. All words may be used in sentences, or the teacher may use homonyms or words likely to be misunderstood in sentences. If the children spell correctly on the average 25 percent or more of the words, it will be advantageous to use the test-study plan in the term's instruction. The differences among children will be such that some may spell nearly all the words correctly and others may misspell half or more

---

[31] *Learning to Spell, A Research Report* (Albany, N. Y.: University of the State of New York, State Education Department, Bureau of Elementary Curriculum Development, 1960), pp. 28–30.

than half of them. In any event, the test-study method is designed to guide each child to study the words that he misspells as he takes the pretests from week to week. If most of the words are misspelled, the study-test may prove advantageous in the beginning of the term. A change may be made to the test-study plan when it becomes evident that children have developed to the point where they know how to spell an appreciable number of the words in an assignment.[32]

## METHOD OF LEARNING TO SPELL A WORD

There are many suggestions in the literature for learning to spell a word. Among the considerations suggested are: understanding of meaning, correct pronunciation, effective presentation, imagery, recall, writing the word, and using the word in communication. A brief summary of these follows. The consensus of opinion of many authorities is that the meaning of a word is highly valuable to its learning and use. Correct pronunciation should be emphasized. The word itself is the important unit of presentation. It may be generally presented visually, and the visual presentation aided by auditory, oral, and kinesthetic activities. The word may be read, listened to, pronounced, analyzed, written, and used in composition. Correct syllabication of the word is helpful. It seems sensible in order to obviate misunderstanding, and because the word is the unit for writing, to begin and end the study with emphasis on the whole word.

Although children learn differently, most children will be aided by the use of all or two or three aids to imagery, rather than the exclusion of all but one. Gradually the child will be helped to good spelling by forming a clear image of the word by one or more of the visual, auditory, oral, and kinesthetic approaches. However, if a child has difficulty in spelling because of his inability to use methods taught to the group, appraisal of his difficulty should suggest guidance of effective imagery.

After the child has perceived the whole word clearly and visualized it part by part, pronounced it as a whole and then slowly syllable by syllable and as a whole word again, he should study the letters in sequence. After seeing the letters in proper sequence, he should recall them. The recall, which may be visual, oral, or kinesthetic should be checked for correctness. Active recall should be dynamic

---

[32] Fitzgerald, *The Teaching of Spelling, op. cit.,* pp. 24–40.

and satisfying. Self-activity in study and checking for accuracy must be developed. To be certain that the spelling is correct, the learner should cover the word and write it. The best test of spelling is the writing of the word in necessary written expression.

Investigations have shown that a systematic method of learning to spell a word generally brings results superior to those attained by haphazard activities which learners devise for themselves without instruction or guidance. The five steps which follow have been used successfully in normal classes in the elementary school.

### Five Steps in Learning to Spell a Word[33]

1. *Meaning and Pronunciation.*   Look at the word. Pronounce the word. Use it in a sentence.

2. *Imagery.*   See and say the word. Hear it. See the syllables of the word. Say the word, syllable by syllable. Spell the word.

3. *Recall.*   Look at the word. Close your eyes and spell it. Check to see whether your spelling is correct. (In case you made an error, do steps 1, 2, and 3 again.)

4. *Writing the Word.**   Write the word correctly. Dot the *i's.* Cross the *t's.* Close the *o's.* Make every letter right. Check your spelling.

5. *Mastery.***   Cover the word and write it. If it is correct, cover it and write it once more. Check the spelling.

If you made a mistake, do these steps again, until you have learned to spell the word.

### THE TEST-STUDY PLAN OF TEACHING SPELLING

### The Essentials of the Plan

The essentials of procedure in the test-study plan are:

1. Pretest over the term's work to determine the achievement of the class and that of the individuals of the class.

2. Pretest on each week's assignment.

3. Each child identifies the words he misspelled.

---

[33] Fitzgerald, *op. cit.,* pp. 30–38.

* Many authorities favor writing the word from memory rather than copying it. To copy the word in the process of learning it is unnecessary for most children if the preceding steps have been successfully carried out.

** For mastery, some children need to cover the word and write it once; others need to repeat the process once more or even twice. This step should fit the needs of the individual child.

4. Each child studies the words he misspelled.

5. Encourage each child to use words of the week in writing.

6. Determine the degree of mastery, for each learner, of the words of the week and of those of two weeks ago.

7. Each child records his weekly achievement on his progress chart.

8. Words missed in the final test of the week are recorded in his individual hard word list by each child.

9. Each learner studies words of the week missed in the final test in preparation for the review test two weeks later.

10. Each learner studies the words of the review lesson of two weeks ago which he misspelled (if any) in the final test and takes a special individual test on them to show mastery.

11. Each learner uses hard words of the lesson in writing, proof-reads his writing, and corrects his mistakes.

12. A final test of the term, comparable to the preliminary term test may be given to determine progress for the class and individuals of the class.[34]

## An Outline of a Week's Work

The assignment for a week will cover from six or seven words in the beginning of the second grade to approximately 20 in the eighth grade. An allotment of from 75 to 100 minutes a week, 15 to 20 minutes a day — five days a week — is ample to carry out the spelling program in normal situations. The weekly program may be undertaken in three days of the week with a time allotment of 25 to 35 minutes a day, in two days of the week with a time allotment of 40 to 50 minutes a day, or even in one day if the schedule requires such a program. The five-day schedule has proved to be highly satisfactory.

The following outline is based upon a five-day program, which may begin on any day of the week in order to best accommodate the schedule.

The plan should be put into operation enthusiastically by the teacher; and to be successful, it should be followed understandingly by the pupils. The plan permits necessary variation in the study of words that children misspell. Note that the testing may be administered to the whole group, but the study must be carried on individually.

---

[34] Fitzgerald, op. cit., p. 42.

*Weekly Program*

FIRST DAY (Monday): *Meaning, Pronunciation, Pretesting, Correction, Studying New Words of the Week*

1. The assignment of the week's work should be clear to every child.

2. Guide children to understand meanings of new words in at least one of the following ways:

   *a*) Reading a story or sentences including new words

   *b*) Matching new words with meanings

   *c*) Matching homonyms and words easily confused in sentences

   *d*) Using the dictionary to study words (usually after the third grade).

3. Teach correct pronunciation of each new word.

   *a*) Each child should listen attentively as the teacher pronounces each new word correctly.

   *b*) Children may pronounce each word in unison with the teacher or after she has pronounced it.

   *c*) Volunteers may pronounce difficult words.

   *d*) The teacher should listen to the pronunciation in order to make corrections when necessary.

   *e*) Children may be guided to analyze pronunciation of words by using the dictionary (usually in the spelling book).

4. Give the first test of the week.

   *a*) Pronounce each word once. Present homonyms in a sentence as follows: "to. He went to town. to."

   *b*) Have papers corrected. Sometimes each child may check his own paper; sometimes he may check his neighbor's; sometimes the teacher may mark the errors. Whatever method is used, the teacher must be certain that the spelling errors are identified. Illegible writings should be checked as errors. There must be no penalties for misspelling on this first test. Children must understand that the purpose of this test is to determine the words that each cannot spell and should study. A child who misspelled no words in this first test may use his time in other subject areas. For example, an experiment in science, a problem in mathematics, or a feature article for the school newspaper may require his effort and engage his interest.

5. Have each child write correctly in a study list the words mis-

spelled in the first test. This should be done carefully for these words make up the child's individual study assignment.

6. Supervise the children in studying words to be learned with the *Five Steps in Learning to Spell a Word.*

**SECOND DAY** (Tuesday): *Supervised Study of New Words and Study Activities*

1. Guide each child to study the words he misspelled in the first test.

2. Supervise his use of the *Five Steps in Learning to Spell a Word* in studying these.

3. Direct each child to begin planned activities on studying, analyzing, building, and using words.

**THIRD DAY** (Wednesday): *Supervised Study of New and Review Words and Other Study Activities*

1. Supervise the completion by each child of the study of new words misspelled in the pretest of the week.

2. See that each child uses the five steps correctly in proper sequence to master the words misspelled in the final test of two weeks ago.*

3. Guide children to complete exercises in studying and using words. These should be designed to help each child to know and use words correctly.

4. Children should be directed to use their time efficiently. If some complete the work of the spelling assignment, they may be permitted to work in some other area.

**FOURTH DAY** (Thursday): *Testing, Correcting, Writing, and Studying*

1. Give the final test of the week over new words and review words (words of two weeks before).

2. Supervise the marking of mistakes and the grading of the papers.

3. See that the words misspelled in the final test are properly written in the hard word list in the spelling workbook or notebook.

4. Direct study by each individual of his hard words with the *Five Steps in Learning to Spell a Word.*

5. Have each child draw a line through or check each of the words in his hard word list of two weeks ago which he spelled correctly in the final test of the present week. This should be a matter of special satisfaction for each child.

---

* The continuing review may be directed to words of one, two, three, or four weeks ago as the teacher finds satisfactory.

6. Direct each child, who misspelled a word of the lesson of two weeks ago, to study that word until mastery has been achieved and checked with a special individual test.

**FIFTH DAY** (Friday): *Record Progress, Mastery, Complete the Unit*

1. Have each child record on his progress chart the number of words misspelled in the final test of the week. Each should compare his record with the scores of previous weeks.

2. Motivate each child, who has not finished his study of the words, to complete the mastery of words missed in the final test of the week.

3. See that children use the *Five Steps in Learning to Spell a Word* in studying hard words of previous weeks.

4. Supervise the completion of all unfinished activities and exercises.

5. After all the work of the week has been completed, some teachers may desire to make the assignment for next week.[35]

### Variations of the Test-Study Plan

Two variations of the test-study plan are worth mentioning. The first permits three tests a week in place of the two suggested in the plan just outlined.

*Three-test plan.* No attempt is made to outline this excellent plan because of limited space. The following partial outline points up the differences in it and the one described in the preceding pages.

**FIRST DAY** (Monday):  Pretest and individual study

**SECOND DAY** (Tuesday):  Individual study of words misspelled by each child

**THIRD DAY** (Wednesday):  Test and study

**FOURTH DAY** (Thursday):  Study by each individual of words misspelled

**FIFTH DAY** (Friday):  Final test of the week followed by study.[36]

In both these plans presented, the procedure is to test before teaching and studying. Gates and Bennett compared the two-test and the three-test modifications of the test-study plan of teaching spelling. The findings favored the weekly two-test plan in grades two, three,

---

[35] James A. Fitzgerald and Patricia G. Fitzgerald, *A Teacher's Manual for Learning Words* (Milwaukee: The Bruce Publishing Company, 1957), pp. 48–50.
[36] Ernest Horn, "Spelling," *Encyclopedia of Educational Research,* 1941, p. 1175.

and low four. In grades high four, five, and six the results were slightly in favor of the three-test plan.[37]

*Team testing for gifted.* In a second variation, the individual who knows most of the words of the term may be guided to clear up the term's core of words in a few weeks or even in a few days. The team procedure may be followed. Two pupils of high achievement in spelling, test each other over the words of the term. Each can make note of the words he misspells and attack them with the *Five Steps in Learning to Spell a Word.* After the two have reason to believe that they have mastered the words they misspelled, each may test the other again. If words are misspelled in this second test, study may be directed to them and a third test may be administered. This procedure of test-study-test may continue until the words of the term are mastered.

*Independent study.* A gifted pupil who easily mastered all the words of the basic core may have specific advanced problems of his own. His projects may call for words beyond the core, needed in connection with special activities he has undertaken. This individual should be guided to attack his spelling independently by careful appraisal of his writing needs and by study of them. A well-developed spelling consciousness will indicate to him a word which may be misspelled and he can use the dictionary to check the correctness of his spelling as well as the propriety of his choice of a word to meet his purpose as he strives to express a particular meaning. With perseverance he can develop a word-attack procedure by using roots, prefixes, and suffixes in building and using derivatives. In such a process, he develops not only correct forms of words, but also meanings of the derivatives, and a facility in the use of them.

## The Importance of the Corrected Test

The corrected test refers to test correction after each test has been given. These testings and the correction of them are highly valuable in the learning process. When a gifted pupil is tested on a word, makes a mistake, corrects the mistake, and writes the word carefully in a study list he may have achieved the necessary mastery of that word. This type of study should be emphasized. Thomas Horn, after investigating the effect of the corrected test on learning to spell by

---

[37] Arthur I. Gates and Chester C. Bennett, "Two Tests versus Three Tests Weekly in Teaching Spelling," *Elementary School Journal,* 34:44–49, September, 1933.

268 sixth-grade children, reported that the corrected test was the "most important single factor contributing to achievement in spelling."[38] He stated that in some classes the corrected test alone was sufficient for mastery or near mastery of the typical spelling assignment by the higher third of the pupils. Horn's results emphasized strongly not only the importance of testing, but also the value of correcting misspellings and taking note of correct spellings.

## Self-Testing and Self-Study

The test-study plan of instruction and the method of learning to spell a word foster self-testing and self-study. Mastery of spelling is based logically on self-testing and self-study of the words misspelled. The *Five Steps in Learning to Spell a Word* combine these procedures. Proofreading and the correction of words lead to the employment of the dictionary and to independence in choice of words, their correct spelling, appropriate use, and legible writing. No spelling program can teach a child all the words he will need to write, but any good program can teach him to test and study the words he needs and to use the dictionary properly in becoming independent.

## Keeping Record of Progress

Valuable records of spelling achievement and progress may be used in motivating spelling. A spelling notebook with a place for "My Hard Words" and a section for "New and Interesting Words" is always conducive to spelling improvement and to good usage. Such records could be kept in a section of the English notebook.

Records of achievement may be kept on a progress chart. A record is valuable because the child can compare his achievement from one week to another and obtain satisfaction in noting his improved scores which generally eventuate as the test-study program progresses.

The individual spelling record for the semester might contain the number of words missed in the pretest of each week, the number missed in the final test of each week, and the number, if any, misspelled in the review test two weeks later. A record of the mastery indicated in special individual tests, if any are necessary, should be stimulating to the pupil.

---

[38] Thomas D. Horn, "The Effect of the Corrected Test on Learning to Spell," *Elementary School Journal*, 47:285, January, 1947.

## THE STUDY-TEST METHOD OF TEACHING

A foreign group, a group with a language handicap, or a slow-learning group might possibly know the spelling of none or of a very few words of the term. In such a situation, the pretest of the week may be omitted and the teacher may present two or three words a day until the words of the week are taught. A workable plan is suggested for the teacher and the child.

*Meaning and pronunciation.* Use the word in a sentence. Explain the meaning and illustrate the word's use. Ask volunteers to use the word. Pronounce the word and have children pronounce it in unison. See that the pronunciation is correct.

*Visualization.* Write the word on the board, saying the letters as you write them. Have children say the letters as you write the word again. Have the children read the word in their workbooks or texts. Let them study the word carefully and have them say the letters in proper sequence. The word should be "seen, heard, pronounced, studied, written, and used in a sentence."

*Writing the word.* After the children have a clear image of the word, they should write it as legibly as possible. If errors are made, they should be corrected. The word should be written again.

*Study for mastery.* Have the children write the word from memory. Check the work of each child. If mistakes are made, have them corrected. Have the pupils write the word again without copying it. Have each child check and, if necessary, correct his spelling. Once again, have the children write the word from memory. Teach other words of the day's assignment similarly.

*Testing.* After the words of the day have been taught, give a test on the new words and on those of the day before. Have the spelling checked, and if necessary corrected. Have each child write in a study list the words he misspelled, if any.

After the words of the week have been studied in this way, give a final test on Friday. If words are misspelled in the final test of the week, they should be written correctly into the hard word list and mastered before the review test is given — two weeks later.

As the children develop in spelling power, it is well to include in the final test of the week the words studied two weeks before. If any of the review words are misspelled by a child, he should be motivated to study these words with the *Five Steps in Learning to Spell a Word* and to accept the responsibility for requesting an individual test to prove mastery of them.

*Individual study.* As soon as possible, the teacher should motivate each child to study individually the words of the lesson and the words he needs.

*Use of words learned.* Spelling words should be used in writing. Unless words are learned for necessary writing, a child will not maintain mastery of them. Proofreading of the writing, therefore, is important.

*Change of method.* As the children develop in language power and gain experience through reading and writing, they will arrive at a point where they know some of the words of the weekly assignment — some children many words perhaps, and others a few. Since it is a tiresome experience to be "taught" words which one can spell, the test-study procedure should at that time supersede the study-test plan. The children will be motivated by a procedure which helps them to determine what words they need to study and guides them to efficient individual study.

## GENERALIZATIONS AND RULES

Principles of spelling that have few exceptions and apply to many words may be developed inductively. Generalizations which cover the adding of common suffixes — *-ing, -ed, -s* — are useful. The *"q* followed by *u"* has no common exceptions. The old rule, *"i* before *e* except after *c* or when sounded as *a* as in *neighbor* and *weigh"* applies to about 110 words in one of the modern spellers in which there are eight exceptions such as *height, either, foreign,* and *leisure.* These words should be taught as exceptions to the rule.

Rules or generalizations should be simple. For example, the rule — "most nouns form their plurals by adding *s* or *es* to the singular" — has two parts. If one is attacked at a time, success may be achieved. The *es* part of the rule is the more difficult part. It may be generalized separately from the easier part — adding *s* to form plurals. For example, children may have reason to use plurals of *church, box, tax, mass, address, branch, wish, class, loss.* They can work on each specific word as it arises from time to time, and they will recognize the fact that the plural of such a word cannot be pronounced properly if only the *s* is added. By a study of like words as they appear in their work, they will understand the need for adding *es* after *branch, dish, class,* and *ax* to form plurals. It is possible for them to discover and formulate the rule — "To form the plurals of words ending in *ch, sh, ss,* and *x,* add *es* to the singular." Dolch who encouraged *thought* spelling believed that generalization in spelling is an extension from specific cases. He pointed out that rules as generally taught are thought out not by the pupil but by the teacher and that they are learned mechanically.[39] Certainly, the memorization of involved rules is questionable. It is much better to understand a principle and apply it to words as the need arises for adding suffixes, for example, than to try to follow a memorized statement.

Many teachers do not believe in teaching rules of spelling. It is true perhaps that pupils learn to spell a list of words as well without them as with them. However, according to Gates, generalization does increase power to spell unstudied words.[40] Since it is an objective in elementary education to strive to develop independence in the pupil, generalization in spelling has its place and should be developed by meaningful and rational activities.

The following generalizations may be developed inductively:

1. The letter *s* is added to the singular of many nouns to form the plural.

2. Words ending in *ss, x, ch,* and *sh* form their plurals by adding *es.*

3. The letter *q* is followed by the letter *u* in all common words in our language.

4. The *i* is written before *e* except after *c,* or when sounded as *a* as in *neighbor* and *weigh.*

5. To form derivatives of words ending in *y* after a consonant, generally change the *y* to *i* except where the suffix begins with *i* (*try, tries, tried, trying*).

6. To form derivatives of words ending in *y* preceded by a vowel, generally keep the *y,* as in *play, plays, playing, playful.* (Some exceptions: *daily, paid, said.*)

7. A word of one syllable or a word of more than one syllable accented on the last syllable, which ends in a single consonant preceded by a single vowel usually doubles the final consonant before a suffix beginning with a vowel, as in *omit, omitted, omitting, regret, regretted, regretting.* Note that when the addition of a suffix causes a

---

[39] Edward W. Dolch, *Better Spelling* (Champaign, Ill.: Garrard Press, 1942), pp. 192–236.

[40] Arthur I. Gates, *Generalization and Transfer in Spelling* (New York: Bureau of Publications, Teachers College, Columbia University, 1935), pp. 41–42.

Spelling demons

shift in accent from the final to another syllable the final consonant is not doubled, as in *prefer, preferring, preferred, preference.*

8. Final silent *e* is usually retained before a suffix beginning with a consonant, as in *lines, lanes.* (Some exceptions: *ninth wholly.*)

9. Final silent *e* is usually dropped before a suffix beginning with a vowel, as in *dining, mining.* (Some exceptions: *peaceable, mileage.*)

## ERRORS AND REVIEWS

The types of spelling mistakes made by children are almost beyond imagination. For example, *stationery* dictated as follows — *"stationery. My teacher writes on good stationery. stationery."* — was misspelled 170 times in 68 different forms by 200 fifth-grade children, missed 185 times in 39 different forms by 200 sixth-grade children, and misspelled 274 times in 23 different forms by 420 seventh- and eighth-grade pupils. *Sincerely* presented in the same manner was misspelled 160 times in 54 different forms by 200 fifth-grade children, 143 times in 47 different forms by 200 sixth-grade children, and 179 times in 39 different forms by 420 seventh- and eighth-grade pupils.[41] Many other striking examples are available.

Each pupil should review the words which he misspells and which he needs to write. The first learning of a word may not be sufficient for permanent mastery. Some words persist as demons throughout the grades and into higher levels. Each child should review his own difficult words with a good method.

The following suggestions may help to guide the teacher in planning reviews. Reviews may be conducted individually by children on the following:

1. Words which were misspelled in the final test of the week
2. Words of the review unit of two weeks ago which were misspelled in the final test of the week
3. Words which are misspelled by individuals in their written work
4. Common homonyms, such as, *to, too, two, right, write, their, there, here, hear,* and others found in the 222 demons
5. Common contractions such as *can't, couldn't, didn't, haven't, I'll, that's, they're, we're, won't, you're*
6. Common abbreviations, such as *Ave., Dr., Mr., Mrs., St.*
7. Common possessives, such as *boy's, boys', teacher's, mother's, father's*
8. The *222 Spelling Demons.* These are a crucial core of useful words of persistent difficulty for elementary school children. These words were used 417,176 times in 682,082 running words written by children in grades two to six inclusive. They were misspelled 23,636 times of the 42,992 misspellings made in the writing of the 682,082 running words. Since they comprise more than half of the words written and caused more than half the misspellings in the writing done by children in these grades, they should be subject matter for dynamic and intensive review by the test-study method before children leave the elementary school.[42]

## DIAGNOSIS AND REMEDIAL INSTRUCTION

If results are not as good as they should be, a diagnostic and remedial program should be instituted. Some brief suggestions follow.

---

[41] Fitzgerald, *The Teaching of Spelling, op. cit.* pp. 61–73.
[42] Fitzgerald, *A Basic Life Spelling Vocabulary, op. cit.,* pp. 144–150.

## Diagnosis

In a thorough diagnosis, tests and other instruments may be used to appraise mental, emotional, achievement, and personality traits. It is possible that a teacher may receive expert help in diagnosis of a child from the school psychologist. Some group tests may be used, but diagnosis must come down to the individual learning-teaching situation. The following questions may help guide the teacher in trying to determine the causes of spelling difficulty in a normal group.

### 222 SPELLING DEMONS

| | | | |
|---|---|---|---|
| about | close | *Halloween | loving |
| address | come | handkerchiefs | made |
| afternoon | *coming | has | make |
| again | couldn't | *have | March |
| all right | *cousin | haven't | maybe |
| along | daddy | having | me |
| already | day | he | Miss |
| always | December | hear | morning |
| *am | *didn't | hello | mother |
| an | dog | her | Mr. |
| *and | *don't | *here | *Mrs. |
| answer | down | him | much |
| anything | Easter | his | my |
| anyway | every | home | *name |
| April | *everybody | hope | nice |
| are | father | hospital | November |
| arithmetic | February | house | *now |
| aunt | fine | how | nowadays |
| awhile | first | how's | o'clock |
| baby | football | I | October |
| balloon | *for | I'll | off |
| basketball | fourth | *I'm | on |
| *because | Friday | in | once |
| been | *friend | isn't | one |
| before | friends | it | *our |
| birthday | *from | it's | out |
| bought | fun | I've | outside |
| boy | *getting | January | party |
| boys | goes | just | people |
| brother | *going | *know | play |
| brought | good | lessons | played |
| can | *good-by | letter | plays |
| cannot | got | like | please |
| can't | grade | likes | *pretty |
| children | *guess | little | quit |
| Christmas | had | lots | quite |

* The fifty words marked with an asterisk are most persistent demons — among the one hundred of four or five of the five grades.

receive
*received
remember
right
said
Santa Claus
*Saturday
saw
school
schoolhouse
send
sent
sincerely
snow
snowman
*some
something
sometime
*sometimes
soon

stationery
store
studying
summer
*Sunday
suppose
sure
surely
swimming
*teacher
*teacher's
*Thanksgiving
*that's
the
*their
them
then
*there
there's
they

they're
think
thought
through
*time
*to
*today
together
*tomorrow
tonight
*too
toys
train
truly
*two
until
vacation
*very
want
was

*we
weather
well
went
were
we're
when
white
will
with
won't
would
*write
*writing
*you
*your
you're
yours

1. Are you enthusiastic about teaching spelling?

2. Are the materials you use appropriate?

3. Are your procedures effective?

4. Do your pupils understand the need for spelling and are they enthusiastic about it?

5. Can learners see and hear the words of the assignment?

6. Are words pronounced correctly by the pupils?

7. Do the pupils write legibly?

8. Do they associate letters and combinations of letters correctly with sounds?

9. Is study time efficiently used?

10. Are tests properly administered?

11. Are pretests, final tests, and review tests carefully corrected?

12. Does each pupil use an effective method to study the words he misspelled in the tests?

13. Do pupils use meaningfully in writing the words they learn in their spelling lessons?

14. Are their mistakes in writing checked and corrected?

15. Does each individual keep a record of his spelling achievement?

16. Does he list words difficult for him, and does he study them systematically?

17. How are you helping him to overcome his difficulties?

18. Is each individual improving his spelling, and if not what are the causes of his lack of improvement?

## Remedial Instruction

A pupil should understand the causes for his difficulties and deficiencies, and then work to overcome them. A curriculum of the correct content and activities must be planned. Some pupils will need a large supplementary list and others may not be able to master or use all of the words which are basic for the normal individual. The teacher must recognize these differences and teach each in accord with his abilities and requirements.

A teacher must appraise the study habits of the individual who is having difficulty. Perhaps he needs instruction on the *Five Steps in Learning to Spell a Word*. Perhaps he needs guidance in pronunciation. A child who writes illegibly should be instructed in writing. He may need help on forming or joining letters. If a child dislikes spelling, he should be shown how valuable spelling is in school and life and how well the method that he uses works when it is correctly followed. A pupil who is discouraged, may be aided by one of his classmates who is willing and able to give him help by studying with him. An individual who spells well in a test but poorly in his composition, needs guidance in proofreading. Whatever may be wrong, or insufficient, or disconcerting, must be recognized and corrected.

## Preventive Measures

Preventive measures are extremely important. Prevention of difficulties is insured generally for normal pupils by putting into operation the test-study plan indicated in this chapter. A teacher however may wish to make notes about how to handle children of differing backgrounds and of varying abilities, interests, and problems. Notes kept from year to year about difficulties of children in learning to spell certain specific words or types of expression are sometimes very helpful in anticipating trouble spots and in guiding children to avoid failure. Careful consideration and appraisal of each pupil from day to day and week to week will help in the understanding of his problems, and in preventing mistakes and failures.

## SUMMARY

A child must be guided to study, as he requires them, the words he needs to write and cannot spell.

The core curriculum for spelling instruction should include the most useful words for writing — the common words needed by child and adult. These have been validly determined by research on child and adult writing. Each pupil should build up his own supplementary word list, words that are of special interest and use to him in fulfilling his writing needs. Each should keep also in a hard word list, words of special difficulty which he misspells frequently. These he should master with an efficient method of learning to spell.

The test-study procedure is generally effective in teaching normal and rapid learners to spell because they usually know the spelling of a considerable proportion of the words of an assignment, and testing before teaching directs them to study words they need to learn. Variations in methods should be made to fit the needs of the class and of the individuals of the class.

Generalizations are best approached inductively. Reviews should be planned to guide the learner to appraise his spelling. Pretests, final tests, and review tests should be supplemented with individual tests and proofreading to indicate to the learner the words which he must continue to study in his drive for mastery.

A program of diagnosis and remediation should be instituted for those who have difficulty. Remediation procedures should be designed to overcome individual difficulties determined by the diagnosis of each child's problems in spelling. Prevention of the development of difficulties is an important factor in achieving spelling proficiency.

### ACTIVITIES, PROBLEMS, QUESTIONS

1. List and analyze the causes of poor spelling.
2. Note the fourteen ways in which the long *a* sound is spelled. List words to show several ways to spell the long sounds of *e, i, o,* and *u.*
3. State the most important aims in learning to spell.
4. Give evidence to show the overlap of:
   a. child and adult vocabularies
   b. reading and writing vocabularies.
5. How valuable are the *350 Most Useful Spelling Words?* How valuable are the *222 Demons?* What evidence is available to show the value of each list?
6. Explain how incidental learning should be used as a basis for systematic spelling instruction.
7. List the *Five Steps in Learning to Spell a Word.* Use these steps exactly in learning to spell a difficult word. Teach these exact steps to your pupils. Appraise the results.
8. Outline the *test-study* weekly method of teaching spelling. State clearly the daily procedures and responsibilities for each child.
9. Compare and contrast the *test-study* and the *study-test* plans of spelling instruction. (*a*) When can you use each of these plans most profitably? (*b*) Why is the *test-study* plan more economical of time for normal pupils?

10. State the generalizations you would use in teaching spelling. Why would you use them? How would you teach the generalizations?

11. Outline a plan for reviews in spelling. Explain the values of such a plan.

12. Define: diagnosis, remediation, prevention. Show how each can be made most useful in a spelling program.

## SELECTED REFERENCES

Dolch, Edward W. *Better Spelling.* Champaign, Illinois: Garrard Press, 1942. 270 pp.

Fitzgerald, James A. *A Basic Life Spelling Vocabulary.* Milwaukee: The Bruce Publishing Company, 1951. 161 pp.

———— *The Teaching of Spelling.* Milwaukee: The Bruce Publishing Company, 1951. 233 pp.

Gates, Arthur I. *A List of Spelling Difficulties in 3876 Words.* New York: Bureau of Publications, Teachers College, Columbia University, 1937. 166 pp.

Greene, Harry A. *The New Iowa Spelling Scale.* Iowa City, Iowa: Bureau of Educational Research and Service, State University of Iowa, 1955. 178 pp.

Hildreth, Gertrude. *Teaching Spelling.* New York: Holt, Rinehart & Winston, 1955. 352 pp.

Horn, Ernest. *A Basic Writing Vocabulary: 10,000 Words Most Commonly Used in Writing.* Iowa City: University of Iowa Monographs in Education, No. 4, 1926. 225 pp.

———— *Teaching Spelling.* What Research Says to the Teacher. No. 3. Washington, D. C.: DCT and AERA of the NEA, 1954. 32 pp.

*Learning to Spell.* Albany: The New York State Education Department, 1960. 59 pp.

Rinsland, Henry D. *A Basic Vocabulary of Elementary School Children.* New York: Macmillan, 1945. 636 pp.

# Chapter XI

## Learning to Write: Manuscript and Cursive

### ORIENTATION

IN ANCIENT as in more recent times, the human being desired to express himself in writing. Not only did he wish to communicate, but he wanted to leave a record of the events which transpired in his life. Picture writing, hieroglyphics, and symbols of various kinds were used successfully to record history. Various forms of writing were developed by different cultures. Some writings were so formed that they were read from top to bottom of the page, and others from the bottom to the top. Some systems were designed to be read from right to left, and others like our own from left to right. Alphabets were invented and small letters and capitals for various purposes were developed. From the earliest times to the present, there has been a constant striving to perfect the means and mechanics of communication by improving handwriting and print.

### Past to Present in America

Handwriting was emphasized in the colonial and pioneer schools of our country. English writing was followed by the Spencerian which in turn gave way to the more practical cursive handwriting necessary in the rapidly growing industry of our developing economy. Because of the difficulties in teaching children the so-called muscular movement of cursive writing with a pronounced slant, vertical writing was introduced. However, because vertical writing did not encourage a sufficiently free movement of the hand across the page, it was discontinued.

Research by Judd, McAllister, and Freeman indicated the impracticality of trying to teach young children the muscular movement. These men demonstrated also the high value of rhythm in writing. They showed the importance of good posture and the need for proper position of hand, instrument (pencil or pen), and paper in handwriting.[1]

Because of the difficulties in teaching cursive writing to young children it followed that innovations were tried. Manuscript writing was introduced into our country from England in the early 1920's. (See chart on page 331 for examples of manuscript and cursive writing.) Its simplicity and usefulness in other language arts has caused its adoption in the primary grades in a majority of schools of the nation.[2] A mild controversy concerning whether it or cursive writing should be taught still continues. There is also some question concerning whether, if taught, it should be superseded by cursive writing and also when the change should be made if a change is to be made.

Templin questions the efficacy of teaching both manuscript and cursive writing because "recent findings seem to indicate" that some adults trained in the two types are less fluent and write more illegibly than those trained in one only.[3]

## Problems in Teaching Handwriting

Teachers, supervisors, and investigators who are concerned with the low standards of handwriting in this country continue to study problems relating to the improvement of the mechanics of written communication. Among the problems and questions being studied are the following:

1. What is the level of handwriting in the country, and what standards should be achieved in the school?

2. What is the importance of handwriting in language areas in and out of school?

3. What are the major objectives in the teaching of handwriting?

4. What types of handwriting — manuscript or cursive — should be taught at the various levels in the elementary school?

---

[1] Frank N. Freeman, "Contributions of Research to Special Methods: Hand-writing," *The Scientific Movement in Education,* Thirty-Seventh Yearbook of the National Society for the Study of Education, Part II, 1938, pp. 91–94.

[2] *Ibid.* See also Margaret B. Parke and William H. Bristow, *Practices and Problems in Handwriting,* Educational Research Bulletin, No. 9 (New York: Board of Education of the City of New York, 1947), pp. 1–2.

[3] Elaine Templin, "Handwriting — The Neglected 'R,'" *Elementary English,* 37:386–389, October, 1960.

5. How may manuscript be introduced most beneficially to young children?

6. Should a change from manuscript to cursive writing be made, and if so, when and how should it be made?

7. What are the essentials of an effective program for the teaching of handwriting?

8. When and how should cursive handwriting be taught?

9. What consideration should be afforded the left-handed child?

10. How can an effective plan of diagnosis and remediation be implemented?

## Levels of Handwriting Today

For several decades there have been sharp criticisms of handwriting, such as the following: the teaching of handwriting is in a confused and disorganized state; handwriting is the poorest taught and most neglected of skills in elementary education; ability in handwriting is the least valued of all elementary school skills.[4] Sheaffer, however, reported that children of today write approximately as well as those of a generation ago, but indicated that considerable improvement could be made in the skill.[5] Grant and Marble reported a survey of 3581 sixth-grade pupils which indicated that more than a fourth of the children were deficient in letter formation, size, slant, and spacing, and these needed individual help in appraisal of difficulties and in remediation. They reported also that the writing of a fifth of the children lacked legibility and required systematic instruction in the essentials of handwriting.[6] The average quality score of 74 seventh-grade pupils in the University of Chicago High School was reported to be 44.3 (less than Grade IV norm) on the Ayres Measuring Scale for Handwriting.[7] Woody reported an average quality of 46.2 (a little more than Grade IV norm) on the Ayres Scale for 2097 sixth-grade pupils in Michigan.[8] These reports seem to indicate the need for

[4] Luella Cole, "Heresy in Handwriting," *Elementary School Journal*, 38:606–618, April, 1938; and *Learning to Write* (Albany, New York: University of the State of New York, State Education Department, Bureau of Elementary Curriculum Development, 1960), pp. 9–10.

[5] Craig R. Sheaffer, "Penmanship Not a Lost Art," *Journal of Business Education*, 26:248, April, 1951.

[6] Albert Grant and Margaret M. Marble, "Results of Cincinnati Handwriting Survey," *School Review*, 48:693–696, November, 1940.

[7] Arthur E. Traxler and Harold A. Anderson, "Group Corrective Handwriting in Junior High School — An Experiment," *School Review*, 41:675–684, November, 1933.

[8] Clifford Woody, *Teaching Practices and Achievement in Penmanship in the*

careful consideration of our handwriting curricula and of the methods used in teaching handwriting.

## Standards of Handwriting

Since handwriting is written to be read as one of the factors of communication, there is reason for judging the quality of legibility — its readability. A second element important to a pupil in school and to an individual outside the school is the speed with which he can write with acceptable quality. It is evident that an individual must vary the speed of writing in different types of situations. In general, the faster an individual writes, the lower is the quality of his writing.[9]

Freeman found, from a survey of 46 cities by use of the Ayres Handwriting Scale, an average quality score of approximately 40 for grade two and one of 54.5 for grade six, with approximate ratings of 42, 46, and 50.5 for grades three, four, and five respectively.[10] He reported also an average speed in letters per minute — determined from surveys of writing — of 30, 40, 50, 60, and 67 for grades two to six inclusive.[11]

These averages of both quality and speed of writing are bases for appraisal of achievement norms, but they are not standards. They should be used with considerateness of the great differences of individuals in each of the successive grades. A child who attains comparable scores without difficulty may be guided to achieve higher standards. A child who has not attained them, should be encouraged to improve both quality and speed of writing. For him these norms may suggest goals to be achieved.

## The Importance of Handwriting

Handwriting is an integrating tool in purposing, planning, and carrying out projects. It is a means of facilitating study and thought both in and out of school. Narrowly considered, handwriting has been thought of as a skill, but it is more, for it is a way of conveying

---

*Public Schools of Michigan.* Bureau of Educational Reference and Research Bulletin, No. 151 (Ann Arbor, Michigan: School of Education, University of Michigan, 1938).

[9] Adrienne Erlebacher and Virgil E. Herrick, "Quality of Handwriting Today and Yesterday," *Elementary School Journal,* 62:89–93, November, 1961.

[10] Frank N. Freeman, *Teaching Handwriting* (Washington, D. C.: Department of Classroom Teachers and American Educational Research Association of the N.E.A., 1954), p. 5.

[11] *Ibid.,* p. 4.

ideas, of describing events, and of expressing emotions. It is used in recording what we hear, what we see, what we think, and what we do. It has value in listening, reading, speaking, spelling, and writing. Handwriting is of help in most aspects of living for writing letters, notes, labels, names, and for filling out blanks. It is valuable in almost every situation that calls for written expression — sometimes the typewriter may be used, but often the employment of any mechanical device is impractical.

When children write their ideas in a real situation, they are expressing themselves purposefully. In order to do this, they need to think and to recall what they have read or heard. Handwriting is an instrument for retention. In order to organize their thoughts some form of it is generally necessary. In revision of a letter or composition, handwriting is obviously useful. As pupils progress they have increasing need for it in connection with the other language arts. Thought, study, and organization of knowledge are enhanced by writing and by the use of handwriting as a means of expression.[12] More and more handwriting is recognized as beneficial in learning to read.

## OBJECTIVES IN LEARNING TO WRITE

The typical child long before he goes to school has a strong desire to express himself in writing. This is evident in the marks he makes upon paper with crayon or pencil. Using that urge, a teacher can motivate the learner to control his scribbling to conform to a pattern of symbols that will be recognizable. In short, then, the child's desire to communicate can be developed. He wants to write, and he is encouraged when he can read what he writes, when others are able to read what he has written, when others answer him in writing, and when he can read their written messages.

In learning to write, the child must be guided to recognize and to achieve four important aims: (1) communication; (2) legibility; (3) speed, and (4) individuality.

Communication objectives grow naturally throughout the grades. From the time in kindergarten or first grade when the child writes a brief message to be carried home to his parents until he leaves elementary school, his desire and ability to communicate by writing

[12] Helen K. Mackintosh and Wilhelmina Hill, *How Children Learn to Write,* U. S. Department of Health, Education, and Welfare (Washington, D. C.; N.E.A., 1953), p. 1.

develop. He has many opportunities for writing, and he will write if he is properly encouraged to so express himself.

Legibility may be purposed and enhanced through motivation by the teacher and through self-motivation of the learner. When a child truly recognizes the need of legibility in writing, he will want to achieve it. When he realizes that his illegibly formed letters and words make communication impossible, he will strive for a degree of legibility that will make his messages readable. When he appreciates that well-formed letters, careful spacing, and uniform size of writing help the reader in receiving his message, he will try to write acceptably.

Speed is an objective which must be purposed. However, rate of writing is of no value if what is written cannot be read. After a degree of legibility has been achieved, the child should try to write with a moderate rate of speed in order to conserve time. Speed will vary among individuals, and it will undoubtedly vary for the different types of writing in which a learner engages. Tables of speed and legibility are only suggestive. They are offered to help the teacher and the child to appraise progress. Each pupil should strive for a balance between legibility and speed. The crux of the matter is that a learner should aim for legible writing at an acceptable and practical speed.

Individuality, an objective which has sometimes been referred to as character, distinguishes a person's handwriting from that of others. While individuality may be considered less important than legibility and speed, it is nevertheless desirable. Character or individuality is recognizable in the form and size of letters, in uniformity of slant, and in beauty. Individuality is necessary in signatures on checks, contracts, and wills. As the individual matures his handwriting changes, and in those changes character develops and becomes recognizable.[13]

Among other objectives of teaching handwriting, whether cursive or manuscript, are the following:

1. To build interest in improvement of handwriting
2. To develop facility in writing automatically while concentrating upon thought and content
3. To guide the learner to practice purposively and systematically the mechanics of handwriting
4. To have the learner understand and practice proper posture and position for writing in a relaxed and uncramped manner.[14]

---

[13] See *Learning to Write, op. cit.*, pp. 13–14; and Freeman, *op. cit.*, pp. 3–4.
[14] Mary T. Sullivan, "A Functional Handwriting Program," *Elementary English*, 30:85–90, February, 1953.

## Cursive Alphabet

*Aa Bb Cc Dd Ee Ff Gg Hh Ii*
*Jj Kk Ll Mm Nn Oo Pp Qq*
*Rr Ss Tt Uu Vv Ww Xx Yy Zz*

*1 2 3 4 5 6 7 8 9 10*

## Manuscript Alphabet

ABCDEFGHIJKLMNOPQR
STUVWXYZ abcdefghijklm
nopqrstuvwxyz 1234567 8 9 10

The Zaner-Bloser Company

CHART III.   MODEL LETTERS AND NUMERALS

## TYPES OF HANDWRITING:
## MANUSCRIPT AND CURSIVE

When a child first goes to school, many problems confront him. He is faced generally with those of adjustment and personality such as getting along with his schoolmates and with the teacher. He is challenged with the problems of learning to read, to write, to listen, and to speak with others in a group. Accordingly, the approach to them should be made as easy as possible for him.

### Principles to Determine Symbols to Be Used

A skill such as handwriting is difficult to learn by a first-grade child because many of the movements are relatively complex for the immature six-year-old. The writing to be used in the beginning should be simple in type and easy to acquire by one who has little control over finer muscular movements and who needs experience and practice in mental and physical coordination. Cursive handwriting can be introduced only after the mechanics of manuscript handwriting have been mastered.

Gray, after studying the findings of research and statements made by handwriting authorities in several nations, set forth principles which should be considered by teachers of handwriting. A summary of conclusions from these principles follows:

1. Attention should be given to each child, and adjustments made to meet his particular needs and problems.

2. Readiness activities, when necessary, should be developed for learning to write.

3. Words rather than elements of words should be the bases for beginning writing experiences.

4. A simple form, such as manuscript writing, is preferable to cursive writing in early school years.

5. Handwriting skill "develops slowly" through "maturation and practice."[15]

### The Individual Considered

Each child, different from every other child, must be understood. His maturation should be appraised, his interests assessed, and his abilities directed. Each individual requires guidance which may vary

---

[15] William S. Gray, *The Teaching of Reading and Writing* (Chicago: UNESCO and Scott, Foresman and Company, 1956), pp. 196–197.

from that necessary for others. The program must be planned for him and adapted to his present needs and to his rate of growth and learning from day to day and month to month. The child of six cannot be expected to use accurately and successfully the complex movements required for cursive writing, but he may be able to learn to use simple lines and curves in his first writing. Even these will require practice and they will be improved as he matures and uses them.

## Use of Manuscript as a Beginning Type of Writing in the United States

The great majority of elementary schools in the United States teach manuscript writing to beginners. Freeman reported from a survey of schools in 48 states that manuscript was taught in more than 84 percent of the city school systems responding to the questionnaire. He stated further that manuscript writing was used in a large majority of schools in grades one and two, but that less than one-fourth as many schools taught it in grade three. It was taught infrequently in the remaining grades.[16] Polkinghorne sampled public schools in some cities of more than 100,000, private schools with enrollments of 100 or more, laboratory schools connected with teachers colleges, and other schools of varying nature in the Chicago area. Her results indicated that more than 89 percent of these schools used manuscript for beginning instruction in handwriting, and more than 93 percent of these began teaching handwriting in grade one. Her findings also indicated that instruction in handwriting most frequently shifts from manuscript to cursive in grade three or above. Less than 18 percent of the schools surveyed used manuscript throughout the grades.[17] Noble reported research which indicated that "manuscript writing is almost universally taught in the first two grades" at the present time. He also reported that in a great majority of systems the change from manuscript to cursive is made early in the third grade.[18]

## Advantages of Manuscript Writing for Beginners

Principals, supervisors, and teachers have the problem of determining the type of handwriting to use both for beginners and for those

---

[16] Frank N. Freeman, "Survey of Manuscript Writing in the Public Schools," *Elementary School Journal,* 46:375–377, March, 1946.

[17] Ada R. Polkinghorne, "Current Practices in Teaching Handwriting," *Elementary School Journal,* 47:218–224, December, 1946.

[18] J. Kendrick Noble, Jr., "Handwriting Programs in Today's Schools," *Elementary English,* 40:509, May, 1963.

who are proceeding through the successive grades in the elementary school. From statements by many teachers and writers the following suggested advantages of manuscript writing have been summarized:

1. Manuscript writing is easier for young children to learn than cursive writing because of the plain strokes — straight lines and simple curves.

2. Children with undeveloped muscular control and unperfected co-ordination can produce fairly legible manuscript writing easier than they can write acceptable cursive. The beginner's manuscript writing is more readable than his cursive writing.

3. A smaller amount of eyestrain develops from manuscript writing for the beginner; tension is lessened because of the simplicity of manuscript writing and because the writing instrument is lifted in moving from one stroke to the next.

4. A child who begins with manuscript writing needs to learn essentially only one alphabet in his first school years because the alphabet for manuscript is quite similar to that of print. Accordingly the learning of reading and writing is coordinated and simplified somewhat for the beginner who uses manuscript writing. If a child begins to write with cursive writing when he begins to read, it is necessary for him to learn two alphabets — one for reading and one for writing.

5. Manuscript writing continues to be socially useful in filling out forms of various types in later life.[19]

## Reasons for Teaching Cursive Writing

Investigators, who indicated that manuscript writing was preferred for instruction of beginners, reported that cursive writing was taught after the second grade. Most frequently given reasons for the use of cursive writing follow:

1. Parents want children to write cursively.

2. Children want to learn to write cursively because it is the type their parents and other adults generally use.

3. Cursive writing is generally considered to be more rapid than manuscript writing.

4. The continuous movement utilized in writing whole words in cur-

[19] See Marion E. Lewry, "Improving Manuscript Writing in Primary Grades," *Elementary School Journal,* 47:508–515, May, 1947; and Archie E. Hendricks, "Manuscript and Cursive Handwriting in Brookline," *Elementary School Journal,* 55:447–552, April, 1955.

sive writing is generally considered to be more efficient and less tiring than the use of short choppy strokes required in manuscript writing.

5. More character and individuality can be developed and maintained in rapid cursive writing than in rapid manuscript writing.

6. The individual can learn cursive writing easier and more adequately at the age of eight or nine after he has had manuscript writing than he can learn it when he is six or seven without previous experience in writing.[20]

Some writers question whether manuscript writing should be superseded by cursive writing after grade two. A sensible view seems to be that manuscript writing may be maintained for certain types of work, and cursive writing may be effectively developed for other types.

## INTRODUCING MANUSCRIPT WRITING TO YOUNG CHILDREN

The need for writing becomes evident to most children in the primary grades. A child wants to write his name on a label for his locker. He wishes to write his name on books and materials that belong to him. He may choose to write a title for a picture which he has drawn, or he may express a desire to write a letter to his brother who has gone into the armed services. He may ask to write to his father who is away on a trip, or to his aunt who is ill in the hospital. Not having one such purpose, he may request to write a letter to his mother to carry home to her. For such activities, the child recognizes the value of handwriting.

### Appraising Readiness for Beginning Manuscript Writing

Children in a class vary in their readiness for writing, and the time for beginning to write depends upon the readiness of the individual. Children who come from homes where writing is done and in which consideration is given to child education are quite frequently ready to learn to write before entering the first grade. At that time, children who are physically or mentally immature will have little desire to write and perhaps not much concern about what to write. Lack of motor coordination, defects in vision or hearing, and confused hand dominance may delay an individual's readiness for beginning writing. Writing should be begun at the right time. If it is started too soon, an undue amount of practice is required to achieve a definite standard or degree

---

[20] Freeman, *Teaching Handwriting, op. cit.,* pp. 26–27.

of skill. In order to learn to write, a child must have control of muscles essential for writing. He must have ability to coordinate physical movement with his mental objectives — to form letters and words. He must have the capability of holding pencil or chalk properly, without undue tension. He must be able to make symbols which are meaningful to him, and which, with some practice, will become readable to his teacher and to others.

The signs of readiness are quite obvious. A child may show a desire to express himself by drawing. He may ask his teacher or his parent to write a word or sentence for him. He may begin copying letters and indicate that he recognizes differences in letters and words. When a child asks to write and when he shows evidence of wanting to copy letters and words, it is probable that he has readiness for beginning writing instruction.[21]

Children who are physically and mentally unready can be helped by engaging in activities both in school and on the playground. They need to develop their muscular control and coordination. Drawing on the blackboard or on large sheets of paper is helpful. Engaging in rhythmical exercises, talking to others, and observing classmates drawing or writing help children to become ready to write.[22]

## Use Child Experiences

Experiencing causes children to recognize the joy and importance of communicating through talking and writing. Thinking about an experience is conducive to expression — both oral and written. Handwriting is studied when a child recognizes it as a way of communicating his thoughts. Children like to talk about their experiences on a trip, and what they saw at the zoo, at a farm, or at the circus. The time comes when they will ask to write about what they saw and heard.

A first-grade class went to a zoo. After returning, the children talked about the many strange animals and birds they had seen. They thought they would like to write a book about the zoo. One of the groups produced the following, which was dictated to the teacher to write in manuscript on the chalkboard:

> We went to the zoo.
> We saw some bears.

---

[21] Parke and Bristow, *Practices and Problems in Handwriting, op. cit.,* pp. 24–25.
[22] *Ibid.*

We saw some deer.
We saw five ducks.
We saw four geese.
We saw other birds.
We had fun.

The children watched the teacher write each word from left to right. They saw how she made the capital letters and the small letters, and noticed that she placed periods at the ends of the sentences. Children who had cooperated joyously in writing the story read it in unison. Later, a child volunteered to read it individually. Children who had written manuscript previously asked if they could write the story. One of them produced it as follows:

The Zoo
We went to the Zoo.
We saw bears.
We saw some deer,
We saw five ducks.
We saw four geese.
We saw other birds.
We had fun.
                                    D. P.

*Situations for Manuscript Writing*

Among the situations that are helpful in a writing program in the primary grades are the following:

1. Writing one's name on labels of possessions and equipment — books, desks, lockers
2. Writing signs: Save. Keep. Be Quiet. Testing. Do not touch.

3. Writing a greeting card — Christmas, New Year, Easter, Thanksgiving, Halloween, Birthday
4. Writing titles for a story, song, or book
5. Writing captions for pictures, exhibits, and collections
6. Writing the names of a committee
7. Writing words for a picture dictionary
8. Writing names of animals, flowers, plants
9. Making a list of materials needed for an aquarium or terrarium
10. Writing numbers for pages in a booklet
11. Writing a letter or a notice
12. Writing answers to questions
13. Copying an assignment
14. Writing a plan or outline
15. Writing a report of an experience
16. Writing a story about a pet — dog, cat, or rabbit.

### Early Instruction in Manuscript

A functional approach to writing is to be desired. The children may dictate a letter or a sentence to the teacher, who writes it on the board. Careful observation of the teacher by the children will be beneficial. Sentences composed of most useful words should be used for practice, as for example: "Here is our dog." "He runs." "He plays with me." Such words will be written over and over in a child's work and throughout life. They are among the 350 most useful words.* The words used in beginning writing are the ones that children require in their spelling. They should be words with which the children are familiar.

In writing at the board, the teacher should use as nearly perfect manuscript as she is capable of writing. She should write large, as she expects the children to do. She should stand in such a position that children can see the movement — the strokes, the forming of letters, and also the forming of the words. Children should be directed to note how letters are made and how they are spaced in the words. They should note also that greater space is required between two words than that required between two letters in a word. They should be encouraged to try to space letters and words correctly as soon as possible.

First writing may well be at the board, or on large sheets of paper. If not at the board, manuscript writing requires that the child should

* See pages 299–301 for this list.

assume a favorable position at a table or desk of the right height. The child should sit comfortably, facing the desk squarely, with both feet on the floor. He should place the paper parallel to the edge of the desk and put his writing arm in a relaxed position so that he can move it without tension across the paper.[23] He should use the model letters and numerals which the school system has provided for manuscript writing. Although practice should generally be upon words, an individual should be directed to practice writing a letter or a numeral if one requires special attention.

## Materials and Instruments for Writing

The chalkboard is useful both for demonstration and for child writing. The easel is quite frequently used also. Unruled white paper is adequate and frequently used in beginning writing in grade one, although colored paper is sometimes used. Inch-ruled paper is useful in grades one and two. Five-eighths-inch ruled paper and ½-inch ruled paper are used in grades one, two, and three. Although there are differences among learners in accommodating themselves to it, ⅜-inch ruled paper fulfills the needs of children increasingly from grade four to grade six and above. The size of the ruling of the paper cannot be dictated for all children of a certain age or grade level. The size should be selected to fit the needs of the individual. Chalk of medium softness is an excellent material for writing on the board. Some authorities suggest yellow or other soft colors for preventing eyestrain. A beginner's pencil with a black lead of moderate softness is advisable for young children. The adult pencil for children above the second grade is acceptable. Fountain pens with stub points, or ballpoint pens have been found to be satisfactory.

## A Beginning Writing Vocabulary

The six words — *the, I, and, to, a,* and *you* — make up about 20 percent of words in children's running writing and are most common also in adult writing. The 100 words presented below are among the 500 commonest words of the spoken vocabulary of young children, of primary reading, of children's writing in life outside the school, of children's writing in school, of adult writing, and of adult reading.[24]

---

[23] It is suggested that teachers of manuscript writing particularly to left-handed children, read E. A. Enstrom, "Paper Placement for Manuscript Writing," *Elementary English,* 40:518–522, May, 1963.

[24] James A. Fitzgerald, "An Integrating Basic Communication Vocabulary," *Elementary English,* 40:283–289, March, 1963.

These words were written 3,482,999 times of the total usage of 6,012,359 in the Rinsland basic data. In fact they made up approximately 58 percent of the running writing in this extensive child writing vocabulary.[25] These words may be used to build practice exercises for handwriting. They may be written in sentences, paragraphs, and little stories. Writing the words may be practiced. If children would learn to write these words legibly, a large percentage of their writing should be readable, for they include all lower-case letters of the alphabet except *q, x,* and *z.* Exercises might be made on such words as *quit, quiet, box, boxes, ax, zero,* and *zoo* to supplement the practices developed from the 100-word list.

### 100 Commonest Basic Words

| | | | |
|---|---|---|---|
| a | get | me | the |
| about | go | mother | their |
| after | good | my | them |
| all | got | name | then |
| am | had | night | there |
| an | has | not | they |
| and | have | now | this |
| are | he | of | time |
| as | her | on | to |
| at | here | one | too |
| back | him | or | two |
| be | his | other | up |
| because | home | our | us |
| but | house | out | very |
| by | how | over | was |
| came | I | play | we |
| can | if | put | went |
| come | in | said | were |
| could | is | saw | when |
| day | it | school | will |
| did | just | see | with |
| do | like | she | would |
| down | little | so | write |
| for | made | some | you |
| from | many | that | your |

## ISSUES: MANUSCRIPT TO CURSIVE WRITING

### Whether to Change

Many authorities have considered the issues of whether and when to change from manuscript to cursive writing. Some schools — a

---

[25] Henry D. Rinsland, *A Basic Vocabulary of Elementary School Children* (New York: The Macmillan Company, 1945), 636 pp.

minority — teach only cursive writing. Others — a minority — teach only manuscript writing. The majority teach manuscript and then cursive. Some systems that teach manuscript in the beginning grades, teach cursive generally in the third grade without concern for keeping up skill in manuscript. Others that begin with manuscript writing in the first two grades, instruct in cursive writing in grades three and above, and encourage children to maintain the manuscript skill for various situations. Other systems which sponsor a change approve individual initiative in practice. If a child desires to practice and use manuscript, he is encouraged to do so in addition to learning and using cursive writing. Many parents, and many children too, favor the change from manuscript to cursive writing.

## When to Begin Cursive Writing

The evidence from various sources and the common practice in the country indicate that a transition is made generally sometime near the beginning of grade three. Some schools promote change in the latter part of grade two; others change in the beginning of or in the first semester of grade three, some later. The evidence seems to show that although manuscript writing is quite easy to learn by children in grades one and two, cursive writing can be learned very effectively in grades three and four after manuscript writing has been mastered. Furthermore, it seems that for rapid work, which becomes more necessary in the middle and upper grades, cursive writing is more efficient. Also, the legibility of manuscript suffers greatly as speed is increased.

Some authorities emphasize that an early transition from manuscript to cursive writing is favorable to success in achieving legibility. All indicate the importance of consideration of readiness of the individual in making the change. There seems to be evidence also that the well-planned instructional and daily practice periods of from ten to fifteen minutes will enable the average third-grade pupil to make the transition successfully.

## Facility for Learning Cursive Writing

The change from manuscript to cursive writing can be effected with little difficulty if the transfer is begun when the child is ready and willing to make it. The change should begin with letters, the forms of which are quite similar in both types of writing. Simple sentences should be used for demonstration. The children should be guided to slant the writing paper properly. They should be shown that letters are joined in cursive writing of a word because the pencil or pen is not lifted. If a comparison is made of a sentence written in both cursive and manuscript, the children will see the similarity in words and letters. Attention should be given to formation of letters, uniformity of slant, alignment, spacing, and quality of line. Letters such as *b, e, f,* and *s* which are formed differently in the two types of writing should be given specific consideration. The cursive *s,* for example, should be demonstrated by the teacher and the form practiced by the pupils. Likewise, the child should practice looping the cursive *e,* and making the two loops properly in writing the cursive *f.*

Practice in and of itself does not develop legible cursive writing. Instruction must be well-planned. Enthusiastic, purposeful, consistent practice on commonly used words, which include letters in varying common combinations, facilitates transition and enhances the legibility of the newly acquired cursive writing.[26]

## *Maintaining Manuscript and Developing Cursive Writing*

The question is not so much when should a child change from manuscript to cursive, or whether he should change, but rather whether he should not build and maintain both skills — manuscript and cursive writing. Confusion about the matter should be allayed. It is doubtful that manuscript writing should be dropped and cursive writing be taught exclusively. The questions really are: *when and how shall cursive writing be taught,* and *how shall manuscript skills be maintained?* Some children will want to begin cursive writing early and others later, and a few, never. Perhaps a deprived few will be better off to learn and practice manuscript for the limited writing that they will need to do in life. For the great majority, there is reason for developing both manuscript and cursive writing — each to be used in situations which are best served by the one or the other.

Children — most of them — will eventually learn to write cursively, either by trial and error, from parents, older brothers and sisters, or from the teacher. Since the school is the most advantageous place for teaching, it seems best that the teacher begin instruction in cursive writing, as suggested earlier, toward the end of the second grade or in the beginning of the third.

---

[26] See *Learning to Write, op. cit.,* pp. 28–31; Freeman, *Teaching Handwriting, op. cit.,* p. 26; Lucy Nulton, "Readiness to Change From Manuscript to Cursive," *Elementary English,* 32:382–383, October, 1955; Parke and Bristow, *Practices and Problems in Handwriting, op. cit.,* pp. 61–62.

Both manuscript and cursive have a place in the writing that a pupil does in language arts, arithmetic, social science, and art. For example, manuscript may be used in filling blanks or labeling, and cursive writing in taking notes while listening to directions or reading for information.[27]

## TEACHING AND LEARNING CURSIVE WRITING

In general, children are ready to learn to write cursively at the approximate age of eight in the third grade. However, readiness will differ from individual to individual. In the American school, a majority of children in the third grade who have used manuscript for two years are ready for cursive instruction and have achieved muscular coordination necessary for the more complex movements required.

By the third grade their field of experience is broadening and as they continue through this grade and on into the middle grades they are challenged by many new and varied learning problems. From this point, they require a legible and comparatively more rapid handwriting than they did in earlier grades. Accordingly, they need to acquire legibility and speed that will be practical in school and in life outside the school.

Cursive writing, properly taught, has important advantages. The movement is more rhythmic than that of manuscript. For example, the word m a n requires seven simple short strokes in manuscript writing. In cursive writing, *man* is written with one continuous stroke. Since the shift to cursive can be made without difficulty, children who begin to learn cursive in the third grade develop a quality in later years approximately equal to that of individuals who began the study of cursive in the first grade.[28] Evidence seems to show that if the transition from manuscript to cursive writing is to be made, it should be made early; for the longer pupils delay it, the more difficult it seems to be and the poorer the handwriting which is developed.[29]

## *Integration versus Separate Approach*

Handwriting is useful in nearly every elementary school area, and in a sense it is an essential part of each subject. It is an instrument

[27] E. A. Enstrom, "After Manuscript Writing — When Shall We Begin Cursive?" *Elementary School Journal,* 61:24–28, October, 1960.

[28] Freeman, *op. cit.,* p. 27.

[29] J. de V. Hesse, "The Use of Manuscript Writing in South African Schools," *Journal of Educational Research,* 40:161–177, November, 1946.

for crossing subject-matter lines, for integrating work in several fields. For example, notes are made from readings for writing a report. Handwriting is used to make study outlines in the social studies. It is used in arithmetic and science. Notes are written while listening to the teacher in subject areas. Written reports in one field become a basis for study in another. Accordingly, handwriting should be appraised for legibility in every use made of it.

However, although handwriting is an integrating agent, it requires well-planned scheduled periods when it should be taught and practiced specifically, when it is the major purpose of instruction. Left to incidental practice, it is likely to be neglected. In a period of from ten to fifteen minutes per day or from fifty to seventy-five minutes a week scheduled in from three to five periods on different days, much can be done to develop handwriting skill. Such periods should be carried on under conditions that bring improvement in the writing of every individual who participates. The practice periods may vary in type, in duration, and in frequency, but they should be planned in consideration of the needs of the individuals.

## The Program of Instruction and Practice

The program of instruction should include:

1. Pretesting to determine the level of the class and the needs of the individuals of the class
2. Teaching the forms of letters and other items to meet the requirements of the class and of the individuals
3. Practice to meet needs of the class and of individuals
4. Appraisal and evaluation to determine achievement and progress
5. Remedial work to overcome deficiencies shown by the evaluative and appraisal procedures.

1. *Pretesting.*   The general quality of handwriting may be tested with the *Ayres Handwriting Scale*[30] which presents a series of specimens with ratings from 20 to 90. *The Freeman Chart for Diagnosing Faults in Handwriting*[31] guides a teacher in appraising five characteristics of handwriting: letter formation, uniformity of alignment, quality of line, spacing, and uniformity of slant. A similar instrument, *Handwriting Faults and How to Correct Them,* amplifies the elements

---

[30] *Ayres Handwriting Scale,* Nobel and Nobel, New York.
[31] Frank N. Freeman, *The Freeman Chart for Diagnosing Faults in Handwriting,* Riverside, Cambridge, Massachusetts.

in the Freeman Chart and suggests procedures for improvement.[32] Teaching should be guided by the results of such pretesting.

2. *Instruction.* Instruction should be given as it is needed — sometimes to the whole class, sometimes to groups, and often to individuals. In the beginning, children should be taught to sit properly, facing the desk squarely, with the feet placed on the floor. The paper should be on the desk correctly — the bottom of the paper at an angle of approximately 30 degrees to the front of the desk and the length of the paper parallel with the writing arm. The 30-degree angle is obviously reversed for right and left-handed individuals. The pen or pencil should be held naturally without undue tension by the thumb and the first two fingers about an inch from the point. The writing movement should be developed in such a way that the child achieves rhythm. He should be guided in the beginning to recognize the similarity of the manuscript and cursive letters which are quite alike and of useful words in which cursive and manuscript letters are similar. For example, words in cursive such as *can* and *cat* are easily recognized from the manuscript  can  and  cat.  Such simple easy words may be written cursively without difficulty by normal third-grade children.

Children should be taught cursive letter forms. Not only should appropriate models of these forms be available for study, but teachers should demonstrate the movement in writing simple words and simple sentences, such as: *We can go. We play. Mother came home.* Children should be instructed concerning the continuous movement required to write the word *can* or *dog* cursively. If they observe the teacher and try to use her movement as a model, they generally will improve. Successful efforts should be rewarded and unsuccessful ones should be corrected considerately. Instruction should begin on words with cursive letters similar to manuscript. Later, the writing of cursive letters that are unlike the manuscript such as *r, k, z,* and *p* may be demonstrated and taught.

Instruction should include consideration of proper spacing of letters within words and between words. Models in copy books and models written by the teacher are helpful in demonstrating appropriate spac-

---

[32] Published by the Zaner-Bloser Company, Columbus, Ohio. Other scales of value are: *Conrad Manuscript Writing Standards,* Bureau of Publications, Teachers College, Columbia University, New York; *American Handwriting Scale,* A. N. Palmer, New York; *Gray Standard Score Card for Measuring Handwriting,* Public School Publishing Company, Bloomington, Illinois.

ing. Children should be shown that they can achieve a good quality of line by holding the writing instrument properly with appropriate relaxation. Models of good quality of line and examples of poor quality will suggest the desirability of good line quality. Models of acceptable uniformity of slant and alignment indicate desirable objectives in these skills. A teacher who can write well can put a model on the board which children should study.

3. *Practice.* Practice must be purposeful and meaningful. Excellence is achieved in many skills such as basketball or typing by meaningful dynamic practice. In handwriting, practice should have desired and attainable objectives. It must be carefully planned in accord with the psychological principles of learning. It should be methodical. It should be interesting and well motivated. Practice for brief periods of time — perhaps for ten minutes four or five times a week may be scheduled for pupils in third and fourth grades. When necessity demands it, the whole class may practice upon the same type of exercise, that is, when such drills have purpose applicable to all. For example, timed drills to attain a standard of quality at a necessary speed may be useful occasionally.

Frequently, however, the class may be divided into groups, the members of which will practice a skill they need. Perhaps most often, an individual may practice to overcome difficulties. Practice should vary in order to present drill as needed by different individuals. For example, one pupil may need to practice forming the letters *g, j, q, p, y,* and *z.* Another may require practice of *l, b, d, k,* and *t,* and another may need to practice the capital letters *B, C, D,* and *F.* Some in the class may require practice on uniformity of slant, others on uniformity of alignment, and some others on spacing. However, when instruction is necessary for several children on a letter or a combination of letters, it will probably be most economical to instruct the group that needs it rather than to rely on individual instruction. Each should work and practice with purpose and dynamic drive under supervision to improve the skills that he requires to meet an acceptable standard.

Handwriting is a most useful and convenient skill. Perfection is not so much an objective as is the development of "automatic-neuromuscular" coordination which is required to write with sufficient legibility, speed, and ease in everyday situations. A person uses handwriting in many ways in many positions for many purposes. One must be able to write what he thinks as he thinks without being concerned about the mechanics of the movements. So he must practice to facilitate the automatic movement needed for the various kinds of jobs to be done.[33] Automatization tends to be achieved by efficient practice. In the early stages of learning to write, the individual should attend carefully to the formation of letters, spacing, and so on. Later, as the result of instruction and practice, the learner becomes more and more free from the burden of the mechanics and attends to the thought and the concepts which he is expressing. In other words, instruction and practice must hold forth these two objectives: (1) learning and improving the skills of letter formation, quality of line, spacing, uniformity of slant and alignment, and speed; (2) improving and perfecting the expression of thought by the "automatic" procedure, handwriting. The major purpose of instruction and practice is that handwriting may be used effectively in communication and recording thought.[34]

4. *Evaluation.* Evaluation should be operative continually. The teacher should observe the child as he writes — his position, his handling and use of paper and pen or pencil, his degree of relaxation, his attitude toward improvement, and his product. She will find it worthwhile to criticize constructively the child's writing from time to time, in practice, in his written reports, and in creative products. She may find it valuable to use one of the handwriting charts to rate quality and deficiencies. Each child should be guided to appraise his own writing to determine the specific letters or the special skills which require improvement and practice. When such evaluation has been made and instruction given, improvement will be facilitated. Progress from one semester to another or from one grade to another grade may be indicated by comparing the handwriting specimens produced at different levels.

## Movement in Handwriting

Handwriting, an intricate operation for a learner, is in the beginning comparatively uncontrolled, nearly unmanageable, because it requires a complex series of movements. As maturation develops and the individual practices, control is enhanced and a readable writing is produced. Furthermore, to achieve muscular control, the child must work purposively because the kinesthetic improvement is built up by planned practice properly executed. Cursive writing includes the mak-

---

[33] See Adelaide B. Curtis, "Minneapolis Suburbs Learn to Write," *The American School Board Journal,* 131:20, December, 1955.

[34] Freeman, *op. cit.,* pp. 17–18.

ing of some bold and large movements, some delicate and small movements, and others of a more moderate type. As the child learns to write he must develop a balance between the many pressures of these movements. The balance which depends upon proper pressures between thumb and fingers and between the first and second fingers must be learned and maintained. Well-motivated practice upon easy sentences with simple letters at first, and upon more complicated sentences which include increasingly complex and difficult letter combinations later are valuable in improving the balance of these pressures.

Rhythmic movement which is important for long periods of writing in upper elementary school, in high school, and in life outside the school will be better developed by practicing on words and sentences than on letters alone. A pupil in cursive writing seldom forms unconnected letters exclusively; he is called upon to write sentences made up of varied types of words with letters joined in many ways.[35] For the young child, the most commonly used words in writing built into sentences are highly satisfactory for practice. The intermediate pupil's practice should include more complex materials. Evidence shows that a learner should be guided to use a combination of hand, arm, and finger movement in order to develop freedom, fluency, and ease of writing.[36]

It is evident that maturation without practice will not develop a graceful handwriting, nor will practice without maturation ensure the character and legibility desirable in handwriting. It seems certain that practice must be given systematically when the learner is ready for it in order to develop the finer as well as the larger muscular movements.

Relaxation is another desirable factor of handwriting. When a child uses finger movements exclusively he tends to develop a cramped position and jerky motion. On the other hand, the arm movement alone results in large characters, slow writing, and fatigue. No skill is really perfected without a degree of relaxation — not complete relaxation, but relaxation sufficient to obviate undue tensions. Freeman indicated that muscles producing a movement must cooperate with one another properly. As one or more muscles contract in making a movement, others must relax accordingly — giving away appropriately for a moment. A moment later, the reverse movement requires the second

[35] Elizabeth H. Irish, "The Principles of Time and Motion Applied to the Teaching of Handwriting" (unpublished Doctor's dissertation, Palo Alto, California: Leland Stanford Junior University, 1948), 121 pp.; and Freeman, *op. cit.*, pp. 14–15.

[36] Marion Little, "Current Opinion, Experimentation, and Study in Handwriting Problems," *Elementary School Journal,* 43:607, June, 1943.

muscle or set of muscles to exert necessary pressure in making a stroke in another direction, and the first muscle or muscles lessen pressure appropriately. Practice will bring about relaxation, as well as balance and rhythm.[37]

## Words, Bigrams, and Trigrams for Practice

The most useful words in writing are highly valuable for practice in handwriting. The fact that the 350 most useful words presented in Chapter 10 make up approximately 74 percent of all the running writing of children is indicative of their significance. They contain such bigrams as *al, an, en, at, he, in, nd, re, ea, ou,* and *th.* They also include such common trigrams as *and, are, tha, the, ere, for, hat,* and *her.* These are useful because they occur frequently in words. In addition, the words of this basic list contain many common prefixes and suffixes such as *re-, be-, in-, pro-, -ing, -er, -s, -es,* and *-ed.* All of these and other affixes are found in common derivatives. Practice upon such common derivatives is of value for improving handwriting.

## THE LEFT-HANDED CHILD — A SPECIAL PROBLEM

In a real sense, our society is dominantly right-handed. Provision is made in business and in industry for the right-handed, generally, not for the left-handed. Simple machines, such as the scissors for example, are made to fit right-handed people.* From 2 to 8 percent of people according to estimates are quite definitely left-handed. Another larger percentage of people, estimated by some to be as high as 30 percent, have some tendencies toward sinistrality. Classes have been shown to vary in the number of left-handed children from none to 25 percent.

It is quite improbable that many people are ambidextrous for this term implies equally good use of both hands. Ambilaterality as suggested by Wills is a more descriptive term because it implies equal inefficiency with both hands.[38] Evidence seems to indicate that relatively more children seem to be sinistral in the lower grades than in the higher grades. In other words, change seems to take place as children mature, and that change seems to tend toward dextrality or right-handedness. This factor of change and its direction should cause teachers to be cautious in judging the handedness of a young child for handwriting instruction.

[37] Freeman, *op. cit.,* p. 17.
* Left-handed scissors have recently come on the market.
[38] Betty J. Wills, "Handedness," *Encyclopedia of Educational Research,* third edition, 1960, p. 613.

## The Importance of Appraising Handedness in Children

Because evidence shows that a pronounced sinistral should be taught to write with his left hand, the importance of determining the truly left-handed children is quite evident to everyone. Since there seems to be a societal advantage in writing with the right hand, everyone who is right-handed should be guided to write with this hand. Because some children by accident, by imitation, or because of environment begin to write with the left hand when perhaps they should use the right hand, the laterality of each child should be carefully determined.

The sinistral is handicapped even in seating because seats are sometimes so placed that light comes in over the left shoulder, or they are built to accommodate the right-hander. The teacher is generally right-handed, and she gives demonstrations which help the right-handed but are less helpful to or even confuse the left-handed child, who cannot imitate the right-handed teacher, but must often devise his own system of letter formation and the making of the movements required in handwriting. Even when the left-handed child assumes a correct position and places the paper properly so that his arm is at right angles to the bottom of the paper, the handicaps are still difficult to overcome. He must push the pen or pencil, more or less, to move it across the page from left to right while the right-handed child more generally pulls the pen with more likelihood of smooth contact.

The decision concerning handedness affects an individual's efficiency not only in school but in life outside the school. It is estimated that left-handed writers on the average write about 20 percent slower than the right-handed. Those who are right-handed, and those who are ambilateral, will be benefited greatly if they learn to write with the right hand.

## Appraisal and Testing for Handedness

A child's handedness should be observed and tested. A child who throws a ball with his right hand, picks up a tool with his right hand, places his book on the desk with his right hand, may be right-handed. If on the other hand, he does these things and other similar acts with his left hand, it is possible that he may be left-handed. However, a teacher must be certain about this tendency to handedness and so in the absence of a specialist she should test the child as carefully as possible.

Such tests as the following should be of some value in determining handedness. These directions may be given:

1. Throw the ball to me. (Take note of the hand used.)
2. Hit the ball with the bat. (Note whether he swings from the right or left side.)
3. Hand me that book. (Note the hand used.)
4. Place this book on the table. (Note the hand used.)
5. Open the book. (Note the hand used.)
6. Drive this nail with the hammer. (Note the hand used to grip the hammer.)
7. Bounce the ball as fast as you can. (Note the hand used. It might be well to have the child bounce the ball first with one hand and then with the other and note with which he is most competent.)
8. Trace the picture with this pencil. (Note the hand used.)
9. Make as many dots (short lines or x's) as you can until I stop you. (Note the hand used.) Have him do this exercise first with one hand and then with the other, and note the one with which he is most capable.
10. Cut this circle out of the paper with the scissors. (Note the hand used.) This last test according to Freeman is quite indicative, if despite the discomfort of using the right-handed scissors, the child uses the left hand. However, there may be an inclination to use the hand that is most comfortable with the scissors.[39]
11. Take this key and unlock the door. (Record the hand used.)

A child who uses his left hand without exception in all these tests is probably left-handed. One who uses his right hand in a majority of them and the left in others is likely ambilateral and probably should use the right hand in cursive writing. If there is uncertainty about the laterality of a child, he should be tested by an expert.

## Teaching the Left-Handed Individual

The procedure for teaching manuscript writing to the left-handed child has much in common with that of teaching it to the right-handed child. The procedures for teaching cursive writing to left-handed children are less similar to those for teaching it to right-handed children. The sinistral should be guided to understand that he has as an objective the learning to communicate his ideas clearly through legible writing. He should not be in any way embarrassed because of his sinistrality. He must be instructed most considerately. A left-handed teacher has an advantage in teaching left-handed children. She can use the chalkboard and show them how to form the letters in the slant best adapted to them. However, a right-handed teacher may with painstaking practice assist the left-hander considerably.

A left-hander should assume a comfortable and relaxed position. He should grasp the pen or pencil an inch or a little more from the point

---

[39] Freeman, *op. cit.*, p. 22.

Penmanship for the left-handed child

so that he will not puncture the paper easily in his movement which requires a comparatively large amount of pushing. For the left-hander, light should come in over the right shoulder.

The paper for a left-handed child writing cursively generally should be placed so that the bottom is at an angle of about 30 degrees to the front of the desk and the long side of the paper parallels the left arm.

After instruction, dynamic practice should be carried out to improve the writing of sentences composed from basic words which include bigrams and trigrams that are most useful in writing in school and outside the school.

## DIAGNOSIS AND REMEDIAL INSTRUCTION

Continuous appraisal in handwriting is necessary. A diagnosis of an individual's handwriting to determine his deficiencies and their causes should be made. After diagnosis, an instructor should guide each individual to correct his mistakes by a program of remediation. In this remedial program, principles of motivation and sound learning procedures should be planned and carried out.

### Some Findings of Research

Guiler analyzed the handwriting errors of a group of seventh- and eighth-grade pupils. Each child was shown his particular difficulties such as: *a*, open at the top; *f*, lower loop too long; *g*, written like *cj*; *k*, made as an *h*; *r*, written as *s*; *t*, not crossed; *i*, not dotted; *w*, made like *u*, and so on. Each child was guided to overcome his own deficiencies. Although there was variance in the improvement of individuals, in twelve weeks — one hundred minutes per week — the average improvement in quality amounted to about a three-year normal gain, and the improvement in rate was appreciable.[40]

After an analysis of 3000 illegibilities, Pressey and Pressey reported that 12 percent involved the letter *r*, and that the letters *a, e, o, n, r, s,* and *t* accounted for more than 50 percent of the difficulties in letter formation.[41] Lehman and Pressey concluded that drill upon specific illegibilities, such as *d* written like *cl*, *n* like *u*, *r* like undotted *i*, and *h* like *li*, is more fruitful than general practice in handwriting.[42]

Newland reported the letters *a, e, r,* and *t* contributed from 45 to 47 percent of the illegibilities. Fourteen unreadable forms on elementary and high school levels made up 50 percent of the illegibilities.[43]

The handwriting of advanced students was analyzed by Boraas by means of a photographic method. The findings disclosed that: straight lines were written rapidly without deterioration; however, curved lines when written too speedily deteriorated into straight lines; speed changes for certain strokes tended to cause erratic writing; simple strokes and simplicity of form in continuous free flowing lines were found preferable to forms of writing involving many pauses, sharp direction changes, and air movements.[44] Kvaraceus presented as demons the letters *a, d, e, f, g, i, r, s, t, y,* and *z,* and found the following types of errors: failure to close letters — *a, d,* and others; failure to form loops in such letters as *f* and *g;* failure to dot the *i* and cross the *t*.[45]

[40] Walter S. Guiler, "Improving Handwriting Ability," *Elementary School Journal,* 30:56–62, September, 1929.

[41] S. L. Pressey and L. C. Pressey, "Analysis of 3000 Illegibilities in Handwriting of Children and Adults," *Educational Research Bulletin,* 6:270–273, 285, 1927.

[42] Hilda Lehman and Luella C. Pressey, "The Effectiveness of Drill in Handwriting to Remove Specific Illegibilities," *School and Society,* 27:547–548, May, 1928.

[43] T. Ernest Newland, "An Analytical Study of the Development of Illegibilities in Handwriting from the Lower Grades to Adulthood," *Journal of Educational Research,* 26:249–258, December, 1932.

[44] Harold O. Boraas, "Photographic Analysis of Certain Letter Forms With Respect to Speed Changes and Stability," *Journal of Experimental Education,* 20:87–96, September, 1951.

[45] W. C. Kvaraceus, "Handwriting Needs of Mentally Retarded and of Children in Regular Classes," *Elementary School Journal,* 55:42–44, September, 1954.

Boyle compared a diagnostic and remediation program with a regular program of handwriting. She used two groups of approximately 150 pupils each equated on the bases of mental ability, quality of handwriting, a diagnosis of faults, and reactions to a handwriting inventory. Content, materials, and procedures were planned for the experimental group on the bases of the diagnosis. Weekly writing tests were administered, scored, and recorded. The control group followed the regular program of handwriting. Pupils in both groups were encouraged to try to improve their handwriting.

Findings after a nine-month period indicated that pupils taught in the systematic diagnostic-remedial program, eliminated significantly more errors in letter formation, spacing, size of writing, and slant, and made significantly greater gains in quality of handwriting than those taught in the regular program. A most significant finding of the investigation was that pupils who became aware of their handwriting errors were able to eliminate them by applying specific remedial technics purposefully and energetically. The regular program, well motivated though it was, was not effective in bringing about the improvement produced by the remedial program.[46]

## Diagnosis

The purpose of diagnosis is to determine the deficiencies in handwriting of specific children, to find the causes of these deficiencies, and to appraise the powers, aptitudes, and interests of each child for writing. The teacher should use the medical and psychological services provided by the school system, and take note of the school reports on health, mental ability, achievement records, and personality. Attention should be given to the history of the child in school and outside the school, of his centers of interest and strength.

A teacher should study faults in formation of letters, uniformity of alignment, spacing, uniformity of slant, and quality of line. She should note the size of letters and slowness of writing. She should notice defects in position, improper holding of the writing instrument, and wrong placement of the paper. She should appraise also peculiarities of movement and tensions. By using scales such as those of Freeman for determining deficiencies and Ayres for appraising legibility, the teacher can recognize generally what is wrong and make judgments concerning what to do.

[46] Sr. Mary Charles Boyle, O.P., "An Experimental Study of a Diagnostic-Remedial Program in Handwriting in the Fourth, Fifth, and Sixth Grades" (unpublished doctor's dissertation, Fordham University, New York, 1963).

## Remedial Instruction

Remedial instruction has for its main purpose the improvement of technics and practices that will eliminate illegible writing and thus improve communication. The purpose is to teach children on the bases of the findings of diagnosis to overcome illegibilities and other faults. It is necessary to emphasize the needs for writing and to develop in the child the desire to improve. Using all the information that she has gained through diagnosis, the teacher must plan a program of instruction and practice for improvement.[47]

Instruction should be planned for those who require it. If two or three children need to learn how to form the capital *A*, they should be shown how to write it properly and given practice. In like manner the formation of other letters may, if necessary, be demonstrated by the teacher for those who require remedial work on them. Individuals should be instructed when necessary on other phases of writing — spacing, alignment, quality of line, and size of characters. Practice periods should be brief, well motivated, and productive of results. If children work with enthusiasm to overcome a deficiency, make progress, and are shown the degree of improvement, they will be convinced that the practice is worthwhile.

Some examples of pointed questions and suggestions for instruction and practice on cursive letter formation follow. Similar exercises may be used for those who need them.

1. Do you write your *i* like your *e*? Make a loop when writing the *e*, but not when you write the *i*. You always dot the *i*, but not the *e*.
   Write carefully: *in, him, pin, fine, climb.* Check your *i*'s.
   Write carefully: *be, see, he, the, she.* Check your *e*'s.
2. Do you make your *a* like *ci*? Note that the *a* must be closed. The *c* and *i* are two letters.
   Write: *at, act, am, an.* Write: *city, circle, citizen, civil.* Check your writing.
3. Do you write your *d* like *cl*? Be sure to close the first part of the *d*. Practice writing these words: *do, dog, did, dig, dot.*
   Write: *clear, clean, clay, claw.* Check. Correct your writing.
4. Do you write *h* like *li*? The first part of the *h* is looped; the second part is rounded.
   Write: *he, him, his, she, hat.*
   Write: *little, light, line, live, life.*
   Correct mistakes, if any.

A model letter may be written on the chalkboard for a pupil who has difficulty. Research shows that diagnosis and remedial work on

---

[47] *Learning to Write, op. cit.,* pp. 42–44.

such specific errors, including instruction and definite practice on correct forms, result in considerable improvement by children properly motivated.

## Motivation and Self-Motivation

Pupils must be motivated to discover their deficiencies. If they are convinced that readable handwriting is important they will strive to achieve legibility. If they understand the value of neatness and quality of line, they will practice to attain those objectives. In like manner, they will strive for an acceptability of slant, alignment, and rate of writing. They can be induced by guidance to self-appraisal and practices that will bring recognizable progress. When an individual understands that he can improve by testing, by studying, by practicing, and again by final appraisal, he will work at handwriting. The most important type of motivation is self-motivation, and the child who practices self-appraisal and engages in self-teaching is making progress toward independence in handwriting.

## SUMMARY

Handwriting is neglected to a greater extent perhaps than any other of the basic skills. The major objectives in teaching handwriting — efficiency in communication, acceptable legibility, moderate speed, and individuality — can be achieved by a well-planned program of instruction and practice.

Because manuscript writing is easier to learn than cursive, it should be taught probably in grades one and two, but because cursive is generally more practical after it has been learned, it should be taught probably near the beginning of grade three and thereafter. Good handwriting is an integrating skill, and instruction and practice should be provided to perfect it. The program should include pretesting, instruction, practice, evaluation, and remediation. Skill in both manuscript and cursive writing will be useful to most individuals in this modern age. Both skills should be developed and maintained.

Careful appraisal of a child's handedness should be made to determine whether he should be taught to write with the right or left hand. Ambilaterals — those equally inefficient with both hands — should generally select the right hand. All dextral children should write with their right hands. The truly left-handed comprising between

2 and 8 percent of the population should be guided to write with their left hands.

Diagnosis and remedial instruction should be planned for children to overcome deficiencies and to develop competency in communication by attaining necessary legibility and a moderate rate of writing.

## ACTIVITIES, PROBLEMS, QUESTIONS

1. What are the reasons that handwriting levels are so low at present?
2. Explain the importance of handwriting:
   a) In life outside the school;
   b) In each of the other language arts;
   c) In other areas in school.
3. State and describe the objectives of learning to write.
4. Why is manuscript well adapted to first-grade children?
5. How would you appraise the readiness of a child for beginning writing?
6. Enumerate the reasons for using The 100 Commonest Basic Words as a basis for formulating exercises in beginning handwriting. Construct examples of three types of such exercises.
7. Analyze the important issues related to manuscript and cursive writing. Discuss each issue critically.
8. Compare the advantages of manuscript and cursive writing.
9. How would you introduce manuscript writing to young children?
10. List the letters that are quite similar in manuscript and cursive handwriting. What use would you make of them in introducing children to cursive writing after they had mastered manuscript?
11. How would you instruct children to learn to write cursively the letters of the alphabet which are not similar in cursive and manuscript writing?
12. Set up a plan for appraising handedness. Why is it important to determine the handedness of children?
13. Contrast the instruction in handwriting of right and left-handed children.
14. What does research show regarding diagnosis and remedial instruction in handwriting?
15. Formulate six exercises useful in diagnosis and remedial instruction in handwriting.

## SELECTED REFERENCES

Clark, Margaret M. *Teaching Left-Handed Children.* New York: Philosophical Library, 1961. 44 pp.

Cole, Luella. *Handwriting for Left-Handed Children.* Bloomington, Illinois: Public School Publishing Company, 1955. 17 pp.

Freeman, Frank N. *Teaching Handwriting.* What Research Says to the Teacher. No. 4. Washington, D. C.: DCT and AERA of the NEA, 1954. 33 pp.

Gardner, Warren H. *Left-Handed Writing Instruction Manual, Prepared for Use in the School, Clinic, or Home.* Rev. ed. Danville, Illinois: Interstate Press, 1945. 28 pp.

Gray, William S. *The Teaching of Reading and Writing, An International Survey.* Chicago: UNESCO. Scott, Foresman, 1961. 281 pp.

Herrick, Virgil E., ed. *New Horizons for Research in Handwriting.* Madison: University of Wisconsin Press, 1961. 308 pp.

Herrick, Virgil E., *et al. Handwriting and Related Factors, 1890–1960.* Washington, D. C.: Handwriting Foundation, 1961. 134 pp.

*Learning to Write: Manuscript and Cursive.* Albany: The New York State Education Department, 1960. 53 pp.

*New Horizons for Research in Handwriting.* Report of the Invitational Conference on Research in Handwriting. Madison: University of Wisconsin Press, 1963. 276 pp.

Slote, Claire T. *Improve Your Handwriting.* New York: McGraw-Hill, 1958. 138 pp.

Voorhis, Thelma G. *The Relative Merits of Cursive and Manuscript Writing.* New York: Teachers College, Columbia University Press, 1931. 58 pp.

# Chapter XII

# Developing Good Usage in Communication

## ORIENTATION

IT IS claimed that elementary school children enter high school with little facility in language usage and that many secondary school pupils enter college without proficiency in speaking or writing simple English. Only 1 percent of nearly a half million high school pupils from all sections of the United States wrote a five-minute composition without committing errors. Thousands are graduated from college unable to write an acceptable 500-word composition.[1] Not only are the graduates of high schools and colleges unable to write well, but many graduate students have great difficulty in producing theses and dissertations satisfactorily. Editors report that many who write articles and books make mistakes in expression and usage.

Adults in general speak and write imperfectly and carelessly. Children are criticized for inability to communicate precisely what they have in mind, and it is doubtful whether they will remedy their deficiencies unless and until their elders have achieved habits of clear expression. There is a tendency among critics to extend the cliche, "Johnny can't read" to "Johnny can't read, write, or talk properly."[2]

### Errors and Deficiencies

Many studies show that the types of mistakes in oral and written expression range from the incorrect use of the comma to intolerable vulgarisms. In oral language, errors and deficiencies are heard in articulation, enunciation, pronunciation, and voice control, and are

---

[1] George B. Leonard, Jr., "Why Johnny Can't Write," *Look,* 25:103–104, June 20, 1961.

[2] Joseph Mersand, "What Has Happened to Written Composition?" *The English Journal,* 50:231–237, April, 1961.

observable in manner and posture; they are evident in conversation, discussion, presenting announcements, making introductions, and in all other kinds of oral expression. In written language, mistakes occur as handwriting illegibilities, misspellings, incorrect punctuation, and as wrong capitalization practices; they are found in letter writing, reporting, outlining, filling in forms, and writing notices, signs, and reports. In both oral and written expression errors are made in use of verbs, pronouns, adverbs, and adjectives; defects in unity, organization, clarity of expression, and sentence structure are frequent.[3]

That mistakes are constantly repeated is shown by normative research. A large number of errors are made on common verbs such as: *begin, come, do, drink, break, go, give, lie, ring, run, see, sing, sit, take, write.* The past tense and past participle forms are foci for errors. Confusions are common, for example, in the use of: (1) *sit, set, sat;* (2) *go, went, have gone;* (3) *lie, lay, laid, lain.*[4]

Charters and Miller reported that 47 percent of errors in written compositions of sixth- and seventh-grade children were made in punctuation and 16 percent were verb errors.[5] Diebel and Sears found that composition form and punctuation made up 61 percent of errors, and verb misuse and syntactical redundancy were responsible for about 20 percent of the mistakes in compositions of children from grades three to eight.[6] Sunne reported that the most common form of errors were in punctuation, capitalization, and sentence structure, and that the most frequent syntactical mistakes were concerned with verbs, pronouns, and adjective-adverb confusions.[7]

Fitzgerald reported studies by several investigators of the errors of sixth-, fifth-, fourth-, and third-grade children's life letters written outside the school. Kremer found that sixth-grade children were deficient generally in specific language skills and sentence consciousness, and that carelessness seemed to be responsible for many errors. Geo-

---

[3] Harry A. Greene and Walter T. Petty, *Developing Language Skills in the Elementary School* (Boston: Allyn and Bacon, Inc., 1959), p. 134.

[4] *Ibid.,* p. 135.

[5] W. W. Charters and Edith Miller, *A Course of Study in Grammar Based Upon the Grammatical Errors of School Children of Kansas City, Missouri,* University of Missouri Bulletin, Vol. 16, No. 2, Education Series 9 (University of Missouri, 1915), 46 pp.

[6] Amelia Diebel and Isabel Sears, "A Study of the Common Mistakes in Pupils' Written English," *Elementary School Journal,* 18:172–185, November, 1917.

[7] Dagny Sunne, "The Effect of Locality on Language Errors," *Journal of Educational Research,* 8:239–251, October, 1923.

ghegan showed that 40 percent of all fifth-grade composition errors were punctuation mistakes, and that 83 percent of these could have been eliminated by mastery of a few uses of the period, comma, apostrophe, interrogation, and quotation marks. Twenty-seven percent of all the mistakes were classified as letter-form errors. Mastery of the form of the heading, salutation, spacing, margins, closing, and signature would have eliminated them. Parks showed that carelessness and lack of standards were to blame for many errors of fourth-grade writing. Knaphle's findings based on third-grade children's letters paralleled those of Kremer, Geoghegan, and Parks.[8]

A survey of the letter-writing errors presented by Geoghegan, Parks, and Knaphle revealed 100 types of language errors. The ten most common types accounting for 50 percent of those mistakes are listed as follows:

1. Omission of the terminal period in a sentence
2. No sentence division
3. Omission of the capital in the first word of a sentence
4. No paragraph division
5. Numerals not written out
6. Omission of the interrogation mark
7. Omission of the comma after introductory words
8. Unnecessary use of the capital
9. Omission of the apostrophe in contractions
10. Homonym confusions.

In addition, six types of deficiencies appeared in the following order: (1) adjective used for adverb; (2) incomplete sentence; (3) omission of capital letter in proper nouns; (4) omission of words; (5) words incorrectly used; and (6) omission of comma in series. The results of these investigative surveys showed that the sixteen types of errors accounted for approximately 64 percent of the total mistakes of the children of the three grades in more or less spontaneous writing.[9]

Little improvement in the elimination of errors from grade to grade and practically no improvement in language usage were obvious from

---

[8] James A. Fitzgerald, "The Letter Writing Difficulties of Intermediate Grade Children," *Twentieth Yearbook of the National Elementary Principal,* July, 1941, pp. 332–338.

[9] James A. Fitzgerald and Lawrence C. Knaphle, "Crucial Language Difficulties in Letter Writing of Elementary-School Children," *Elementary English Review,* 21:14–19, January, 1944.

the data. It seemed clear that the writers of these letters lacked an understanding of the sentence.

In view of the evidence, it follows that these simple principles should be discovered, learned, and practiced by elementary school pupils:

1. A sentence expresses a complete thought.

2. A sentence should begin with a capital letter.

3. A declarative sentence ends with a period, and an interrogative sentence with a question mark.

4. Words, such as *yes, no, well,* should be set off from the rest of the sentence with a comma or with commas.

5. Proper nouns should begin with capital letters.

6. The apostrophe is necessary in contractions and in some possessives.

7. The use of abbreviations in context is seldom desirable.

8. Simple homonyms, such as *to, too, two,* and *there* and *their* should be understood and used properly.

9. Words should be used correctly in communication.

10. Slang and vulgarisms should be avoided.

11. The simple paragraph should be understood and its use practiced.[10]

## Problems

Communication connotes: (1) a speaker, an oral message, and an audience (a listener or listeners), or (2) a writer, a written expression (letter, article, book, or note), and a reader (or readers). In order to be understood correctly and completely, a speaker must know his audience and comprehend his message, its purpose, and content. In order to be understood correctly, a writer must know his readers and the purpose and content of his communication. If the one who is communicating fails to achieve rapport with listeners or readers, or if he does not express his thoughts clearly, he likely will fail to achieve his purpose. The many barriers to effective communication must be avoided. Many types of problems in efficient communication must be solved by speakers and writers. Among them, those concerning usage should be considered.

1. How can the learner be motivated to want to speak and write correctly?

---

[10] James A. Fitzgerald and Patricia G. Fitzgerald, *Methods and Curricula in Elementary Education* (Milwaukee: The Bruce Publishing Company, 1955), p. 215.

2. How can the learner be guided to understand the importance of good usage in speaking and writing?

3. How can the learner be made aware of the needs for considerate communication, clear speaking, and accurate writing?

4. How can acceptable usage be developed by the learner?

5. How necessary is grammar, and how can it be taught and learned?

6. What is the relationship between instruction and practice in developing good usage?

Interest in desiring to communicate well is basic to learning. The child will purpose acceptable usage if he realizes its importance. He will enjoy dynamic practice if well-planned instruction makes clear the value of it.

## OBJECTIVES OF GOOD USAGE

Varying ideas are expressed about developing good usage and grammar. Some confusions and disagreements about what should be expected of elementary school children in language are evident. On one extreme there is a tendency to permit a great deal of latitude; on the opposite extreme there is a demand for strict exactitude in grammar and form. It is important, however, to consider what good usage entails. A teacher must have objectives which promote good usage, good form, social grace, and excellence in language. It seems sufficient in this presentation to suggest that a learner should develop: (1) ability in communicating his thoughts accurately; (2) acceptable form in communication; (3) considerateness and poise in manner of communicating; (4) desire to achieve excellence in speaking and writing; and (5) habits of evaluating his own written and oral communications.

### Communicating Accurately

Accuracy of communication can be achieved by thinking, by purposing, planning, and expressing, and by selecting the right words and correct grammatical construction to convey the meanings. For example, the statement, "After planning our assembly project, the rest of the work was undertaken," does not communicate accurately what is probably intended. A complete revision of the sentence is necessary to make the meaning clear. The child perhaps intended to write: "After we had planned our assembly program, we formed committees for working out the preparation of the program."

The speaker should decide before speaking just what the purpose of his statement is, what it should convey, and then he should give the message accurately and simply. A child in the third grade used three sentences in conveying the information about the class program: "We made a plan for our assembly program. We formed five committees. Now each committee is working on its part of the plan."

## Learning to Use Acceptable Forms

A youngster who said, "This is mine; that is yourn," needed instruction which guided him to say, "This is mine; that is yours." Likewise the child who said, "He hurted hisself," should be aided to use instead, "He hurt himself." The expression, *have saw,* should be replaced by *have seen*. The *here* in "This here is mine," should be dropped, and in "Them pupils are going by bus," the *them* should be changed to *these* or *those*.

## Developing Considerateness

The type of language used depends to some extent upon the situation. For example, a child would hardly greet the wife of a teacher or the mother of a schoolmate with "Hi" or "Hiya" but more likely with, "I am glad to meet you," or "It is good to know you." Different situations permit varying types of expression. A learner should be guided to practice courtesy in listening, speaking, and writing. The tone of a letter becomes evident "between the lines" if not in the wording. The tone of a speaker is evident in the inflection, pitch, and degree of loudness of his voice. The attitude and concern of a speaker are recognized in gestures, facial expression, voice, or in the manner of address. The attitude of the listener is evident by his manner or the degree of his attention. There are many occasions in the curriculum of the school and in the cocurricular activities for the development of courtesy. In the relationships with the teacher and also with classmates, a pupil should know the importance of polite expressions — *please; thank you; please excuse me; I am sorry to interrupt* — used at the proper times. The control of behavior and of voice is to be practiced. Waiting patiently and deferring to others graciously are to be desired. Asking a question in a polite but confident manner and giving an opinion considerately, although different from that of another, are to be developed. The avoidance of talking too much and the practice of attentive listening to the views of others are important in language training. A teacher may plan situations in which a youngster has an opportunity to meet people, act as host to visitors, and greet parents who have come to attend an assembly. Evaluation of a child's behavior and conduct in the classroom, in the halls, in the gymnasium, and on the grounds should be carried on. Practice of desirable skills should be motivated.[11]

## Developing a Desire for Excellence

Despite the tendency toward informality and slang in expression, there is need for excellence in both informal and formal communication. Not only should a learner sense that he may talk differently in various situations, but he should also become aware of the value of improving his ability to communicate effectively in various ways. A teacher should recognize the great differences in ability to develop language excellence. It is her responsibility to motivate each child to achieve the highest possible skill. All learners should be able to communicate graciously, correctly, and in good colloquial form in the situations that call for such communication. The gifted learner should appreciate the great importance of perfecting skills in various types of speaking and writing. Excellence should be an objective of the gifted, particularly in the use of English.[12] All learners have a right to instruction which conveys to them the emphatic need for acceptable oral and written language and the right to learn how to become independent in planning and communicating.

## Developing Habits of Self Evaluation

In addition to the evaluation by the teacher, self evaluation should be developed. Self-questioning and self-criticism of an oral or written communication will generally lead to improvement in speaking and writing.

### MINIMAL STANDARDS OF USAGE

Good usage does not require literary English in the communications of ordinary living. Although a teacher should recognize change in language forms, she should keep well within the limits of conformity in instruction. While good colloquial language is permissible in talking, a learner should not be satisfied with illiterate or vulgar speech.

---

[11] *The Language Arts: A Handbook for Teachers in Elementary School,* Kindergarten, Grades 1–6, Bureau of Curriculum Development (Albany: State Education Department, 1957), p. 145.

[12] John W. Gardner, *Excellence* (New York: Harper and Brothers, 1961), 171 pp.

## Some Tentative Standards

The replacement of undesirable forms by acceptable expressions would go far to improve standards of communication.

Pooley prepared a list of items of usage which he considered essential to accurate communication and which met the minimal standards of social acceptability. It was his hope that they might be found valuable for instruction in usage. The order of presentation is approximately that "in which the usage decisions become significant in the student's command of his language."[13]

1. The elimination of all baby talk and "cute" expressions
2. The correct use of *I, me, he, him, she, her, they, them* (Exception, *it's me*)
3. The correct use of *is, are, was, were* with respect to number and tense
4. Correct past tenses of common irregular verbs such as *saw, gave, took, brought, bought, stuck*
5. Correct us of past participles of the same verbs and similar verbs after auxiliaries
6. Elimination of the double negative: *We don't have no apples,* etc.
7. Elimination of analogical forms: *ain't,* \* *hisn, hern, ourn, theirselves,* etc.
8. Correct use of possessive pronouns: *my, mine, his, hers, theirs, ours*
9. Mastery of the distinction between *its,* possessive pronoun, and *it's,* it is
10. Placement of have or its reduction to *'ve* between *I* and a past participle
11. Elimination of *them* as a demonstrative pronoun
12. Elimination of *this here* and *that there*
13. Mastery of use of *a* and *an* as articles
14. Correct use of personal pronouns in compound constructions; as subject (*Mary and I*), as object (*Mary and me*), as object of preposition (*to Mary and me*)
15. The use of *we* before an appositional noun when subject; *us* when object
16. Correct number agreement with phrases *there is, there are, there was, there were*
17. Elimination of *he don't, she don't, it don't*
18. Elimination of *learn* for *teach, leave* for *let*

---

[13] Robert C. Pooley, "What Is Correct English Usage?" *NEA Journal,* 49:18, December, 1960.

\* *Webster's Third New International Dictionary* (Unabridged) states that *ain't* though disapproved by many and more common in less educated speech, is used orally by many cultivated speakers especially in the phrase *ain't I.* It is the opinion of the authors that the word *ain't* should not be taught.

19. Elimination of pleonastic subjects: *my brother he; my mother she; that fellow he*

20. Proper agreement in number with antecedent pronouns *one* and *anyone, everyone, each, no one*. With *everybody* and *none* some tolerance of number seems acceptable now

21. The use of *who* and *whom* as reference to persons (but note, *Who did he give it to?* is tolerated in all but very formal situations, in which *To whom did he give it?* is preferable)

22. Accurate use of *said* in reporting the words of a speaker in the past

23. Correction of *lay down* to *lie down*

24. The distinction between *good* as adjective and *well* as adverb; e.g., *He spoke well.*

25. Elimination from writing of *can't hardly, all the farther* (for *as far as*) and Where is *he* (*she, it*) at?[14]

Correction of language mistakes pertaining to these items would be useful in language instruction today. As the years go by, new items may require consideration.

## Changing Standards of Usage

Most of us were taught to distinguish between *shall* and *will,* but usage has changed the necessity for such differentiation according to Pooley who listed eight items which still remain as cautionary matters to be taught or not according to the teacher's discretion.

1. Making no distinction between *shall* and *will*
2. The split infinitive
3. The use of *like* as a conjunction
4. The use of "different than" as in "He's different than me."
5. The pattern "she is one of those girls who are"
6. The pattern "The reason I did this is *because* . . ."
7. The pattern *myself* as a substitute for *me* as in, "I understand you will meet Mrs. Jones and *myself* at the station."
8. Not using the possessive case with the gerund. "What do you think of Jean coming here?"[15]

While the teacher should use discretion in teaching these borderline items, a pupil who desires the preferred forms, should use them.

It is difficult, as Pooley intimated, to say that a certain item is absolutely correct. An item of usage might be acceptable in one situation but not in another. The learner should become sensitive to the communication needs in different circumstances and should select

[14] *Ibid.,* pp. 18–19. Acknowledgment is made to the *Journal of the NEA* and to Dr. Pooley.
[15] *Ibid.,* p. 19. Permission has been given by the Journal of the NEA.

appropriate and considerate types of language for each. A point to emphasize is that the usage should clarify the communication. Is the usage the best possible to convey meaning in this situation? If it is, that is a point in favor of using it. On the other hand if an item is illiterate or obnoxious, it should be replaced by a literate expression.

As Pooley so well explained, communication is the primary objective and the main goal of a speaker or a writer. Correctness is frequently a secondary objective or goal because it contributes to the accurate transmission of the message. As a learner develops, he will perfect his judgment and taste in choosing a way of expression because it serves the purpose of effective communication.[16]

## Discovery

Instruction should motivate the spirit of discovery in language. It is impossible to direct the child specifically by rules for every eventuality, but it is possible to teach him the importance of making choices. It is conceivable that an interested pupil will develop a strong desire for effective communication of thought, for original expression which meets the standards of usage, and for pleasant and considerate relationships in oral and written language. It is possible to have him objectify the need for excellence. Instruction should place the pupil in a position in which he will understand that the purposes of communication are to convey appropriately a message to a listener or reader in an effective manner. To achieve the goals of accurate expression, the pupil requires practice after he understands the aims. As he practices, he needs constructive criticism in order that he may discover and improve form and mechanics of expression. Writing and speaking in real situations aid a pupil not only because of the study and practice involved, but also because they add to experience and assist in developing judgment and self-evaluation. In fact, the concept of discovery should be ever present with the learner who would achieve excellence in communication.

## GRAMMAR AND LANGUAGE USAGE

### An Issue: Formal Versus Functional Grammar

An important issue in teaching language concerns grammar. Shall formal or functional grammar be used in teaching good usage? Each

---

[16] *Ibid.,* p. 20.

type of approach has a place in teaching correct language, depending upon purposes, needs, and abilities of learners.

Formal grammar refers to the rules and principles which relate to syntax of language. Functional grammar is concerned with those aspects of usage which assist a pupil to improve his specific communications. Functional grammar considers the learning of good usage through active effort in improving speech and writing.[17] In the elementary grades, the major emphasis is upon developing acceptable usage and skill in language through using it. It is doubtful whether there is much value in the memorization of rules or in diagramming sentences.[18] Formal grammar is most important as an instrument for editors and language specialists. Meade showed that high-school seniors who placed in the lower 50 percent in verbal intelligence did not succeed in learning formal grammar.[19] Communication of elementary school children does not seem to be improved by a formal approach to the problem.[20]

The essence of the approach through functional grammar is learning to do by doing. A learner strives to use language better by learning what he needs when he needs it, by checking his errors to overcome his language shortcomings, and by experiencing the satisfaction of speaking and writing appropriately in real situations.

When a pupil has something to say, he will talk. When he knows that his speech is deficient, for example, in pronunciation, enunciation, or grammar, he will, under the direction of his teacher or because of his own appraisal, determine how to improve it by use of a dictionary, a language book, or other aid. When a pupil has been named the chairman of a panel, he may realize the need for determining what his duties are. Consequently, he is motivated to search through books of usage or style books to determine the manner for carrying out effectively the functions of a chairman.

When a child is faced with the desire to write a letter of appreciation for a favor received, he may need information about the correct form and the proper wording of such a letter. He can choose one of

[17] Carter Good (ed.), *Dictionary of Education* (New York: McGraw-Hill Book Company, Inc., 1959), p. 252

[18] Lois Gadd Nemec and Robert C. Pooley, "Children's Experiences With Usage and Functional Grammar," *Children and the Language Arts* (Englewood Cliffs, N. J.: Prentice-Hall, 1955), p. 289.

[19] Richard A. Meade, "Who Can Learn Grammar?" *The English Journal,* 50:87–92, February, 1961.

[20] Greene and Petty, *op. cit.,* pp. 340–341.

Exercises in grammatical relationships

several ways to gain the information he needs: he can ask the teacher; he can look for the solution in his language book; he can consult sources in the library. A pupil should be stimulated to become independent in solving his own problems by using his textbook, and, if necessary, sources in the library. These examples indicate the functional approach. The teacher motivates the child to "want" to learn. This approach is enhanced by problems recognized and solved by active effort. The outcome is experience which is fruitful. It is obvious that memorized rules may be forgotten even before application can be made of them, but it is evident that when the correct way of expressing a thought is learned in a challenging situation it is not easily forgotten.

## Grammar: Helpful in Usage

Rules of grammar sometimes can be applied with reservations. The rule regarding the use of a complete statement must be tempered to fit the needs of a situation. For example, if asked by a neighbor, "May I borrow your dictionary?" the answer would most likely be, "Yes," rather than, "You may borrow my dictionary." If a child is asked, "Where is your notebook?" the answer, "On my desk," would be thought of as meeting the needs of this situation.

A child talks before he comes to school; sometimes because of his background, he speaks quite correctly. More often, his speech contains errors. It is a mistake to think that a normal child can eradicate these errors only by learning formal rules of grammar. Explanation concerning the difference between the correct and the incorrect forms, understanding the superiority of the correct form, purposeful, persistent use of the correct form, and sufficient practice will generally change a wrong habit to acceptable usage. This type of grammar is most valuable.

When emphasis is placed upon accurate communication, the pupil will become alert to accept a correct way of talking or writing. The understanding of grammar terms is quite necessary in the consideration of errors and in the effecting of good usage to overcome them. For example, the pupil and the teacher may need to talk about a *noun* or the *subject* and a *verb* in considering the correction of the sentence, "Mr. Jones don't walk rapidly." Likewise, the term *verb* or *predicate* is used in the discussion of the word *runs* in the incorrect sentence, "Edward and Henry runs the truck." The term *pronoun* will be advantageous in discussing the words, *he, she, it, I, her, him,* and *whom.* If there are confusions of *adverbs* and *adjectives* these terms should be carefully studied and properly used. A pupil should understand that *adverbs* are words which often limit, qualify, or modify the verb, adjective, or other adverb by answering questions — when? how? where? and to what degree? A pupil will use the term *adjective* in describing the qualities of the subject of a sentence. The pupil needs instruction in usage which involves grammar. After instruction, he will be benefited by practice. Dynamic drill will be necessary to fix the correct use. After near mastery of a grammar form, the appraisal of the usage will be helpful so that correction of faults may be effected.[21]

## Need for Terms

In the intermediate grades and throughout high school and college, there will be increasing need to understand and use terms of language and grammar. It is suggested by the New York State Department of Education that when terms are required, these presented are quite acceptable. If elementary school pupils need such terms, it is thought

[21] Greene and Petty, *op. cit.,* pp. 342–345.

they should learn the ones commonly used. With that idea, the following outline is presented.

1. **The Material of Speech**

THE PARTS OF SPEECH

| | |
|---|---|
| Nouns | Adverbs |
| Pronouns | Prepositions |
| Adjectives | Conjunctions |
| Verbs and Verbals | Interjections |

*Nouns*

| | |
|---|---|
| Kinds | Gender |
|   Common |   Masculine |
|   Proper |   Feminine |
|   Collective |   Neuter |
| Number | Case Form |
|   Singular |   Possessive |
|   Plural | |

*Pronouns*

| | |
|---|---|
| Kinds | Person |
|   Personal |   First |
|   Interrogative |   Second |
|   Demonstrative |   Third |
|   Relative | |
|   Indefinite | |
| Number | Gender |
|   Singular |   Masculine |
|   Plural |   Feminine |
| |   Neuter |

Case Forms
  Nominative
  Objective
  Possessive
  (Teach case of personal pronouns and of *who*)

*Adjectives*

Comparison
  Positive      Comparative      Superlative

*Verbs*

| | |
|---|---|
| Kinds | Tense |
|   Transitive |   Present (simple) |
|   Intransitive |   Past (simple) |
| Person |   Future (simple) |
|   First |   Present perfect |
|   Second |   Past perfect |
|   Third |   Future perfect |
| Number | Verbals |
|   Singular |   Gerunds |
|   Plural |   Infinitives |
| Voice |   Participles — present past |
|   Active | |
|   Passive | |

*Adverbs*

Comparison
  Positive          Comparative          Superlative

*Conjunctions*

Kinds
  Coordinate        Subordinate          Correlative

## 2. The Use of the Material of Speech

*Sentences*                         *Clause*

Kinds                               Independent
  Declarative, interrogative        Dependent
  Exclamatory, imperative
  Simple, complex, compound
Subject                             Complements
  Simple subject                      Object of verb
  Complete subject                    Indirect object of verb
  Compound subject                    Predicate nominative
                                      Predicate adjective

Predicate                           Appositives
  Verb                              Expletives
  Complete predicate                  Use in the Sentence (this
  Compound predicate                    expression is used in-
                                        stead of "syntax") [22]

## LANGUAGE DEFICIENCIES AND REMEDIATION

The language used on the streets, in business places, and in schools leaves much to be desired. Various causes seem to operate which promote improper speech and writing. McKee suggested several which seem sensible. Children in learning to speak develop incorrect patterns which become firmly fixed, and which are difficult to break. The language instruction, although meaningful enough, lacks the drive which would perfect skills and make them permanent. Furthermore, practice of correct habits is not emphasized sufficiently in school to overcome the bad procedures in life outside the school. There is probably too much speaking and writing without thinking and planning, and without evaluation of content and form. Poor speech and faulty written work have been permitted without proper diagnosis and remediation. There seems to be indifference concerning usage. Learners in all levels of school do not seem to be motivated to achieve excellence in speaking or writing. Practice materials are not fitted to the

---

[22] *The Language Arts: A Handbook for Teachers in Elementary Schools,* Kindergarten, Grades 1–6, Bureau of Elementary Curriculum Development (Albany, New York: State Education Department, 1957), pp. 189–190. By permission of the New York State Education Department.

needs of many individuals. Sometimes the practice materials have been badly prepared, poorly chosen, or improperly used.[23]

To achieve good usage, a teacher will plan instruction in situations that call for communication; both content and form of composition should be considered in the various types of oral and written language. In types in which mistakes are made, there is need for diagnosis and remediation measures and for practice. There is no reason for ignoring incorrect usage, for permitting unevaluated communication, and for accepting without concern illiterate speaking and writing. If our society requires clear thinking and effective communication, good usage must be emphasized. Instruction, practice, and correction must fit the needs of each child. McKee presented data on errors in the use of nouns, verbs, pronouns, adjectives, adverbs, prepositions, and conjunctions.[24] Greene and Petty charted the skills in oral and written language and enumerated errors in tense, word confusions, agreement, and redundancy.[25] Research has identified the language errors that are most frequently made in elementary pupils' letters. It has indicated also the skills that are more frequently needed in elementary school letter writing.[26] Since it is probable that letter writing will be the most frequent type of written communication for which the majority of children should prepare, it is thought that a consideration of the important skills and those in which the most frequent mistakes are made would be helpful in language instruction.

## The Sentence and Sentence Structure

Although it is probably quite correct to say that one learns to write by writing, it is also proper to indicate that a pupil must know how to remedy deficiencies and to improve his first drafts. Among the many shortcomings of writing is that of the imperfect sentence structure. Investigations indicate the need for developing understanding of the sentence, for the sentence is the basic instrument for communication.

*The sentence.* The sentence is a necessary thought conveying medium. It consists of a word or a group of related words that "expresses an assertion, a question, a command, a wish, or an ex-

---

[23] See Paul McKee, *Language in the Elementary School* (Boston: Houghton Mifflin Company, 1939), pp. 53–54.

[24] *Ibid.,* pp. 285–294.

[25] Greene and Petty, *op. cit.,* pp. 133–147.

[26] Fitzgerald and Knaphle, *op. cit.*

clamation."[27] In speaking, the sentence is made clear phonetically by various patterns of emphasis, pitch, and pauses. In writing, the sentence begins with a capital letter and ends with a period, interrogation mark, or other appropriate terminal punctuation. If a sentence is well structured, thought may be communicated precisely, but if its structure or form is defective, communication is imperfect.

"Go!" is a sentence as well as, "Father drives a car." "Hush!" is a sentence just as surely as, "May I go to the circus tomorrow?" These types are common to the experience of young children before entering school.

*Considering sentence structure.* It is evident that a child must be made aware of the simple sentence, but instruction is not enough; there must be practice and evaluation. There should be instruction on the simple sentence such as *John runs.* There is nothing wrong in having a child know that *John* is the subject, the name of the doer, and that *runs* is a verb — a predicate — which agrees with the subject. The child should be corrected if he writes *John and Mary runs.* Correction should be made at the proper time. It is a faulty philosophy to presume that to correct a child's language will frustrate his personality. It is good methodology to have the child know what a sentence is, practice talking and writing sentences, discover his own mistakes, and make necessary corrections under guidance. If a child is permitted to express himself incorrectly repeatedly, the improper type of expression is being condoned, accepted, and made habitual. The simple sentence is the beginning of communication, and the correct simple sentence is a basis for the extension to more complex expression. Clarity of thinking will lead to clarity of expression both in oral and written communication. The thought is of course most important, but the message will be vague and uncertain unless the form is correct.

## The "Incomplete Sentence"

Among the common deficiencies of child speaking and writing is the "incomplete sentence." Typical is the written fragment of expression of a third-grade child, "Both your mother and yourself," or that of a fifth-grade pupil, "Or maybe four or five." Consequently, the child must be impressed with the concept of the sentence as a complete thought. To memorize the statement that "A sentence is a group of words which expresses a complete thought," is not sufficient for understanding, and probably not advisable. The child should study

---

[27] *Webster's Third New International Dictionary,* 1961, p. 2068.

statements made by himself and his classmates, evaluate and criticize them, and determine whether they are meaningful. After studying several voiced or written statements, he should know what makes a statement acceptable. He will realize that there is in a simple declarative sentence a subject and a predicate. In the beginning, the teacher may write simple declarative statements on the board:

Mary talks.                    Father works hard.
Ann sings.                     Mother cooks the dinner.
Tom whistles.                  James plays ball.
Frank shot the snake.

Each simple sentence is understood because it conveys a thought. Every child in the class understands each statement and knows that it is a sentence. In such exercises as the following, complete sentences and "incomplete fragments" should be identified:

1. Running to the train
2. On the top of the mountain
3. The full moon is beautiful.
4. Some celery, potatoes, and bread
5. Mother bakes delicious pies.
6. The soldiers ride tanks.
7. The boy seeing the rabbit
8. The little group trudged slowly up the icy road.

Children may change the "incomplete fragments" to complete sentences. Varying completions will be interesting. In completing 2, for example, one child may write, "There were no trees on the top of the mountain." Another might write, "We stood on the top of the mountain." A third could write, "We stopped on the top of the mountain to look at the beautiful view." After learners master the simple sentence, approach may be made to more complex types.

### Run-on Sentences

Common among the structural errors is the run-on type of expression. A run-on sentence is one that rambles by the addition of successive clauses without punctuation. These are not infrequent in child communication. A study of the following examples of slightly different kinds shows the confusion and the difficulty of understanding such expressions.

A third-grade child wrote, "How are you getting along we are all feeling good is Bobby still going to school."

A fifth-grade child expressed himself, "We had final tests and when does your school get out our school goes out April the 4 and do you have a picnic we have a picnic."

Another fifth grader wrote, "This morning I saw a gopher and a dog and the dog chased the gopher and the gopher ran into a hole in the ground and the dog could not go down the hole."

If an individual knows what a sentence is, he may be guided to avoid the run-on type of expression. Pupils can be directed to identify the sentences in the above examples and to cross out unnecessary words. Suggestions may be made to capitalize the first word of each sentence and to place a period or other terminal mark at the end of each. Some children will need additional instruction, but others will write for the first exercise, "How are you getting along? We are all feeling well. Is Bobby still going to school?" The second exercise will probably be handled as easily. The third one will require the crossing out of unnecessary words.

The child will receive additional benefit in correcting his own creative expression. The recognition of the need for correct sentence structure, capitalization, and punctuation is in itself a motivator.

## Double Negatives

One of the faults found frequently both in oral and written language of elementary school children is the double negative. Children verbalized: "I do not go no more." "My brother isn't not working now." "I haven't nothing to do." "There isn't hardly a minute to play."

A sixth-grade girl in an economically deprived home wrote sadly, "I don't see no use trying any more when you know you just can't get no place."

Although each child's expression should be carefully appraised for such types of incorrect usage, it is likely that such exercises as the following will be helpful in clarifying the uselessness of the double negative.

Directions: *Mark the incorrect sentences and correct them:*

1. There wasn't no one at home when the fire started.
2. We haven't any money to buy a car.
3. There hasn't been no party since August.
4. We had scarcely no provisions when the storm came.
5. They can't never fly again.
6. They can never fly no more.
7. I saw no one on the road.
8. They don't want no trouble.
9. She can stay only two days.
10. You didn't break no record at the track meet.

It may be well to have pupils write the equivalent of negatives in another manner. For example, a child may be asked to change the wording of "He hasn't any money," and he will express the same thought thus: "He has no money." In the following, the child should be directed to write the thought of each sentence in a different way:

1. We have had no breakfast.
2. He can't work any more.
3. They haven't seen anyone.
4. There isn't any food for us.

To be able to make a choice between two correct statements of a thought is often an invitation to discovery which leads eventually to originality in expression.

## Misplaced Modifiers

A modifier should be placed near the word modified if clarity requires such placement. Many child writers by wrong arrangement of words cause uncertainty for the reader or listener. For example, the misplaced modifier *only* is quite confusing in the statement, "This is the car I only ever drove." The speaker no doubt meant to say, "This is the only car I ever drove."

After explaining the importance of the position of the modifier, the teacher may distribute mimeographed copies of exercises such as those below. After each exercise has been read and corrections made, each child's paper should be evaluated. If many errors are made, a class discussion will be useful. If only a few children make errors, they should be instructed on the exercises which they write incorrectly.

Directions: *Rewrite each sentence placing the modifier properly:*

1. The auto was leading in the race with the long hood.
2. My brother only has one helper on the farm.
3. The young girl spoke graciously with blond hair.
4. The tornado struck just as we approached with great fury.
5. The stranger was found in the forest who was lost.
6. Mr. Smith saw a flock of sheep going to the banquet last evening.[28]

## Pleonasm

In the written work of elementary school children and also in oral language, there is a considerable amount of pleonasm, such as the following: "John he is going away soon." "Mary she will be married

[28] See Maude McBroom, *The Course of Study in Written Composition for the Elementary Grades* (University of Iowa Monographs in Education, First Series, No. 10, 1928), 104 pp. for many further excellent suggestions.

next June." Instruction should help the child to see that the word *he* in the first sentence and the word *she* in the second are unnecessary.

In exercises such as the following, the unnecessary words should be deleted:

Direction: *Strike out the unnecessary words:*
1. The sky it is cloudy.
2. My employer he has great wealth.
3. It is still raining yet.
4. This is a true fact.
5. We two both had steak for dinner.

The appraisal of oral and written language will guide a teacher in applying remedial measures. Although instruction and practice are helpful, the pupil should appraise his own work and make corrections when necessary.

## Capitalization

The correct use of the capital letter should be taught in the primary grades. According to McBroom, the capital letter may be taught in grade one in the following: the beginning word of a sentence, the child's own name, and the capital *I*.[29] Greene and Petty agree with the above and suggest in addition the name of the teacher, school, town, and street.[30] These authorities suggested for the primary grades: capitalization of the date, of proper names of persons and places, and of the first and important words of titles. Among the items that require capital letters in early grades are names of holidays, geographical places, months and days, the first word of a salutation in a letter, first word of the close, *Mr., Mrs.,* and *Miss,* and the name of *God.* The capitalization of the first word of a direct quotation, a line of poetry, and the names of race and nationality may be taught.

Research has shown that more than 5 percent of all language mistakes in third-, fourth-, and fifth-grade letters were made by failing to capitalize the first word of a sentence, and that unnecessary use of capitals made up approximately 2.4 percent of all language mistakes. Since surveys have shown that there is little improvement from grade three to grade five, it is fair to infer that the teaching of capitalization can be improved.[31] It is suggested that dynamic instruction and motivating drill be planned to teach these most frequent and basic capitalization skills.

---

[29] McBroom, *op. cit.,* p. 55.   [31] Fitzgerald and Fitzgerald, *op. cit.,* p. 214.
[30] Greene and Petty, *op. cit.,* p. 115.

## Verb Usage

*Verbs.* Third-grade children wrote the following sentences: "The valentine you *give* me was pretty." "I think Clara is *come* to school today." "I had wrote a letter March 4." Fifth-grade children continued to confuse the tenses in expressions such as the following: "We *have went.*" "On last Sunday, I *go* with my father to town." In letters by elementary school children there was frequent lack of agreement of the subject and the verb in such statements as: "We *was* there." "He *don't* like cake." "Mamma and the baby *is* fine." According to some studies, the use of verbs did not seem to be much better in the later intermediate grades than in the second and third grades. Accordingly, instruction should be motivated, and purpose and need clarified. Thoughtful practice should be organized to foster correct form. Mistakes should be discovered and corrected if possible by each pupil.

*Verbs and simple predicates.* In helping children to speak and write correctly, a teacher will find it necessary to consider particularly main and auxiliary verb forms. What a child writes is a record that can be studied and faulty usage can be objectively marked. Investigation has shown that many language mistakes involve tense, agreement, and word confusion. Main verbs and auxiliary verbs are misused. Instruction about agreement of subject and predicate and correct tense is helpful, but the diagnosis of each child's oral and written language is most important. Among the purposes should be the identification and correction of faulty verb usage. Not all mistakes should be discussed in the same lesson or interview. One fault should be corrected and one skill should be mastered at a time. Exercises should be devised to assist a group with common difficulties.

Verb-form errors such as the following should be eliminated: *come* for *came, have came* for *have come, has ran* for *has run, has did* for *has done, done* for *did, seen* for *saw, has went* for *has gone.* Examples of exercises follow:

> Directions: *Check each incorrect sentence. Mark the incorrect verb usage and write each statement correctly.*
>
>   1. He don't like cabbage.
>   2. Mary has came for Christmas vacation.
>   3. My uncle has gone to New York on business.
>   4. We have ate our supper.
>   5. They have begun their long trip.
>   6. The boys seen the show yesterday.
>   7. I knowed my lesson today.
>   8. Mother set the baby on the floor.

9. Judy sets beside the baby.
10. He will lay down at ten o'clock tonight.
11. John will lie down now for an hour before going on his trip.
12. He has ran away.
13. Dad and mamma is gone.
14. Jim, Robert, and George are coming home.

Sentences may be discussed with those who fail to appraise them correctly. In the event that all pupils in a group use an incorrect form, exercises can be presented to the group for instruction and practice. Another effective procedure calls for teams of two or three to work together in mastering forms which give difficulty.

### Pronouns

Pronoun mistakes should be indicative of instruction required. The following indicate the more prevalent types of mistakes: "Me and Frank played together today." "We have a new neighbor but they are away." A discussion of the first sentence should guide the child to say, "Frank and I played together today." The child can be helped to correct the second sentence which involves nonagreement of the pronoun with its antecedent. Teaching the child to think clearly and to say what he thinks is important. The pupil should be helped to see that if there is only one new neighbor, the proper pronoun is either *he* or *she,* but if he is talking about neighbors he should change the statement to read, "We have new neighbors, but they are away." Practice in saying and writing sentences to develop correct usage is worthwhile.

Such exercises as the following may be used for practice on pronoun usage:

*Directions: Identify incorrect sentences. Write a correct one for each faulty one. Explain each change.*

1. Us girls are going to the party.
2. Tom and me are home.
3. Teacher helped James and I.
4. The award will be given to her or me.
5. Please give the book to him or I.
6. Either one or the other is guilty.
7. Everybody must correct his paper.
8. Everybody has enjoyed their vacation.
9. Each one is asked to correct his paper.
10. Everyone of the men have their job planned.
11. Anyone is happy to be an American.
12. The country expects every soldier to do their best.
13. Neither Bill nor Jim are ready for the test.

## Confusion of Adjectives and Adverbs

Adjectives are frequently substituted for adverbs in elementary school letter writing. Among the typical third-, fourth-, and fifth-grade confusions of adjectives and adverbs are the following: "I was sure glad to get your letter." "We stopped quick." "We won easy." "He did good." "She drove careful." "He acted strange."

Other types of errors concerned the comparison of adjectives and adverbs. "This is a gooder book than that one." "Chicago is more far from us than Detroit." "This is the most beautiful picture of the two." "This is the bestest of all the fruit."

Instruction, practice, and games may be planned to overcome these difficulties. Generally individuals should practice on items with which they have difficulty but not necessarily upon items which they have mastered. A test may be given, such as the following, with the direction to cross out the incorrect word:

1. He worked (careful, carefully).
2. John is the (better, best) of the three workers.
3. The boy walked more (rapid, rapidly) than the man.
4. The little girl learned to eat (slowly, slow).
5. We could see the mountain (clear, clearly).
6. Jim is the (stronger, strongest) of the two boys.

## Homonyms and Words Easily Confused

A third-grade child wrote, "I am in the third grade to." A fifth-grade child wrote, "Jim one the race." Other mistakes were: "Uncle came hear last Sunday." "We went their to play." "We have too cars." The homonyms *here, hear, there, their, to, too, two, right,* and *write,* were misspelled more than 6 percent of the total misspellings of writing in grades two to six.[32] A large proportion of these misspellings were caused by confusion or misunderstanding of the homonyms. These and several other homonyms such as *no* and *know, piece* and *peace,* and *sea* and *see* are troublesome for young children and for pupils even in high school. The following are a few of the homonyms and other word confusions which present difficulty for some children in writing:

| | |
|---|---|
| bin and been | sum and some |
| clothes and close | stationary and stationery |
| forth and fourth | whether and weather |
| hear and here | their, there, and they're |

---

[32] James A. Fitzgerald, *The Teaching of Spelling* (The Bruce Publishing Company, 1951), p. 172.

| | |
|---|---|
| isle and I'll | to, too, and two |
| maid and made | wood and would |
| hour and our | your and you're |
| cent and sent | scent and sent[33] |

## Contractions and Possessives

Contractions are hard spots in writing. The following gave difficulty in child writing outside the school:

| | | | | |
|---|---|---|---|---|
| can't | couldn't | didn't | don't | haven't |
| how's | I'll | I'm | isn't | it's |
| I've | that's | there's | they're | we're |
| won't | | | | you're |

These seventeen contractions were misspelled 30 percent of the times they were written by children of grades two to six. Sometimes they were confused with possessives as: *its* and *it's,* and *their* and *they're.* The apostrophe was omitted frequently in such contractions as *don't* and *didn't.* One child wrote, "*Id* like you to answer my letter."[34]

The possessive form was sometimes confused with the plural as *boys* for *boy's* and *boy's* for *boys.* The apostrophe was omitted in the possessive as, "My *teachers* name is Mary Smith."[35] Knowledge of meaning of the possessive and of the plural form is helpful in obviating the difficulty.

## Miscellaneous

Miscellaneous errors in the free writing of children from grade three to six follow with examples of incorrect usage:

1. Unnecessary abbreviation of names or places — "We are going to G. I. tomorrow." "R. S. sure likes school."
2. Unnecessary repetition — "Can you go can you?" "Tell me tell me your teacher's name."
3. Unnecessary words — "I came home a long time ago already." "We didn't complete it all either though."
4. Numerals not written out — "I am 8 years old." "I got 25 candy eggs this year."
5. Omission of a necessary word — "I went bed then." "I didn't go school yesterday."
6. Slang or vulgarisms — "I hadn't ought to say no more so will stop." "Gee that redhead kid is fat." "I ain't got a pencil."

Because of differences in pupil needs, individual instruction is well adapted to correction of such faulty expressions. The attention a teacher gives to the language of a pupil is well received if the learner

---

[33] *Ibid.,* p. 65.      [34] *Ibid.,* p. 185.      [35] *Ibid.,* pp. 173–174.

understands the importance of the correct usage. An instructor should plan to correct not more than one or two types of error in one session.

## Paragraphing

In paragraphing, two types of mistakes are frequently made: (1) paragraph divisions are not indicated; (2) unnecessary paragraph divisions are made. The child should know that a good paragraph possesses unity and coherence, and that it is a natural expression unit in which there is generally a topic sentence followed by related sentences to round out the details of thought and to complete the presentation. The learner should understand that a paragraph may be thought of as a short unit of composition made up of a group of sentences dealing with a single topic. If children can read several simple well-written paragraphs and if they think about them — noting the topic sentence and the other related sentences — they can comprehend the nature and structure of the paragraph. After understanding, writing may be undertaken. At first, a group may formulate a paragraph under the teacher's guidance and with her cooperation.

The paragraph may be dictated, sentence by sentence, and written on the board. After the first draft is completed, revision takes place. Better choices of words may be made. The topic sentence may be reworded to give purpose to the whole thought of the paragraph. The sequence of sentences may be changed. Sentences may be deleted because they are not relevant, or sentences may be added to give completeness and coherence to the whole. Mastery of paragraph writing should be achieved by practice after understanding and purpose have been provided.

## Punctuation

Punctuation errors generally comprise a large proportion of the mistakes made in compositions or letters of elementary school children. In the third grade the punctuation items most frequently misused were the period, the comma, interrogation mark, apostrophe, and quotation marks in that order.[36] In the fifth grade, the comma seemed to be the most frequently misused punctuation mark. Following in order of frequency of misuse in this grade were the period, apostrophe, interrogation mark, and quotation marks. Seldom used were the semicolon, hyphen, colon, and exclamation mark.[37] It is suggested,

---

[36] Fitzgerald and Knaphle, *op. cit.*
[37] *Ibid.*

therefore, that emphasis be placed upon the proper use of the comma, period, apostrophe, interrogation mark, and quotation marks. Other punctuation marks may be considered as individuals need them.

It is difficult to state the exact grade level for the mastery of different punctuation items because of individual differences. In general the following list of items arranged in stages or levels may be helpful as a guide for presentation and a norm for evaluation of punctuation items:

Stage 1. — *First and Second Grades*
1. Period at end of a declarative sentence
2. Period after numbers in a list of items or questions
3. Question mark at the end of an interrogative sentence
4. Comma after salutation and after close in friendly letter
5. Comma between the name of the city and state
6. Comma between the day of the month and the year.

Stage 2. — *Third and Fourth Grades*
1. Review of items taught in grades one and two
2. Period after initial letters of a name
3. Ending an abbreviation with a period
4. Comma in series
5. Apostrophe in some possessives and in contractions
6. Quotation marks around title of a story or article
7. Underline title of book or name of magazine
8. Comma generally before and usually after an appositive
9. Hyphen separating syllables of a word divided at end of line.

Stage 3 — *Fifth and Sixth Grades*
1. Necessary review of items taught in grades one through four
2. Periods after numerals and letters indicating items in outline divisions
3. Colon before list of items
4. Hyphen in some compound words
5. Quotation marks around a direct quotation
6. Comma to set off direct quotation
7. Semicolon between independent clauses in a compound sentence when a conjunction is not used.[38]

## LETTER-FORM TECHNIQUES

*Results of Survey of Letters*

In a study of 735 life letters of third-grade children, Knaphle found an average of 7.63 letter-form errors per letter. These mistakes involved spacing and margin, heading, closing, salutation, signature,

---

[38] See McBroom, *op. cit.,* pp. 53–54. See also other courses of study.

and miscellaneous types. The most prevalent were related to deficiencies in or lack of side margins. Among the heading errors were omissions of punctuation between city and state, omission of the period in abbreviations, and the omission of the comma between the month, date, and year. In the close, the youngsters omitted punctuation and capitalization or inserted unnecessary capitalization. Inappropriate forms and incorrect placement of the close occurred frequently. In writing the salutation, pupils omitted or used incorrect punctuation. Signature shortcomings involved incorrect placement, unnecessary punctuation, and placement of signature on more than one line. Untidiness, illegibilities, and improperly appended notes comprised the principal types of miscellaneous imperfections.[39] The letter-form errors made so frequently by the third-grade children indicated need for instruction.

In a study of 748 life letters of fifth-grade children, Geoghegan reported an average of a little less than five letter-form mistakes per letter. Closing errors, spacing and margin errors, heading errors, salutation errors, and signature errors occurred in that order. The specific mistakes were similar to those of the third grade.[40]

The incidence of error in letters of this grade was still amazingly high. While there was improvement from third to fifth grade, the degree of change was disappointing. Children should be interested in writing real letters and should be motivated to write them correctly. Instruction about acceptable form as well as about appropriate content should be begun early.

## Some Suggestions

After motivation has been provided, general instruction to offset common difficulties, specific drill for correcting individual defects, and the prevention of shortcomings by careful attention to each child's needs should be carried out.

It is suggested that acceptable forms be presented to pupils. Such forms may be found in language books, stylebooks, or in courses of study developed by a school system.

Too frequently opportunities are missed for the writing of letters

---

[39] Lawrence C. Knaphle, "Language and Letter-Form Errors of Third-Grade Children's Life Letters" (unpublished master's thesis, Fordham University, New York, 1941), pp. 77–81.

[40] Patricia S. Geoghegan, "Composition and Letter-Form Errors in Fifth-Grade Children's Letters" (unpublished master's thesis, Loyola University, Chicago, Illinois, 1934), pp. 75–119.

in appropriate forms. If real situations are utilized improvement can be achieved.

A fourth-grade child read about a new type of science gadget. The teacher, after noting the boy's great interest, suggested that he write a letter to a company that sold it to find out about it. She helped him obtain information concerning companies that handled the gadget, and guided him further in composing a request for information. The letter was mailed, and the boy forgot about it. One morning two or three weeks later, the boy ran in and expressed himself with great joy and enthusiasm.

"Look, the company answered my letter. See, the letter is addressed to me; it has my name and address. I can't believe it! Look, see my name and everything."

The boy read his letter to his classmates. At the suggestion of the teacher the boys and girls studied the heading, salutation, close, and signature. Thus the real situation lent itself to the study of form.

## SUMMARY

In order that it be most effective in modern living, communication requires correct speech and writing. Good usage is necessary so that the reader will comprehend the writer's thought, and the listener the speaker's message. In order to convey thought properly, the speaker and the writer must select appropriate forms of expression. The prime purpose of good usage is accuracy in transmission of thought rather than correctness of form. Usage changes to meet the requirements of a living, growing society. Forms and standards change.

When a child enters school, he has used considerable language, but his usage, flavored by his peculiar background and unique experience, requires appraisal and generally remediation. Research has indicated many of the errors made in the use of the sentence, parts of speech, punctuation, and capitalization; these should be detected for each learner and corrected. Homonyms, contractions, and possessives are, for example, centers of difficulty, particularly in writing. Instruction and practice exercises should be arranged for those pupils who require them.

The situations which arise in social and business communication should be utilized to motivate a strong desire for appropriate correspondence and for developing proper technics. Grammar, particularly functional grammar, deftly employed is important in guiding learners to acceptable language usage. Nothing is ever lost by a speaker or a writer who chooses correct forms of grammar for the purpose of meaningful communication.

## ACTIVITIES, PROBLEMS, QUESTIONS

1. How can the ideal of excellence in communication be best promoted in the elementary school?

2. What has research shown about usage mistakes in grades three through six?

3. Make a list of the errors you hear in talking during a day. Analyze them as to type. What remediation measures can be effected?

4. List the errors made in the written compositions of your class. Place them in categories. How can these be corrected?

5. Collect fifty letters written outside the school by elementary school children. Identify the mistakes in usage and grammar. Compare them with the mistakes made in class compositions.

6. Formulate a plan for improving language usage.

7. What methods do you find most effective in teaching sentence sense to pupils of an elementary grade?

8. Set up exercises to help pupils to overcome such errors in usage as the following: (a) incomplete sentence; (b) run-on sentence; (c) double negative; (d) misplaced modifier; (e) pleonasm; (f) parts of speech errors.

9. Explain how to teach the paragraph most effectively.

10. After reviewing the results of studies on letter-form errors, explain how you can teach the essentials of letter form to elementary boys and girls.

11. Compare and contrast functional and formal grammar for teaching language usage.

12. How should criticism be used for improvement without frustrating or discouraging learners?

## SELECTED REFERENCES

Allen, Harold B., ed. *Readings in Applied English Linguistics.* New York: Appleton-Century-Crofts, 1958. 428 pp.

Anderson, Paul S. *Language Skills in Elementary Education.* New York: Macmillan, 1964. 447 pp.

Braden, Waldo, ed. *Speech Methods and Resources: A Textbook for the Teacher of Speech.* New York: Harper, 1961. 568 pp.

Burrows, Alvina. *Teaching Composition.* What Research Says to the Teacher. No. 18. Washington, D. C.: DCT and AERA of the NEA, 1959. 32 pp.

Conlin, David A. *Grammar for Written English.* Boston: Houghton Mifflin, 1961. 341 pp.

Dawson, Mildred A., Marian Zollinger, and Ardell Elwell. *Guiding Language Learning.* 2nd ed. New York: Harcourt, Brace & World, 1963. 430 pp.

Eisenson, Jon, and Mardel Ogilvie. *Speech Correction in the Schools.* 2nd ed. New York: Macmillan, 1963. 400 pp.

Gleason, Henry A., Jr. *An Introduction to Descriptive Linguistics.* Rev. ed. New York: Holt, Rinehart & Winston, 1961. 503 pp.

Golden, Ruth I. *Improving Patterns of Language Usage.* Detroit: Wayne State University Press, 1960. 196 pp.

Greene, Harry A., and Walter T. Petty. *Developing Language Skills in the Elementary Schools.* Boston: Allyn and Bacon, 1963. 572 pp.

Herrick, Virgil E., and Leland Jacobs, eds. *Children and the Language Arts.* Englewood Cliffs, N. J.: Prentice-Hall, 1955. 524 pp.

Jesperson, Otto. *Growth and Structure of the English Language.* 9th ed. Garden City, New York: Doubleday, 1956. 274 pp.

Long, Ralph. *The Sentence and Its Parts.* Chicago: University of Chicago Press, 1961. 536 pp.

Pooley, Robert C. *Teaching English Grammar.* New York: Appleton-Century-Crofts, 1957. 207 pp.

Shaw, Harry. *Errors in English and Ways to Correct Them.* New York: Barnes & Noble, 1962. 375 pp.

Wolfe, Don M. *Language Arts and Life Patterns.* New York: Odyssey, 1961. 615 pp.

See also references for Chapters II and IX.

# Chapter XIII

# Developing Vocabulary and Language Power

## ENGLISH: A LIVING, GROWING LANGUAGE

THE purpose of this chapter is threefold: (1) to indicate briefly that English is a living, growing language; (2) to suggest procedures for developing a rich and effective vocabulary in language; and (3) to describe some methods for developing power in communication. Linguists have given increased emphasis to the understanding of words and the structure of language. Power of communication is based upon the use of words in sentences structured purposively and properly.

Words and their use are necessarily centers of interest. When we listen, we hear words in context to understand or to enjoy; when we speak, we enunciate words in sentences to convey meaning; when we read, we recognize words through written or printed symbols and comprehend meaning based upon our experience and knowledge; and when we write, we transmit our thoughts by words expressed in manuscript, cursive, or type. A word is an utterance, a speech sound, or a series of speech sounds. It may be a written or printed letter or character or a combination of letters which represents a speech sound.[1] The word itself is a symbol or combination of symbols by which a thought may be communicated. Generally a combination of words is used to express a thought by a speaker or writer, and accurate reception is essential for comprehension by the listener or reader.

### English: an Enriched Language

English has grown throughout the centuries, until today it is a magnificent medium for communicating among English-speaking peo-

---

[1] *Webster's Third New International Dictionary* (Springfield, Mass.: G. and C. Merriam Company, 1961), p. 2633.

ples. The changes are astounding and are going on every day to accommodate the needs of those in various communities and vocations of life. The *Oxford English Dictionary,* Funk and Wagnalls, and the Webster series of dictionaries give testimony to the richness of the language. The authors, editors, and compilers have tried to express and to record, as accurately as possible, words, uses, pronunciations, and meanings important for communication.[2] Some unabridged dictionaries contain from four hundred thousand to six hundred thousand entries of various types. Revisions have attempted to make the expressions and recordings more useful, explicit, valid, and up to date. The sources for entries in *Webster's Third New International Dictionary* include: the *Oxford English Dictionary,* a comprehensive and valuable historical record of the English language; the Merriam-Webster dictionaries with especial use of the Second Edition; and a file of about four and a half million quotations of recent oral and written language, each of which illustrates a usage of a word.[3]

Anyone who wishes to study the English language and who desires to utilize its vast resources would do well to develop efficient dictionary technics and effective dictionary habits.

### English Language Changes to Accommodate Expanding Needs

Our language is changing to meet the needs of society. New words are developed as they are required for communication. Science, space, invention, medicine, law, sociology, economics, citizenship, and mathematics constantly require improved expression. The necessity for reporting discoveries in any field demands additional words. *Webster's Third New International Dictionary* contains fifty thousand words not presented in the earlier editions of the dictionary. It presents also about fifty thousand new meanings for previous entries.[4]

*Changing parts of speech.* The English language is continually being adapted to the needs of users to facilitate expression, and such adaptation is conducive to more effective communication. Many words have been used as various parts of speech over the years; some are

---

[2] See Philip B. Gove, "Linguistic Advances and Lexicography," *Word Study* (Springfield, Mass.: G. and C. Merriam Company, 1961).

[3] Sumner Ives, "A Review of Webster's Third New International Dictionary," *Word Study* (Springfield, Mass.: G. and C. Merriam Company, Vol. 37, No. 2, December, 1961), pp. 3–4.

[4] *Ibid.,* p. 5.

used as a noun and a verb; some are used as a noun, a verb, and an adjective; others may sometimes be used as a noun, verb, adjective, and adverb. The word *time* is an example: It is *time* to go. Please *time* the race. The train was destroyed by a *time* bomb. She made the mistake *time* and again. Note the noun, verb, adjective, and adverb uses of the word *right:* People have the *right* of freedom. *Right* the boat before it overturns. Reading is a *right* use of leisure. Hold the book *right*. Twenty-two adjective entries for the word *right,* fifteen noun entries, ten adverb entries, and five verb entries, recorded in *Webster's Third New International Dictionary,* indicate the many uses of the word and its value for facilitating expression. In addition, compound forms are presented with meanings and synonyms with examples of usage to enrich understanding.[5]

Interesting are the shifts in usage of "body" words. Many such noun words are frequently used as verbs. The following are examples of only a few conversions of these words from one part of speech to another:

| | |
|---|---|
| *stomach:* | I cannot *stomach* eels. |
| *scalp:* | They *scalped* the prisoners. |
| *head:* | He *headed* for the fort. |
| *bone:* | She *boned* the turkey. |
| *beard:* | He *bearded* the lion in his den. |
| *eye:* | He *eyed* the beautiful toys in wonder. |
| *elbow:* | He *elbowed* his way through the crowd. |
| *hand:* | She *handed* me the fork.[6] |

Pupils can illustrate verb usages of such words as *chin, heel, nose, leg, thumb*. A game may be played in which they find as many conversions as possible for "body" parts.

Coard illustrated the use of animal names as verbs. The following words are indicative of the shifting of usage:

| | |
|---|---|
| *badger:* | Tom *badgered* the witness until he became angry. |
| *skunk:* | Our team *skunked* the Tigers today. |
| *ape:* | He *aped* his father in every movement. |
| *fish:* | She *fished* for trout early each morning. |
| *wolf:* | He *wolfed* his dinner as if he had been starved. |
| *buffalo:* | I knew he was trying to *buffalo* me by his loud talk. |
| *fox:* | The dealer tried to *fox* us, but we would not be fooled.[7] |

---

[5] *Webster's Third New International Dictionary, op. cit.,* pp. 1955–1956.

[6] Robert L. Coard, "Shifting Parts of Speech," *Word Study,* Vol. 37, No. 3, February, 1962, pp. 5–6.

[7] *Ibid.*

A competition among interested pupils in finding animal words and making conversions to verb uses will enhance facility of communication.

Shifting of noun and verb meanings in various occupations is illustrated:

| | |
|---|---|
| *clerk:* | He will *clerk* in the store this summer. |
| *butcher:* | Packers *butcher* steers and hogs. |
| *nurse:* | His wife *nursed* Henry back to health. |
| *pilot:* | June will *pilot* her new boat in the bay.[8] |

Children are interested in selecting items of furniture or common articles in homes or schoolrooms and indicating verb meanings for them. The following are examples:

| | |
|---|---|
| *table:* | The club *tabled* the motion for a bond issue. |
| *chair:* | Florence will *chair* the society meeting tonight. |
| *pen:* | George *penned* a note of thanks to the librarian for her help. |
| *picture:* | The process will be *pictured* on the screen. |
| *bed:* | The farmer will *bed* down the horses in the barn. |

Many other words can be found in the categories listed to illustrate the use of a noun as a verb, and many other categories are available for study of shifting parts of speech.

*Compounding of words.* Among the developments which have increased the facility of English is the compounding of words. A few examples will motivate children in searching for other common ones.

| | | | |
|---|---|---|---|
| airfield | fly ball | home run | study hall |
| baseball | folklore | ice-cold | sun lamp |
| basketball | head cold | listening post | sun porch |
| beach fly | headlight | love-sick | thanksgiving |
| blackboard | head-on | love song | throughway |
| clockwise | heartache | machine gun | timetable |
| color-blind | heart failure | notebook | traffic light |
| downstairs | high-pressure | picket fence | turnpike |
| everybody | high school | pocketbook | typewriter |
| father-in-law | hillside | schoolhouse | waterfall |

Attention should be focused upon the three types of compounding: (1) the open, as *sun porch;* (2) hyphenated, as *love-sick;* (3) joined, as *heartache.* Some compound words are presented in two spellings, as *sun lamp* or *sunlamp.* The compounding of words in more than one way and the discovery of other compound words in each of the three categories are interesting activities.

Compound words are developed from year to year. The following presentation illustrates this tendency:

---

[8] *Ibid.*

| | Webster's New International Dictionary, Second Edition, Copyright | Webster's New International Dictionary, Second Edition, Addenda Section, Copyright | Webster's Third New International Dictionary, Copyright |
|---|---|---|---|
| | 1934 | 1939 | 1961 |
| expressway | No | Yes | Yes |
| freeway | No | Yes | Yes |
| frequency modulation | No | Yes | Yes |
| jet propulsion | No | Yes | Yes |
| jet stream | No | No | Yes |
| radio telescope | No | No | Yes |
| traffic divider | No | No | Yes |
| traffic circle | No | Yes | Yes |
| wire recorder | No | Yes | Yes |
| tree farm | No | No | Yes |

These ten words were not recorded either in the new-word section or the main section of Webster's Second Edition of 1934. Six of the ten were presented in the addenda section with copyright of 1939. All ten words were listed with meanings in the *Third New International Dictionary,* 1961. It is likely that usage will change some of the open to closed compound words in the coming years.

## Slang Versus Good Usage

Slang, a volatile part of our language, should be analyzed by people who desire to understand fully the expression of thought. Words sometimes thought of as slang are not necessarily so, and other expressions not considered to be such are slang. Heffron asserted that slang is "an integral part of our language, and, as such, has to be recognized, is not accepted."[9] Her enlightening presentation differentiates slang from other forms of the language.[10] In this connection, slang is considered to be "a non-standard vocabulary composed of words" and other expressions of somewhat excessive informality or "extravagant, forced, or facetious figures of speech" which frequently come into the language quickly and sometimes disappear quickly.[11]

The following are examples of words used as slang and in ordinary accepted usage:

---

[9] Pearl M. Heffron, "Our American Slang," *Elementary English,* 39:429, May, 1962.

[10] *Ibid.,* 429–434, 465.

[11] *Webster's Third New International Dictionary, op. cit.,* p. 2137.

| Slang | | Not Slang |
|---|---|---|
| *baloney:* | What Joe said is *baloney.* | Buy some *baloney* for lunch. |
| *blows:* | Jim George *blows* about his large allowance. | The wind *blows* fiercely tonight. |
| *cluck:* | The prisoner was a *cluck.* | The hen will *cluck* to the chicks. |
| *cat:* | He is a *cat* about music. | My *cat* is an Angora. |
| *neat:* | We have a *neat* automobile. | She is a *neat* housekeeper. |

In good usage, the word *baloney* refers to meat, but as slang it refers to something false or rather insincere. Some pupils might be interested in determining the differences in meanings of *blow, cluck, cat, neat,* and other words used as slang or in accepted expression. For example, the words *clobber* and *jive* are common as slang expressions, but *skinflint, crackpot, sourball,* and *beatnik* are words of good usage. They add to the vigor of expression when employed properly.

## DEVELOPING VOCABULARY OF BOYS AND GIRLS

Children who talk and listen understandingly know thousands of words when they first come to school, and they increase their vocabularies through continued listening, speaking, reading, writing, spelling, and handwriting. Their vocabularies are enlarged and made more meaningful also through experiencing, seeing, observing, and reacting in and out of school. Normal children listen to broadcasts and view and listen to telecasts. They look at pictures in periodicals, and read, as soon as they are able, the textbooks and supplementary books provided in school. Because of differences in growth processes, some learn rapidly, many others moderately fast, some others slowly, and still others more slowly — at a "snail's pace." Low-normal children and those who are deprived in one way or another, have a difficult time in achieving vocabulary growth and competency in expression. They should be helped by all possible means. The objectives for all pupils are to develop a useful meaningful vocabulary and to enhance ability to use this vocabulary in the situations requiring communication.

### An Integrating Communication Vocabulary

Because vocabulary is developed in many ways and through many avenues, it was thought important to present in this book *A Basic Integrating Communication Vocabulary* compiled from most valid investigations in the various arts of language to be used as a basis for communication power. The most frequently used 340 words are presented in Chapter V, and the remaining 304 are listed below.

## 304 Additional Words of an Integrating Vocabulary

| | | | | |
|---|---|---|---|---|
| across | chimney | farmer | I'd | nose |
| afraid | church | feel | isn't | nothing |
| airplane | city | fill | I've | nut |
| almost | climb | fine | kid | O |
| alone | clock | finish | kite | oak |
| along | close | flowers | kitten | ones |
| already | clothes | food | kitty | orange |
| animal | comes | foot | lady | ought |
| answer | coming | fork | last | outside |
| apples | cook | fox | late | own |
| apron | cooky | friend | lay | pan |
| arm | couldn't | front | leave | paste |
| asleep | count | full | left | pet |
| balloon | country | fun | leg | pick |
| bark | cows | garage | let's | picnic |
| bath | cradle | gate | letter | pictures |
| beat | crayon | gee | light | pie |
| beautiful | cry | gets | lion | piece |
| bee | cup | getting | looked | pink |
| began | danger | gingerbread | looks | played |
| begin | dear | glad | lost | playing |
| bigger | didn't | goat | lot | pony |
| birdie | dig | gold | lots | pumpkin |
| birds | dinner | good-by | love | pussy |
| block | dirty | grandfather | makes | rat |
| bluebird | dish | grandma | making | read |
| board | dishes | grandmother | maybe | real |
| bought | doing | grandpa | mean | rest |
| bow | draw | grew | meat | ring |
| bowl | drum | half | men | road |
| bows | dry | handle | met | roll |
| break | each | hands | mew | rooster |
| breakfast | ear | hasn't | mice | rope |
| bridge | early | haven't | might | run |
| bright | earth | heard | mine | same |
| broke | Easter | hen | miss | sand |
| broom | eggs | here's | monkey | Santa |
| brought | eight | he's | moon | sat |
| build | elephant | hey | more | says |
| butterfly | else | hid | mouse | sea |
| can't | end | hide | mouth | seat |
| cape | enough | hit | move | seed |
| catch | everybody | hop | Mr. | seen |
| cent | everything | horn | near | set |
| chairs | eye | horses | need | sheep |
| chick | eyes | hungry | nice | she's |
| chickens | fan | hurt | nine | ship |
| child | far | ice cream | noise | shoes |

### 304 Additional Words of an Integrating Vocabulary (cont.)

| | | | | |
|---|---|---|---|---|
| should | sugar | tiny | warm | whole |
| sick | Sunday | tomorrow | wash | windows |
| side | sunshine | toy | wear | wolf |
| sled | sure | toys | wee | woman |
| small | tail | trees | well | won't |
| soft | talk | try | we'll | wouldn't |
| somebody | ten | turkey | we're | yard |
| something | that's | upon | wet | year |
| sometimes | there's | wagon | what | yesterday |
| star | they're | wait | what's | yet |
| stocking | things | wall | wheat | you're |
| straight | thought | wanted | where's | yours |
| string | through | wants | while | |

The *value of this vocabulary.* This vocabulary comprises 644 words basic to speaking, listening, reading, writing, spelling, and handwriting vocabularies of children and adults.[12] It is an integrating core valuable for normal primary school children. It is also valuable in developing competency for intermediate pupils who are slow in vocabulary development or who have been handicapped by a deprived background. The following figures show the relative importance of these 644 words:

*a*) 639 are of high importance in Madeline Horn's vocabulary for speaking and listening of young children before entering the first grade.

*b*) 637 are included in the Gates primary-reading vocabulary.

*c*) They include all but one of the Dolch 220 basic sight words and all but one of his 95 common nouns.

*d*) 643 — all but one — are presented in the McKee-Fitzgerald vocabulary based on child letter writing outside the school.

*e*) All are included in the school composition word list.

A careful check indicated that they were used 4,753,844 times — more than 79 percent of the basic running writing — in the Rinsland *A Basic Vocabulary of Elementary School Children.*

This vocabulary has great permanent value also. All except 21 words, such as *balloon, chick, dolly, fox,* and *Santa,* are repeatedly used in Horn's adult basic writing vocabulary, and all, except those with slight inflectional changes from the base word, such as *chairs, boys, dishes, doing, horses,* and *pictures* are present in *The Teacher's Word Book of 30,000 Words* — the Thorndike-Lorge comprehensive reading list.[13]

---

[12] For the method of developing this vocabulary, see Chapter V.
[13] *Ibid.,* Chapter V.

*The use of this core vocabulary.*   This core because of its immediate and permanent value in every kind of communication is worthwhile in vocabulary and meaning development. Every normal primary grade pupil should be able to recognize, use, and understand these words. He should become master of their meanings and use, of their pronunciations and correct spellings. These will be not only most useful in communication, but they will facilitate further language development, for many of them are basic for building vocabularies — compounds, derivatives, and inflectional forms. It is obvious that the words commonly used in speech and listening will be more easily understood and learned in reading than will strange words. Similarly, the words a child employs in conversation and reading will be more readily written and spelled in nonoral communication than unknown words. This vocabulary will therefore be of the greatest service particularly in the primary phases of the communication arts because it is an integrating instrument in language.

Although these words should not give difficulty to normal children, some deprived pupils will be helped by using them in one or more of the following ways:

1. Reading stories containing these words

2. Listening to these words, used correctly by teachers or other pupils

3. Composing stories made up principally of words from this list

4. Writing sentences and phrases using this vocabulary

5. Learning to spell the words failed in trial tests or in writing

6. Practicing writing, either in manuscript or cursive, the words written illegibly

7. Selecting from this list names of things and using them in sentences

8. Selecting action words and using them in sentences

9. Writing sentences telling what is liked

10. Matching word and phrase cards with words and phrases written in sentences

11. Playing word games to develop meaning and facility

12. Matching nouns and verbs selected from this core vocabulary

13. Selecting compound words from the list such as *airplane, everybody,* and *thanksgiving*

14. Building compound words from the words of this vocabulary such as, *bellboy, boxwood, bread-and-butter, breadboard, breakdown,*

*cat-and-dog, crybaby, cupful, dinner table, flower girl,* and *garden-gate.*

15. Finding homonyms such as, *to, too, two; their, there; right, write,* and using them in sentences

16. Using contractions such as, *can't, couldn't,* and *don't* in sentences, and writing words for which each stands

17. Using possessives such as *his* and *yours* in sentences.

These suggested exercises and activities have been concerned generally with words within this core. Many similar exercises may be designed and initiated to stimulate further vocabulary expansion and communication facility.

### Vocabulary: Roots, Affixes, Derivatives

Roots, prefixes, and suffixes, coming as they do from many languages, have made English a rich medium of communication. A basic core vocabulary is helpful in beginning language, but if an individual is to develop power in language it is necessary for him to study roots and affixes in order to understand and use derivatives. Word relationships are interesting to children in the elementary school, and a teacher should make the most of them. Words can be learned in families — words with common roots, words with common prefixes, and words with common suffixes. For example, there are several words with the combining form *tele* (far off) such as *telephone, telegraph, television, telescope, telephonic, telephotograph,* and *teletype.* Such words stimulate discovery of other words and provoke thought by pupils. When a child begins to recognize common roots, prefixes, suffixes, and other combining forms, vocabulary growth and meaning development are stimulated.

*Roots.* A root is a word — English, Latin, Greek, or other — or part of a word or simple element that serves as a basis for deriving other words by phonetic change, by inflectional endings, or by adding prefixes or suffixes, or both. In this section, suggestions are made concerning vocabulary growth by combining roots and affixes. For example, *arm* is the simple element or base word in *armory, armistice, armament, rearm, disarm, unarmed. Am* (from *amare,* to love) or *amic* (from *amicus,* a friend) is the simple element or root in *amiable,* meaning agreeable, good-natured; *amity,* meaning friendly relations; *amicable,* meaning peaceful; *inimical,* meaning unfriendly, hostile. These derivatives are formed by combining stems or roots with affixes. Henkin indicated that ten roots from the Latin — *cap, duc, fac, fer, mit, plic, pon, spec, ten, tend* — and two from the Greek — *graph* and *log* — are basic to about 2500 English words.[14] Osburn showed that 4382 — about 30 percent — of the 14,571 words in the Rinsland list have Latin roots, and 289 — about 2 percent — have Greek roots.[15] As a beginning it is well to use only a few of the commonest roots. A spirit of discovery by which children find roots in larger words and try to develop other derivatives by combining roots with affixes stimulates vocabulary growth. A few common roots are presented here which may be used to build vocabulary.

## Roots and Derivatives

| Root | Meaning | Derivative Examples | | |
|------|---------|------|------|------|
| act | do, perform | action | actor | active |
| audi, audit | hear, listen | auditory | audience | audible |
| cap, capt | take, head | capital | caption | captor |
| cor, cord | heart | cordial | concord | accord |
| crat, cracy | rule | democracy | autocrat | plutocracy |
| cred | believe | credible | credit | discredit |
| dic, dict | say, speak | diction | dictate | dictaphone |
| duc, duct | lead | conduct | duct | conduit |
| fac, fact | act, do, make | facile | facilitate | factory |
| fer | bring, carry | transfer | defer | ferry |
| fort, force | strong | comfort | effort | force |
| graph | write | autograph | biography | telegraph |
| greg | group, herd, flock | congregate | segregate | aggregate |
| mit, mis | send | emit | mission | submit |
| mon, mono | single, alone | monologue | monopoly | monoplane |
| pon, pos | place | opposite | opponent | pose |
| port | carry | export | transport | report |
| rupt | break | rupture | disrupt | interrupt |
| scrib, script | write | transcribe | manuscript | inscription |
| ten, tent | hold | tenant | tentacle | tent |
| tort | twist | distort | extort | tortuous |
| ven, vent | come | advent | convene | event |
| vid, vis | see | vision | visit | video |
| voc, vok | call | evoke | invoke | advocacy |

*Derivatives.* It is necessary to understand derivatives to comprehend some sentences. Exercises are helpful in motivating learners to study derivatives based upon a root element such as *faith* in *faithful, faithfully, faithless, unfaithful,* or *form* in *formed, forming, formidable, reform, reformatory, inform, information, informing, reforming, reformation.*

---

[14] Leo J. Henkin, *Five Steps to Word Mastery* (New York: Henry Holt and Company, 1954), p. 129.

[15] Worth J. Osburn, "Teaching Spelling by Teaching Syllables and Root Words," *Elementary School Journal*, 55:39, September, 1954.

A prefix may be thought of as a letter, syllable, or combination of syllables placed before a word or root and connected with it to modify or adjust its meaning. Note the examples, *ante-* in *antedate* and *ab-* in *absent*. While roots give the central meaning to a derived word, the prefix guides the meaning or redirects it in a special manner. Note the prefix derivatives: *subject,* to bring under; *reject,* to refuse to take.

A suffix is a letter, syllable, or more than one syllable joined to the end of a root or word in order to adapt, modify, or qualify the meaning. Note the examples of derivatives made by adding suffixes in this manner: *fearful,* full of fear; *cheerful,* full of cheer; *thoughtful,* having thought; *harmful,* having a tendency to harm; *pailful* or *handful,* enough to fill the pail or hand.

To illustrate, the root *loc* means place. *Locate* means to find a place. Obviously the suffix signifies action in the derivative. If *dis-* is added to *locate* to form *dislocate* — put out of place — the meaning is redirected. A study of *loc* and the derivatives illustrate the power gained in using affixes.

The importance of derivatives formed by using prefixes and suffixes is attested to by research. Stauffer reported that 4922 or 24 percent of the Thorndike 20,000 most important words have prefixes.[16] A representative sample of Horn's 10,000 words most commonly used in adult writing indicated that the proportion of words with prefixes is well over 25 percent.[17] Eight hundred and forty or approximately 31 percent of 2650 words most frequently used in writing are derivatives formed by the addition to roots or other elements of such simple suffixes or endings as: *-able, -age, -ance, -ant, -ard, -ary, -ation, -dom, -ed, -en, -ence, -ent, -er, -ern, -ery, -es, -est, -ful, -hood, -ing, -ion, -ity, -ive, -let, -ly, -ment, -ness, -or, -ous, -s, -ship, -some, -teen, -ty, -wards, -wise,* and *-y.*[18]

1. *Using prefixes to form derivatives.* A prefix may be employed to convey several meanings. The prefix *a-* may signify on, in, at, to, from, position, motion, condition, or manner. In *aboard,* it suggests in or on; in *abandon,* it signifies from; in *ahead,* it suggests at; in *asleep,* it indicates condition. Some prefixes are spelled varyingly. For example,

[16] Russell G. Staufer, "A Study of Prefixes in the Thorndike List to Establish a List of Prefixes That Should Be Taught in the Elementary School," *Journal of Educational Research,* 35:453–458, February, 1942.

[17] Ernest Horn, *A Basic Writing Vocabulary,* University of Iowa Monographs in Education, First Series, No. 4 (Iowa City: University of Iowa, 1926), p. 225.

[18] James A. Fitzgerald, *A Basic Life Spelling Vocabulary* (Milwaukee: The Bruce Publishing Company, 1951), pp. 50–127.

Derivatives

*ad–* as a prefix generally remains *ad-* before a vowel and before *d, h, j, m,* and *v*. It changes to *a-* before *sc* (ascend), *sp* (aspire), and *st* (astringent). It assimilates to *ac-* before *c* or *q*, to *af-* or *ag-* before *f, g, l, n, p, r, s,* and *t*. The list below offers some of the many examples.

### Prefix Derivatives

| Prefix | Meaning | Derivative With Meaning | Other Examples |
|---|---|---|---|
| ab– | away; from; | absent: being away | abduct  abdicate |
| abs– | separation | abstract: to remove | |
| ad– | to; toward | admit: to permit entry | adapt  adjoin |
| | | adhere: to cling | |
| ante– | before; in front of | antecedent: previous | antemeridian antechamber |
| be– | thoroughly (intensification) | berate: to scold | befall  belittle |
| | | become: come to be | |
| bi– | two; twice | bicycle: two-wheeled vehicle | bifocal bipartisan |
| circum– | around; about | circumference: line that encircles | circumscribe circumnavigate |

| com– | with; together | combine: to join | compact |
| | | | committee |
| con– | with; together | conjoin: to join together | convene |
| | | | conform |
| contra– | against | contradict: to disagree with | contrast |
| | | | contravene |
| de– | put down | describe: write down, explain | depose |
| | | | detract |
| dis– | separation; opposite of | distribute: to divide | dissolve |
| | | disappoint: fail to please | dishonest |
| ex– | out of; from | exclude: to keep out | extinguish |
| | | expel: to drive out | extract |
| extra– | beyond; outside of; excessive | extraordinary: most unusual | extravagant |
| | | | extracurricular |
| fore– | before; in front | forebode: predict | forecast |
| | | | forerunner |
| in– | not | inanimate: lifeless | incapable |
| | | | incorrect |
| im– | not | immaterial: not important | impartial |
| | | | immature |
| il– | not | illiterate: untaught | illegal |
| | | | illegible |
| inter– | among; between | interlude: between acts | interfere |
| | | | intercession |
| | | | interrupt |
| mis– | bad; wrongly | misbehave: behave or act badly | mismanage |
| | | | mislead |
| non– | not; opposite | nonsense: foolish acts or talk; not sensible | nonessential |
| | | | nonagreement |
| ob– | against | object: be opposed | obstinate |
| | | | obstruct |
| per– | throughout; completely | perfect: complete; excellent | pervade |
| | | | perfuse |
| pre– | before | precede: to go before | preface |
| | | | preclude |
| post– | after; later | postpone: to put off until later | postscript |
| | | | postmortem |
| re– | back; again | refrain: to hold back | reflect |
| | | recite: go over again | renew |
| sub– | below; down; beneath | subdue: to overcome or bring under | submerge |
| | | | subordinate |
| super– | over; above | supervise: to look over | supernatural |
| | | | supersede |
| trans– | across; over | transport: carry from one place to another | transfer |
| | | | transaction |
| un– | not; contrary | unkind: harsh; not kind | unhappy |
| | | | unlike |
| under– | below in position | underline: to draw a line under | underestimate |
| | | | underlie |

2. *Using suffixes to form derivatives.* A suffix may be added to roots or base words to form derivatives. For example, the suffix *-ant*

suggests one who acts. Assist + ant — *assistant* — means one who
assists; attend + ant — *attendant* — means one who attends. In like
manner, -ery suggests act, as in *robbery,* or place where, as in *grocery.*
Pupils may be motivated to develop derivatives other than the ones
listed below by using the suffixes and other roots.

### Suffix Derivatives

| *Suffix* | *Meaning* | *Derivative With Meaning* | *Other Examples* |
|---|---|---|---|
| –able | fit to be | eatable: fit to be eaten | readable<br>curable |
| –age | collection; act of | luggage: traveling bags; belongings carried | shortage<br>breakage |
| –ance | act of; process | assistance: process of helping | reliance<br>importance |
| –ant | one who acts | assistant: one who helps | servant<br>attendant |
| –ard<br>–art | one who does something excessively | braggart: one who boasts | coward<br>drunkard |
| –ary | one engaged in; place | notary: one who notarizes | missionary<br>aviary |
| –ation | act of; state or quality | visitation: act of visiting | narration<br>starvation |
| –dom | state or condition | freedom: state of being free | wisdom<br>boredom |
| –ed | having characteristics of | moneyed: having money | cultured<br>honeyed |
| –en | made of; to render | golden: made of gold | wooden<br>frighten |
| –ence | state of; quality | independence: being independent | existence<br>confidence |
| –ent | one who; being | student: one who studies | opponent<br>dependent |
| –er | one who does | employer: one who employs | baker<br>runner |
| –ery | act; place where | robbery: act of robbing | grocery<br>surgery |
| –es | suffix to form plurals of some nouns | churches: more than one church | ladies<br>knives |
| –est | most | dearest: most dear | earliest<br>fondest |
| –ful | full of; tending to | beautiful: full of beauty | successful<br>truthful |
| –hood | state; character of | boyhood: as a boy | brotherhood<br>likelihood |
| –ing | act of doing | writing: act of making letters, words | going<br>running |
| –ion | act; process | adoption: act of adopting | selection<br>graduation |

| | | | |
|---|---|---|---|
| –ity | quality of | sincerity: being sincere | agility<br>security |
| –ive | tending to | active: tending to act | creative<br>decorative |
| –let | diminutive;<br>something<br>worn | booklet: a small book | ringlet<br>bracelet |
| –ly | like in manner<br>or appearance | fatherly: like a father | queenly<br>ghostly |
| –ment | act or state of | arrangement: act of<br>arranging | development<br>government |
| –ness | quality or condi-<br>tion of being | goodness: being good | greatness<br>kindness |
| –or | doer; agent | instructor: one who<br>instructs | orator<br>donor |
| –ous | full of | joyous: full of joy | dangerous<br>humorous |
| –s | suffix forming<br>plurals of<br>most nouns | boys: more than one boy | girls<br>pupils |
| –ship | state; office of | leadership: being a leader | friendship<br>authorship |
| –some | like; tending to;<br>causing | troublesome: causing<br>trouble | lonesome<br>wholesome |
| –ty | state of;<br>condition | safety: being safe | liberty<br>sovereignty |
| –ward | direction or<br>course | forward: going ahead | homeward<br>onward |
| –wise | way; manner;<br>direction | clockwise: in direction of<br>hands of a clock | sidewise<br>edgewise |
| –y | full of; tending<br>to | guilty: full of guilt | icy<br>watery |

## DEVELOPING COMMUNICATION POWER

### Power in Language

One might know all the words in the dictionary, if it were possible, and still be a failure in communication unless he purposed to communicate — express and be receptive — with understanding and consideration. Words in and of themselves are not important unless they are used meaningfully. President Lincoln, more than a century ago, put together a few hundred simple words to pronounce perhaps the greatest message ever delivered in the English language. Such an address was not created in a few hours; it was the result of years of study, understanding, and thought. It was the consummation of dedication to the "proposition that all men are created equal" and to the further proposition that a nation upholding that principle can endure. Lincoln's address was a masterpiece of diction, of meaning, and of emotion. Such a piece of literature can be understood if boys and girls study it. To understand it, it is necessary to know the situation in which it was delivered, to read it, and to think about it; it is well to listen to it, to speak it, and to feel the power of it expressed in faultless simple language.

The power of well-selected words used effectively must not be negated. A story is told of Daniel Webster, who speaking to a scholarly audience, stopped to select the most suitable word to express an important thought. The audience waited expectantly as he seemingly examined word after word until he finally chose one so appropriate for conveying his exact shade of meaning that a spontaneous burst of applause followed its pronouncement. President Franklin D. Roosevelt knew well the importance of right words and also the great value of speaking them with correct emphasis and inflection. In order to improve his delivery, it is said that he had his addresses recorded and played back for appraisal.

## Understanding and Symbolism — Bases of Communication

When a pupil hears or "reads" words or other symbols that he cannot understand, he does not profit from the content and communication is thwarted. When a pupil speaks or writes words or symbols he does not understand he cannot possibly convey effectively a purposeful message. Language, whether written or spoken, requires both understanding and symbolism. In fact, language is the most subtle, the most complex, and the most highly developed form of symbolism; all in all, it is also the most effective means of expressing, recording, and transmitting thought.[19] Because of the rich vocabulary and abundant forms, it is possible to communicate more adequately in English than in a simple primitive language. To learn to use English understandingly and expressively is however a truly involved process. Yet, the result is worth the effort. Despite its many intricacies, English can be mastered, and the young person who learns to speak, write, and read it has a most powerful vehicle for understanding and expression.[20]

A word or a sentence may be meaningful to one individual and not to another depending upon the different experiences of the two persons. A word is truly meaningful only when it is used correctly in

19 S. I. Hayakawa, *Language in Action* (New York: Harcourt, Brace and Company, 1941), p. 30.

20 Frederick Bodmer, *The Loom of Language* (New York: W. W. Norton and Company, Inc., 1944), p. 2.

context, for it may be thought of as a means for conveying several possible ideas. The word *cut* for example may convey scores of verb meanings — such as to make an incision in, to hurt the feelings of, to turn off (a motor), to hit and propel as in baseball. *Cut* also has scores of noun meanings as for example, a severed part, a slice of food, a share, a passage. In addition, there are several adjective uses and some combined forms. Perhaps no one uses *cut* to convey all these meanings, and only a small percentage of people know all the possibilities. Certainly, no one would be able to guess except by chance what a person is thinking when the word *cut* is expressed in isolation. Only when the word is used in a well-thought-out sentence is it effective in either giving understanding or in conveying a specific definite idea.[21]

Making language meaningful is an important phase of teaching. A dictionary definition may or may not be helpful; it is certainly not helpful when one abstract term is offered in place of another. A definition can be useful when it touches the child's experiences or knowledge, or when it builds upon what he has learned. It is developed positively through needs arising from problems, projects, and activities in and out of school. Drill upon forms and memorizing words and their definitions may be of little value to the ordinary pupil. The result of such efforts often is a type of verbalism with little worthwhile understanding. Real experiences are, on the other hand, valuable for interesting young pupils in processes and products which in turn may stimulate genuine study of words, meanings, and power in using language. Learning to understand ideas and practice in using words to comprehend and to express ideas are two very useful bases for developing power in language.

## Teaching Language as Communication

The teaching of language is a complex project. True, it must be the instructor's purpose in the first place to teach the child how to think clearly the message to be spoken or written and how to plan effective delivery; it must be a second purpose of the teacher to cause the child to consider the listener or the reader so that his objective will be achieved according to plan; the teacher must in the third place consider how to instruct the learner to select, organize, and use language which will best achieve his goals. The right words must be combined

---

[21] See C. K. Ogden and I. A. Richards, *The Meaning of Meaning* (New York: Harcourt, Brace and Company, 1938), pp. 9–10.

with the most effective presentation by speaker or writer to achieve the most desirable reaction and outcomes in the minds of the listeners or readers.[22] As Dowling phrased the process, communication involves the sender, encoding, the message, decoding, and the receiver.[23] Each is a subject of immense importance and concern to the teacher. Briefly stated, the pupil communicator must be trained to use all his rather as yet undeveloped powers to sense the situation and comprehend the need and purpose for expression. He must plan his message carefully, select the most suitable words he knows for expressing it, and consider the receiver's ability and limitation to understand. In addition, he must use language as considerately and adequately as possible in giving the message — whether spoken or written. The message itself must be tested for validity and clarity. The receiver also should be motivated to listen or read with attention in order to comprehend and interpret the message.

Because the communication process is tremendously complex, an experienced teacher usually will plan programs of instruction in which there is opportunity for expression and reception. The communicatee must have a part, for communication is a two-way process. If a presentation is not clear, the listener should have an opportunity to raise questions, overcome his uncertainty, and straighten out his interpretation. In a discussion, the listener asks questions and makes comments. In reading, the reader can reread to comprehend purposes, the presentation of each main point, the transition from one main point to another, and the precise summary.[24]

*Interest and motivation.* Interest in talking is developed quite naturally by most youngsters in elementary school. Boys and girls converse about a "hundred and one" topics. They communicate about activities, events, and happenings of the day or of the current period. A party, a picnic, a parade, a circus, an accident, a new automobile, the decoration of a home, and many school events are ready topics for conversation. The language used is not always the most adequate or appropriate for the type of expression desired. The improvement of speech should be one of the most important objectives of elementary education, and yet it is one of the most neglected. It is the classroom teacher who must interest children in appropriate speech. It is she who

---

[22] Dora V. Smith, "Teaching Language As Communication," *English Journal,* 49:167–172, March, 1960.

[23] Fred R. Dowling, "The Teacher and Communication Theory," *Education,* 81:181–184, November, 1960.          [24] *Ibid.*

must motivate a desire in pupils to develop poise, good enunciation, proper pronunciation, acceptable usage, and adequate organization in speaking and writing.

*Experience as a basis for communication.* If a pupil is to learn, he must experience. Boys and girls who experience intensely and are able to think objectively and creatively, generally communicate with some degree of clarity and enthusiasm. A child who sees a swan in a park and looks at it in open-eyed wonder, will talk about it and may write about it — even in verse. A boy who sees Willie Mays overhaul a long-hit ball in far-out left centerfield will think about it and express himself exuberantly to his friends. He too may write about this as one of the most interesting experiences of his life. Through experiences, a pupil builds concepts or improves his already partially developed concepts. Horn said, "Ideas must be built by the student out of the materials of his experience."[25] Such experiences do affect the progress of his life. Among the examples of outside school experiences which would make learning real and often stimulate dynamic expression are the following:

1. Visiting an alligator farm or a fish hatchery
2. Attending a fair, a concert, opera, or symphony
3. Visiting the World's Fair
4. Being in a storm — a tornado, a hurricane, a blizzard
5. Seeing a wreck — ship, train, or airplane
6. Attending a convention of scouts or a track meet.

Among the school activities which have helped to develop concepts and improve expression are the following:

1. Building a science aquarium or terrarium
2. Publishing a school annual
3. Planning and laying out a softball diamond
4. Discussing bus discipline and etiquette
5. Planning and carrying out a health and physical education program
6. Planning a safety drive — making posters, writing articles, and being active in fire and accident prevention.

*Reading as a basis for communication.* Reading is a major factor in communication. It is a complex core of mental processes, the most basic of which is thinking. As Young phrased it, "The chief element in reading is thinking, not the motor or mechanical processes of eye movements, eye-span, vocalization, and the like."[26] Meanings are the

---

[25] Ernest Horn, *Methods of Instruction in the Social Studies* (New York: Charles Scribner's Sons, 1937), p. 130.

[26] William E. Young, "The Relation of Reading Comprehension and Retention to Hearing Comprehension and Retention," *Journal of Experimental Education,* 5:30–39, September, 1936.

important outcomes of thoughtful reading, and they are a major basis for expression. A student cannot hope to build all his concepts by direct experiencing; accordingly, it is necessary for him to obtain ideas by study, use them in thinking, and so validate and facilitate his oral and written expression. It should not be forgotten that in order to understand what he reads, a student must also utilize prior experience, activities, and events. All his experiencing — real and vicarious — and all his study in school and outside the school are bases for the interpretation of symbols when he reads. In almost every vocation, reading is used to obtain facts, to understand relationships, to discover principles for organizing plans, and even to convey them and their importance to other people.

If reading is to contribute its full share to communication, it must be meaningful and it should be critical. It is only through critical reading that a reader may interpret facts and recognize truths. In interpretation, the reader must consider whether the writer is an authority and whether he is capable of expressing worthwhile thoughts on the subject. The reader must weigh the statements and expressions of the writer against known facts and principles and the assertions of others. He must consider the clarity of the language and appraise the thought in the light of his background. In other words, a reader cannot accept everything he reads at face value. It is necessary to test the essence and the detail of the materials and sources.

If reading is to enhance communication to the maximum, a child should learn to read creatively. Creative reading is not just giving back the words or even the thought of the author.[27] It is thinking stimulated by reading. When one really reads, he understands the meaning of the author and he interprets the thought. With his understanding and critical appraisal as a basis, he creates ideas of his own about the content and generalizations set forth. For example, when a pupil reads an imaginative story, it is possible that he will be motivated to express himself originally about an experience, or write a poem or story which, while prompted by his reading, is nevertheless original. So he develops his language power.

*Thinking critically and communication.*    It has been suggested that thinking can be based upon experience, reading, discussion, listening, instruction, and audio-visual presentations of various types. Talks by

---

[27] Walter B. Barbe and Thelma E. Williams, "Developing Creative Thinking in Gifted Children Through the Reading Program," *The Reading Teacher,* 15:198–201, December, 1961.

the teacher or by lecturers may seem to be spontaneous, but generally they have been prepared and organized with great care. The most important procedure by which the speaker or writer has arrived at his product is thinking. The thinking by elementary school children can be improved. A question requiring study calls for careful reading in order to formulate an intelligent answer. Such a thought question demands critical evaluative thinking.

The solution of problems that are real requires systematic organized thinking. For example, a group of sixth-grade pupils who planned to visit the United Nations in New York, in working out their project, encountered many problems. One problem is sufficient for illustration: How much money will we need for the trip? This was a limited problem in a situation of uncertainty essential in planning the project. They began to assess their needs: transportation, food, lodging if the trip entailed an overnight stay. The pupils discussed the types of transportation — bus, train, air, automobile. It was necessary to obtain schedules to determine cost of fares. They became aware of bargain rates. They learned that by leaving at seven o'clock in the morning they could arrive at the United Nations buildings at ten. They found also that visiting there from 10:30 until 3:15 with time out for lunch, they could achieve their purposes. They decided this schedule to be satisfactory. Accordingly, they planned for an early dinner and for transportation at 6:30 p.m. for their return home. The expenses of transportation, lunch, dinner, and incidentals were carefully determined.

The following types of thinking and communication were necessary in solving this problem and others in the total UN project:

1. Class discussion of the purposes and values of the visit
2. Interviewing the principal to obtain permission for the trip
3. Interviewing parents and guardians concerning expense money and permissions
4. Visiting transportation offices to determine costs of train, bus, airline tickets, excursion rates, and schedules
5. Writing a bus company for cost of a chartered bus trip
6. Writing the proper UN office for permission for the group to visit the various halls and rooms
7. Discussing details, behavior, and discipline of travel.

Other activities after the return from the trip are examples of thinking and communication:

1. Reporting and discussing the UN procedures
2. Evaluation of the results of the trip and the learnings acquired
3. Formulating a written report and letters of appreciation to those who made the trip possible and to those who helped make it a success.

In the United Nations transportation problem and in other related activities many types of communication were used: experiencing richly; listening attentively; talking clearly; observing carefully; reading understandingly; and writing appropriately. Such an undertaking properly planned and carried out guides youngsters to develop their interests, knowledge, thinking, and attitudes.

A teacher, supervisor, and children in appraising such a project and other activities should ask:

1. Was the activity valuable? Were truths and principles acquired?
2. Did the pupils develop their communication skills and abilities appreciably? What was their improvement in listening, talking, reading, writing, spelling?
3. Were purposes, plans, activities, appraisals, properly thought out and organized?
4. Were the goals achieved excellently, moderately, or poorly?
5. Were there evidences of improved thinking individually and by the group?
6. Was the thinking useful in developing power of communication in the various language arts?

In motivating boys and girls to think critically, it is important to strengthen their desires to learn. When a pupil asks a pertinent question, it is well to influence him to study that question and to guide him in finding materials for studying it critically. Strickland suggested the need for "open-ended questions."[28] Critical thinking is exemplified when a learner determines an important issue or question, recognizes basic assumptions, appraises the worth of authorities, evaluates the facts and evidence, and draws from his study conclusions which are valid.[29] It is obvious that many children, particularly the gifted, mark time in the schools because they are not challenged to study properly. In promoting thoughtful study, children can be guided to critical and creative thinking and to effective communication which becomes a concomitant of it.

*Striving for power in speaking.* Speech and listening make up a major portion of the communication activities of people. The classroom teacher has a highly important role in guiding the improvement of oral language. Although the most difficult cases should be handled by a speech therapist, the pupil who says *ah* for *I, dat* for *that, readin* for *reading,* and voices *uh, uh, uh,* while groping for words needs

---

[28] Ruth G. Strickland, "Creating a Challenging Classroom Environment," *The Reading Teacher,* 15:195–196, December, 1961.

[29] Edgar Dale, "Teaching Critical Thinking," *Education Digest* (reported from the News Letter of the Ohio State University, 24:1–4), 24:29–31, May, 1959.

help every day and it falls to the classroom teacher to guide him. So also the child who says, "He don't" for "He doesn't," "We 'uns" for "We," "We goes" for "We go," and "They isn't here," requires considerate instruction and guidance. Deficiencies and errors in usage and pronunciation should be remedied.

Learning should be motivated by stimulating the pupil to want to improve his language. Instruction should be made pleasant. Undue tension should be avoided. If the pupil with a minor deficiency is a normal member of a group in every other facet of school activity, he can gain a great deal from the performance of his teacher and classmates. A conversation or discussion is a natural situation for speech; in it, there develops a desire to communicate both by listening and talking. Attentive listening will help pupils to note the best way of saying a word, and comparison by the child of a correct pronunciation with his faulty one is valuable.

A speech therapist or a speech clinic should, it is hoped, be available for treatment of severe speech defects. Hinze reviews briefly different theories for speech improvement. Her presentation provides a helpful bibliography.[30] Among the suggestions made for speech improvement in a classroom are: purposing, using a tape recorder, utilizing a record player, informal discussions about speech and what makes good speech, describing causes of indistinctness in speech, stimulating the desire to speak clearly, imitating sounds, acting as a chairman of a meeting, listening to stories read by able readers, reading stories, a storytelling program, mock telephone conversations, panel discussions, and dramatization of stories.[31]

Effective speech should be an objective of every class whether in English, social studies, science, reading, or mathematics. If children are to become excellent in speaking, it is necessary for them to understand its importance, to purpose with determination to achieve excellence, and to plan talks and reports thoughtfully. An elementary school pupil can make a logical outline, and can prepare an introduction, a discussion, and an ending. He can find pertinent facts, put them in the proper place, omit irrelevant materials, arrange and revise the sequence until it seems perfect, memorize the outline, think the whole report through, and practice its delivery. In practicing, it may be well for

---

[30] Helen K. Hinze, "Speech Improvement: An Overview," *Elementary School Journal,* 61:91–96, November, 1960.

[31] B. Barton Gallegos, "Toward Better Speech," *Elementary School Journal,* 62:375–379, April, 1962.

children to work in teams. One child may listen to another and *vice versa.* Critical appraisal by each of the other will result in improvement of content and delivery. Considerate appraisal and constructive criticism by the teacher and the class should provide encouragement and suggestions which can be of value in succeeding lessons. Teacher motivation and guidance and pupil striving and self-help are necessary to achieve progress and some degree of power in oral communication.

*Striving for power in writing.* Children can write if they want to write. The key to the solution of the problem of causing pupils to want to write is in using interesting situations which are real or lifelike. A child who has received a gift from an uncle is presented with an opportunity to write a "thank you" note. A child who has gone to summer camp also faces a situation in which he should write to his parents. Children will write if they understand that writing at such times is a duty and if they learn how to write appropriately. This, they *must* learn.

Creative writing can be stimulated in many ways. Among the real situations are: telling about a trip or a picnic, writing a story or editorial for the newspaper, or writing a report of a scout conference. Other stimuli for writing may be provided: pictures of a lake, of a wild animal, or of a mountain. A motion picture, a football game, a title, word, or phrase may motivate writing. Pupils have written rather acceptable poetry about trees, flowers, rain, the moon, a surprise, and the sea.

Power in writing involves selecting the right words for a purpose and in using them correctly. Archer gives an amazing example of selection by a fourth-grade class of words to be used in place of the overworked *said.* In 20 minutes the pupils thought of 44 words which were acceptable. By the time the project was completed a few days later, 104 words had been listed, among them such words as: *exclaimed, suggested, declared, yelled, cried, commented, stated, stammered, claimed, admitted, remarked, conceded,* and *mumbled.*[32] It should be made clear to a pupil that while these words may be used in place of *said,* they should be studied in order that the proper word be selected to convey just the shade of meaning that a writer desires to impart.

To improve meaning and to develop power of written language, pupils should be motivated to write both the practical and also the creative types of communication. Whether composing poetry, writing

---

[32] Marguerite P. Archer, "Building Vocabulary With a Fourth-Grade Class," *Elementary English,* 37:447–448, November, 1960.

memoranda, filling blanks, making outlines, answering questions, reporting a project, or summarizing a science experiment, the pupil will not develop power if he neglects the essentials — words, sentences, paragraphs.

The learner must be made aware of the need for studying words — most useful words, necessary words for a purpose, abbreviations, contractions, possessives, and homonyms. These should be mastered by instruction, study, and practice. Pupils should be educated to employ the dictionary to appraise spelling, meaning, and worth of less frequently used words. The dictionary habit is to be developed in striving for vocabulary improvement and word power.

The sentence is important in communicating correctly and excellently. Creative writing is not creative if sentences are ambiguous. Pupils will require help in mastering the simple, complex, and compound sentences as well as the declarative, interrogative, imperative, and exclamatory sentences. A stylebook is a necessary instrument for boys and girls. Pupils should learn how to use such a source and develop the habit of referring to it when necessary.

A third essential of power in writing is the paragraph. Pupils who learn that a paragraph is composed of sentences relating to a main thought expressed in a topic sentence should practice the art in writing. Instruction in arranging the sequence of sentences in a paragraph is helpful in showing the relationships of sentences.

To achieve power in writing, it is necessary to select most useful words, to formulate appropriate and expressive sentences, and to compose paragraphs which convey the thought desired.

## SUMMARY

Consideration is given in this chapter to English as a living, growing language, to procedures for vocabulary growth, and to suggestions for developing communication power.

English has grown through the centuries, becoming rich from roots and other accessions from many languages — ancient and modern — until today it is a most influential medium of communication throughout the world. Among the features of its strength, English shows facility for meeting new needs as they arise. Among the strands of development of the language are: changing parts of speech of many words, the compounding of words, and the coining of words for new communication requirements.

To facilitate word development of boys and girls in beginning elementary school, a basic integrating vocabulary was prepared from valid research from all fields of the language arts — listening, speaking, reading, writing, spelling, and handwriting. The employment of such an integrating core of words fosters communication and presents a firm basis for growth by study of roots, prefixes, suffixes, and derivatives.

The development of word power is considered, and suggestions concerning symbolism and understanding are offered. In guiding the learner to improve power in communication, emphasis is placed upon motivation, experiencing, reading, thinking, speaking, and writing.

## ACTIVITIES, PROBLEMS, QUESTIONS

1. Explain how English became such an enriched language.
2. Why does language change so rapidly?
3. Give several examples of the development of compound words in the past fifty years.
4. Use the basic communication vocabulary of 340 words in Chapter V, and the 304 words listed in this chapter to build exercises for developing word power of primary grade children.
5. Indicate why this core of words is so important in communication both in child and adult life.
6. Enumerate twelve frequently used Latin and Greek roots and explain their values in vocabulary growth.
7. Select several important prefixes and suffixes and use them in developing useful derivatives.
8. Explain the importance of the use of words and sentences in achieving power in communication.
9. What is meant by "teaching language as communication"?
10. Describe the value of symbolism in language and communication.
11. Explain the significance of Dr. Horn's statement: "Ideas must be built by the student out of the materials of his experience."
12. How is language power enhanced by: thinking, interest, experience, reading, speaking, writing?
13. Analyze the type of thinking and communication used by a fifth- or sixth-grade class in planning and executing a project.
14. Appraise your communication procedures and indicate ways by which you can improve them.

## SELECTED REFERENCES

Dale, Edgar, and Taher Razik. *Bibliography of Vocabulary Studies.* Columbus, Ohio: Bureau of Educational Research and Service, Ohio State University, 1963. 257 pp.

Deighton, Lee C. *Vocabulary Development in the Classroom.* New York: Teachers College, Columbia University Press, 1959. 62 pp.

Dickens, Milton. *Speech: Dynamic Communication.* New York: Harcourt, Brace, 1954. 440 pp.

Hatfield, W. Wilbur, chairman. *An Experience Curriculum in English.* New York: Appleton-Century, 1935. 323 pp.

Hayakawa, S. I. *Language in Action.* New York: Harcourt, Brace, 1941. 345 pp.

Holt, Alfred. *Phrase and Word Origins.* Rev. ed. New York: Dover, 1961. 254 pp.

Hunnicutt, Clarence W., and William J. Iverson, eds. *Research in the Three R's.* New York: Harper, 1958. 446 pp.

Mearns, Hughes. *Creative Power: The Education of Youth in the Creative Arts.* Rev. ed. New York: Dover, 1959. 272 pp.

*Teaching Language in the Elementary School.* Forty-Third Yearbook of the National Society for the Study of Education, Part II. Chicago: University of Chicago Press, 1944. 257 pp.

Thorndike, Edward L., and Irving Lorge. *The Teacher's Word Book of 30,000 Words.* New York: Teachers College, Columbia University Press, 1944. 274 pp.

Torrance, E. Paul. *Creativity.* What Research Says to the Teacher. No. 28. Washington, D. C.: DCT and AERA of the NEA, 1963. 32 pp.

See also references for Chapter XII.

# Chapter XIV

# Integration, Enrichment, and Mass Media

## INTEGRATION

THE child who came home early from school gave as his reasons, "I can't read, I can't write, I won't listen, and she (the teacher) won't let me talk." This child pointed to major problems of integrating reading, writing, listening, and speaking. Although present-day children seem to be superior to those of the preceding generations in communication, they are in need of considerate guidance and instruction in preparing to meet today's challenges. The normal child, who goes into the first grade having spoken and heard millions of words and thousands of sentences, must learn to understand the sentences he hears and to develop the vocabulary required in communicating with others.

### Effective Communication Dependent Upon Integration

To communicate effectively, there is need for integrating the facets of language. There is no communication when a person talks to one who will not listen, cannot hear, or does not understand. Attentive listening does not make a message clear when a speaker talks incoherently. An efficient reader cannot obtain clear understanding from ambiguous paragraphs or jumbled sentences. An individual, reading without adequate background or with insufficient comprehension skills, gains little benefit from the best books in the world.

### Integration of the Language Arts, a Necessity for Perfecting Communication

Each of the arts contributes to the others. Reading and listening parallel each other and are in general intake avenues for comprehen-

The Flight of the Astronaut

Current events: a basis for communication skills

sion. Talking and writing, parallel processes for outgo, are reciprocal to listening and reading. A person may speak and another listens, and then the second person may speak and the first listens. So also, people write and read in turn reciprocally.

Effective teaching by parents causes the child to speak when he needs something or has a thought to express and stimulates him to listen when it is necessary or considerate to do so. When he enters school additional instruction is given. Children should, under teacher and parental guidance, acquire the discipline for listening attentively and understandingly and for talking thoughtfully and effectively. Although some children read before entering school, most acquire reading skills in school. Children generally are active and eager to learn. They view pictures, engage zestfully in activities, and listen to instruction. They read books and other available materials, engage in conversation and discussion, and cooperate in writing a newspaper, logs, and booklets. In other words, youngsters communicate best when they integrate listening, talking, reading, writing, spelling, handwriting, observing, and other experiencing.

## Experience and Knowledge Foster Communication

In order to talk or write well an individual must have a background of knowledge and experience. Experience is built from activities in life outside the school and from work and study in school. It comes from interacting with and reacting to what is heard and observed. Knowledge grows from background — reading, listening, studying, observing, and thinking about real and vicarious experiences. Knowledge evolves from recognizing and solving problems, from planning and executing projects, from study of significant units, from worthwhile and stimulating reflection upon materials, and from the interpretation and evaluation of them. Experience and knowledge foster both receptive and expressive communication, and integrate them one with another.

## CURRICULUM ENRICHMENT

Communication is stimulated through various activities. It is developed through instruction and improved by practice. Direction by the teacher is important, but the teacher must in the final analysis make herself superfluous and so guide the pupil that he will be able to "go it alone." Constructive and creative ideas are born through thinking about materials and experiences. Curriculums must be planned; the objectives must be defined; instruction must be forward-going. There must be time for thinking and reflection. Opportunity for originality should be arranged, and creativity cultivated.[1]

## Definition and Aim of the Curriculum

The curriculum is all the guided experiences, activities, unit study, problem-solving, project building, practice, and drill carried on under the direction of the school. It should be systematic and directed by the teachers; it should not only permit, but motivate youngsters to exercise freedom to work their problems and carry out activities. It should promote study of needed materials and encourage pupils to think constructively and creatively in acquiring the skills, abilities, attitudes, and habits necessary to achieve communication goals. Bobbitt listed ten types of curriculum activities — language, health, citizenship, social, recreational, mental health, religious, home and parental, practical, and vocational.[2] Each of these is important, but it is evident that

---

[1] Ruth Strang, "Creativity in the Elementary Classroom," *NEA Journal,* 50:20–22, March, 1961.

[2] Franklin Bobbitt, *How to Make a Curriculum* (New York: Houghton Mifflin Company, 1924), p. 8.

all are necessary to provide an integrating curriculum. Each taught in isolation is inadequate. All should be merged to effect the development of individual goals.

The curriculum should be planned to meet the aims and needs of every child in the class. Each must have an opportunity to learn what he needs when it is vital to his development. To accomplish this purpose, there should be varied and rich materials available for use by individuals. The principle of readiness entails appraisal of individuals. Readiness requires, for example, that although one child should read a book when it is appropriate, another child in the same class, not ready to read that book, should not be forced to use it until ready. The proper guidance of a pupil demands recognition of his development and difficulties so that instruction will begin for him at the right time with appropriate materials. Because interests and needs differ, each pupil must make use of the opportunity for real learning when it arises.[3] In a real sense, each pupil must under the guidance of the school actually carry out his own curriculum.

## The Influence of the Teacher

The teacher influences communication development in many ways. Obviously her intelligence, personality, knowledge, language facility, understanding of growth and development, and the utilization of principles and practices of learning and instruction influence the achievement of goals in the language arts. Carr emphasized for teacher preparation four ingredients — broad general education, expert knowledge in a field of instruction, mastery of teaching techniques, and understanding of human growth and development.[4]

The personality qualities of a teacher rank high in guiding a child to effective communication. Courtesy, self-control, patience, and poise are recognized by pupils and the response to these qualities is reflected in learning products. Enthusiasm, interest, and naturalness are desirable. A teacher interested in pupils, who loves books and talks about men and women in fields of history, literature, science, health, citizenship, and current affairs, will inspire a desire for both receptive and expressive communication in the members of her class.

Knowledge of pupils' likes and dislikes in poetry, literature, and

[3] Isabel Craig, "The Opportunity to Learn," *Education,* 82:387–390, March, 1962.
[4] William G. Carr, "The Teacher and the Professor," *NEA Journal,* 50:45–47, November, 1961.

reading is important in guidance. Pupils generally react favorably to an instructor's sense of humor, ability to tell a story, knowledge of source materials, and effective presentation of content.

## Sharing Experiences

Backgrounds differ from individual to individual. They may be rich for a favored few in the group. Contrary to what is often thought, they are often limited for children in suburbs as well as in slums. Every child in a class has had experiences which differ from those of every other child. Only one pupil of a class may have made a trip to Europe. Charlie Smith, a shy boy in the fifth grade, went with his father to Alsace-Lorraine — his father's old home — and visited Paris and other parts of France. Not only did this trip enrich his background, but it increased the knowledge of the members of the class, a committee of which kept account of Charlie's travels. Charlie wrote a letter once or twice a week. His letters mentioned many unusual and interesting places. They stimulated the class to study France and particularly Alsace-Lorraine. Maps were drawn, geography was studied, and history was learned. The pupils talked about the trip, viewed a motion picture, discussed scenes of France, and wrote letters. Many language skills were used. After his two-month trip, when Charlie returned, he told about the trip in an assembly. Pupils asked questions about the people, the cities, and the rural areas also, and enjoyed and profited by the answers.

Sharing does much to develop a feeling of "belongingness." A pupil, who may otherwise be an isolate, becomes a "star" for a day or for a longer period of time because he relates to his classmates experiences which they have not had. Every pupil has something to give, if not an event, perhaps a song or an ability to design a cover for a class book. Every child will express if he is properly motivated. Showing a possession or sharing a gift is a basis for understanding and for good relationships.

## Interests and Activities

"Interest is the secret." Interests can be determined by inventories made up from categories such as the following. Reactions of pupils are useful in selecting activities which stimulate communication.

a) Desired vocations
b) Favorite games, sports, play
c) Motion pictures liked best

*d*) Radio programs listened to and television programs viewed
*e*) Favorite subject areas
*f*) Favorite books, stories, poems
*g*) Favorite characters in books, stories, movies, television
*h*) Favorite kinds of language — listening, talking, reading, writing, spelling, handwriting
*i*) Favorite listening activities — opera, lectures, songs, music
*j*) Favorite kinds of oral reading — poetry, stories, dramatics
*k*) Favorite kinds of talking — conversation, discussion, debate
*l*) Favorite newspapers and magazines
*m*) Favorite sections of newspapers — sports, comics, features, news, society, gossip, editorial, others
*n*) Favorite hobbies, pastime, recreation
*o*) Peoples you like best to hear of, read about, or talk to: peoples of other lands; Indians; soldiers; pioneers; farmers; knights; police; firemen
*p*) Kinds of writing activities liked: plays, records, logs, news items, letters, reports.

Such items can be arranged in a form or pattern to fit the requirements and maturity levels of the boys and girls whose interests are to be appraised. Reasons for preferences are useful cues for instruction. There should be freedom to respond or not to react to any of the items or stimuli. Thus, replies will be worthwhile in motivating reading, writing, talking, and listening.

## Motivation

Pupils will desire to learn if stimuli are impelling. Motivation can be promoted by showing the degree of progress achieved. Purposes must be clear and attractive. The more real the situations are, the better. A life situation is generally interesting and alluring. A lifelike situation is useful also for engendering attitudes for improving, for example, talking or writing. Understanding the value of practice will promote dynamic effort. A pupil who practices a communication art to improve a skill will work hard and will be far more successful than one who does not understand clearly why he is carrying out the exercise. The more desired the aim and the more enticing the work, the greater are the benefits. If he knows the penalty attached to failure and the advantage of success, a pupil will be likely to strive diligently for competency. If the goal is kept constantly in mind, the learner will with an effective method, make progress toward it. If a pupil, for example, who has difficulty in writing legibly is introduced to a method for appraising his needs, he will generally respond enthusiastically to specific practice to overcome his deficiencies. In like manner, when he becomes aware of the necessity for proofreading an article for a school paper, he will scrutinize his capitalization, punctuation, and usage carefully to achieve a satisfactory product.

The principle "success succeeds" emphasizes the importance of knowing what progress is being made. Acceptable achievement by the dynamic employment of an effective procedure begets even more drive, greater accomplishment, and higher success. Evidence of improvement resulting from a plan of working is in itself a highly motivating factor for success. Without knowledge of success a pupil will not make the effort that he would if he were aware that he is overcoming obstacles to progress, and is moving forward toward perfection of a skill or to the solution of a problem.[5]

## In-School Learning and Instruction

Communication is a two-way process. It has been proved repeatedly that telling by a teacher is not sufficient for effective understanding. The learner must be active in purposing what he desires to learn, active in planning processes to achieve his objectives, critical of his products and outcomes, and aware of his success. Kennedy reported an experiment which demonstrated that the give-and-take two-way communication by instructor and learner was much more effective than one-way directions by the instructor in attempting to guide the learner to understanding and achievement.[6]

Communication is enhanced by three types of learning situations: (1) incidental, (2) systematic, and (3) integrative. A pupil learns incidentally in situations such as the following: reading signs or notices, talking to a classmate on the way to school, writing a note telling his mother of a phone call, or listening to the weather report. A pupil learns systematically when he studies all the words he cannot spell in a semester's list, proofreads his writing, keeps a hard word list of his spelling demons and masters them by energetic practice. Integrative learning occurs when a pupil uses several of the communication arts in the study of a unit, a problem, or an activity, as he needs them. Frequently, a pupil uses everyone of the language arts — listening, speaking, reading, writing, spelling, handwriting — and in addition televiewing, observing, and evaluating in a unit of study. The three

---

[5] Isidoro Panlasigui and F. B. Knight, "The Effect of Awareness of Success or Failure," *Twenty-Ninth Yearbook of the National Society for the Study of Education,* 1930, pp. 611–619.

[6] W. Henry Kennedy, "Communication is a Two-Way Street," *NEA Journal,* 48:45, March, 1959.

types of learning are useful and effective in mastery of the facets of language. Insofar as it goes, incidental learning may be intensive, but it is desultory and not all-embracing in any field. Systematic learning should take up where incidental learning leaves off, but sometimes it is likely to isolate knowledge in more or less closed subject compartments. Learning must be such that an individual will be able to use it when he needs it. In life, one listens, talks, reads, and writes when he needs these skills in his daily work. In school, boys and girls profit from integrative learning in units, problems, projects, cooperative activities, practices, and drills. As Dewey stated nearly sixty years ago, "All waste is due to isolation. Organization is nothing but getting things into connection with one another."[7]

*The unit approach to learning.* One of the most important curriculum procedures is the unit. The unit procedure, properly planned and executed is practical, integrative, and motivating. Unfortunately, the term unit has been used to mean many different things. However, according to Morrison a learning unit is "a comprehensive and significant aspect of the environment, of an organized science, of an art, or of conduct, which being learned results in an adaptation in personality."[8] A unit is a core of experiences and related subject matter which comprises varying activities, problems, projects, and practices that contribute materially to the development of the learner's understanding, appreciation, and adaptation. The unit emphasizes significance, comprehensiveness, unity, sequence, interest, enrichment, and integration, and these are eventuated by and through the language arts.[9]

The comprehensive plan for a unit may include the following: (1) introduction and overview; (2) approaches; (3) objectives — child and teacher; (4) teacher procedures — testing, guidance, motivation, and appraisal; (5) bibliographies — teacher and child; (6) selection of materials useful in the unit; (7) child activities; (8) integration; (9) culminating activities; (10) outcomes; and (11) evaluation.

In planning and carrying out a unit properly motivated, pupils engage in the work enthusiastically. Sometimes they select the unit and under the guidance of a teacher, formulate the objectives to be achieved, set up procedures, solve problems, find solutions, appraise

---

[7] John Dewey, quoted in Carr, *op. cit.,* p. 45.

[8] Henry C. Morrison, *The Practice of Teaching in the Secondary School,* revised edition (Chicago: University of Chicago Press, 1931), pp. 24–25.

[9] James A. Fitzgerald and Patricia G. Fitzgerald, *Methods and Curricula in Elementary Education* (Milwaukee: The Bruce Publishing Company, 1955), p. 280.

Dynamic integration of material and skills

them, and revise them. The work will include generally listening, speaking, reading, writing, spelling, and handwriting.

Among the possible pupil activities involved in unit study are the following: (1) problem-solving; (2) projects; (3) library work and research; (4) planning the use of materials necessary to the development of the unit; (5) committee work which includes purposing, planning, carrying out plans, and evaluating the work; (6) organizing and outlining materials and content discovered; (7) writing and revision; (8) observation of phenomena and behavior; (9) interviewing people; (10) planning trips or excursions; (11) reporting findings of study or results of project planning and presenting assembly programs; (12) doing creative work; (13) developing and improving study skills.

Many ways to assist boys and girls to integrate subject matter and skills can be devised. A unit generally cuts across subject-matter lines and requires varying materials and skills for achieving its objectives.

A unit on Holland, for example, would consider materials of history, geography, government, culture, literature, mathematics, science, art, music, industry, agriculture, health, and education. It would require thinking, study, observation, listening, discussing, reading, writing, spelling, handwriting, perhaps drawing and making charts and tables. Skills in each of these would be developed and habits of study would be formed and practiced. Dynamic direction of a unit leads to enthusiastic study, intensified interests, and expanding experiencing, and effective expression.

The culminating activities of a unit are rich in impression and expression; they may consist of exhibits of work; they may develop creative expressions such as plays, panel discussions, or books of creative writing; they may eventuate in creative art — drawings, pictures, or murals; they may be evidenced in creative writing — poetry, stories, or history of a community.

The outcomes of units of learning include work accomplished and the products developed and exhibited. They result in improvement of communication skills, development of research abilities, changes in attitudes toward discovery of knowledge, widening of horizons for understanding, intensification of desire for learning, expansion of appreciations, inculcation of improved procedures of discrimination, and the furtherance of thought processes.

Standards for evaluation, although often thought of as the province of the teacher and the supervisor, can be formulated and should be practiced by pupils. Criteria may be developed by which boys and girls appraise their attitudes concerning the unit. Pupils may inquire concerning their progress and achievement: Have we improved in communication? Do we converse and discuss better than we did in the beginning of the unit? Do we listen better? Do we write more clearly and spell more perfectly? Do we plan our work more adequately? Is our organization more effective? Do we know where to find source material? Have we improved our use of the card catalog, the indexes, encyclopedia, the dictionary? Do we read more comprehendingly? Are we able to achieve improved understanding through listening? Do we gain more from the observation of a film or from the demonstration of a process than we did formerly? Was the unit enjoyable? Accordingly, a unit of learning which is truly significant and comprehensive should be an experience of worth and an activity of value.[10]

*The integrating cooperative activity.*    Activities in the modern school

---

[10] *Ibid.*, pp. 276–313.

are legion, but not all are equally effective in promoting learning. Several language activities have been shown to be of value in the preceding section. The integrating cooperative activity is a continuing useful process, an enriching group enterprise in a real situation. Such cooperating activities as publishing a school newspaper, operating a school library, keeping a bulletin board display, or conducting a drama club, a poetry club, or a literary club are group enterprises. These are particularly rich in receptive and expressive language. If participants have a hand in initiating, planning, operating, and evaluating such an activity, they most certainly will achieve many valuable benefits.

In a cooperative group enterprise such as running a library, there are opportunities for many language activities in reading, discussion, inspection, comparison, and evaluation of books, periodicals, and other materials. In publishing a school newspaper, there are activities of news gathering, reporting, writing, art work, planning successive issues, evaluating the writing, revising and correcting the context, spelling, punctuation, and capitalization. All of these are carried out not in isolation but in integration as they are needed. In a cooperative enterprise of a literary club, the group must determine how to achieve the objectives of the club by following the guiding principles formulated and expressed in the constitution and bylaws. In order to achieve the goals it is necessary to read purposively, to think reflectively, to plan creatively, to write and to talk, to appraise and to revise.

If a cooperative activity functions properly, there will be abundant outcomes. Individuals are enriched by their own efforts, by sharing the work and the products, and by enjoying the presentations of others.

*Materials and procedures for enrichment.* The literature of our culture is rich and challenging, and the pupils who are properly guided, love it. Generally it is poor pedagogy to force them to read either prose or poetry. Accordingly, a wide selection of materials — history, literature, poetry, prose, science, and citizenship materials should be available to meet every educable taste. Some children like the comics for various reasons, but intelligent children and the better readers prefer more challenging reading materials. Children enjoy humorous stories, as well as adventure tales and exciting episodes. Listeners will be impressed with the enthusiasm with which pupils recall some of the fascinating scenes and actions.

A storytelling club has great possibilities not only for the telling of tales but because storytelling motivates reading and discussion. Tooze writes glowingly of stories, the storyteller, the telling, what makes the story good to tell.[11]

Arbuthnot indicates the importance of authentic books in every aspect of the sciences, poetry, choral speaking, biography, fiction, and in other fields at every level.[12] Her references include thirty-two items such as Beatrix Potter's *The Tale of Peter Rabbit,* Virginia Burton's *The Little House,* A. A. Milne's *Winnie the Pooh, and* May Hill Arbuthnot's *Children and Books.*[13] Poetry too, should be read. Every child should know and enjoy the poetry of Rosemary and Stephen Benet, Walter de la Mare, Eleanor Farjeon, Vachel Lindsay, James Whitcomb Riley, Christina Rossetti, Robert Louis Stevenson, Rose Fyleman, Eugene Field, and many others.

*An enumeration of some activities.* The following is an incomplete list of games, activities, and projects which will help to enrich the language-arts curriculum.

1. Class or assembly program — relating stories, presenting a play, reading poetry, discussing leaders in the fields of science, history, literature
2. Dramatization of episodes of history or scenes in literature
3. Telling original impromptu tales
4. Pantomiming Mother Goose or other types of literature
5. Quiz programs on poets, poetry, authors, literature
6. Literary society meetings, parliamentary practice, panel discussions
7. Imitation of songs of birds and sounds of animals
8. Puppet shows
9. A quotation competition between two groups
10. Choral reading and speaking
11. A biography competition — identification of prominent literary men, statesmen, historical figures, or heroes after one, two, or three or more statements have been made about the individual
12. Searching in the library for a suitable story or poem to read to the class
13. Making book collections
14. Arranging a book or other type of collection for exhibit
15. Organizing a book fair for book week
16. Making a collection — individual or group — of anecdotes, or quotations of literary, patriotic, biblical, or poetic statements
17. Making a collection of book jackets for display
18. Charades — words represented alternately by each of two sides or groups in dramatic action for guessing by the other
19. A free choice period in which members of a class may work individually, in groups, or as a whole class on selected activities

---

[11] Ruth Tooze, "Storytelling," *Literature With Children* (Washington, D. C.: Association for Childhood Education International, 1961), pp. 37–42.

[12] May Hill Arbuthnot, "Stories and the Curriculum," *Literature With Children, op. cit.,* pp. 15–18.

[13] *Ibid.,* p. 18.

20. Writing an original play, story, or poem for presentation or publication
21. Writing a log of group or class events
22. Staging a play, a pageant, or an historical event
23. Illustrating by drawing a scene of a story or poem
24. Devising a format for a school newspaper
25. Making a mural
26. Using a style book or grammar to determine correct form
27. A competition in speaking, listening, or reading.

## Environment, Objects, Devices, Machines, and Procedures

Many teachers find that objects, devices, and machines, used reasonably, make learning more interesting and fruitful. In using them, it is necessary to keep a right perspective. They are not the goal; they are aids to instruction and learning. Dale presented factors which range from real experiences to abstract symbols in his cone of experience as follows: direct, purposeful experiences; contrived experiences; dramatized experiences; demonstrations; field trips; exhibits; television; motion pictures; recordings; visual symbols; verbal symbols.[14] If these factors are understood, it is possible to arrange learning situations effectively in achieving the highest type of communication possible. An inexperienced pupil can understand and appreciate real intensive situations with impelling experience, but he would be lost in verbalism if we used only highly abstract symbolism. For example, in teaching reading we lead from real experiences gradually to the pages of print. Barnes presented four major levels of abstraction: actual materials used in reality, manipulative materials, pictorial materials, and symbolic materials.[15] A child is helped at first by experiences with materials in actual situations. Then he becomes able to manipulate objects — marbles, balls, or discs — which he counts, identifies, compares, and groups. Next he is introduced to pictorial materials — still pictures, motion pictures, charts, or films. Finally, he comprehends thought through symbols or he listens to words and interprets them in the light of his experience and background.

*Use of objects, bulletin boards, flannel boards, models, and exhibits.* Children in the primary grades can organize an interesting bulletin board. They will use a flannel board effectively in placing figures, words, and sentences. They can arrange an exhibit of book jackets

---

[14] Edgar Dale, *Audio-Visual Methods in Teaching,* revised edition (New York: Dryden Press, 1954), p. 43.

[15] Fred P. Barnes, "Using the Materials of Learning," *NEA Journal,* 50:54–56, September, 1961.

and of books. They may develop a plan of a town or house or store to suit their experience or fancy. In such exercises, they talk, listen, think, and construct. They begin to use the chalkboard and paper and pencil for expression. They make drawings and begin to write. Some children in the second grade have learned to use the typewriter quite effectively in expressing themselves. They manipulate marionettes and puppets, use them to dramatize life with dynamic imagination and evident enjoyment, and in the process they improve their speech and other communication arts. The children of the primary grades often make collections of various kinds — stamps, rocks, fossils. They build scrapbooks and albums. They may have as a purpose the equipping of a museum or a terrarium. In all such projects, pupils must purpose, plan, carry out the plan, and appraise their work if it is to be of appreciable value to them.

*Programed instruction and teaching machines.* In recent years programed instruction and teaching machines have come upon the educational scene. The machine at first made a strong appeal; at present, increasing attention is given to theory and practices of programed instruction.[16]

As Eigen pointed out, programed instruction is more useful than conventional teaching in some cases, but not so valuable in others. It is not the panacea that some enthusiasts predicted it to be.[17] However, thousands of users are trying out the programs and the machines as they should. There is no doubt that many of them will be discarded or replaced by improved materials and instruments in the future. Programing is now being investigated and developed, and no school can afford to neglect the findings of studies which are being reported from month to month.[18]

There is a tendency upon the part of some school and commercial people to accept programed materials and instruments with insufficient proof of their utility. Feldhusen presented evidence to indicate the importance of proceeding slowly and of questioning and evaluating the excessive claims of some publishers.[19] Despite the controversy that

---

[16] Leon Mones, "Automation of Teaching and Learning," *The Clearing House*, 38:136–138, November, 1963.

[17] Lewis D. Eigen, "Programing Poses Problems," *Phi Delta Kappan*, 44:242, March, 1963.

[18] Lawrence M. Stolurow, "Let's Be Informed on Programed Instruction," *Phi Delta Kappan*, 44:255–257, March, 1963.

[19] John F. Feldhusen, "Taps for Teaching Machines," *Phi Delta Kappan*, 44:265–267, March, 1963.

Understanding charts and maps

is being carried on, many reliable investigators have published their findings concerning both the programed instruction materials and teaching machines.[20] A careful appraisal of these results will guide teachers and administrators in the selection and use of such materials.

*Visual materials.* Great strides have been made in the last two decades in producing audio-visual materials. Pictorial materials range from diagrams, accurate drawings, and photographs to sketchy cartoons. They are available in books, pamphlets, periodicals, dictionaries, and encyclopedias. Pictures motivate both the receptive and the expressive language arts. Children make posters and write notices which include drawings and printed or written suggestions or directions announcing an approaching event, a thrift campaign, a need for safety, a warning against infraction of regulations, or a suggestion for right attitudes and behavior.

Pupils may become aware of the value of charts such as those suggesting their daily program, duties, health and safety practices, and correct language usages. They keep a record of the books they read.

<hr>

[20] See "The Teacher and the Machine," *The Journal of Educational Research,* 55:407–531, June-July, 1962.

See also, "A Special Issue on Programed Instruction," *Phi Delta Kappan,* 44:241–298, March, 1963.

They learn to use maps and globes to find cities, distances, and altitudes. They are helped by practice cards of words, phrases, and sentences.

Among the devices which are useful are filmstrips, opaque projectors, overhead projectors, and lantern slides. These may be used as many times as necessary to present a chart or scene, and the children may question the procedures and organize their learnings to meet their purposes. It should be remembered that some pictorial materials cannot portray a whole panorama. Their use is limited, but they are highly valuable in depicting clearly a specific view.

*Oral and auditory methods and materials.* For centuries, the lecture or the oral instruction has been most important in teaching youth. Although "telling" has been overdone in the past, speaking to a whole class or group is still important if the instruction is well organized and enthusiastically presented. Oral guidance is necessary and should be used as perfectly as possible. Talks by a teacher in overviews, presenting problems, describing processes, making transition from one topic or problem to another, summarizing work done, and planning for further work are worthwhile in curriculum and instruction.[21] Radio broadcasts are conducive to improvement of listening abilities and habits. Critical listening will lead to discriminatory and evaluative habits and practices.

Recordings too, are helpful. From a recording, a pupil can recognize, for example, the importance of voice control, and the need for clarity in enunciation. He is benefited by listening to the playback of a recording made of a report. He will listen with enjoyment to recorded songs, ballads, addresses. Many children's stories, beautifully arranged with musical background and related by expert storytellers have been recorded. These promote in boys and girls an appreciation of poetry, other literature, and history.

*Audio-visual devices.* Audio-visual devices combine listening and viewing. Appealing to the eye and ear alike, they generally have a peculiar fascination for young learners. Sound motion pictures have a place in language learning and an important future in class instruction. When so used, pictures must be most carefully selected with a specific purpose in mind. Previewing by the teacher is necessary, and the class should be well prepared for the presentation. The showing should be carried out under favorable conditions for listening and seeing. The

---

[21] Ernest Horn, *Methods of Instruction in the Social Studies* (New York: Charles Scribner's Sons, 1937), pp. 300–303.

sound motion picture is a one-way avenue; that is, the children view and listen. They can, however, react and vocalize about the program; in the postdiscussion, pupils voice their questions and appraise the content. They sometimes criticize and often commend certain points. They may make suggestions concerning further study and action.

*Educational television.* Educational television is becoming an increasingly important factor in elementary school instruction. "Closed" television programs and series in which schools cooperate with state departments and local television stations are multiplying rapidly.

The Public Schools of Scranton, for example, in cooperation with Station WDAU-TV, offered in the Spring of 1964 a series of science lessons running through the semester. *Exploring in Science* presentations by the Pennsylvania State Department of Public Instruction were viewed by fifth- and sixth-grade pupils and *Primary Concepts in Science* lessons were shown to third- and fourth-grade children. These were highly effective in both cases.

Mr. Terrence Gallagher, Supervisor of Art in the Scranton Public Schools, conducted live lessons in art which were televised to thirty-four elementary schools. These programs, excellent in the quality of instruction, motivated interest and diligence in pupil viewers. Before actual viewing, teachers used a prepared guide to interest and instruct the classes as to what to expect and how to benefit from a specific program. During a presentation an individual made note of procedures which he thought would help him in his work.

In a follow-up session, pupils discussed principles and technics learned in both the art and science fields. Thus, these series were not only conducive to art and science learning, but they promoted language skills of listening, speaking, and writing, and challenged pupils to act upon their learning and thinking.[22]

*The cross-media approach.* It is important to understand which types of audio-visual devices and materials are most adaptable for varying purposes in different situations. Sometimes one is best, and other times another. Slides, filmstrips, motion pictures, or still pictures should be used as they meet the needs of a situation. There is some evidence to indicate that combinations of these employed in the proper proportion for varying purposes produce near maximum results. It is evident that if leisurely or repeated viewing is necessary, a filmstrip or other type of still picture is effective, but if activity

---

[22] "Elementary Science and Art Instruction Presented in TV Series," *Scranton Public Schools Newsletter,* February, 1964, p. 3.

and verbal effects are required the sound picture is advantageous. The cross-media approach with properly selected devices is efficient, for example, in vocabulary development. Pupils who used appropriate combinations of audio-visual materials displayed interest and enthusiasm in their efforts to learn.[23] This approach has been used to teach reading, listening, speaking, and writing on secondary and college levels and the results have been equivalent to those of conventional teaching.[24]

## MASS MEDIA AND COMMUNICATION

Since skill and facility in the language arts are acquired outside the school as well as in the school, it seems appropriate to consider briefly the impact of mass media upon communication. Important types of mass media are: newspapers, magazines, comics, television, radio, motion pictures, recordings, and books. Research and authoritative statements have shown the importance of these media, and many just criticisms of them have been made, but nevertheless, a great deal of value is attached to them. In this section it shall be the purpose to offer some advantages and disadvantages of these media as they pertain to instruction.

### Newspapers

The newspaper is one of the most effective ways by which individuals in a free society can study the happenings in the locality, state, nation, and world. It is an educative agency for free peoples; through a free press, we are able to determine truth about problems, processes, conflicts, and events. Although some newspapers may overemphasize certain bizarre and spectacular types of news, others present the important activities in their proper perspective. Daily papers feature the news, financial, sports, society, travel, editorial, political, and other current aspects of life. Elementary school pupils should learn how to read newspapers and to appreciate the various sections. They should learn to discuss important items and critically appraise controversial issues objectively. In these activities, they will grow gradually toward maturity of judgment and develop a sense of values. A metropolitan newspaper and a local paper should be available to boys and girls in

---

[23] Walter Arno Wittich, "Effective Use of A-V Materials," *National Elementary Principal*, 40:12–14, January, 1961.

[24] Samuel L. Becker, "Teaching of English in the Mass Media," *Elementary English*, 38:250–258, April, 1961.

the library. A pupil should strive to evaluate what he reads, differentiate fact from opinion, appraise the source of news stories, and strive to determine the impact of events. He should not only read, appraise, and comment upon the news, but he may, when he feels it important, make notes upon subjects of interest and value to him. Accordingly, the reading of newspapers should aid in motivating both receptive and expressive language.[25]

## Magazines and Comics

Current literature will probably be selected for reading according to preferences, and there is evidence which a teacher or a librarian uses in the selection of periodicals. Lazar indicated that the following types of magazines interested boys and girls in the following order:

| Boys | Girls |
|------|-------|
| 1. Detective and mystery | 1. General story |
| 2. Science and mechanics | 2. Movies and theater |
| 3. Children's | 3. Children's |
| 4. Adventure | 4. Detective and mystery |
| 5. General story | 5. Household |
| 6. Aviation | 6. Serious — popular |
| 7. Serious — popular | 7. Science and mathematics |
| 8. Comics | 8. Literary |
| 9. Sports | 9. Comics |
| 10. Movies and theater | 10. Adventure[26] |

It is important to know what types of periodicals interest growing youngsters for it is a responsibility of the teachers and the school to guide them to extend and possibly to improve their reading preferences. For example, a pupil who reads only mystery and adventure, may shift a considerable portion of his reading to science and aviation periodicals if they are made available. As a pupil expands and intensifies his interests, he may begin to read periodicals such as *United States News and World Report, Newsweek,* or *Time.* Gifted young citizens who have interest and capacity for reading should be able to select materials which will help them understand national and world problems, to critically appraise proposals for solutions, and to evaluate social processes.

[25] See Per G. Stensland, "The Classroom and the Newspaper," *Mass Media and Education,* Fifty-Third Yearbook of the National Society for the Study of Education, Part II (Chicago: University of Chicago Press, 1954), pp. 217–242.

[26] May Lazar, *Reading Interests, Activities, and Opportunities of Bright, Average, and Dull Children.* Contributions to Education No. 707 (New York: Teachers College, Columbia University, 1937).

The reading of current literature in addition to providing up-to-date information aids pupils to develop other communication arts as well. They will report their readings and discuss what they have read. They learn by listening to other points of view, by critically appraising them, by making statements and summaries, and by preparing outlines and reports. Such are the results of reading well-chosen periodicals.

The comics have been a problem, but evidence seems to indicate that boys prefer seven other types of periodical literature to the comics, and girls eight. A wide selection of children's works with a positive approach to reading on appropriate levels is one of the most important means for negating comic books and promoting better materials.[27]

## Motion Pictures

Motion pictures have been a dynamic type of entertainment in our culture for about fifty years. The Payne Fund Studies revealed their influence upon millions of youth who view pictures weekly or more often. Boys and girls remember much of what they see and hear in this medium; their attitudes are changed and their emotions are often aroused by action and sound. Their conversations are affected, and sometimes their sleep is disturbed by motion pictures.[28] A worthy picture is a valuable experience, but unworthy pictures have been shown to leave undesirable impressions upon some sensitive young minds and personalities. The problem of picture viewing has been a difficult one to solve for society. It is obvious that there are objectionable pictures as there are undesirable television programs, harmful comics, and bad food. It is natural and ethical to protect the young from contaminated food and improper diet until they are able to differentiate proper food and diet from the unhealthful. Just as considerate parents and teachers would shield young children from danger and instruct them about safety in crossing the street or railroad tracks, they should take measures to protect them from unwholesome pictures. As children grow, they should be guided to know that worthy pictures are educative, healthful, and desirable. Many good pictures have been produced.

If the purpose is entertainment, the picture should be wholesome. If the purpose is educational, it should be valuable. The habit of going to movies too frequently should no doubt give way in part

[27] Ibid.
[28] The Payne Fund Studies (New York: Macmillan Company, 1933–1935).

at least to more purposeful and vital types of activity.[29] The normal and particularly the superior individual, has a duty and a responsibility, which the teacher should help him to understand — that of doing his part in improving motion pictures. Dale suggested that it may be as simple as attending worthy pictures and recommending them.[30] It should be strongly emphasized that a child who, through the guidance of parent and teacher, develops ability to discriminate between worthy and unworthy films should have no hesitancy in avoiding the vicious and harmful and in using his influence to guide those less fortunate and less able than he to view commendable and wholesome films.

## Television and Radio

The problems of television and radio have much in common with those of motion pictures. During the past decade, broadcasts and telecasts together, have become the most popular mass media of a majority of people. A large percent of homes have television sets and many have two or more receivers. In 1961, Witty and Kinsella reported that elementary school pupils spent an average of about twenty hours a week televiewing, that their parents spent about the same number of hours, and that teachers averaged approximately eleven hours.[31]

Nearly everyone listens to radio. Omitting the advertising, which is a very important feature particularly from the viewpoint of the producer, a large percentage of radio time is devoted to the entertainment types of program — music, drama, "soap opera," domestic, mystery, and quiz programs. A much smaller percentage of time is allotted to information-type programs, and to orientation programs — religion, talks, forums, and panels.[32] Disregarding advertising time, television programs allot similarly much the largest percentage of time to entertainment. Information-type programs hold second place, and orientation third. Drama utilizes the highest percentage of broadcasting time in the entertainment category; crime and western programs

---

[29] Edgar Dale, "Teaching Discrimination in Motion Pictures," *Mass Media and Education,* Fifty-Third Yearbook of the National Society for the Study of Education, Part II (Chicago: University of Chicago Press, 1954), pp. 243–259.

[30] *Ibid.,* p. 257.

[31] Paul A. Witty and Paul J. Kinsella, "A Report on Televiewing in 1961," *Elementary English,* 39:25–26, January, 1962.

[32] Dallas W. Smythe, "The Content and Effects of Broadcasting," *Mass Media and Education,* Fifty-Third Yearbook of the National Society for the Study of Education, Part II (Chicago: University of Chicago Press, 1954), pp. 195–199.

also are presented frequently. Despite the efforts to educate the public as to the great values of good programs and the devastating dangers of bad ones for the young, many children's viewing habits include much that is unsavory. In the offerings which children view there is a great deal of law violation — murder, robbery, and violence.[33]

Television and radio are influential agents in the development of children, their thinking, feeling, and behavior. It is probable that the drama viewing, particularly the crime and the western, results for many in tensions and maladaptive traits. Undesirable programs have a tendency to defile character and degrade behavior of young viewers.

As Smythe pointed out, allotting of so much time to radio and television may preclude many more valuable activities such as good reading. Another possible effect is that people who become engrossed in mystery and other types of programs to which they give attention slavishly, may lose themselves in unreality and avoid the down-to-earth problems of the home, community, state, and nation.[34] Such a result could lower the vitality of our citizenry.

In a recent study of 9000 fourth-, fifth-, and sixth-grade pupils' television practices of 39 selected elementary schools in Brooklyn and Rockville Centre, it was reported that about 99 percent enjoy televiewing, and that 92 percent received parental restrictions. Curtailments were made because of homework, bedtime, and the unsuitability of programs. The youngsters reported that humor was their main reason for the selection of a program, although boys favored adventure also.

The data showed that 346 different TV programs received first-choice mentions. Favorite programs were categorized as follows: comedy, adventure, western, musical, children's, crime, fantasy, drama, and sports. Among the desirable concepts identified were: courtesy, prudence, worthy leisure activity, kindness, love, and humor. Rudeness, slang, assault, slapstick, and untruthfulness were frequent among the undesirable concepts. Respect for life was supported in the telecasts less often than it was violated in this appraisal. Among the findings, the following are pertinent: Children preferred adult programs to children's. They preferred programs that were amusing, exciting, humorous, and recreational. Boys were interested in violence and adventure more than girls. Children who viewed crime and western TV programs particularly were exposed to much harmful content.[35]

---

[33] *Ibid.*, pp. 199–205.  [34] *Ibid.*, pp. 205–212.
[35] Sister Esther R. Monahan, "A Critical Study of the Content of Television

Witty and Kinsella's findings similarly show that children's favorites are not educational presentations, but include westerns, variety, adventure, crime, science fiction, and comedy shows.[36]

It is necessary that the effects of television and radio be carefully assessed. Teachers and others who purpose and plan for the best education of children should recognize the faults and deficiencies of these media and do everything in their power to improve them. Nevertheless, there are many advantages to be gained from these media; through them children become interested in current affairs, in reading, history, science, social studies, music, art, aviation, and transportation. It is possible that the most worthwhile benefits are achieved by the more able individuals who avoid the undesirable and use the valuable presentations. Teachers and parents have opportunities and responsibilities to guide the young to use these media for what they can be worth in information, entertainment, and orientation.

*Miscellaneous*

In addition to the media considered in the foregoing, others have great potentiality. FM radio offers much to those who desire knowledge and culture. Paperbound books include some excellent materials. Recordings are produced which offer help in speech, vocabulary, and language; many of the finest literary and musical productions are available for listening. Such media offer opportunties for self-education. These, particularly the paperbacks, should be critically evaluated and selected with care.

An important factor which relates to all mass media concerns the source of revenue for their support. Many of them — the major ones — are supported commercially by advertising, and advertising presents many problems because it is a powerful and gigantic medium in our present-day life. Printed spreads in newspapers and magazines should be recognized for what they are. Some advertisements of moving pictures, for example, are undesirably sensational. Statements made on radio or television require educated judgment in arriving at truth about products they offer in superlative language. On the other hand, advertising must be recognized as important in communication. Everyone who reads knows the many beneficial notices of new processes,

---

Programs Preferred by Catholic School Children of the Intermediate Grades," (unpublished doctor's dissertation, Fordham University, New York, 1962).

[36] Witty and Kinsella, *op. cit.,* pp. 27–28.

useful products, and improved instruments that are appearing every day in the scientific, industrial, agricultural, and manufacturing fields. Salespeople know that it is profitable to advertise, and consumers know that it pays to read advertisements. Youth must learn to interpret them with understanding and discernment.

## SUMMARY

Effective communication, a most important objective in the education of youth, is enriched by the integration of experience and knowledge.

The curriculum composed of the activities and enterprises provided by the school in cooperation with home and community, develops effective communication. Enriched communication enhances not only the development of ability, interest, and practice of listening, speaking, reading, writing, spelling, and handwriting, but the integration of these arts, each with the others. Enriching procedures for integrating communication are the unit and cooperative activities which promote project-planning, problem-solving, and evaluative technics. Enrichment and integration function through use of books, visual materials, auditory procedures, and audio-visual devices.

Mass media, which makes intensive and lasting impressions upon the pliant mind and personality of the child, should be used intelligently. Children should receive instruction about newspapers, periodicals, motion pictures, television, and radio. These offer many exciting advantages, but they present grave dangers which pupils should be taught to recognize and avoid. The benefits that may come of mass media are unlimited when they are supervised for the good of all by intelligent democratic policies of school and society.

### ACTIVITIES, PROBLEMS, QUESTIONS

1. Why is effective communication enhanced by integration of language arts and skills?
2. Define curriculum. How should a curriculum be planned? Who really carries out a curriculum?
3. State several factors which are most useful for promoting curriculum enrichment.
4. How can a curriculum be enriched by the following: (a) the teacher; (b) pupil sharing; (c) interests and activities; (d) mass media?
5. Explain how the unit approach promotes curriculum enrichment. Show also how an integrating cooperative activity enriches a curriculum in elementary school.

6. State the advantages of teaching machines and programed instruction. State disadvantages of each.

7. Make a list of most useful instruments and procedures for promoting language enrichment. Explain the values of each.

8. Read and evaluate critically a metropolitan newspaper. Prepare a chart indicating the most desirable features, and the less desirable or undesirable qualities.

9. Make a list of acceptable periodicals for elementary school pupils. State the attractive qualities of each.

10. List several educational TV and radio programs for elementary school pupils. Explain the worth of each.

11. Summarize the values and dangers of mass media in the school and outside the school.

## SELECTED REFERENCES

*American School Curriculum.* Thirty-First Yearbook of the American Association of School Administrators. Washington, D. C.: NEA, 1953. 551 pp.

*Audio-Visual Materials of Instruction.* Forty-Eighth Yearbook of the National Society for the Study of Education, Part I. Chicago: University of Chicago Press, 1949. 320 pp.

Boutwell, William D., ed. *Using Mass Media in the Schools.* New York: Appleton-Century-Crofts, 1963. 320 pp.

*The Community School.* Fifty-Second Yearbook of the National Society for the Study of Education, Part II. Chicago: University of Chicago Press, 1953. 292 pp.

Dale, Edgar. *Audio-Visual Methods in Teaching.* Rev. ed. New York: Dryden, 1954. 534 pp.

*Enriching the Curriculum for the Elementary School Child.* Eighteenth Yearbook of the National Elementary Principal. Washington, D. C.: NEA, 1939. pp. 229–704.

Horkheimer, Mary P., and John W. Diffor, eds. *Educators Guide to Free Films.* 23rd ed. Randolph, Wis.: Educators Progress Service, 1963. 662 pp.

*Mass Media and Education.* Fifty-Third Yearbook of the National Society for the Study of Education, Part II. Chicago: University of Chicago Press, 1954. 290 pp.

Schramm, Wilbur, Jack Lyle, and Edwin Parker. *Television in the Lives of Our Children.* Stanford, Conn.: Stanford University Press, 1961. 324 pp.

Sechrist, Elizabeth H., ed. *One Thousand Poems for Children.* Philadelphia: Macrae Smith, 1946. 601 pp.

Shane, Harold G., and E. T. McSwain. *Evaluation and the Elementary Curriculum.* New York: Holt, 1951. 477 pp.

Smith, Mary H. *Using Television in the Classroom.* Midwest Program on Airborne Television Instruction. New York: McGraw-Hill, 1961. 118 pp.

Wendt, Paul R. *Audio-Visual Instruction.* What Research Says to the Teacher. No. 14. Washington, D. C.: DCT and AERA of the NEA, 1957. 32 pp.

# Chapter XV

# Evaluation: Appraisal, Measuring, Testing

## PURPOSES AND CONSIDERATIONS

THROUGHOUT this book, the purpose of which has been to suggest procedures for the development of reading and other communication arts, there have been suggestions for evaluation because instruction can never be perfected without adequate testing, measurement, and appraisal. As Dressel indicated, the "ultimate purpose of all evaluation must be that of increasing the amount of learning which takes place."[1] To simplify this presentation, the term "evaluation" will be employed to encompass appraisal, measurement, and testing of communication.

### Purposes of Evaluation

Evaluation should contemplate understanding the child, his objectives, efforts, interests, deficiencies, and problems. Evaluation should consider incentives both of the teacher and the learner for achieving the goals of growth, power, and mastery in listening, speaking, reading, writing, spelling, and handwriting. The child's behavior, attitude, personality, learning, development, achievement, and progress should be continually observed and appraised. Among the important considerations are the following:

1. Does the child understand the aims and objectives of communication?

2. Does he show positive or negative attitude toward listening, talking, reading, writing, spelling, and handwriting?

3. Is he ready to study the communication skills which will enable

---

[1] Paul L. Dressel, "The Evaluation of Reading," *The Reading Teacher,* 15:362, March, 1962.

him to acquire and use language effectively in the situations of school and of life?

4. Are available materials appropriate to the needs of individual children for acquiring the skills and habits necessary in each field of the language arts?

5. Are the programs for learning well devised and planned?

6. To what degree does the child react favorably or unfavorably to the instruction?

7. Is improvement in interests, attitudes, and skills in the receptive and expressive language discerned?

8. Is there evidence of development in social relationships?

9. Does the pupil cooperate in purposing, planning, carrying out, and evaluating the units of communication undertaken?

Evaluation is an important part of both instruction and of learning. Unless evaluation is valid, instruction and learning cannot achieve their most important goals. The incorrect appraisal of achievement or progress is often the cause of inadequate instruction, misdirected guidance, and inferior learning.

## Some Suggestions for Procedures in Evaluation

A fairly complete view of a child, his potentiality and personality, his maturation and successes, his learning difficulties and deficiencies, and his achievement and progress are required in charting a communication program for him. Tillman suggested that since many types of information required may not be available from the standardized testing program, a teacher should employ health records, sociometric devices, interest inventories, questionnaires, anecdotal records, rating scales, observation, conferences, and checklists.[2] Certainly, because of the great differences in individual abilities, interests, and progress among children in a class, it is necessary for a teacher to develop a procedure for determining the essential facts about each pupil in her charge. Such facts make appraisal more accurate, evaluation more valid, and guidance and instruction more fruitful and effective.

When should testing be done and appraisal be made? Research has given us the answer in some of the areas of the language arts. Measurement before teaching and learning, testing during teaching and learning, appraisal after teaching and learning, and evaluation of the degree of progress evidenced have proved effective in spelling

[2] Rodney Tillman, "What Is a Good Measurement Program?" *The National Elementary Principal,* 41:15, September, 1961.

and writing.[3] Accordingly, as learning is a continuing process, so must evaluation go with it as a concomitant guiding procedure. Testing and appraisal are important before teaching to determine the knowledge, interests, and attitude of the learner. It is obvious that a child who knows the correct spelling of a word should not be forced to study its spelling. It is clear that if a child continually begins a proper name with a lower case letter, but knows how to spell the word, he should be guided to remedy his writing of the capital letter. A child who is not ready to read as determined by a readiness test and by conference between child and teacher should not be forced to try to read, but should be guided to readiness by language activities appropriate to his purpose. It seems clear also that a child who has a poor attitude toward listening, requires the development of incentive, and this may be effected through interesting activities, for example, through games or recordings which entice listening.

Testing during teaching is also a guide for learning and teaching. Testing oneself while memorizing a poem or prose quotation is an effective way to guide study. Children learning to write a paragraph often encounter difficulties which must be overcome when teacher testing or self-appraisal suggests the need for corrective measures. In a class or smaller group, it is probable that different individuals will not encounter the same difficulties — certainly not at the same time. Accordingly, each should be guided to study the problems he faces and not those, necessarily, of his neighbor or classmate. He should be prompted to correct his own errors and practice the skills which he must learn.

Testing after teaching or study is necessary also to appraise achievement and progress. An individual may master correct usage in class and fall into errors outside of school when he is called upon to converse with a stranger. Incorrect forms of speaking in life situations should be noted and efforts made to replace them with acceptable language. A pupil may learn that slang and illiterate expressions are not desirable in conversation, but revert to them repeatedly because of a strongly established habit. Only through evaluation, self-appraisal, and constructive criticism by teachers, companions, or parents will he be guided to habitual acceptable usage.

It is not enough to say that evaluation should be made before,

---

[3] James A. Fitzgerald, *The Teaching of Spelling* (Milwaukee: The Bruce Publishing Company, 1951), pp. 202–207.

during, and after teaching; evaluation must be a continuous process in learning and living. Situations of life vary so greatly that oral language which is acceptable on one occasion may be entirely out of place on another. For example, a child should understand that a response quite proper to a question by his little playmate, Leroy, may not be appropriate in answering a like question by Leroy's mother. A learner must realize that conversing with a brother or sister does not require the same social conduct as that when interviewing the principal of the school or the cashier of a bank to which a group is making an excursion. In like manner, a pupil should become sensitive and alert to the varying situations in which he is called upon to write. The writing of a letter ordering a book from a publishing house differs from the writing of a note of thanks to the donor who contributed generously to a library fund. Thus the differences in situations should be comprehended and the need for varying types of communication should be understood through well-planned instruction and constructive criticism based upon valid appraisal.

## USING TESTS AND EXAMINATIONS

Studying without some kind of testing or appraisal is a very unsatisfactory and unprofitable process for children. Since many books are available on testing and measurement it is not the purpose here to repeat or summarize what is presented in them. It is the intention, rather, to present some brief suggestions which may help in coordinating testing with teaching and learning language skills.

### Informal Testing in Language and Communication

Several types of examination — intelligence, standardized, survey, achievement, diagnostic, personality, aptitude, and informal classroom tests — are useful. A test highly valuable in one situation may not be valid in another. Accordingly, the importance of selecting the best available instrument and procedure for each situation should be emphasized.

Purposes of testing are: to determine readiness for a unit of work, to discover a pupil's attitudes and interests, to determine his powers and capacities, to find out what he has learned and what he needs to study, to know whether he has achieved mastery or what degree of mastery has been attained, to diagnose his difficulties, to formulate a program for instruction, and to ascertain how he applies his learnings. Tyler indicated that great care should be taken in deciding what the objectives are, how they should be stated, and how testing can be used to assist in guiding activities to achieve instructional objectives.[4]

Three types of teacher-developed technics may at appropriate times be used: oral questions, informal objective tests, and constructive essay examinations. These are considered briefly.

*Oral examinations.*   In pioneer times, the oral question was frequently used, but it lost status because of the large groups which overcrowded the classrooms in the first half of the twentieth century. However, for testing an individual, or individuals in a small group, it has a place. A competent teacher uses the oral question to determine whether the child comprehends the import of a selection, the trend of a story, or the meaning of a critical passage in reading. When a pupil makes an oral report on the results of problem solving or when the chairman of a committee reports on the progress made in writing a class play, the oral presentation is an opportunity for appraisal. When each of a group of children in the fifth grade tells an interesting current event, the delivery of the report is a valuable type of test which may be evaluated not solely by the teacher but also by classmates and by the pupil himself. Listening to the playback of a discussion previously taped is becoming an increasingly useful type of oral testing. For oral language and oral reading, appraisal by listening is effective in a variety of ways.

*Informal objective tests.*   The informal objective test is used when it is necessary to test a large group in a limited time. These tests properly prepared are reliable, timesaving, and discriminatory. Their results are useful in guiding pupil study. On the other hand, they have dangers, such as placing too much emphasis on mere facts, testing items sometimes of minor importance, ignoring the more worthwhile factors, omitting the opportunity for organization and expression of thought, and promoting guessing. In view of the rather contradictory arguments about informal teacher-made paper and pencil tests, it is likely that the commendations came about from situations in which well-constructed tests were administered, interpreted, and used properly. It is probable also that the criticisms eventuated from improperly selected instruments for situations where other types of testing would have been more effective.[5]

---

[4] Ralph W. Tyler, "Educational Measurement — A Broad Perspective," *The National Elementary Principal*, 41:8–13, September, 1961.

[5] Mary Hughie Scott, "Teacher-Made Tests? It All Depends —" *The National*

Among the most useful of the informal objective types are the simple-recall, the sentence-completion, the paragraph-completion, the alternate-response, multiple-choice, matching, identification, and classification tests. A brief consideration of these with examples follow:

1. *The simple-recall test item.* This is sometimes referred to as a free-response item.[6] It may require the completion of a partial statement, or it may be a simple question which requires generally a short answer. Items should be clearly stated but not in the phraseology of the text. Two types of examples follow:

*a*) The first word of a sentence should begin with a . . .  ——

*b*) What punctuation mark do you use after a salutation in a friendly letter? . . . . . . . . . . . . . . . . .  ——

The simple-recall item can be used to test factual knowledge. Its proper use should motivate mastery of facts required for thinking.

2. *The sentence and the paragraph-completion test items.* The sentence-completion test item is similar to the simple-recall exercise, and quite similar also to the paragraph-completion exercise. If the blanks are arranged in the right margin, scoring is facilitated. An example of three sentences in a simple paragraph with directions follows:

*a*) *Directions*

Your words for study are: *likes, kitty,* and *my.* Read the paragraph of three sentences below. Think of the word that best fits blank 1. Write this word in the number 1 blank at the right. Write the words for the other blanks in like manner.

*b*) *Exercise*

I like __(1)__ kitty. He __(2)__ milk. The __(3)__ is playful.

1. ——
2. ——
3. ——

*c*) *Suggestions*

These completion exercises should be constructed for brief answers. The wording of items should be clear. One blank or at most two should be incorporated in a sentence. Such items may be used to test comprehension in reading and study.

3. *The alternate-response test item.* The *true-false* is probably the most commonly used of the alternate-response test items, although

*Elementary Principal,* 41:37–41, September, 1961. See Harry A. Greene, Albert N. Jorgensen, and J. Raymond Gerberich, *Measurement and Evaluation in the Elementary School* (Chicago: Scott, Foresman and Company, 1953), pp. 160–198.

[6] Walter W. Cook, "Tests, Achievement," *Encyclopedia of Educational Research,* revised edition, 1950, pp. 1467–1468.

the *yes-no* is frequently employed. An example of each type is presented.

    *a) True-false items.* Put a ring around the *T* if the statement is true. Ring the *F* if the statement is false.

    1) A conjunction connnects words or groups of words in a sentence . . . . . . . . . . . . .    T    F

    2) A noun is an action word . . . . . . . .    T    F

    *b) Yes-no items.* If the answer is *yes,* circle the *yes* at the right of each statement or question. If the answer is *no,* circle the *no.*

    1) May a pronoun be used in place of a noun?  .  .    Yes    No

    2) Does a sentence always end with a period?  .  .    Yes    No

    *c) Suggestions.* Alternate-response items should be unquestionably true or false. Ambiguities in writing the alternate-response items are avoided only with care. The double negative should be avoided in writing statements. Items should be arranged in random order. Both responding to items and scoring them are facilitated by provision for marking answers on the right-hand side of the page.[7]

4. *Multiple-choice test items.* Multiple-choice items vary in form. A simple general type is an incomplete statement or a question followed by four or five responses or partial statements, one of which is the best answer. The others are incorrect responses, or vary in degree of correctness with which they complete the statement. The item may consist of a paragraph, a chart, graph, diagram, or map followed by the responses. The responses may be in the form of numbers, words, phrases, or sentences. The item may require the selection of an incorrect response or of an answer that is most faulty. It may test reasoning, aptitude, comprehension, or the application of facts. It is easy to administer and easy to score but not easy to construct properly. Practice on constructing such items, keeping a record of items used in former tests, and of the incorrect answers made by pupils to objective test items, make improvement of this type of test possible. Some examples of multiple-choice items follow:

    *a) Directions:* Write the letter preceding the correct response in the blank at the right of each item.

    1) Which is a homonym? (a) spot, (b) boy, (c) hole, (d) himself . . . . . . . . . . . . . .    \_\_\_\_

    2) Which of the following is a contraction? (a) girls, (b) boy's, (c) good-by, (d) doesn't . . . . . .    \_\_\_\_

    3) The punctuation mark used after a question is: (a) ? (b) ! (c) ; (d) : . . . . . . . . . . .    \_\_\_\_

    4) Which is a complex sentence? (a) The man did not come. (b) When he comes, we shall go. (c) You may ride and I shall walk. (d) Hurrah! . . . . . . .    \_\_\_\_

---

[7] Cook, *op. cit.,* p. 1469.

*b) Comments.* Items should be positively stated without ambiguity. Four choices are considered quite practicable for classroom use. All choices should be plausible, but clues of any kind should be avoided. An item should not reveal the answer to another item of the test. Correct responses should vary among the four different positions randomly.

*5. Matching exercises.* Matching exercises are useful in reading, spelling, vocabulary, and usage. A list of words may, for example, be set up in one column and definitions in a second column. The purpose is to match the definitions and the words.

*a) Exercises*
1) Write the number of each word in the correct blank at the right of its definition.

| 1. remembered | Made one think of . . | —— |
| 2. remind | Recalled  . . . . . | —— |
| 3. repeat | Ready to act . . . . | —— |
| 4. speaking | One who writes  . . . | —— |
| 5. writer | Talking . . . . . . | —— |
|  | Say again  . . . . . | —— |

2) Write in the correct blank at the right, the number of the word that is an example of each term.

| 1. baseball | A pronoun . . . . . | —— |
| 2. friendly | A base word . . . . | —— |
| 3. ask | A proper noun  . . . | —— |
| 4. John | A homonym  . . . . | —— |
| 5. too | A conjunction . . . . | —— |
| 6. him | Derivative  . . . . . | —— |
| 7. Dec. | Possessive  . . . . . | —— |
| 8. teacher's | Abbreviation  . . . . | —— |
|  | Compound word . . . | —— |

*b) Comment.* Prepare a small number of items — four or five for the primary grades. A larger number may be presented to the pupils in the upper elementary school. Materials in matching exercises should be homogeneous,[8] for example, only words and definitions are presented in exercise 1, and language terms and examples in exercise 2. One or two extra responses for which there is no matching item should be presented as in these examples.

*6. Identification test.* The identification test is a form of objective test in which ideas, concepts, pictures, parts of maps, or graphs are identified. The test may be oral or written. For example, when a child is asked to name several playthings, one at a time, he is taking an identification test. A child identifies words of varying forms in reading as a part of his reading skill. The following is a type of identification test which may be written.

---

[8] Cook, *op. cit.,* p. 1470.

*a*) *Item.* Write the words in the following list that have the sound of long *a:*

can     man     tame     ran     came     fame     name     had

*b*) *Item.* Write the words in the group below that have suffixes, and after each word write the suffix:

| behold | unknown | stationary | comfortable | even |
|--------|---------|------------|-------------|------|
| greatest | confidence | prevail | proposition | restless |
| arise | leakage | medical | subway | gladness |

7. *Classification test.*   This is similar to the identification test, but offers opportunity for differentiating items into categories. It may be used to classify words, terms, pictures, statements, concepts, and various types of expression. It can be employed readily in word study, word usage, or literature. The following is an example.

*a*) *Directions.*  Classify the following words. Write the numeral 1 in the blank at the right of each noun. Write 2 in the blank at the right of each pronoun. Write 3 in the blank at the right of each adjective. Write 4 in the blank at the right of each adverb. Write 5 in the blank at the right of each verb.

| nation | —— | fiercely —— | fought —— | her | —— |
|--------|-----|-----|-----|-----|-----|
| faithful | —— | narrow —— | officer —— | calmly | —— |
| very | —— | he —— | cared —— | rang | —— |
| pocketbook —— | | it —— | greater —— | you | —— |

*b*) *Comment.*  Care should be exercised in selecting elements that fit only one group or category particularly for primary children. In intermediate grades, it may be challenging for pupils to find that a word may function as a noun or a verb. For example, the word *hit* may be used as either a verb or a noun. The classification test may be given orally in identifying colors of balls, of cloth, or of paper. For example, the child can be asked to separate the blocks according to colors: green, red, blue, yellow.

8. *Some general suggestions for composing informal objective tests.* An informal objective test may include one or more sections — completion, multiple-choice, true-false, matching, classification — which fit the purposes of instruction. The following suggestions may be helpful in writing these tests:

*a*)  Formulate the purpose of the test.

*b*)  The purpose, it must be remembered at all times, is to test — not to confuse.

*c*)  Make a plan for the test which involves scope, adequate sampling, and proper length.

*d*)  Formulate test items carefully. Write statements in the form desired.

*e*)  Make a key for each item as it is constructed.

*f*) Edit all irrelevant confusions from each statement.

*g*) Blanks at the right of items are best for reacting by pupils generally.

*h*) Appraise, revise, and rewrite items as necessary.

*i*) Write clear and specific directions for reading and taking the test. State exactly what the pupil should do.

*j*) Write fore-exercises, if necessary, to illustrate the method of reacting to items.

*k*) Arrange items in order of difficulty, if possible.

*l*) Duplicate test for class use, and prepare scoring key.

*m*) After the test has been administered and scored, test papers may be returned and questions by the pupils answered.

*n*) Use the results of the test to improve learning and instruction.

*Essay examinations.* Essay examinations have been improved in the last two or three decades. The well-planned essay tests give pupils an opportunity to think analytically, to organize, to critically appraise, to express themselves creatively, to draw inferences, and to formulate conclusions. Although such a test may be constructed carefully and administered properly, its scoring and rating require critical reading and interpretation.

Stalnaker stated the values of the essay question as freedom of response, direct approach to important goals, emphasis on the total theme, attitudes, creativity, and insight.[9] He further concluded that although values claimed for the essay have not been achieved, it may yet be developed to measure significant aspects of learning that have not been measured.[10]

The chief criticisms of essay examinations can be summarized as follows: (1) poor coverage due to inadequate sampling, (2) lack of validity because of hasty construction, (3) unreliability due to subjectivity of scoring. It is alleged further that essay testing promotes measurement of nonrepresentative tasks and allows writing mechanics to interfere with the measurement of abilities or achievement purposed to be measured. It often permits bluffing, and requires an undue amount of valuable time in grading papers.

1. *Suggestions for constructing essay tests.* While it is obvious that for a quick survey of a unit or course, the informal objective types of items are useful, it is important to realize that for examining

---

[9] John M. Stalnaker, "The Essay Type of Examination," *Educational Measurement* (Washington, D. C.: American Council on Education, 1951), pp. 507–513.
[10] *Ibid.,* p. 530.

depth of understanding, for determining ability to organize, and for appraising reasoning, constructive essay questions are superior. Accordingly, the following suggestions for construction of essay questions should be studied.

*a*) An essay examination should be constructed to meet the objectives of the curriculum and the purposes of the examiner.

*b*) Questions should bring out the important factors, concepts, and processes of the unit or course covered.

*c*) If short answers are desired, such words or phrases as *what, when, where, how many, definite, identify, list, select,* and *state* are useful.

*d*) In planning to appraise understanding, analysis, reasoning, and originality, such queries as *how, why, compare, outline, construct, summarize, explain, interpret, evaluate,* and *develop* are useful.

*e*) Such directions as "discuss," "comment on," "write what you can on," may lead to bluffing or avoidance of the essential points desired.

*f*) Questions should be arranged in order of difficulty, especially if there is a time limit for the examination.

*g*) The first draft of the examination should be carefully appraised, revised, and rewritten.

*h*) Directions for writing the examination should be explicit in order to avoid careless and ambiguous answers.

*i*) The examination should be accurately and neatly duplicated.

*j*) The scoring key for each question should be carefully constructed.

2. *Suggestions for reading and rating essay examinations.* The following suggestions have been found helpful by some teachers.

*a*) Set up directions for reading and rating papers.

*b*) Do not identify the writer of an examination until after the paper has been completely rated.

*c*) Refer to the scoring key when necessary in grading a paper.

*d*) It seems to be a good practice to read and rate answers to one question on all papers before beginning on the second question, and so on.

*e*) Rereading answers to some questions may be necessary.

*f*) Incorrect constructions, faulty spelling, and careless handwriting may be penalized in language examinations if the types of penalties to be assessed are made clear to pupils beforehand.

*g)* Mechanics should not be permitted to overshadow or obscure the important goals sought in a course or a unit of work.

*h)* Score the tests as objectively and accurately as possible.

*i)* Use the tests and examinations as a basis for remediation of errors as well as a partial basis for awarding final marks.

## Standard Tests and Examinations

Brief comments about standard tests and scales follow. Those needed most are: (1) tests of mental ability, (2) achievement tests, and (3) diagnostic examinations.

*Testing mental ability.* It is important to know the mental ability of the child — whether he is gifted, mediocre, or mentally retarded. Some schools appraise the mental ability of children at least twice during the elementary school period.

1. *Group tests of mental ability.* Among the widely used group tests of intelligence are the following: the Kuhlmann-Anderson Intelligence Test,[11] the California Test of Mental Maturity,[12] the Detroit Beginning First-Grade Intelligence Tests,[13] the Pintner General Ability Tests,[14] the Otis Quick Scoring Mental Ability Tests,[15] and the SRA Test of Mental Maturity.[16] Competent teachers can administer and score these tests and determine with fair accuracy the performance of individuals of a class. Manuals present directions for using, scoring, and interpreting scores. The Buros Mental Measurements Yearbooks review these and other tests adequately, and such reviews are worthwhile in test selection.[17]

2. *Individual intelligence examinations.* A child who is severely retarded in language, reading, handwriting, or in some other way may not do himself justice on a group test. In that case the results of an individual intelligence examination can improve the appraisal of his mental ability which is important in assessing the causes of difficulty. The Revised Stanford-Binet Scale, Form L-M,[18] and the Wechsler Intelligence Scale for Children[19] are widely used. These are ade-

---

[11] Published by the Personnel Press, Inc., Princeton, N. J.

[12] Published by the California Test Bureau, Los Angeles, Calif.

[13] Published by the World Book Company, Yonkers-on-Hudson, N. Y.

[14] *Ibid.*

[15] *Ibid.*

[16] Published by Science Research Associates, Chicago, Ill.

[17] Oscar K. Buros, *The Fifth Mental Measurements Yearbook* (Highland Park, N. J.: The Gryphon Press, 1959), 1292 pp.

[18] See *ibid.,* pp. 543–548.

[19] See *ibid.,* pp. 555–561.

quately evaluated in *The Fifth Mental Measurements Yearbook*. They should be given by one who has competence in administering and interpreting individual intelligence test results. Detailed manuals are available, adequate for administering, scoring, and interpretation of the results of these examinations.

*Achievement tests and batteries.* An experienced teacher knows which standardized test or battery is best suited to her situation. A teacher with little experience in testing will be able to obtain help from the supervisory staff of the school system. The Stanford Achievement Test,[20] the Iowa Every Pupil Tests of Basic Skills,[21] the Co-ordinated Scales of Attainment,[22] the Metropolitan Achievement Tests,[23] measure among other areas, language-arts skills in general from the first, second, and third grade through grade eight. They have generally several forms and are evaluated in *The Fifth Mental Measurements Yearbook* or in previous Measurements Yearbooks.[24] The reading of critical reviews of these and other tests will assist a teacher in test selection. Each of these batteries offers a manual with necessary directions about administering, scoring, and interpretation.

*Diagnostic tests in reading.* Many books have been written about diagnosis and remediation in reading. Bond and Tinker present some excellent approaches to appraisal and correction which are helpful to anyone with pupil reading problems.[25] The Bond-Clymer-Hoyt Silent Reading Diagnostic Tests[26] based upon extensive research can be applied to eleven areas such as word recognition and letter sounds. These are group tests and may be administered by the classroom teacher. The Gates technic is described in *The Improvement of Reading*.[27] The Gates Reading Diagnostic Tests[28] are designed to identify most kinds of reading difficulty, but they are best administered by a trained clinician. An excellent system for diagnosing individual reading difficulties has been developed by Durrell and others. The

---

[20] Published by World Book Company, Yonkers-on-Hudson, N. Y.
[21] Published by Houghton Mifflin Company, Boston, Mass.
[22] Published by Educational Test Bureau, Educational Publishers, Inc., Minneapolis, Minn.
[23] Published by World Book Company, Yonkers-on-Hudson, N. Y.
[24] Buros, *op. cit.*
[25] Guy L. Bond and Miles A. Tinker, *Reading Difficulties, Their Diagnosis and Correction* (New York: Appleton-Century-Crofts, Inc., 1957), 486 pp.
[26] Published by Lyons and Carnahan, Chicago, Illinois.
[27] Arthur I. Gates, *The Improvement of Reading*, third edition (New York: The Macmillan Company, 1947), 657 pp.
[28] Published by Bureau of Publications, Teachers College, Columbia University.

Durrell Analysis of Reading Difficulty[29] is practicable for use by well-trained and experienced teachers. One of the most carefully planned programs was put into operation three decades ago by Marion Monroe who used Gray's Oral Reading Examination, Monroe's Iota Word Test, Monroe's Word-Discrimination Test, and other technics to identify faulty vowels and consonants, reversals, additions and omissions of sounds, substitution of words, repetition of words, addition and omission of words, and refusal of words. This system is explained adequately in *Children Who Cannot Read*.[30]

*Some tests for appraisal in language, handwriting, and spelling.* Various attempts to measure written composition were made four or five decades ago. The Hillegas Scale[31] and the Hudelson English Composition Scales[32] were among the first planned to measure general merit of written compositions. The Willing Scales for Measuring English Composition[33] were set up to measure story value and form value. These comprised specimens for comparing and rating original compositions. The Wilson Language Error Test[34] is an example of tests which assist in surveying the general form and to some extent the errors of compositions.

The Ayres Handwriting Scale,[35] The Freeman Chart for Diagnosing Faults in Handwriting,[36] and The Conrad Manuscript Writing Standards[37] have been used satisfactorily for appraisal of handwriting. Commercial scales published by the Palmer Company and by Zaner-Bloser are also helpful in determining deficiencies in handwriting. Such tests used properly are useful in applying remedial technics.

Spelling scales have been produced in the last forty years by Ashbaugh, Bixler, and Greene. These present important words for testing the spelling ability of pupils. Greene's The New Iowa Spelling Scale — the most recent and the most comprehensive offers 5507 words drawn from the most valuable spelling vocabularies. The test-

---

[29] Published by World Book Company, Yonkers-on-Hudson, N. Y.

[30] Marion Monroe, *Children Who Cannot Read* (Chicago: University of Chicago Press, 1932), 205 pp.

[31] Published by Bureau of Publications, Teachers College, Columbia University, New York.

[32] Published by World Book Company, Yonkers-on-Hudson, N. Y.

[33] Published by Public School Publishing Company, Bloomington, Ill.

[34] Published by World Book Company, Yonkers-on-Hudson, N. Y.

[35] Published by Russell Sage Foundation, New York.

[36] Published by Houghton Mifflin Company, Boston, Mass.

[37] Published by Bureau of Publications, Teachers College, Columbia University, New York.

ing of words of this list was nationwide and involved 230,000 pupils in approximately 8800 classrooms in 645 school systems. Twenty-three million spellings are basic to the data presented in this scale. Teachers may use these materials in grades two to eight in determining the difficulty of the words selected for spelling.[38] Greene offers suggestions for testing of various types. Because of the size of the word list and the validity of the sources from which it was compiled, this is an excellent instrument for appraisal of pupils' spelling and for the evaluation of spelling programs.

Help can be obtained in the text on testing and measuring in the elementary school by Gerberich, Greene, and Jorgensen.[39] Their text contains test descriptions, evaluations, and bibliographies in most elementary school areas. Wrightstone, Justman, and Robbins offer excellent guidance in important types of evaluative practice in education.[40]

## SOME PRACTICES AND TECHNICS FOR EVALUATION

Evaluation should continue from day to day, month to month, and year to year. It cannot be valid if only the results of tests given intermittently are taken into account. Evaluating is a two-way process — by the teacher and by the pupils. A teacher who is concerned with growth must have many queries — some voiced and some not spoken — such as: How is John doing today with the writing of his story? Is Mary overcoming her reluctance to talking in a group? How can I help her to feel at ease when speaking to the class? Why can't Bill improve the skills of word identification more rapidly? What can Wayne do to develop more adequately his power of critical thinking? How can I guide Joseph to improve legibility in handwriting? How can Ann increase her ability to comprehend more adequately through listening? How can June enlarge her vocabulary? How can Tom facilitate his power of expression? These and one hundred other questions arise in a teacher's day. They are evaluative questions which must be considered in the development of language. The question for Tom must be answered in relation to his specific problem.

---

[38] Harry A. Greene, *The New Iowa Spelling Scale* (Iowa City, Iowa: Bureau of Educational Research and Service, State University of Iowa, 1955), 178 pp.

[39] J. Raymond Gerberich, Harry A. Greene, and Albert N. Jorgensen, *Measurement and Evaluation in the Modern School* (New York: David McKay Company, Inc., 1962), 622 pp.

[40] J. Wayne Wrightstone, Joseph Justman, and Irving Robbins, *Evaluation in Modern Education* (New York: American Book Company, 1956), 481 pp.

Mary's problem is different from those of others. Each child's difficulty must be considered so that remediation will be effected where and when it is needed.

In addition to teacher evaluation, appraisal is carried on by pupils. The boy who yawns in language class is a victim of ennui. The girl who gazes covertly at the picture of a handsome actor while the teacher tries to interest the class in sentence structure has evaluated the teaching-learning situation and decided that other things are more satisfying than classwork. Such situations must be remedied. Learning must be made challenging and stimulating. When Mark Atwood, a junior high school pupil forty years ago, asked scores of times, "What do we have to do that for?" referring to the many activities in various fields of study, it became apparent then that evaluation was not only a function of the teacher but certainly an opportunity for the learner, and a very important one. The experience with Mark and others clarified and emphasized the proposition that evaluation is a most necessary part of learning as well as a useful part of instruction. It became evident then that the pupil profits when he evaluates and that he benefits by evaluative and appraisal activities when properly planned and carried out, properly interpreted, and properly used to direct learning — both developmental and remedial.

Appraisal must be purpose-centered; it must be specific as well as general; it must be two-way. The teacher must understand the pupil's world and see his problems as if through his eyes, and the pupil should realize that the teacher desires to understand him — his problems, his difficulties, and his potentialities. The pupil must realize that the teacher is striving to help and guide him in ways that will add to his progress and achievement. If he is sure of this, he will accept constructive criticisms and corrections with appreciation. If he feels that the teacher does not understand him or does not have the right attitude toward him, he is likely not to improve as he should from appraisal.[41]

### Teacher Appraisal

The teacher may employ many technics in the appraisal of the child and his communication — among them informal consideration of oral and written work, observation, interviews, the sociogram, and the cumulative record folder. By their use in connection with the

---

[41] Robert E. Cummins, "Evaluating and Grading," *Education,* 82:403–405, March, 1962.

results of testing, she will strive to understand causes of difficulty and build instruction on the bases of her evaluation.

*Observation and listening.* A pupil's performance in telling a story, making a report, or reading a poem offers information to a talented observer. The background and maturation level should be taken into consideration in guiding the child to know his strength and his difficulties. His problems should be recognized. Deserved praise for what is good should be given, and constructive criticism offered. Sometimes members of a group may give helpful suggestions for improving oral communication. In some cases, however, a teacher-pupil conference is more effective in handling problems. Good organization and preparation should be commended, as should intensive interest and notable effort. Certainly, improvement of communication from one situation to another should be noted and recorded.

*Appraising written specimens.* The purpose, content, and form of writing should be evaluated. The following questions about written products may be helpful:

1. Is the purpose correctly stated by the writer?
2. Is there a well-designed plan for communication?
3. Are the tone and form of writing appropriate to the situation?
4. Is the content or message so presented that it will be understood?
5. Is there an adequate close or succinct summary?

In the writing of a letter, is the purpose achieved by the thought presented, and is the form appropriate to the type of letter? In creative writing, does the child show originality? Are the plot, the conversation, the delineation of characters, and the climax properly presented? Sometimes, a group discussion about an original writing is helpful not only for a writer but also for other members of the group. Children properly motivated may give excellent suggestions to a classmate, and in the same exercise may profit from suggestions of others.

The teacher and the pupils also should attempt to discern growth. Samples of writing kept in individual cumulative folders should be reviewed from time to time. The pupil receives satisfaction by noting improvement in facets of writing, and benefits by overcoming deficiencies which appear repeatedly in the specimens kept throughout a semester or a year.[42] The pupil who really strives will, with adequate guidance,

---

[42] Ruth G. Strickland, "Evaluating Children's Compositions," *Elementary English,* 37:321–331, May, 1960.

eliminate errors by critical evaluation of his work and develop good usage by thoughtful practice.

*The interview.* In the elementary school, the interview may be quite informal and even casual. When the child comes to the desk to ask a question, the teacher has an opportunity to observe his manner, his tension, his way of talking, and use of words and sentences. In such face-to-face meetings, attitude, interest, and effort can be appraised. The teacher may determine in a few moments what she might not recognize in a month of group teaching. The interview is flexible because it is a two-way technic. The interviewer may lead off, but the interviewee may redirect the trend of the meeting. While the teacher frequently purposes to gain information, she will permit pupil latitude in advancing information on his own initiative pertinent to the problem for which the interview was undertaken. Individual experiences and background which may not be appraised by any other data gathering device become quite obvious.

An interview in which Tommy or Annie responds to questions or reacts to simple statements may indicate Tommy's brashness and Annie's tension.[43] Such information is of importance in guiding Tommy to improve his manners, and Annie to feel more secure when she realizes that the teacher is truly interested in her welfare.

Recording the essence of an interview is sometimes a problem, but in the elementary school this is generally easily handled because of the simplicity of the purpose of the meeting. A tape recording of an interview made when necessary, and when both the teacher and the child are agreeable to it, is extremely valuable in analyzing deficiencies.[44]

*Sociometric procedures.* Since communication must always be directly or indirectly social, a technic such as the sociogram that will indicate mutuality or lack of it among members of a class is of significance. One crucial purpose of sociometry is to identify members of a group who are in need of assistance in "getting along" with other members. Questions which are important to the teacher are: How well has the pupil adjusted to the class? How well is this pupil accepted by his classmates? Would other children like to play with him? Would other children like to work with him? Would other children accept him as a member of a team in a language activity? In any group, it is probable that some individual is lonely,

43 Wrightstone, Justman, and Robbins, *op. cit.,* pp. 148–152.
44 *Ibid.*

isolated, shy, or unpopular. The purpose of a sociogram is to identify the "isolates" (the unwanted) and also the "stars" (the popular).

A teacher may ask the question: With whom would you like to work on our writing project next week? Pupils may make first choices, second choices, and if it is thought advisable, third choices. The choices may be recorded on a table or graphed in the form of a sociogram.[45] While there is a possibility of the isolated pupil becoming aware of his rejection, much good can eventuate through the efforts of a teacher who recognizes his difficulty and arranges an opportunity for him to tell of an interesting project or describe perhaps an exceptional experience about which other members of the group are unaware.

It should be realized that children of primary and intermediate grades change quite frequently and sometimes suddenly in their likes and dislikes. No one should assume permanency of the results of a sociogram. It is valid only for the time that it is administered. Guidance based upon the use of the sociogram technic will produce sometimes amazing changes in youngsters who once felt rejected but later developed a feeling of acceptance in a group.

*Use of the cumulative individual record folder.*    Evaluation should primarily concern the child, his health, his attitudes, his abilities, and his incentives for and progress in learning. A practical means for progressive study of the child's learning and development is set up by organizing a cumulative individual folder in which a record is kept. The folder for a child may contain information under headings which are thought necessary, such as the following.

### THE CUMULATIVE INDIVIDUAL RECORD FOLDER

A. *Examination, appraisal, evaluation, and diagnostic data*
   1. Personal data — name, address, age, grade
   2. Home and environmental history, facts, conditions
   3. School history, transfers, progress, success, failures
   4. Test data — mental age, IQ, achievement
   5. Physical data — health records, records of physical examinations, physician's reports, accident records, vision, hearing, and so on
   6. Correspondence concerning the child — from parents, guardians, and former teachers
   7. Records of interviews with parents and conferences with pupil in school or home

---

[45] *Ibid.,* pp. 210–211. See James A. Fitzgerald and Patricia G. Fitzgerald, *Methods and Curricula in Elementary Education* (Milwaukee: The Bruce Publishing Company, 1955), pp. 496–497.

8. Records of attendance, absence, tardiness
9. Records of observation of behavior and discipline
10. Personality ratings and appraisals
11. Interest inventories and records of activities and experiences
12. Records of:
    a. Courses taken
    b. Teacher tests
    c. Standard tests results
    d. Reports of special accomplishments
    e. Special disabilities or abilities
    f. Readings — books, magazines
    g. Assignments
13. Reports of appraisal of aptitudes for development of communication
14. Other communications and reports.

B. *Progress and development*
    1. Assignments completed and work accomplished
    2. Goals achieved and aims attained
    3. Progress charted month to month and year to year
    4. Remedial measures carried out in communication areas
    5. Successes and failures noted
    6. Records of activities and practices perfected
    7. Specimens of work
        a. Showing defects
        b. Indicating progress
        c. Suggesting aptitude and promise
        d. Creative writing, handwriting, spelling, usage.

C. *Recommendations*
    1. Teacher plans
    2. Pupil's plans
    3. Physician's comments
    4. Supervisor or special teacher's observations and notations.[46]

The materials in the cumulative folder should be checked critically from time to time. Those which are no longer useful should be discarded as new and more pertinent materials are added. Necessary notations should be entered into the permanent record. Such a record faithfully kept reveals useful data in individual development in many areas of activity and learning; it provides composite evidence of the

------

[46] Fitzgerald and Fitzgerald, *Methods and Curricula, op. cit.,* pp. 503–504.

Self-appraisal and correction

school's impact on the child — a picture of progress and difficulties, and a basis for a plan for his future activity.[47]

## Self-Appraisal

It is a truism that every individual must educate himself and it is probably even more correct to affirm that every individual has the first right and duty to educate himself. If these statements are true, it is also a fact that every individual must therefore evaluate his performances continually. In the communication arts, a child should learn to appraise his listening, speaking, reading, writing, spelling, and handwriting. He must ask himself: Can I hear and under-

[47] Royce E. Brewster, "The Cumulative Folder," *School Life,* 42:16–17, September, 1959.

stand what is spoken by another? Can I speak acceptably, thought-fully, and fluently? Can I read comprehendingly and critically? Can I write correctly and clearly? Do I spell correctly the words I write? Do I write legibly? Every individual who evaluates his work critically, takes the trouble to determine his deficiencies, and makes the effort to improve his skills will in time achieve some degree of excellence. If an individual can bring himself to the point where he will not be satisfied with anything other than the best that he is capable of, he is on the way to successful education. For every project in communication which a pupil undertakes he should: (1) test his skills to find out what he does not know; (2) study and learn what he needs to improve his skill or ability; (3) appraise his work to determine the de-gree of improvement; (4) study again what he requires for mastery; (5) evaluate his product and continually strive for correctness and ultimately for greater perfection. Such evaluation and self-teaching should continue with emphasis upon overcoming weaknesses, remedy-ing imperfect skills, and striving for mastery of communication in its complex relationships.

The following generalizations about self-evaluation may be helpful in guiding pupils:

1. The pupil should participate in appraisal of his work.

2. He should compare his present and past performance to deter-mine his progress.

3. It is worthwhile for him to recognize newly impinging objectives and seek to achieve them with determination and persistence.

4. Objectives must be purposed by the pupil if they are to result in individual development.

5. The gifted pupil may compare his attainments with those of a master in striving for excellence.

6. A pupil should test himself on newly acquired competencies in real situations in order to determine whether his learning has be-come assimilated into his behavior.

7. The pupil should be stimulated to devise his evaluation technics and to use them ever more perfectly.

Pupils require considerate guidance in their activities. Those who have been motivated to seek excellence will show ingenuity in de-veloping and using technics in evaluating their work. They will use progress charts, set up graphs, and formulate scales for rating them-selves in reading, spelling, writing, talking, listening, and handwriting.

No one should expect that elementary pupils will use the highest type of adult judgment in evaluation; however, no one should criticize the pupil for trying to evaluate his performance. Pupils are capable with guidance of setting up standards for themselves, and they are capable of determining how well they have achieved these goals. By so doing, individuals are assuming responsibility for learning and mastery to a degree greater than that assumed when they have no voice in planning or evaluating their work. As individuals learn to communicate, they must learn to evaluate communication.

## CRITERIA FOR TESTING AND APPRAISAL

Whether a teacher is using a newer type of evaluative practice, a standardized examination, a teacher-made test — it is necessary that she be concerned about the qualities of her appraisal instrument. The following questions pinpoint important criteria of any evaluative practice or measuring instrument:

1. Does the instrument measure what it is supposed to measure?
2. Does the test discriminate adequately among responses and abilities of those being tested?
3. Does the examination measure consistently what it does measure?
4. Is the test practical, economical, administrable, and easy to score?
5. Are the test results objective — free from bias and opinion?
6. Are the results useful in developmental and remediation activities?

### Validity

Without validity, a test or other evaluative technic fails to achieve desired results. A valid test tests what it purports to test. It should be recognized, however, that a test valid in one situation may not be valid in another, or a test valid for one group might not be valid for a second group. Accordingly, tests should be constructed or selected to meet the needs of a class, group, or individual in a specific situation.[48] Evaluative practices may be used effectively or ineffectively. If an evaluative practice, although properly planned and designed to determine information attained or attitudes developed, is poorly administered or if the results are improperly interpreted, the appraisal

---

[48] Donald Ross Green, "Tests Are, Tests Are Not," *The National Elementary Principal,* 41:18–22, September, 1961.

will not be valid. Accordingly, validity is not achieved by having an appropriate instrument available; it can be achieved to some degree however by administering the valid instrument effectively and by interpreting the results properly.

One of the factors which makes a valid test highly useful is its discriminatory factor. A test or other instrument that will determine differences among individuals in certain specific skills is valuable. A valid test should not only identify superior students, medium students, and poor students, but it should indicate the degree of goodness or poorness of individuals in the specific skills being tested. For example, a truly valid instrument may well distinguish clearly between the performances of the two highest achievers in a class. Similarly, it should differentiate the achievements or products of the other members of a group. An instrument or practice which indicates for two individuals on the same level, differences in weakness or strength is highly valuable. Although the basic criterion is validity, testing is also dependent upon such other qualities as reliability, objectivity, scorability, and usefulness.

## Reliability

Reliability indicates the consistency with which a test measures what it does measure. However, a really reliable test may not always measure what a teacher purposes to measure. In other words, one may administer the most reliable test in the world and not test what is desired. On the other hand, lack of reliability does limit validity. Because reliability is desirable and necessary a teacher should determine as well as possible the reliability of a test she wishes to use. Manuals on standard tests generally present a reliability coefficient which must be interpreted in the light of the range of talent tested. The same coefficient of reliability — .90 ± .04, for example — would be considered high for a group on one grade level, but much lower for a group of youngsters ranging from grade three through eight.

A teacher who builds an informal objective test of one hundred well-selected multiple-choice, matching, completion, and true-false items taken systematically from the main sections of a unit will have a much more adequate sampling of the learning desired in the unit than one who writes out five essay questions. Certainly, her sampling is more representative. However, with these, she may be unable to test critical thinking about the important questions of the unit. She may have constructed a fairly reliable examination, but not perhaps a valid one. It is necessary in making a test to be concerned with validity. Will the test test what she wants it to test? It is likely that a combination of the informal objective and the constructive essay may be the answer to the problem of achieving an acceptable degree of validity and reliability.

## Objectivity

Objectivity is that quality in a test which eliminates personal judgment, bias, or opinion from affecting scoring. It is achieved when the score on a test arrived at by any number of persons is the same. Objectivity can be achieved when a properly constructed multiple-choice or matching test is scored with an accurate key. Standard tests and informal objective tests are generally scored objectively with a prepared key. Essay questions are frequently quite subjective, and the scoring may vary greatly according to the background of the scorers. Yet, essay tests, if constructed properly, may be rated quite objectively. When a test maker formulates questions carefully and constructs a key which provides acceptable answers for the questions, he is on his way to some degree of objectivity. Objectivity should be sought in an essay test because a low degree of objectivity in scoring tends to reduce both validity and reliability.[49] Although objectivity does not assure validity, it is one of the qualities which a truly valid test should possess.

## Practicality, Economy, Administrability

Practicality, economy, and administrability are related. Many qualities bear upon practicality. It may not be practical to use an otherwise good test because it is too lengthy, too complicated to administer, or too difficult to score. Of two tests quite equal or similar in other qualities, a teacher in elementary school will generally desire the one that can be administered in a class period rather than one twice or three times as long. However, a test should be long enough to test a unit or skill adequately.

Economy in testing refers to costs in time, money, or nervous energy in its use and relates to practicality. Economy should be computed upon the value received rather than upon the amount of money expended. Some tests are too expensive at any price; a higher price is not too much to pay for a valid, reliable, objective, and usable test. Such properties as organization, readability, administrability, scorability, for-

[49] Green, *op. cit.*, p. 20.

mat, and size of type should be considered in selecting or constructing tests. In making a test, a teacher should strive to produce an instrument that will meet her purpose of testing what has been taught in the course. Such a test should be well organized, economical to administer and score, and practicable to use.

A well-constructed test or a properly selected test should be easily administered. If the instructions are clear both to the teacher and the child, effective administrability is promoted. The print should be readily readable at the level on which the test is used. The child should know from the directions and fore-exercises just how he should work and where he should place his responses; he should understand when and where he should stop working and whether to wait for a further signal to continue. The administration of a teacher-made test requires carefully formulated directions. In each session of testing, pupils should exercise adequate discipline and appropriate behavior in order to achieve the most desirable results. A teacher should have everything prepared for testing in a room in which there will be no disturbances. Youngsters should be habituated to have pencils and pens at hand and booklets available, to be alert and ready at an appointed time. There should be an atmosphere of willingness to think, to work, and to write.

## Usefulness

Good testing is useful in guiding learners to success in achieving their purposes. Alternate forms are helpful in measuring progress from one semester to another. Standards and norms are valuable in comparing achievement and progress of one group with another. A teacher may compare the performance of her present group with the performance of groups in past years. To be most usable, the scores of a test should be easily interpreted and the results applicable to the learning problems of the individuals. Tests given without the consideration of objectives may be a complete waste. Tests administered without proper interpretation and effective use are wasteful also. Used properly, tests are an essential in teaching and learning; used improperly, they are of little value and may be positively harmful.[50]

---

[50] See Resolution No. 13 adopted by the American Association of School Administrators in Convention, February 18, 1959, quoted in *School Life*, 42:5, September, 1959.

## Other Desirable Considerations

In addition to the major criteria discussed, other considerations relating to tests and testing follow:

1. *Do the pupils recognize the value of testing?*   They must learn its value in studying. If they understand that through testing they can achieve their purposes better and enhance their learning effectively, they will profit more than if they feel that testing is only another type of monotonous exercise which they must endure.

2. *Are the pupils challenged by the testing?* For example, in spelling when a child understands that the pretest on a unit helps him to select the words which he cannot spell, he will study them with a method by which he can learn to spell them. When he finds out by means of a final test that he has learned all but one of the words which he studied he will be encouraged. If he recognizes the word misspelled as a useful word which he needs in writing, he will concentrate on it at perhaps the first opportunity to make mastery complete.

3. *Do pupils enjoy the testing program?*   The testing period can be one of enjoyment as well as of profit. With proper stimulation, members of a class will look forward to testing as satisfying and will strive to achieve high scores and to correct deficiencies which the test reveals.

*Résumé.*   Tests and appraisal instruments must be evaluated. Important criteria for evaluation are validity, reliability, objectivity, practicality, and usefulness. Pupils should understand the purposes of testing, be challenged by tests, and enjoy the experiences of testing in order to profit from them.

## EVALUATIVE RESULTS: BASES FOR DEVELOPMENT AND REMEDIATION

Evaluative results should be used to guide the pupil's learning activities, to correct his deficiencies, to develop his powers, and to perfect his competencies. In the communication arts, almost every child can profit from teaching and learning based upon appraisal and diagnosis. The slow pupil requires a great deal of instruction in order to acquire the essentials of reading and language. The normal individual needs to study efficiently and intensively to master skills required in modern life. Even the gifted requires guidance of one type or another to achieve the excellence of which he is capable. In the communication arts particularly, there is need for evaluation, diagnosis, remediation, and preventive measures.

## Diagnosis

Diagnosis is concerned with testing, appraisal, and evaluation of the child to assess his powers, interests, and drives, to identify his difficulties and deficiencies, and to determine causes of trouble. The purpose of diagnosis is to prepare a valid basis for planning and carrying out a program of either a developmental character or remedial nature. The evaluative procedures outlined in this chapter are useful in preparing for instruction which will fit the needs and meet the difficulties of the normal healthy boy and girl in reading and language skills. If an individual is severely handicapped in one or more of the communication arts it is probable that a thorough diagnostic program will be necessary to determine the reasons for his limitations. In such a procedure, it may be necessary to use psychological, medical, and clinical examinations.

## Remediation

The purpose of remediation is to guide the individual to overcome his difficulties and to correct his deficiencies in the reading or language skills in which he has trouble. If the causes can be determined, remedial measures may be applied which will help the child to achieve progress. In a program of remediation, the individual should be supplied with appropriate and interesting materials and directed to use effective and stimulating methods. Brueckner and Bond offer programs of diagnosis and treatment of difficulties in reading, language, spelling, and handwriting.[51] Bond and Tinker present excellent suggestions for both diagnosis and corrective procedures for those who are limited in the field of reading.[52] Among others who have offered much in the field of remedial work are Gates, Gray, Betts, Marion Monroe, Helen Robinson, and Durrell. The investigations by these and other authorities give valuable guidance for evaluation.

## Prevention and Development

Preventive measures are important in teaching and learning, and they are economical in the long run. In short, prevention suggests the

[51] Leo J. Brueckner and Guy L. Bond, *The Diagnosis and Treatment of Learning Difficulties* (New York: Appleton-Century-Crofts, Inc., 1955), 424 pp.

[52] Guy L. Bond and Miles A. Tinker, *Reading Difficulties, Their Diagnosis and Correction* (New York: Appleton-Century-Crofts, Inc., 1957), 486 pp.

use of well-selected developmental procedures of learning and instruction which protect a child from retardation or failure by proper use of appropriate materials and activities. Just as the study of health emphasizes the use of diet, exercise, vitamins, and vaccine to prevent illness of various types, so can preventive measures be applied effectively to insure the attainment of the goals of communication. For example, in learning to speak, a child should be given opportunity to listen to correct colloquial language. If he hears good pronunciation and engages in pleasant conversation devoid of slang, illiterate expressions, and baby talk, his chances of developing acceptable speech are enhanced. If on the other hand he is exposed to vulgarisms, slang, and slovenly language, he probably will require diagnostic and remedial measures sooner or later. If a child is taught to read by invalid methods, he will not develop reading skills as he would if he were guided to read through a well-planned intrinsic program which includes interesting and appropriate materials, effective instruction, and tested practices. If a pupil is directed to study difficult and uninteresting tasks without understanding the reasons for the work and without knowledge of the degree of his success, uncertain progress will result. On the other hand if success is achieved and progress is charted, his probability of mastery will be improved.

## Guidance and Motivation

Remediation in the language arts is necessary not only for slow learners. The normal and the rapid have difficulties also, and guidance is generally essential for them in achieving their goals. The emotions should not be lost sight of in guiding pupils. Harris suggested five technics — association, substitution, release, redirection, and self-direction — for improving learning of individuals.[53] These technics are exemplified briefly. Healthy association is used when a pupil enjoys a thrilling story or reads to determine how to preside at a dinner meeting. Thus reading is associated with enjoyment or an essential learning. Substitution is practiced when an individual writes a feature story about an event interesting to him in place of an assigned composition. Release from tiresome (to him) textbook study of geography is enjoyed when a pupil views a motion picture showing life of a foreign people about whom he is studying. Redirection is operative in handwriting when a pupil uses appraisal to determine his illegibilities

[53] Fred E. Harris, "What Emphasis Should Be Placed on Emotions?" *Elementary School Journal*, 44:590–593, June, 1944.

and engages in successful corrective practices rather than the copying procedures which he had been using. Self-direction is developed when a pupil purposes, plans, writes, revises, appraises, and perfects an original play for the class assembly. Association, substitution, release, redirection, and self-direction have important emotional and educational values because they make study and learning satisfying, attractive, and effective. Motivation should cause the child to want to learn, and guidance should provide suitable materials and effective procedures for mastering the essential communication skills.

## SUMMARY

Evaluation, appraisal, measuring, and testing are component parts of the learning and teaching of reading and the other communication arts; properly used, they direct teaching and redirect study.

Evaluation considers the whole child — his health, abilities, attitudes, interests, desires, difficulties — and also his efforts, problems, and progress. Appraisal and testing may be applied to listening and talking in conversation and discussion, to skills, abilities, and activities in oral and silent reading and study, and to writing, spelling, handwriting, language usage, vocabulary, and power in communication.

Oral and informal objective tests, and essay and standardized examinations offer means for measurement, appraisal, and evaluation of progress in communication. Teacher appraisal of oral language and written expression is a valuable means for the guidance of study by each child. Useful also for appraisal and evaluation are such technics as the interview and sociometric procedures.

To achieve the most accurate and worthwhile evaluation, it is necessary to use technics of appraisal and instruments for testing and measurement that meet the criteria of validity, reliability, objectivity, practicality, and usefulness. A testing instrument or evaluative procedure should test effectively what it purports to measure, and the results should be useful for interpretation and guidance. Testing should be interesting and challenging to the learner and offer him incentives for improvement.

Evaluation should be a continuous process in order to facilitate and direct learning. Principles should be formulated and practices should be developed which lead pupils to necessary self-evaluation and self-guidance.

## ACTIVITIES, PROBLEMS, QUESTIONS

1. Make a list of the essential measurement and appraisal instruments and technics for each of six major language arts.

2. Why are testing and evaluation necessary in learning and teaching?

3. Critically appraise each of the eight types of informal objective tests discussed in the chapter.

4. Construct an informal test using at least four of the types described to test a group of pupils in one of the communication arts. How well did your test test what you wanted to test?

5. Make an essay test covering the same area. Try it out on a group. Compare the procedure and results of this test and the objective type test suggested in 4 above.

6. Describe the following: (a) mental tests; (b) achievement tests; (c) diagnostic tests. What are the values of each?

7. What are the advantages and disadvantages of the following: (a) interviews; (b) sociometric procedures; (c) cumulative record folder?

8. State what can be the values of self-appraisal. What dangers must be avoided?

9. Define: validity, reliability, objectivity, practicality, economy, administrability, and usefulness of tests. Explain how each can be attained.

10. Outline a program of diagnosis and remediation in reading.

11. Explain the worth of a program of prevention and development.

12. How can guidance be made useful in helping pupils to avoid mistakes and difficulties in one (select one) of the communication areas?

## SELECTED REFERENCES

Ahmann, J. Stanley, Marvin Glock, and Helen Wardeberg. *Evaluating Elementary School Pupils.* Boston: Allyn and Bacon, 1960. 435 pp.

Austin, Mary C., *et al. Reading Evaluation: Appraisal Techniques for School and Classroom.* New York: Ronald, 1961. 256 pp.

Baron, Denis. *Evaluation Techniques for Classroom Teachers.* New York: McGraw-Hill, 1958. 297 pp.

Brueckner, Leo J., and Guy L. Bond. *The Diagnosis and Treatment of Learning Difficulties.* New York: Appleton-Century-Crofts, 1955. 424 pp.

Buros, Oscar K., ed. *The Fifth Mental Measurements Yearbook.* Highland Park, N. J.: Gryphon Press, 1959. 1292 pp.

Chauncey, Henry, and John E. Dobbin. *Testing: Its Place in Education Today.* New York: Harper and Row, 1963. 224 pp.

Furst, Edward J. *Constructing Evaluation Instruments.* New York: Longmans, Green, 1958. 335 pp.

Gerberich, J. Raymond, Harry A. Greene, and Albert Jorgenson. *Measurement and Evaluation in the Modern School.* New York: David McKay, 1962. 627 pp.

Green, John A. *Teacher-Made Tests.* New York: Harper and Row, 1963. 141 pp.

*Handbook of Research on Teaching.* N. L. Gage, ed. Chicago: Rand McNally, 1963. 1218 pp.

*Impact and Improvement of School Testing Programs, The,* Sixty-Second Yearbook of the National Society for the Study of Education, Part II. Chicago: University of Chicago Press, 1963. 304 pp.

Robinson, Helen M., ed. *Evaluation of Reading.* Supplementary Educational Monographs, No. 88. Chicago: University of Chicago Press, 1958. 208 pp.

Rothney, John W. *Evaluating and Reporting Pupil Progress.* What Research Says to the Teacher. No. 7. Washington, D. C.: DCT and AERA of the NEA, 1955. 33 pp.

Smith, Edward W., Stanley W. Krouse, and Mark Atkinson. *The Educator's Encyclopedia.* Englewood Cliffs, N. J.: Prentice-Hall, 1961. 914 pp.

Wrightstone, J. Wayne, Joseph Justman, and Irving Robbins. *Evaluation in Modern Education.* New York: American Book, 1956. 481 pp.

# Index